Right Hon

History of England

During the Reign of George the Third

Right Hon

History of England
During the Reign of George the Third

ISBN/EAN: 9783742816436

Manufactured in Europe, USA, Canada, Australia, Japa

Cover: Foto ©ninafisch / pixelio.de

Manufactured and distributed by brebook publishing software (www.brebook.com)

Right Hon

History of England

A HISTORY OF ENGLAND

DURING THE

REIGN OF GEORGE THE THIRD.

VOL. IV.

LONDON
PRINTED BY SPOTTISWOODE AND CO
NEW-STREET SQUARE

A

HISTORY OF ENGLAND

DURING THE

REIGN OF GEORGE THE THIRD.

BY

THE RIGHT HON.
WILLIAM MASSEY.

EDITION, REVISED AND CORRECTED.

IN FOUR VOLUMES.

VOL. IV.

1795 — 1801

LONDON:
LONGMANS, GREEN, AND CO.
1865.

CONTENTS
OF
THE FOURTH VOLUME.

CHAPTER XXXVI.

Expedition to Quiberon—Naval Operations—Coercive Acts—Negotiation for Peace.

	PAGE
Plan for invading Brittany	2
Failure of the plan	2
The Channel fleet	4
Disappointment of De Puisaye	4
Landing in Quiberon bay	5
The Royalists inefficiently supported	7
Results of the failure at Quiberon	9
Plans of De Puisaye	10
Charette in Poitou	12
Vacillation of the Ministry	13
Affairs in the West Indies	14
Political meetings	15
Outrage on the King	16
Proceedings in Parliament	16
Act to repress public discussion	17
Reception of the measure	18
Petitions against the Bills	20
Political pamphlets	21
Barracks	22
Loan and new taxes	23
Selfish conduct of the landed interest	24
Cessation of the Reign of Terror	24
Opposition against negotiation	25
Persistence of the Ministry	26
Failure of negotiations	27
Impossible terms of the French propositions	29
Dismissal of Lord Malmesbury	31
Intrigues of the French in Spain	32

CHAPTER XXXVII.

Bank Restriction Act—French Invasion of Wales—Mutiny in the Fleet—Conference of Lisle—Battle of Camperdown—Financial Measures—Patriotic Fund—Change in Public Opinion.

	PAGE
New Parliament	33
New loan	34
Drain of specie	36
Meeting of merchants	37
Arguments against the Act	38
The Dutch fleet	39
Loss of the English	44
Peerage and pension of Jervis	45
Anonymous letters of complaint	45
Demands of the mutineers	47
Earl Spencer goes to Portsmouth	48
Mutiny at St. Helen's	50
Lord Howe at Portsmouth	51
Admiral's flag hauled down	54
Reply of the Admiralty	54
Earl Spencer at the Nore	55
Alarm at Sheerness	56
Parliamentary denunciation of the mutineers	56
Execution of Parker	59
Ill-usage of the seamen common	60
Increase of the national debt	61
Supplementary loan	62
Motions for a change of Ministry	63
French commissioners	65
Divisions amongst the French	65
Proposals to Austria	69
Ionian Islands ceded to France	70
French invectives against the British	70
Projects for invading England	71
Equality of the forces	72
Factious conduct of the Opposition	73
Unconstitutional conduct of the Whigs	74
Mr. Tierney	75
The Budget	75
Opposition to the Budget	76
Prospect of invasion	79
Defence of the country	79
State prosecutions	81
Change in public opinion	84

CHAPTER XXXVIII.

State of Ireland—The Rebellion—The Union.

	PAGE
Remedial measures in Ireland	90
Treasonable projects of French invasion	90
Duke of Portland's policy	91
Overtures made to Grattan	92
Fitzwilliam's arrival in Dublin	93
Influence of the Beresfords	97
Panic amongst Irish officers	98
Animosity against Fitzwilliam	98
Letters of Fitzwilliam	100
Lord Camden made Viceroy	101
Beresford's house attacked	102
Orangemen	103
United Irishmen change their tone	104
Disordered state of the country	104
Violence of the Protestant party	105
Troops billeted on Catholics	106
Preparations for a general insurrection	106
Sir James Stuart's proceedings	108
Suppression of the 'Morning Star'	109
Dissolution of Parliament	109
Fresh applications to France	110
Extent of the conspiracy	111
Reynolds the informer	111
Apprehension of the Sheares's	115
Dr. Esmonde	116
Attack on Naas and Kilcullen	116
Daff's attack on the rebels	118
Wexford address	119
Proclamation of an amnesty	121
Virulence of the Loyalists	121
Bonaparte's distrust of the Irish	123
Promptitude of Lord Cornwallis	126
Suppression of the rebellion	127
Union proposed	131
Opening of Parliament	133
Chancellor Clare	134
Royal message	134
Revival of agitation in Ireland	135
Address to the Crown	138
Duke of Portland's instructions	141
Resolutions moved by Pitt	146
Irish Houses prorogued	153
Trial of Fitzgerald	157
Arrest of Mr. Scott	158
Use of torture	160

	PAGE
Lord Cornwallis's Government	164
Murder in Wicklow	169
Court-martial dissolved by Cornwallis	170
Prorogation of Irish Parliament	173
Pitt's speech on the representation	181
Sixth Article of Union	183

CHAPTER XXXIX.

French Expedition to Egypt—Battle of the Nile—Naples and its Court—Campaigns in Europe—Expedition to the Helder—Siege of Acre—Fall of Seringapatam.

Fleet sails from Toulon	188
Nelson sent in pursuit of the French	190
Nelson's complaint of want of frigates	195
His presence of mind	195
Nelson created a peer	198
Exultation on the Continent	199
Nelson sails for Naples	200
Movement of Russia	204
Movements of Austria	208
Macdonald at Naples	209
Prince Caracciolo	212
Seizure of Caracciolo	213
Defeat of the Dutch	212
Difficult nature of the country	222
Sir Sidney Smith	225
Siege of Acre	227
Bonaparte's despatch	229
British before Seringapatam	234

CHAPTER XL.

Income Tax—Bonaparte's Letter proposing Peace—Hadfield's Attempt on the King's Life—Scarcity—Prosecution of the Corn Factors—Measures of the Government.

Bonaparte's reception in Paris	240
Bonaparte's letter to the King	240
Lord Grenville's speech	241
Debate in the Commons	243
Attempt to shoot the King	249
Public expression of loyalty	253

Concessions of Austria	263
Isolation of England	266
British embargo	271
Extent of private benevolence	282

CHAPTER XLI.

First Parliament of the United Kingdom—Catholic Question—Change of Ministry—King's Illness—Addington succeeds Pitt—Proceedings in Parliament—Battle of Alexandria—Expedition to the Baltic—Peace of Amiens.

First United Parliament	285
Election of Speaker	285
Dundas at the King's levee	286
Discussion in the Cabinet	286
Castlereagh's promise	288
Proposed measures for Catholic relief	289
The Cabinet assembled	290
Loughborough's breach of confidence	290
Loughborough and Castlereagh	291
The King's reply to Pitt	295
Pitt's offer to resign	295
Attempt of Addington to dissuade Pitt from resigning	298
The new Cabinet	299
Health of the King	305
The opinion of Dr. Willis	306
The King's inquiries	309
Addington Premier	314
Resignation of Cornwallis	316
Personal character of Addington	317
Complaint of Pitt's friends	318
Popular dissatisfaction with Pitt	319
Addresses of Cornwallis to the Catholics	321
Grenville's defence of the late Ministry	322
Addington's parliamentary success	325
Proceedings of the Ministry	328
Affairs of Egypt	330
Treaty of El Arish	332
Position of the French	334
British expedition to Egypt	335
Misinformation as to the French army	338
Convention of Cairo	342
Negotiations for peace accelerated	343
Subserviency of Russia to French interests	344
Sailing of the fleet	346
Frivolous punctilio of Sir H. Parker	346
Council of war	349

	PAGE
Nelson goes on shore	352
Nelson's letter to the Crown Prince	353
Conclusion of an armistice	354
Evasive conduct of the Swedes	355
Change of Russian policy	356
Recall of Sir H. Parker	357
Dissolution of the Northern League	360
Grenville's attack on the Northern convention	365
Definitive treaty	367
Difficulties in adjusting the terms	368

A HISTORY OF ENGLAND

DURING THE

REIGN OF GEORGE THE THIRD.

CHAPTER XXXVI.

EXPEDITION TO QUIBERON—NAVAL OPERATIONS—COERCIVE ACTS—NEGOTIATION FOR PEACE.

The campaigns of 1794–5 were, in all their results, and in most of their details, favourable to the French. The conquest of Holland was completed early in the year 1795, although the remnant of the British army did not evacuate the territory of the states until April. The Duke of York had been removed from the command in December.

The King of Prussia made a treaty of peace with the French Republic early in the year. Spain, and the military principality of Hesse, concluded similar treaties during the summer. The Emperor remained firm in alliance with Great Britain, on condition of a loan of four millions six hundred thousand pounds, for the purposes of the war, being guaranteed by the British Government. England also obtained a new ally in the Czarina, who undertook to furnish a small contingent of twelve thousand troops in exchange for the services of twelve ships of the line. This alliance was of little value, Catherine being at that time fully occupied in providing for the military occupation of the vast territory, of which, in conjunction with Frederic of Prussia, she had recently despoiled the Poles. Under these circumstances, England was not in a condition to engage in extensive military enterprises; and the only military adventure in which she did embark ended in disaster and confusion.

In the autumn of the preceding year, the Count de Puisaye, a Breton nobleman, and chief of a Chouan band, had submitted to the English Government a project for raising a Royalist insurrection in Brittany. He proposed that an expedition, comprising ten thousand English troops, and a corps of emigrants should enter the province at different points, and effect a junction at the capital city of Rennes, the possession of which would put the expeditionary force in possession of ample magazines and munitions of every kind, if it did not, as was probable, insure the immediate success of the enterprise. From Rennes, the insurrectionary army was to extend its operations to Normandy, Maine, and Poitou; and, finally, it was intended that the Count d'Artois should be invited to assume the chief command.

The British Cabinet having consulted Lord Cornwallis, the first military authority in the service, approved of this plan; and it was determined that the British contingent should be commanded by the Earl of Moira, the officer who had served with so much distinction as second to Cornwallis in the American war.

Many months, however, were consumed in this negotiation, notwithstanding the urgent representations of De Puisaye that every day's delay was injurious to the cause. The Bretons, already in arms, were dispirited by the protracted absence of their leader. The emigrants in London, who were not admitted to the counsels of the Chouan chief, became jealous of his secret correspondence with the British Government, and sought to frustrate his efforts. Through the envy, if not the treachery, of these people, intelligence reached Paris, and preparations were set on foot to counteract the formidable enterprise which had been planned at London. Cormatin, who commanded the Chouan bands in the absence of De Puisaye, following the example of Charette, made peace with the Republicans; and the Royalist levies dispersed and returned to their homes. Such were the unhappy results of hesitation and delay. The British Government, taking advantage of their own wrong, retracted the promise of immediate military aid, and confined their assistance to a small sum of money, and a supply of stores. The gallant spirit of the Chouan chief bore up even against this last cruel disappointment; and it was ultimately decided that the attempt should be made with a few French regiments in British pay, amounting to between four and five thousand men. If these could hold their ground, hope was held out that they would be reinforced by the British contingent, upon the original co-operation of which the plan of the Royalist General had been principally based. Not content with thus dashing down, at the last moment, the hopes with which they had so long amused these devoted men, the English Government interposed objections with regard to the conduct of the expedition. De Puisaye wished to land on the northern coast of Brittany, where he was sure of being surrounded by friends and followers; but the Cabinet of St. James's determined that he should land in the south, and Quiberon was chosen as affording a convenient station for the fleet. The chief of the expedition was not permitted even to select his second in command; and, instead of an officer in the vigour of life, with enthusiasm and *dash*, the essential qualities for such a service, the Ministry named a certain Count d'Hervilly, an old military formalist of the monarchy, without an idea beyond routine, a General who might have commanded a division in a campaign upon the Rhine without discovering his incapacity, but who was destitute of every qualification which enabled the Bonchamps, the Cathelineaus, and the Larochejaquelins to guide the ardent peasantry of the Loire. That nothing might be wanting to complete the unfortunate character of this appointment, it so happened that D'Hervilly had commanded in Brittany before the Revolution; and, by the rigour with which he suppressed a local disturbance, had earned a reputation extremely odious to the common people.

The transports which conveyed this expedition were under the convoy of a squadron commanded by Sir John Borlase Warren. The French, who were well informed of the movements of the Royalists, sent out a fleet to intercept them; but Lord Bridport, who commanded the Channel squadron, kept the French Admiral in check, and took two of his ships. The crews of these captured ships were, with rash precipitation, drafted into the ranks of the Royalist regiments intended for service in Brittany.

When the transports were under weigh, De Puisaye congratulated himself on having at length surmounted his most formidable difficulties. But he soon found he was mistaken. Before the troops were landed, D'Hervilly insisted that his commission entitled him to the command of the expedition, and positively refused to abate his claim without fresh instructions from the British Government. As it was impossible to await the result of a reference to London, De Puisaye was compelled, for the present, to yield the point, though not without apprehension that it might involve the fate of the enterprise. On the 25th of June, the fleet anchored in Quiberon bay, and two Royalist officers of rank came on board to report that everything was prepared for the reception of the troops and the co-operation of the native forces. De Puisaye proposed, therefore, that the disembarkation should be effected immediately. But D'Hervilly, tenacious of his newly asserted authority, would by no means consent, until he had himself reconnoitred in due form. It was in vain De Puisaye urged that he might rely on the reports of competent officers, and that he could form no opinion for himself without landing. The punctilious pedant, nevertheless, sailed deliberately round the bay, glass in hand, although, from the nature of the coast, he could see nothing.

The troops and their officers, mad with impatience, were still detained on board by the petty scruples of their Commander; and had it *Landing in Quiberon bay.* not been known that the Count was as loyal and honest as he was dull and formal, it might have been thought that he intended to ruin and betray the whole undertaking. At length, finding nobody to listen to his difficulties, D'Hervilly gave the order to disembark; and on the morning of the 27th of June, the troops were safely landed before the small garrison town of Carnac. A force of two hundred Republican soldiers, which occupied the place, offered resistance; but a body of Chouans advancing on their flank, they dispersed without a shot having been fired on either side.

The troops were welcomed by the country people with the greatest enthusiasm. Those who were on the beach rushed into the sea with loyal shouts, and would hardly permit the boats to land before they took out the chests of arms and ammunition; others, men, women, and children, harnessed themselves to the gun-carriages, and dragged them ashore. Cartloads of provisions and other necessaries arrived from the interior, and were eagerly forced upon the soldiers. D'Hervilly was shocked at these irregular proceedings, so contrary to the usage of war, and so subversive of discipline. A slight accident had nearly been aggravated by the folly of the Royalist General, into a serious rupture between the troops and their irregular allies. A stand of arms, intended for the service of D'Hervilly's own regiment, had, by mistake, been distributed among a band of peasantry; and a dispute arose, in consequence of an attempt of the French sergeant to disarm the Breton regiment by force. D'Hervilly, hearing the commotion, ordered the drums to be beat, and the boats to be got ready for re-embarkation, loudly declaring that the Chouans were attacking his soldiers. Fortunately, however, the men on both sides had more sense and temper than their Commander; and when De Puisaye, with several other chiefs hastily summoned, arrived at the scene of disorder, they found good humour and cordiality restored.

The first military operation was to take possession of the fort Penthièvre, which connected the small peninsula of Quiberon with the mainland. D'Hervilly, however, could not think of approaching a fortified place without a battering train; but when De Puisaye ridiculed the idea of a siege, and offered to take the place with a handful of Chouans, the old General, satisfied by the proposal of an assault, a mode of offensive warfare justified by military precedent, consented to the undertaking. The garrison, which consisted of seven hundred men, many of whom were supposed to be well affected to the royal cause, offered no resistance, and surrendered at discretion. Four hundred of the prisoners immediately availed themselves of the permission offered them to assume the white cockade.

De Puisaye, knowing that inaction must be fatal to the enterprise, and hopeless of moving his slow and punctilious colleague but by regular steps, himself pushed forward with his Chouans. Hoche, who commanded the Republicans, had, at that time, only five thousand men under his command; and his position, in a hostile country, at a great distance from his communications, was very precarious. A vigorous blow at this moment might have placed the whole country watered by the Loire in the hands of the Royalists. Had the Breton chief been supported by a coadjutor of ordinary skill and activity, the movement could hardly have failed; but D'Hervilly, despising his irregular auxiliaries, had withdrawn the artillery and supports from Moudon, the advanced post of the Chouans, in order to aid in the reduction of Penthièvre, which made no resistance. Hoche, taking prompt advantage of this error, assumed the offensive, and, driving the Chouans back in confusion, encamped upon the heights of St. Barbe, which commanded the fort. It became necessary, therefore, to dislodge the French General before any other step was taken. But the tide of fortune was changed. The attack on the French camp was repulsed; after an obstinate engagement, in which D'Hervilly was disabled by a wound, the Royalists retreated to Penthièvre, under cover of a heavy fire from the English fleet.

Penthièvre was strong enough to hold out until the arrival of the reinforcements which were anxiously expected; but the army of Hoche was rapidly augmented, and the Royalists, closely invested, saw their bright prospects rapidly fade away. The tempestuous state of the weather kept the English transports at sea; and the Count de Sombreuil, a young nobleman in command of a small body of emigrants, was the only officer who succeeded in landing his men. This tardy and scanty reinforcement greatly depressed the spirits of the Royalists, who had been taught to expect prompt and powerful support from Great Britain. Treachery,

The Royalists insufficiently supported.

also, which might have been kept down by success, was encouraged by misfortune, and completed the ruin of the expedition. The French prisoners who had been received into the ranks of the invaders, merely on their representations that they were willing to serve on the opposite side, only waited for an opportunity to rejoin their former comrades. These men, who cared more for the military glory of France than the colour of their flag, had no vocation to support the forlorn hope of a falling cause; and it soon became known in the camp of Hoche that the Republicans had friends in the garrison of Penthièvre. Many desertions took place; and a night attack on the garrison was planned in concert with the traitors. The surprise was successful. On the night of the 21st of July, amidst storm and tempest, the Republicans were admitted into the fort. The Governor and the emigrants within the walls were immediately massacred; in a few minutes, the three-coloured flag was raised upon the ramparts; and the cannon of the fort was turned upon the peninsula, along which the corps of Sombreuil, alarmed by the sound of musketry, was rapidly advancing, amidst the roaring of the waves and winds, from its cantonments at the extremity of the land. But it was too late. The advanced guard of the Royalists was swept down as soon as they advanced within range of the cannon of Penthièvre. The main body was pressed by the columns of Humbert; and, under cover of the guns of an English corvette, which with difficulty maintained a position within range of the shore, the discomfited Royalists, intermingled with a terrified crowd of peasantry, retreated to the sea in the hope of regaining the boats, which lay tossing on the raging surf. Humbert, unwilling to risk an engagement with desperate men, halted his troops at the extreme point of retreat. A parley took place between the Republican General and the Royalist Chief;

and after a few minutes, De Sombreuil, returning to his ranks, announced that he had concluded a capitulation with Humbert, and ordered the men to lay down their arms. The greater number obeyed, and were marched off as prisoners of war; some, who dispersed rather than yield, or trust to the faith of the Republican leader, either perished by the sword, or sought a voluntary death. The remnant of the expedition, consisting of nine hundred men, together with several hundred Chouan militia and peasantry, was brought off by the English fleet. Tallien, the Commissioner of the Convention, at the head-quarters of Hoche, refused to ratify the convention under which the emigrants had surrendered to Humbert. The Republican Generals, from fear of this infamous wretch, and the power which he wielded, were base enough to palter with their plighted words, and affected to question the validity of the capitulation. Sombreuil, when led forth to execution, solemnly affirmed that he had capitulated on an express stipulation that his soldiers should be treated as prisoners of war. Other officers of rank were executed with their noble and chivalrous leader. The venerable Bishop of Dol, who had favoured the Royalist cause, underwent the same fate. All the prisoners, with the exception of a few boys, were put to death.

The expedition to Quiberon has been often quoted as one of the many proofs of Pitt's incapacity as a war minister. The censure is just. The plan, as propounded by its able and energetic author, appears to have been the best military plan which had yet been submitted to the English Government. It was designed to revive and support the insurrection in La Vendée, and to organise an insurrection in Brittany, which was ripe for revolt. A junction with the army of the Upper Rhine, by way of Franche-Comté, or Alsace, was

Results of the failure at Quiberon.

contemplated as the result of these operations. The plan had been framed by De Puisaye, in concert with the Breton leaders, with whom, as well as with the people of the province, he had unbounded influence. The alarm of the French Government at the condition of the insurgent provinces had been shown by the policy of conciliation which they had anxiously pursued. The haughty Republicans, who had no terms but those of defiance for the powers of Europe, condescended to treat with the leaders of Vendéan and Chouan bands on terms of equality and even of concession. While De Puisaye was negotiating in London, Charette, the most formidable of the Vendéan chiefs, concluded a treaty of peace with the Republic, by which, in return for their recognition of the Republic, the Vendéans were to receive a large indemnity for their losses in the war, and many privileges which were not accorded to the French people in general.* A similar treaty, though not so favourable, was made with some of the Chouan chiefs. Even these terms were assented to by the insurgents only as a truce; and many of the patriotic chiefs refused any terms whatever. The principal Chouan leaders remained in arms; and Stofflet, the rival of Charette, in La Vendée, rejected the overtures of the Republicans.

M. de Puisaye accompanied the complete statement of his plans and resources, which he laid before the English Cabinet, with an emphatic intimation that their early decision, one way or the other, was of urgent importance. Yet four months were frittered away in negotiations and conferences; and it was not until the arrival of a deputation from the Breton leaders, urging the immediate return of their chief, that the Government determined upon supporting the expedition with an

* The Treaty is dated March 7, 1795, and is to be found in the *Annual Register* of that year, p. 255.

auxiliary British force of ten thousand men. De Puisaye was impatient to convey this joyful intelligence in person to his friends; but the ministers detained him in England to organise the expedition. The preparations were making rapid progress, when it became known in London that Cormatin, who commanded in the absence of De Puisaye, had entered into a truce or treaty with the Commissioners of the French Convention. The Ministry became alarmed; it was in vain they were told that Cormatin had exceeded his authority; that of one hundred and twenty-five chiefs, twenty-two only had signed the treaty; and that Cormatin himself had declared that it was only a temporising measure to obtain a suspension of arms until the opportunity for action should arrive. The English Government retracted their offer of ten thousand men, and offered a subsidy of ten thousand guineas instead. The men were to follow, in the event of the expeditionary force of a few French regiments being able to obtain a footing in the country. De Puisaye was not even consulted in the appointment of his principal officers; the most unfit man that could have been selected was forced upon him as his second in command, with a commission so obscurely drawn, that the Lieutenant claimed, and for a time exercised, to the serious hazard of the enterprise, the chief authority.* Had the British succours accompanied, or promptly followed, the expedition, it is all but certain that it would have been successful. It was not without much hesitation that Hoche, one of the most enterprising of the French Generals, ventured to attack Penthièvre, even after he had occupied the adjacent heights;

* D'Hervilly was brought off with the remnant of the expedition, and died of his wounds in England, four months after the action on the heights of St. Barbe. This brave and loyal, though sadly incompetent, officer frequently expressed his regret for the errors into which he had been led.

and it is hardly possible that he could have gained the heights, or attempted a forward movement, in the presence of ten thousand British soldiers. But, as it had been at Toulon, and as it had been in the former war of La Vendée, so it was at Morbihan. The British aid was too late. While the shattered remnant of the emigrant corps was retreating to the sea, along the peninsula of Quiberon, the advanced transports of the British regiments were tossing in the Channel, waiting for a favourable wind.

With this expedition, the cause of the Royalists may be said to have perished. Another insurrection, indeed, had taken place in Poitou; Charette was again in arms, and using every effort to obtain the aid of the British force which had been destined for service in Brittany. The first detachment of that force sailed towards the coast of Poitou, and Charette was led to believe that he might rely on its co-operation; but after a Council of War, it was determined that the troops should be landed at L'Isle Dieu, to await the arrival of the transports which were conveying the remainder of the force. At L'Isle Dieu, the army was, for the first time, joined by the Count d'Artois, who had given his authority to the expedition, and had promised to place himself at its head. The appearance, at Quiberon, of the first prince of the blood,[*] might, in a great measure, have compensated for the delay of the British regiments; but the Republican force, which, in June, when the expedition landed at Quiberon, did not exceed five thousand men, had been increased to forty thousand when His Royal Highness landed at L'Isle Dieu, in October. Still it was not too late. The Prince's name, coupled with the promise of British reinforcements, had enabled Charette to col-

[*] The unhappy child of Louis the Sixteenth had lately died, a victim to ill-treatment; and Monsieur had consequently assumed the title of Louis the Eighteenth.

lect an army of fifteen thousand men in a few days, and the presence of the Count d'Artois at their head would soon have doubled their numbers, and inspired a confidence which no other event could have secured. But the Count d'Artois remained at L'Isle Dieu with the British regiments, while Charette, with his brave and devoted comrades, were left to their fate. That fate was not long delayed. Deserted by their Prince, disappointed by their allies, and closely pressed by the savage legions of the Republic, the brave Royalists in vain maintained the conflict. They fought desperately; but they were overwhelmed. Those who were not slain in the field perished by the murderous vengeance of the enemy. Charette and Stofflet, the last of the famous leaders who had so long defied the regicide Government, were among the last who were taken and put to death. Even when the cause was hopeless, and further resistance was vain, the gallant spirit of Charette was unbroken. Hoche, admiring his valour, or unwilling to tempt the last effort of despair, offered the Royalist chief a ship to convey himself and his friends to Jersey. But Charette replied, that all the ships of the Republic would not be sufficient to remove the loyal adherents of the Crown from the territory where he commanded.

The vacillation and inconsistency of the English ministers, throughout this unhappy business, gave rise to an imputation on their sincerity and good faith. It was said, not alone by disappointed partisans, but by writers on both sides, that Pitt, actuated by an impartial animosity to the French people, had artfully fomented their dissensions, and had amused one party with promises of support, which he never intended to realise. It was even alleged that, on the fatal morning when the Royalists were driven in wild disorder from Penthièvre to the sea, the British gun-boats and ships of

Vacillation of the Ministry.

war fired indifferently upon the advancing columns of Humbert and the retreating emigrants. No English writer can condescend to vindicate the Government of this country from a charge which could be invented only by the extreme of ignorance and malignity. The expedition to Quiberon, so far as the English Ministry were concerned, was, like almost every other transaction of the war, marked by a degree of incapacity seldom exceeded in the administration of public affairs; but there is not the smallest pretence for accusing Pitt and his colleagues of conduct which would have exhibited a refinement of cruelty and treachery more atrocious than that of Tallien and his infamous coadjutors.

The successes of the British navy hardly compensated for the inaction of the army during this year. A few detached engagements, in which the English had mostly the advantage, had no effect upon the fortunes of the war; but a masterly retreat of Admiral Cornwallis, from a position which exposed his squadron to great danger, proved in a signal manner the superiority of British seamanship and skill. The two small West India islands of St. Lucie and St. Vincent were taken by the French. On the other hand, the important island of Ceylon, with the Malaccas, and all the Dutch settlements on the southern continent of India, yielded to the British arms without resistance. The valuable settlement of the Cape of Good Hope likewise surrendered.

Affairs in the West Indies.

The domestic condition of the country during this year was not prosperous. A succession of bad harvests combined, with the increasing pressure of taxation, and the languor of trade, to inflict severe privation on many classes, but more especially on the labouring people. The times were, therefore, favourable to those persons who, from ignorance or malignity, are always ready to persuade the populace that distress is entirely owing to political causes, and that the only remedy is to be found in organic changes in the constitution of the country. The agents of sedition did not fail to take advantage of this season; and their efforts were more successful than they had been since the commencement of the French Revolution. Immense assemblages were gathered in London and the great towns, Political meetings. to hear how bread was made dear, and how taxes were heaped upon an overburdened people for the purposes of an effete monarchy, and a grasping aristocracy; and how universal suffrage and annual Parliaments were the only cures for all these evils. Many riots took place, and a turbulent spirit of discontent became manifest throughout the country. Seditious hand-bills and ribald ballads were widely circulated among the common people, while persons of better education were supplied with publications in which revealed religion was assailed, together with political establishments. Paine's 'Age of Reason' appeared at this time, and being written in a more popular and plausible style than any of his former works, which had, from time to time, controverted the truth of Christianity, it was eagerly read by thousands, who were deluded with the idea of a new era of freedom, from which the restraints of religion and law should be alike banished.

The ministers were so much alarmed at this state of the country, that they thought it necessary to call Parliament together in the autumn, in order that the Government might be armed with new powers for the maintenance of order, and the suppression of dangerous opinions. The Corresponding Society, which had taken the lead in the propagation of the new revolutionary doctrine, organised an immense demonstration three days before the meeting of Parliament. They fixed upon some open ground in the parish of Marylebone, called Copenhagen Fields, a district now covered with streets and terraces, and there they collected an assemblage amounting, it was said, to a hundred and fifty thousand persons. An address to the King was voted, praying for reform in Parliament, the dismissal of ministers, and peace with the French Republic.

The immediate result of this meeting was an outrage upon the King, when he went in state to open the session of Parliament. A vast concourse of people filled the streets, and the procession was followed by a rabble, vociferating against the war, the ministers, and the King. In Pall Mall, opposite the Ordnance Office, the window of the state coach was perforated by a bullet, and His Majesty, on arriving at the House of Lords, announced to the Chancellor that he had been shot at. On his return, the carriage was attacked with greater fury, and was with difficulty saved from destruction. At St. James's, the King quitted the state coach, dismissed the guard, and proceeded in his private carriage to Buckingham House. He was still pursued by the infuriated populace, who threatened to pull him out of the carriage, and would probably have done so, but for the rapid driving of the coachman, and the timely arrival of a troop of Life Guards.

Outrage on the King.

These violent proceedings prepared the way for measures of a very stringent character, to which the ministers had already determined to require the assent of Parliament. A proclamation was, in the first place, issued by way of introduction to two Bills; the one for the repression of seditious meetings, and the other for extending the definition and penalties of high treason. The last-mentioned Bill was introduced in the Lords. Its provisions extended the crime of treason far beyond any limits which had been hitherto assigned to it. Writing, *preaching*, and speaking, which, under the existing law, would be criminal only if accom-

Proceedings in Parliament.

panying overt acts, were themselves constituted overt acts, and rendered the offender guilty of treason. A new offence was created, which subjected to the penalties of a high misdemeanour any person who by writing, preaching, or speaking, should incite or stir up the people to hatred or dislike of His Majesty's person, or *the established Government and Constitution of the realm*. Under the last words, it is obvious that the liberty of speech and the liberty of the press might have been wholly destroyed, had it not been for the recent Libel Act, which happily deprived prerogative judges of the exclusive right of interpretation in questions of libel. The Bill was denounced in the strongest terms by the Whig lords; and Grenville, who introduced the measure, could refer to no better times than those of Elizabeth and Charles the Second, as precedents for such unconstitutional legislation.

The second of this pair of Bills, which was brought forward in the Commons, was intended to restrict freedom of discussion, and to render it hardly possible to hold meetings for any political purpose without infringing on the law. Every public assembly, relating to any matter concerning the Church or State, was to be held by previous advertisement, signed by resident householders; and all assemblages not convened in this manner were declared illegal. The next clause of the Bill was of the most arbitrary character. It subjected any meeting, legally constituted, to the summary provisions of the Riot Act, if, in the opinion of any two justices, such meeting was dangerous to the public peace. By another provision, lecture-rooms, and even gatherings in the open air, to which admittance was obtained by payment, were required to be licensed, and were placed under the observation of the police.

This measure was received by the few members of

the House of Commons who were neither the obsequious followers of the minister, nor unmanned by exaggerated terrors, with every mark of amazement and disgust. Fox had been hardly able to restrain himself, while the minister, in stately periods, sought to demonstrate, that the partial excesses of the untaught populace, irritated by temporary causes, were a sufficient reason for retrenching some of the most valuable liberties of Englishmen. When Pitt sat down, the Whig leader, fired with a generous indignation, started up, and denounced the measure in words of vehemence and power, which even he himself had never surpassed. He said it was better at once to declare that, after experience, and upon a review of the present state of the world, a free constitution was no longer suitable to this country; but he hoped that the people, while they were yet allowed to meet, would assemble and express their abhorrence of these measures; for if they were to be denied a legal mode of making known their grievances, they would be reduced to the level of those unhappy creatures who have no alternative between abject submission and armed resistance. This Bill, and Lord Grenville's, commonly distinguished by the names of the 'Treason Bill' and the 'Sedition Bill,' were carried through both Houses by the commanding majorities which usually supported the Ministry. Fox and his friends, however, abated none of the vehemence of their opposition. When the Bills were advanced to that stage in which the details should have been discussed, Fox declined to discuss them, and hoped that they might pass in their integrity, that the people might fully understand the nature and extent of the attack which had been made upon their liberties. As to their *obedience* to such laws, that, said the great Whig chief, is a question, not of duty, but of prudence. Such language as this, of course, drew down

upon the intrepid orator the solemn censure of the
head of the Government. He was told that he had
preached rebellion, that he had recommended an
appeal to the sword, that he desired to involve the
country in anarchy and bloodshed. The strong
words of the Opposition leader became the text for
many a Tory speech and pamphlet; they inflamed
still further the overheated loyalty of the gentry,
clergy, and freeholders, throughout the kingdom;
and convinced, if conviction were wanting, the upper
and middle classes of the necessity for rallying round
the altar and the throne. Moderate men shook their
heads, while the violent and revolutionary party alone
applauded the bold language of the Whig leader. It
is not easy to defend a statesman who suggests resistance
to the laws made by competent authority,
unless he is prepared for the consequences to which
he points. It is certain, that Fox did not mean to
incite the people to rebellion; but it was well that at
a time when the current of public opinion ran violently
in a direction opposite to freedom, and when
the Government, instead of moderating the rage of
the friends of order, were doing everything in their
power to aggravate alarm, a great Englishman should
stand up, even if he were alone, and vindicate those
high principles of liberty for which the Eliots, the
Hampdens, and the Sidneys had sacrificed their lives.
'The principles of freedom of speech and freedom
of the press,' said Fox, 'I have learned from my early
youth, from Sidney and Locke, from Sir George
Savile and the Earl of Chatham; but,' he added, 'if
there were no authority for them, I would maintain
them by myself. I may be told these are strong
words, but strong measures require strong words.'
The rash impetuosity of Windham, excited by this
speech, hurried him into language, in the opposite
sense, still more objectionable. He accused Fox of
appealing to force, and declared that, in such case,

the Ministry were determined to exert *a rigour beyond the law*. Loud cries of 'Take down his words' forced the minister, courageous as he was, to retreat upon an explanation, tantamount to retractation. But these rash words, as well as another insolent phrase dropped by Bishop Horsley, in the Upper House, *that the people had nothing to do with the laws but to obey them*, were long remembered, and quoted by those who would represent the Court as engaged in a systematic design to subvert the liberties of the nation.

While these angry debates were agitating both Houses of Parliament, the political associations in the metropolis and in the principal towns were preparing petitions against the further progress of the Bills. The Corresponding Society, however, thought it prudent, in the first instance, to set themselves right, if possible, with the country, by issuing a paper, in which they disclaimed all connection between the meeting at Copenhagen Fields and the tumultuous attacks which had been made on the person of the Chief Magistrate, as they affected to designate the King. The Whig Club also thought it necessary to make a distinct statement of their principles. Their manifesto was carefully drawn: it enunciated no doctrine which was not accepted by constitutional authority, and contained no approval of universal suffrage and annual Parliaments, which were avowed as the basis of the affiliated societies. The appeal to public opinion against the Bills was, on the whole, a failure. Many petitions, indeed, were presented, but the bulk of them was got up under the immediate superintendence of the Corresponding Society, and emanated from the metropolitan districts. Four counties only petitioned, and two of these were Middlesex and Surrey. On the other hand, the petitions in favour of the Bills were almost as numerous as the petitions against them; showing that there was a powerful party in the country resolute to support the Government in any measure to put down the societies which adopted the principles, the language, and the nomenclature of the French Republic. The Bills passed both Houses; but an important modification of the Sedition Bill was effected by omitting the clause which empowered the magistrate to dissolve a meeting merely on his own judgment that it was dangerous to the public peace. The Bill was limited to three years; and it expired by efflux of time, without having, in any instance, been put into operation. The Treason Bill was limited to the duration of His Majesty's life, and likewise remained a dead letter.

A curious instance of the inconsistency into which the blindness of party can betray its ablest leaders and most shining lights was exhibited during this session. One Reeves,* who held a small place in one of the public offices, a courtier and a man of some learning, with more zeal than ability or discretion, had rendered himself obnoxious to the revolutionary party by his activity in organising an association to counteract their proceedings. While the Treason and Sedition Bills were pending in Parliament, this man, intending to serve his party, published a bulky pamphlet, which he called 'Thoughts on the English Government.' It was a mere farrago, which showed that the author was wholly ignorant of the subject on which he professed to write; the only intelligible proposition to be extracted from it was, that the British constitution was a monarchy which could dispense with Lords and Commons. The style of this piece was as contemptible as the matter; and it is difficult to conceive that any person should afford the leisure to look through it; still more that it could influence the opinion of

Political pamphlets.

---

* He was the author of a book with the ambitious title of 'A History of the English Law.' It is a mere compilation.

any educated man, woman, or child. The treatise of Filmer on Divine Right, to which we are indebted for Locke's admirable essay on Government, was an able and moderate performance compared with the work of Mr. Reeves; yet such was the irritable state of the popular party, within as well as without the walls of Parliament, that this insignificant author was assailed with a vehemence and pertinacity as if he had been the most formidable opponent of the liberties of the nation. Erskine, fresh from the defence of Hardy and Thelwall, loudly called for prosecution against a dangerous and malicious libeller. Fox declared, that this unreadable treatise had a far more dangerous tendency than anything which had emanated from the Constitutional and Corresponding Societies. Sheridan insisted, that the audacious pamphleteer should be prosecuted by the Attorney-General, that the Crown should be addressed to dismiss him from his employment;* that he should be summoned to the bar, reprimanded by the Speaker, and made to disown his published opinions, and that his tract should be burned by the hangman. Ultimately the Attorney-General was directed to prosecute; but the jury had the good sense to see that speculative writings, however dull and absurd, were not fit subjects for penal procedure. Mr. Reeves was, therefore, very properly acquitted.

An attempt was made to cast censure on the Government for having expended a considerable sum in the erection of barracks within the United Kingdom, as if a design had been entertained of overawing the people by the establishment of inland fortresses. But the old constitutional jealousy of standing armies, however suitable to the times in which it prevailed, had now become obsolete; and, notwithstanding the unconstitutional restrictions

---

* He held a small place in Lord Hawkesbury's office.

on freedom of discussion, which had recently been imposed, it was too late to alarm the people with any serious apprehension that their liberties were in danger from military power. If, then, the exigencies of modern times required the presence of an army within the realm, it was but reasonable that it should be housed. The practice of billeting soldiers had, from early times, been complained of as one of the grievances of the subject; and it was only a mitigation of the grievance, that one particular class of tradesmen should be compelled to entertain these unwelcome guests. Much nonsense was talked about the British soldier not having divested himself of the character of a citizen; a theory from which it was to be inferred, that an ale-house was the best place for maintaining this composite character. But a soldier without discipline is useless, and dangerous to everybody but the enemy; and discipline cannot be maintained for any length of time, over an army cantoned in the public-houses of populous towns. The extension of the barrack system was generally acknowledged to be one of the most useful measures of the administration.

The Chancellor of the Exchequer brought forward his budget before Christmas. He borrowed eighteen millions, and among the new taxes which he proposed, to defray the interest of this loan, were a duty on legacies, and a duty on collateral successions to real estate. The former tax, after some discussion, was voted by the large majority which usually supported the Government, especially on questions of finance. But the succession duty met with a different reception. It was pursued through all its stages with violent opposition, the country gentlemen following Fox and Sheridan, instead of the leader whose call they usually obeyed with implicit submission. At length, the third reading of the bill was carried only by the casting vote of the Speaker. The consequence was, that this part of the measure was abandoned. The landed interest wholly failed to establish a claim to exemption from a burden which they willingly imposed on personal property; and their conduct on this occasion was a far weightier argument for a reform in the representation than any which had been discovered by the Corresponding Societies, or the demagogues of the platform. The vote on the succession-duty was an abuse of power; it was a vote which could hardly have been agreed to by an assembly, the majority of which acknowledged constituents to whom they were responsible.

Selfish conduct of the landed Interest.

The cessation of the Reign of Terror in France, and the establishment of institutions which made provision for a regular and responsible Government, afforded the English Cabinet the much-desired opportunity of making overtures for peace. Accordingly, on the day after he had opened his budget, the minister brought down a message from the Crown, announcing that His Majesty was ready to open a negotiation with the French Government. The royal message anticipated a motion to the same effect, of which Grey had given notice. But the Opposition were not disarmed. They were shocked at the inconsistency of the ministers, in proposing peace with a Government composed of the same persons whom they had before objected to as incapable of making a binding treaty; and an amendment to the address was moved, because the message implied, that if the French Government should happen to undergo another change, the negotiation might be broken off. Grey himself asserted that the object of the message was merely to favour the contractors for the loan. But the recognition of the French Republic, though it must be the consequence of a treaty, and might be insisted on as a preliminary to negotiation, could hardly, with due regard to the dignity

Cessation of the Reign of Terror.

of Great Britain, be conceded upon the first overture for peace. Another party in the country, still smaller than that of the regular Opposition, objected to treat with the French Government on plainer grounds. This was the original war party, comprising, at one time, the great majority of the upper and middle classes, who entered upon the war, not for the purpose of vindicating the inviolability of the Scheldt, but to put down democracy in France. To this idea, long since exploded by statesmen as a principle of action, a few precise politicians still adhered. Lord Fitzwilliam maintained this principle, which had at the outset been avowed by the Duke of Portland, and the other Whig chiefs, who had joined the administration. Windham, though he continued in the Cabinet, also disapproved, on the same ground, of any attempt to make peace. Fitzwilliam, however, found no support, so weary of the war had all classes become. The cavils of the Opposition were equally discouraged, and their amendments to the address were negatived without division in both Houses. Nevertheless, the peace was conducted as languidly as the war. It was not until three months after the King's message to Parliament, that the proposal to treat was first communicated indirectly to the French Government. The French minister at Berne was requested, through the British plenipotentiary at the same Court, to ascertain whether his Government were willing to settle, in Congress, the terms of a general peace? And if so, upon what basis they would be prepared to discuss such a proposal? The answer of the French Directory was prompt and decisive. They intimated, in a tone and language hitherto unknown to diplomatic courtesy, that the offer of the British Government was insincere and delusive, and only made with the view of acquiring that character for moderation which attaches to the first proposal for a cessation of hostilities. But lest this rebuff should not be sufficient, they went on to declare, that no proposal would be listened to which involved the cession of any territory annexed to France; in other words, that they meant to retain the Low Countries. This reply, of course, put a stop to further negotiation; and the Court of London had only to address a note to their allies, pointing out the inadmissible pretensions which precluded the possibility of laying the basis of a treaty.

The Opposition, who found fault with the Ministry for the attempt to make peace, were indignant at the failure of the attempt; and so little did they regard the temper of the nation, and the plain sense of the proceeding, that they undertook to defend the insolence and arrogance of the French democracy. Fox moved an address to the Crown, in which the argument of the French reply to the English overture was amplified, and its offensive language even was adopted. Pitt had an easy victory in repelling such an attack as this; several members of the Opposition joined the large majority which rejected Fox's motion.

Opposition against negotiation.

Nevertheless, the Ministry were so intent on peace, that they determined to persevere in their endeavours to open a negotiation. They tried the mediation of the King of Prussia, but without success. They then engaged the good offices of the Danish Ambassador at London to solicit, through the agent of his Government at Paris, a passport for an English plenipotentiary. Even this advance was rejected. The domineering Republic refused to listen to a proposal for peace through any intermediate channel; and required the plenipotentiary of their enemy to attend at the French frontier, there to await the pleasure of the Directory. England was not quite so reduced as to supplicate for peace in this way; but the Government were not deterred from making a final effort to obtain a hearing. They

Persistence of the Ministry.

made a direct demand for passports, to enable an ambassador, with full powers, to proceed to Paris.* As it was difficult to find a decent pretext for rejecting solicitations so pressing, the passports were forwarded; but, at the same time, to show how unwelcome and how futile the English mission would be, two very significant notes were promulgated, by the order of the French Directory. In these documents, one of which appeared on the day after the passports had been sent, England was charged with perfidy, with intrigue, with bribery, and ambition. It was argued, that she could not possibly be sincere in her desire of peace, the effect of which must be to reduce her pretensions to ascendency on the seas, and to elevate into rivals those maritime states which had hitherto been her dupes. Her overture for peace, they maintained, was merely a pretence, to amuse an impoverished and discontented people, and to furnish a pretext for the imposition of new burdens.

It was easy to foresee the result of a negotiation which was to be opened in this spirit. *Failure of negotiations.* Nevertheless the Ministry persevered, and on the 22nd of October, Lord Malmesbury presented his credentials at Paris, and delivered a memorial,

---

* The reasons which influenced the English Cabinet, in thus seeming to court insult and humiliation, are given (not very intelligibly) by Lord Grenville. 'The Directory has sent us the most insolent answer that can be conceived; but, as the substance of it is in some degree ambiguous with respect to the main question of granting or refusing the passport, it has been thought better not to leave a loophole or pretence to them, or their adherents here, to lay upon us the breaking the business off. Another note is therefore to be sent to-day, by a flag of truce from Dover, in which the demand of the passport is renewed in such terms as seem most likely to bring that point to a direct issue, Aye or No. In other times, this last step would not only be superfluous but humiliating; in the present moment, the object of unanimity here, in the great body of the country, with respect to the large sacrifices they will be called upon to make, is paramount to every other consideration.'—*Courts and Cabinets of George the Third*, vol. ii. p. 350.

stating in general terms the principle on which he was authorised to treat. He proposed, that a general peace should be negotiated on a basis of mutual concession, and such an adjustment of territory as should be satisfactory to the allies of Great Britain, as well as to Great Britain herself, and be conducive to the maintenance of the balance of Europe. To this memorial, a derisive and insolent reply was returned by order of the Directory. The British Ambassador was told that his proposal was dilatory and delusive; that he had no power to treat on behalf of any Government but that by which he was accredited; that a vague enunciation of a principle of retrocession was not a sufficient basis; and that a belligerent whose principal allies had become hostile or neutral was not in a condition to retain the conquests he had made. As if this was not enough, the French note proceeded broadly to insinuate, that Lord Malmesbury's secret instructions were at variance with his ostensible powers; that his real objects were to prevent any other power from making a separate peace with France—to obtain from the people of England the means of carrying on the war—and to cast upon the Republic the odium of refusing reasonable terms. To this offensive paper, Lord Malmesbury was instructed to reply that his Government declined in any way to notice the offensive and injurious insinuations which it contained; that he was empowered to conclude a general peace; but that the conditions of a treaty could not be framed without the concurrence of His Majesty's allies; and that, before inviting them to accede to a treaty, he was to demand from the French Government whether they assented to the principle which he had proposed as the basis of negotiation? The French minister retorted, by requiring Lord Malmesbury, *without the smallest delay*, to define expressly the objects of reciprocal compensation which he had to propose; and upon the Ambassador inquiring whether this peremptory demand was the answer which he was to transmit to his Government, he was informed by M. Delacroix that it was; and the impertinent question was added, whether, on every communication, he thought it necessary to send a courier to London for fresh instructions? At length, after an interchange of several notes to the same purport, an interview took place between the two ministers. At this interview, Lord Malmesbury presented a memorial containing the final instructions from his Court. It placed the basis of the negotiation on the *status ante bellum*, which was explained as meaning the restoration of the Netherlands to the Emperor; the evacuation of Italy by the French troops, and peace with the Germanic Empire, on terms which should secure the balance of Europe. On the other hand, England offered to restore all her conquests in the East and West Indies, together with the islands of St. Pierre and Miquelon, and the fishery of Newfoundland. The only reserve made was of the Spanish portion of the island of St. Domingo, the cession of which to France would give that power an undue preponderance in the Archipelago.

It would have been impossible for this country at that time to conclude a peace which should have abandoned the Netherlands to France; but it is hardly credible that the English Cabinet should have believed that the French Directory would, for a moment, entertain the proposition which was laid down as the first article of the treaty. The possession of Belgium and of the Milanese had, for centuries, been the dream of French ambition; Belgium and Milan were now occupied by the armies of the Republic; and it was at this moment that England came forward and offered, as an equivalent for these magnificent conquests, two or three paltry sugar islands, and a

Impossible terms of the French propositions.

fishing bank in the northern seas. Such a proposal,
under the circumstances, gave some plausibility to
the French taunt, that the importunity of the English
Government was only simulated for the purpose
of persuading the people of England that peace was
impracticable, and that they must be content to furnish
the means of carrying on a war, however wearisome
and hopeless. M. Delacroix informed Lord
Malmesbury, at the outset of their conference, that
the Netherlands were now a part of France, and that,
by the constitution of the Republic, they could not
be given up. The Ambassador replied, that a municipal
law could not be set up as a bar to treaties with
foreign powers; that the allies had bound themselves
to treaties, known to all Europe, not to lay down
their arms without restitution of the territories of
which they had been dispossessed during the war;
that these treaties were older than the French constitution,
and anterior to the annexation of Belgium
to France. Pressed by this argument, the French
minister shifted his ground, and disclosed his real
meaning. He said that the great continental powers,
by the partition of Poland, and England, by her vast
colonial possessions, had altered the balance, and that
it was necessary for France to extend her dominion.
'We are no longer,' said he, 'in the decrepitude of
the monarchy, but in the vigour of the young Republic.'
Upon which Lord Malmesbury remarked
that if France, as a decrepit monarchy, was considered
an object of jealousy by the other powers,
how much more formidable was she in her new form
of a vigorous Republic; but M. Delacroix assured
him that the Republic would become the most quiet
and pacific power in Europe. He proceeded to throw
out some suggestions for indemnifying the Emperor
for the loss of Belgium, by the annexation to his
hereditary domains of some of the minor States of
Germany. His proposal, in fact, contemplated the

entire dismemberment of the Germanic body. The British Envoy, though he declined to discuss a project so extensive in the absence of the Emperor, nevertheless hinted that France might be compensated for the Netherlands by some of the Germanic States adjacent to her frontier, in addition to Savoy, Nice, and Avignon. The French minister's reply brought back the controversy to his original proposition. He said that these possessions were already part of the territory of France, and could not constitutionally be severed from it. Upon this, Lord Malmesbury declared, in distinct terms, that if such a principle was to be adhered to, negotiation would be useless, as his Government never would consent that the Netherlands should be permanently annexed to France. The interview might then have terminated; but it was prolonged upon secondary points, which might easily have been adjusted, if the main obstacle could have been overcome. But the truth is, that England was not, at that moment, in a position to maintain the *status ante bellum* as a basis for negotiation.

On the day after his long interview with Delacroix, Malmesbury received a note from the French minister, requiring him to sign the memorandum which he had delivered on the preceding day, and to deliver his ultimatum, in an official form, within twenty-four hours. With this arrogant and unusual demand, the Ambassador, after some hesitation, thought fit to comply. The Directory, having thus arrived at the end of the series of affronts which they had put upon the English Government, thought fit to bring it to a close by the last indignity they could offer. In a short note, drawn up without any attention to the forms of diplomatic courtesy, Lord Malmesbury was informed that the Directory would listen to no terms contrary to the constitution of the Republic; and that, as it

Dismissal of Lord Malmesbury.

appeared he was merely the passive agent of his Government, his continued presence at Paris was useless; he was, therefore, desired to take his departure in forty-eight hours. The paper concluded by intimating the pleasure of the Directory that any further communication on the subject of the peace, which the British Government might desire to make, should be on the basis laid down by the Republic, and conveyed to Paris by a courier.

A few days before Lord Malmesbury's arrival at Paris, the French had succeeded, through the agency of the Camarilla at Madrid, in obtaining a declaration of war by Spain against England; and while the forms of negotiation were proceeding at Paris, an envoy of the Directory was actually engaged at Vienna in endeavouring to detach the only remaining ally of this country. The pride of the Imperial Court had, however, been too deeply wounded by the campaign in Italy, and the insults to which they had been subjected by Bonaparte. The reverses which the French arms had experienced on the Rhine counterbalanced, in some degree, their success in Italy; and it was hoped that the possession of Mantua by the Austrian General might check the career of French conquest. These considerations determined the Emperor to try once more the fortune of war.

CHAPTER XXXVII.

BANK RESTRICTION ACT—FRENCH INVASION OF WALES—MUTINY IN THE FLEET—CONFERENCE OF LISLE—BATTLE OF CAMPERDOWN—FINANCIAL MEASURES—PATRIOTIC FUND—CHANGE IN PUBLIC OPINION.

THE Prorogation had been followed by a General Election, and vigorous efforts were made by the regular Opposition, in conjunction with the popular party, to improve their position in the House of Commons. But though all parties were weary of the war with the exception of Windham, Lord Fitzwilliam, and a few remaining disciples of the school of Burke, there was no party, beyond the avowed Republicans, willing to conclude a peace on any terms. The landed interest, which returned the majority of the House, retained undiminished confidence in Pitt. French principles of equality found little favour among the middle ranks of the English people; always more jealous of the lower than they are envious of the upper classes. The multitude had little or no share in the representation; but, on the whole, they seldom manifested any sympathy with the demagogues, who would persuade them that their interests lay in the destruction of the aristocracy, and a political revolution. The result of the General Election, therefore, was to leave Mr. Pitt in possession of the unparalleled parliamentary power which he had hitherto maintained.*

New Parliament.

---

* The King nevertheless appears to have thought it necessary to make extraordinary efforts to support the ministerial majority. In a letter to Pitt, a year following this election, he says:— 'I have some debts, of which the sum borrowed for the late elections makes the most considerable part, which I am by instalments paying off.'—EARL STANHOPE'S *Life of Pitt*, vol. iii. append. xi.

The new Parliament assembled while the negotiations, already described, were in progress at Paris. The Opposition found it difficult to quarrel with a measure which, during every period and circumstance of the war, they had constantly commended; but they vehemently denied the necessity of taking any precaution against the invasion which the French rulers had so loudly menaced.

They did not, however, venture to divide against the Bills for the establishment of a reserve of militia, of a body of irregular cavalry, and for the addition of fifteen thousand soldiers and sailors to the regular services by levies on the parishes; but their unpatriotic and unreasonable objections were generally disapproved, and elicited even from the smooth and cautious Wilberforce the sharp remark, that though the Opposition might not go the length of wishing for an invasion, they would not be displeased at some disaster befalling the country if they could thereby promote their party objects.

Financial affairs, and the fiscal policy of the Government, became the most important topics of debate during this session. The Budget was opened in December. A sum of eighteen millions, required for the military service of the year, instead of being raised, as in former years, by contract, had been obtained by open subscription, with a facility which proved at once the undiminished credit of the Government, and the resources of the country. It was contended, indeed, that the terms on which the loan was effected were unduly favourable to the moneyed interest—an argument which seemed to be supported by the eagerness with which subscriptions were sought. But the transaction which gave rise to the most serious attack upon the ministers was the advance of one million two hundred thousand pounds to the Emperor, out of the vote of credit of the preceding year. There is no point on

New loan.

which the House of Commons is so constitutionally jealous as its absolute dominion over the appropriation of the supplies. A vote of credit is not unfrequently granted as a temporary and provisional expedient; but such a vote is nothing more than an anticipation of the regular supply, and, as a general rule, should be applied only to ordinary purposes, or to those which Parliament has already sanctioned. The appropriation of any portion of such a grant, as a loan or subsidy to a foreign ally, in time of war, might be within the purpose or policy of the grant; but it would be a highly exceptional act, and justifiable only where the emergency was so urgent, that the sanction of Parliament could not be previously obtained. The first instalment of this subsidy had been paid while Parliament was sitting; and the only reason which the minister gave for his reserve was, that the money market would have been disturbed by the knowledge that so large an amount of specie was going out of the country. So far, however, was Pitt from putting forward this explanation by way of excuse, that he demanded a farther vote of credit of three millions, with the view of making any advances, within that sum, which the Government might think proper, to any of their allies in arms. And, in making this demand, Pitt maintained that a vote of credit entitled the Government to apply the money so voted to whatever purposes they might deem proper. But this doctrine, to be consistent with the sacred principle of appropriation, must be limited to cases in which the exigencies of the public service may require an expenditure which cannot be ascertained at the time when the vote or supply* of credit is granted. Pitt referred to several precedents in support of his position; but all these precedents were acts of power, carried, in defiance of strong

---

* Speaker Onslow always more properly termed it a 'supply of credit.'—3 HATSELL's *Prec.* 213 note.

opposition, by corrupt majorities, and reprobated by writers on constitutional law. The particular precedent on which the minister relied as precisely in point was one of the most questionable * of the bad catalogue which he cited. The Whigs were justly indignant, and many of his supporters were offended at the insolence with which Pitt, secure in his parliamentary following, thought fit to trample on the constitutional privileges of the Commons. The vote of censure, moved by Fox, it was not thought prudent to meet by the direct negative; an amendment approving the measure as a measure of policy, but disavowing it as a precedent, was ultimately carried; but the minority in favour of the original question was unusually large.

During the Christmas recess, an exigency of a novel and alarming character demanded the prompt and decisive interference of the Government. For some time past, an unfavourable balance of trade, combining with, or consequent upon, the loans to foreign powers, had drawn an unusual quantity of specie from this country. The Government, also, had drawn heavily upon the Bank. The country people, alarmed by the increasing rumours of invasion, took their paper to the banks, and hoarded the gold which they received in payment. Many of the provincial establishments, depending almost wholly on their paper circulation, sank under

---

* 'All things were very quiet in Parliament till the Christmas. The first attack was in the Committee of Supply, when a demand was made for nine hundred and odd thousand pounds, advanced to the Duke of Savoy, and Prince Eugene expended on my Lord Rivers's expedition, over and above the supplies given the last session of Parliament; they carried this so far that they moved a censure upon the Ministry for it. It was a long and warm debate, and, upon the division, we carried it in favour of the service 211 against 105.'—*Sir R. Walpole to Horace Walpole*, Feb. 12, 1706. — *Walpole's Correspondence*; Coxe's *Walpole*, vol. ii. p. 6. Pitt described the Ministry, in this instance, as receiving the thanks of the House!

the pressure. The Bank of England maintained its credit undiminished; nevertheless, the Directors thought fit to contract their issues; and as banknotes soon became as scarce as gold, the rate of interest rose to seventeen per cent.* The Directors, also, gave notice to the Treasury, that their advances on Treasury notes could not, in future, exceed half a million. They yielded, nevertheless, to the pressing solicitation of the minister to such an extent, that the coin and bullion in the Bank vaults, which had amounted to nearly eight millions in March, 1795, was reduced, on Saturday, the 25th of February, 1797, to one million two hundred and seventy-two thousand pounds;† and it was certain that the demand for gold on Monday would exhaust this balance. The country was in fact within forty-eight hours of bankruptcy.

The Governor and Deputy-Governor of the Bank hurried to Downing Street, and in an interview with Mr. Pitt, it was determined that cash payments should be immediately stopped by an Order in Council; that a meeting of bankers and merchants should be assembled in the City early in the ensuing week, and that Pitt himself should see some of the principal bankers at his office on the following day. The King, prompt as ever in the performance of his public duty, immediately came to town, and on the following day, although Sunday, a Council was held, at which a proclamation was issued in conformity with the arrangement above mentioned.

On Monday, the Lord Mayor convened a meeting of commercial men, and a resolution was unanimously adopted, that the paper of the Bank should be received and paid as cash in all their transactions. This resolution was afterwards signed by upwards of three thousand persons engaged

Meeting of merchants.

* Thornton on *Paper Credit,* p. 73. † Smith's *Wealth of Nations.* M'Culloch's *Note on Money.*

in business. The stocks immediately rose two per cent., and the success of the measure was completely assured. On the motion of Pitt, a committee of the House of Commons was appointed to inquire into the affairs of the Bank of England; and its report was such as to restore public confidence in the stability of that great institution. It appeared that, besides the advances to the Government of nearly twelve millions in course of repayment, there was a clear surplus of nearly four millions. A bill to prohibit the Bank from paying in cash any sum exceeding twenty shillings, and from making advances to Government of any sum exceeding six hundred thousand pounds, while cash payments were suspended, was passed, after considerable opposition. The duration of the Act was limited to seven weeks; it continued in operation twenty-two years.

There were, of course, not wanting many weighty arguments, both in and out of Parliament, against the suspension of payments by the Bank of the State, even for a few weeks. It was said, that the Bank should have been permitted to pay in cash while there was a coin in its coffers; and that the interference of Parliament was an arbitrary and unjust alteration of a contract between the Bank and the public, of which every note in circulation was, in itself, legal and conclusive evidence. It was feared, not without reason, that such a proceeding would give a shock to public credit from which it might never recover; and the example of France, led on to bankruptcy and disgrace by the facility of creating fictitious money, which the issue of assignats afforded, was held up as a warning to this country. These arguments were not easily answered; but, like many other arguments apparently as sound, they were refuted by time and experience. Public credit was unhurt, and commerce throve under laws which, so far as they extended, were a legislative declaration of national insolvency. Not only was it so, but there arose a school of economists who taught that this anomalous state of things was the sound condition of trade and commerce; that an inconvertible paper currency was the best security for public and private credit; and that a metallic circulation was only fitted for a primitive state of society.

At the same time that the country was in the crisis of a financial convulsion, its soil was in imminent danger of foreign invasion. *The Dutch fleet.* While Lord Malmesbury was amused with pretended negotiations for peace at Paris, active preparations were making in the harbour of Brest, and in the Dutch port of the Texel. A formidable fleet of line-of-battle ships and transports, destined for a descent on the coast of Ireland, was ready for sea at the beginning of the year; but the prevalence of storms and contrary winds detained the fleet in port. A few of the French ships and transports, however, succeeded in crossing the Channel, and appeared in Bantry Bay, on the 24th of December; but they were unable, from the state of the weather, to effect a landing; and far from being aided by an insurrection of the people, as the French had been led to expect by the representations of Irish emissaries, they found that ample preparations had been made for the defence of the island. The expedition, therefore, returned to Brest, with the loss of four ships of the line and eight frigates, which were either sunk or captured.

Another expedition, upon a still smaller scale, and apparently of an experimental character, was despatched in February to attempt a landing on some remote and defenceless part of the south-western coast of the British Islands. Hoche himself had undertaken the command of the force destined for the invasion of Ireland; but for the particular service on the coast of England he was content to detach a small body of twelve or fourteen hundred men, composed of convicts, and volunteers from the military prisons of Brittany and La Vendée. This marauding band was sent forth under the orders of one Tate, an Irish adventurer, who held the rank of Colonel in the French army. Tate's instructions were to enter the Bristol Channel, and to land his troops on the right bank of the river Avon, within five miles of Bristol. He was then to advance rapidly at night; to fire the city, the docks, and the shipping on the windward side. This being done, he was to scatter his force in predatory detachments, so as to spread confusion and dismay through the surrounding country. The main object was to effect a diversion which should aid the grand expedition intended for the regular invasion of the island. This daring scheme might have been attended with a momentary success. It was not improbable that three or four ships should elude the vigilance of the Channel cruisers; and the landing once effected, the march to Bristol, and the destruction of property, might easily have been accomplished. But here the success of the expedition must have ended. The handful of invaders, whether they held together, or dispersed in detachments, must have fallen an easy prey to the local force which would have been assembled in a few hours, unless the whole populace had risen in their favour. But this daring enterprise was not attempted. Instead of obeying his orders by sailing up the Severn, Tate did not even venture to enter the Bristol Channel. On the 22nd of February, the little squadron, consisting of two frigates, a corvette, and a lugger, anchored in a roadstead off the iron-bound coast on the northern extremity of Pembrokeshire; and in the course of the afternoon the French legion disembarked in perfect order at a desolate place called Cerrig Gwasted Point, about three miles from the town of Fishguard. They brought with them a large quantity of ammunition and small arms, but no artillery. One of the boats, which sunk in the surf, was supposed to have contained some field pieces. The troops, as they landed, dispersed over the country, plundering the cottages and farm houses. On the following morning the whole force, with the exception of a few stragglers, was drawn up on a high hill; and shortly afterwards the French frigates, on a signal from Tate, weighed anchor, and sailed away. The troops, indignant and alarmed at this unexpected desertion, became mutinous; and it was evident to the Commander that no reliance could be placed on their stability. Meanwhile the surrounding country was in motion. Lord Cawdor, who resided about thirty miles from Fishguard, having heard of the landing of the French on Wednesday night, had hurried to Lord Milford, the lieutenant of the county. But Milford, being aged and infirm, delegated his authority to Lord Cawdor; and this nobleman, though only a captain of yeomanry, by his vigour and conduct gathered around him in a few hours all the available strength of the immediate neighbourhood. During Thursday a force of six hundred and sixty men, consisting of the Fishguard volunteers, one hundred and twenty of the Cardigan militia, and his own troop of yeomanry, were mustered under Lord Cawdor's command. None of these men had ever seen a shot fired, but on parade; yet Lord Cawdor hesitated not a moment to lead them against the enemy, and they were equally willing to follow their able and gallant leader. A crowd of country people armed with scythes and other rude weapons were disposed, in such order as was practicable, in the rear of this little army. The French force, comprising many good soldiers, the flower of the army of La Vendée, and numerically superior to the raw levies of the Welsh captain of yeomanry, was drawn up in a position almost impregnable. Nevertheless, the French General, on the appearance of the English troops, offered to surrender upon terms. But he was peremptorily required to surrender at discretion; and in obedience to this summons early the next morning, the Frenchman laid down his arms. Such was the inglorious and somewhat ridiculous close of an invasion which lasted little more than twenty-four hours. Had Tate risked an action, it is hardly possible that the handful of militia opposed to him could have maintained their ground. But the alarm had spread; regular troops would soon have assembled in overwhelming numbers, and the small body of foreigners must, in their turn, have yielded to superior numbers, and to discipline equal to their own. According to his own statement to Lord Cawdor, Tate was determined to surrender by various reasons. He was disappointed at the want of co-operation from the country people which he had been led to expect, from the representations made to the Directory by Price of Bristol, and other persons among the dissenting interest, of the disaffected state of the population in the west of England: he was harassed by the jealousy and intrigues of Le Brun, his second in command; and by the mutinous state of his troops, already demoralised by plunder, and enraged at the desertion of the ships. These were the reasons which the French brigadier assigned for declining a conflict which, whatever might have been its immediate result, could only have caused a useless effusion of blood. Another reason has been mentioned for the hasty capitulation of the French. It is said they were frightened by an army of Welsh women in red cloaks and round hats, whom they mistook for soldiers; a tale which would have been unworthy of notice, had it not passed into popular belief. It is possible that among the crowd of peasantry which assembled in the rear of Lord Cawdor's column, the country-women in their national costume might have gathered on the distant heights; but the soldiers of Hoche, and the brave Bretons who had fought at Quiberon and followed Charette, were not so easily alarmed; even if such an absurd mistake could for a moment have been made, a field-glass would at once have betrayed the real character of Lord Cawdor's imaginary reserve. To complete the failure of this expedition, the frigates which conveyed it to the Welsh coast were captured on their return to Brest.*

A few days before Tate and his little band of adventurers sailed from Brest, the great Spanish fleet of twenty-seven sail of the line and ten frigates, under Don Joseph de Cordova, put to sea. The 'Santissima Trinidada,' mounting four decks and one hundred and thirty-six guns, the largest ship of war that had ever been built, and six other ships of the first rate, formed part of this mighty armada. When the Spaniard sailed from the port of Carthagena, a British squadron of nine sail, under Sir John Jervis, was cruising in the Mediterranean. But before he came in sight of the enemy, Jervis was reinforced by five sail of the line under Parker, and, what was of hardly less importance, was joined by Commodore Nelson, with his ship, bringing exact information as to the strength and position of the enemy. The

* A letter appeared in the *Times* newspaper of December 19, 1859, signed Edward Tate, and dated from Leicester Square, professing to vindicate the memory of the writer's relative from imputation on account of this prompt surrender. The letter was fictitious; it was from the pen of a distinguished correspondent of the journal. In addition to the ordinary sources of information, I have, by the kindness of the Hon. George Denman, been enabled to refer to an authentic account of this transaction, in the 'Journal of a Nobleman,' privately printed by Mr. Brettel, of Rupert Street. The journalist was the late Duke of Rutland, who derived his information from Lord Cawdor, when on a visit at Stackpole Court, shortly after the invasion. The present Earl Cawdor has also kindly furnished me with some facts, and referred me to a letter which the late Earl addressed to the *Times* in December, 1859.

object of the Spaniard was to effect a junction with the French and Dutch fleets at Brest and the Texel, in which event the British Channel would have been swept by seventy sail of the line. To intercept this formidable movement was a service of such urgent importance, that notwithstanding the enemy outnumbered him by twelve ships and twelve hundred guns, Jervis, with Nelson at his side, determined to fight. Accordingly, during the night of the 13th of February, the British fleet was prepared for action, and at daybreak the next morning, the long line of the Spanish fleet was seen off Cape St. Vincent. Before they could form in close order, Jervis bore down upon them, and, by a feat of consummate seamanship, succeeded in separating one-third of the Spanish ships, and excluding them from any share in the action which ensued. The conflict raged from half-past eleven o'clock in the forenoon until five in the afternoon, when four of the Spanish ships struck; but the nine ships, which had been cut off in the morning, having by this time regained the line, Cordova was in a condition to continue or resume the engagement had he thought fit. But the Spanish Commander, unwilling to risk further loss, retired into the port of Cadiz.

The English loss was three hundred; that of the Spanish six hundred and three. Nelson bore the most conspicuous part in this brilliant affair. At one time, his ship, the 'Captain,' a seventy-four, was engaged with the 'Santissima Trinidada,' and five other ships of the line. Trowbridge, Collingwood, and Frederick, gallantly supported him; but the 'Captain' was battered to a wreck. Nelson finished the day by boarding the 'San Josef,' of one hundred and twelve guns, and receiving the sword of the captain on his own quarter-deck.

This exploit, so honourable to British seamanship and valour, was welcomed with the pride and exultation which England never fails to bestow on the achievements of her favourite service. Admiral Jervis was raised to the peerage, with the rank of Earl, and the proud title of St. Vincent. A pension of three thousand pounds a year was also conferred upon him. Nelson was rewarded with the Order of the Bath. The thanks of both Houses, and of the principal cities in the kingdom, were given to Earl St. Vincent, and the fleet under his command. A liberal provision was also made, by subscription, for the widows and orphans of the brave seamen who fell in the performance of their duty.

Peerage and pension of Jervis.

Hardly had the rejoicing for the victory of St. Vincent begun to subside, when the country was imperilled by an event far more alarming than any danger which was to be apprehended from the foreign enemy, or from domestic treason. Early in March, Lord Howe, who commanded the Channel fleet, received several anonymous communications, drawn up in the form of petitions, praying for redress of grievances, and purporting to come from the seamen of the fleet. These papers, being all couched in the same terms, the Board of Admiralty agreed with Lord Howe, and the principal officers of the fleet, that they were the work of some mischievous individual, and unworthy of notice. But it soon transpired, that a conspiracy had been formed among the crews at Spithead, to place the officers under restraint, and to take possession of the ships. No sooner was the intelligence communicated to the Admiralty than an order was sent, by telegraph, to put to sea. Accordingly, Lord Bridport, who commanded in the absence of Earl Howe, made the signal to weigh anchor. This signal, it had been agreed, should be the signal for the commencement of the mutiny. Three cheers were given by the crew of the 'Queen Charlotte,' the flag-ship, and

Anonymous letters of complaint.

instead of mustering at the capstan, they ran up the shrouds. Their example was instantly followed by every ship in the fleet, and not an anchor was lifted. The commands and remonstrances of the officers were wholly disregarded; all authority was at an end. The next day, delegates from every ship in the fleet took possession of the cabin of the flag-ship; the obnoxious officers were sent on shore, and ropes were run out at the fore-yard-arm by way of intimidation. The first act of the delegates was to draw up a petition to the House of Commons. They desired the repeal of the Act of Charles the Second, which fixed their wages on a scale that had undergone a depreciation of thirty per cent. from the original standard. They complained that Lord Howe had disregarded their representations, and they pointed out some particulars wherein the army and militia seemed to have advantages in respect of pensions and allowances. This petition was signed by two men from each of the ships at Spithead. A petition, entering more fully into their grievances, was, at the same time, addressed, by the same parties, to the Board of Admiralty. In this paper, they demanded a re-adjustment of wages, in conformity with the present value of money; that their provisions should be of better quality and full weight; that they should be supplied with fresh bread and vegetables when in port; that the sick should be better cared for, and that the necessaries provided for them should not be misappropriated; that they should be allowed more liberty to go on shore; that when a man was disabled from duty by wounds received in action, his pay should not be stopped. And they concluded by limiting their grievances to these heads, that their countrymen might be convinced they asked nothing which might not be granted without detriment to the nation, or injury to the service.

These demands must be considered, in the main,

moderate and reasonable; and dangerous as it was that men, with arms in their hands, should approach Parliament in the guise of petitioners, and that mutineers should dictate terms to their superiors, it was more discreditable for the Government to have suffered such grievances to exist than for the men to complain of their existence. In fact, the state of the navy had not been much improved since it was described, with such terrible humour, by Smollett, in the novel of 'Roderick Random.'* Officers owed their promotion, in great measure, to family connections and parliamentary interest, and consequently, the service was infested with Whiffles and Oakums, who were either ignorant of their duty or abused their power. The ships' companies were defrauded of their right, first by the contractors, and afterwards by the pursers, until gains, which began in peculation, were openly claimed and recognised as perquisites. An almost incredible example of this prescriptive robbery is to be found in one of the grievances enumerated by the sailors in their petition; the practice, namely, of abstracting about one-fourth of the rations to which they were legally entitled. The power which is necessarily entrusted to the superior officers of a man-of-war, after every possible limitation has been imposed upon it, is so extensive, that the comfort of a ship's company depends mainly on the good sense and moderation of the captain and his lieutenants. British seamen are remarkable for their discernment of the professional qualifications of their officers, and for their obedience and fidelity to the commanders who are worthy of their confidence and respect. The frequency of mutinous conduct may, therefore, be taken as a strong test of incapacity, or wanton tyranny, or vexatious discipline on the part of the officer. No less than seventy-nine cases of

---

* First published in 1748.

mutiny and mutinous conduct had been tried by court-martial within the year.*

The First Lord of the Admiralty, Earl Spencer,
Earl Spencer goes to Portsmouth. with two other members of the Board, hurried down to Portsmouth at the first intelligence of the mutiny. The demands of the delegates from the 'Queen Charlotte' received, therefore, an immediate answer. An increase of wages, on the scale of four shillings, three shillings, and two shillings per month, to three classes of men respectively, was offered, and that pay should no longer be suspended during disability from wounds received in action; but the official reply was silent upon the other points mentioned in the memorial. The men refused to give way until their grievances were fully redressed, and an act of indemnity passed by Parliament. After two more days had been wasted in attempting to bring them to terms, partly by concessions, and partly by threats, it was determined that three flag officers should be sent on board the 'Charlotte' to confer with the mutineers. Accordingly, Admirals Gardner, Colpoys, and Pole, went alongside, and were received with the respect due to their rank. But the delegates, though respectful in their language and demeanour, were inflexible in their demands. Gardner lost his temper, and, seizing one of the delegates by the collar, swore they should all be hanged, together with every fifth man in the fleet. This rash ebullition nearly produced disastrous consequences. The crew, enraged at the insult offered to their representative, rushed towards the quarter-deck, and in the excitement of the moment

* Barrow's *Life of Earl Howe*, p. 321.

Lord Collingwood's opinion on the subject of the mutiny is, I believe, that of most officers of experience and good sense. When complaints were made of conduct which was designated as mutinous, Collingwood would exclaim, 'Mutiny, sir! mutiny in my ship! If it can have arrived at that, it must be my fault, and the fault of every one of the officers.' —*Memoirs and Correspondence of Lord Collingwood*, vol. i. p. 71.

the choleric Admiral hardly escaped with his life. The conference was abruptly broken off, and the delegates, returning to the 'Royal George' in high indignation, reported what had occurred. The red flag was immediately displayed; and at the sight of this terrible emblem, Lord Bridport ordered his flag to be struck. The guns were then loaded; watches were set; in every ship the officers were detained prisoners on board; and some dreadful event was hourly expected. On the next day, however, the men repented of their violence, and addressed a dutiful letter both to the Board and to their Admiral, Lord Bridport. These overtures led to a speedy settlement of the dispute. The demands of the delegates were granted in full; the Admiral's flag was again displayed, and the King's proclamation of a free pardon came down from London. The crews of all the ships at once returned to their duty.

Throughout these proceedings, the men, conscious of the justice of their cause, were careful that their conduct should be consistent with the moderation of their professions. They maintained an exact discipline in every ship; they punished drunkenness with flogging; and every other offence received its appropriate penalty. No man was allowed to quit his ship, nor was any letter permitted to be sent on shore. Every officer was superseded, but none, however odious, was ill-used. The frigates, with convoy, were allowed to sail, that no unnecessary injury might be inflicted on commerce.

While the mouths of all men were full of thanksgiving for their happy deliverance from a new and fearful peril, it was announced that the mutiny had broken out afresh. The Admiralty, which by its negligence had been the cause of the first outbreak, was, by its folly, the cause of the second. To save their credit and authority, so grievously impaired by the late transactions, the Board thought fit, a few days after their unconditional submission to the seamen, to take a step well calculated to excite jealousy and resentment throughout the fleet. On the 1st of May, an order was issued from Whitehall, referring to the late disturbances, and enjoining upon the officers a strict attention to their own conduct, with the view to the maintenance of discipline and the prevention of discontent. So far this was well; but, in a succeeding paragraph, the captains were instructed 'to see that the arms and ammunition belonging to the marines be constantly kept fit for immediate service, as well in harbour as at sea; and that the captains and commanders be ready on the first appearance of mutiny to use the most vigorous means to suppress it, and to bring the ringleaders to punishment.'

Mutiny at St. Helen's. Fired with indignation at this threat of keeping them in awe under the bayonets of the marines, and believing that the order itself was significant of an intention to break faith with them, the crews of the ships at St. Helen's, to which the main body of the fleet had been recently moved, again revolted against their officers, again appointed delegates, and despatched some of their number to claim the co-operation of the 'London' and the 'Marlborough,' which remained at Spithead. Admiral Colpoys, whose flag was flying in the 'London,' in obedience to the recent order, summoned his officers, put the marines under arms, and refused to let the delegates come alongside. The crew of the 'London,' after some hesitation, came aft, and demanded that the delegates should be admitted. The officers ordered them to go below; but a few only obeyed, and one man proceeded to unlash a gun and point it towards the quarter-deck. He was instantly shot dead by a lieutenant. This was the signal for a general insurrection. The men ran for their arms;

the marines joined them; the officers were disarmed, and the lieutenant, who had performed his duty with such stern decision, was about to be hurried to the yard-arm, when the Admiral interposed, avowed the lieutenant's act, and declared that it was done in pursuance of the orders of the Lords Commissioners of the Admiralty. This saved the officer's life; but the triumph of the seamen was complete. The 'Marlborough' quickly followed the example of the 'London,' and both ships weighed anchor, and joined the rest of the fleet at St. Helen's.

Lord Howe, the Commander-in-Chief of the Channel fleet, oppressed by sickness and infirmity, had been detained at Bath during the disturbances at Spithead. But, in the present extremity, Howe was justly deemed the person of all others most fitted to bring back his mutinous fleet to a sense of their duty. Accordingly, the venerable Admiral went down to Portsmouth, determined to visit every ship, and to ascertain, by personal communication with the seamen, what they wanted. Lord Howe was, in age, experience, and reputation, the foremost officer in the service. A man of birth, a courtier, a diplomatist, and a person of high accomplishments, he nevertheless adapted himself to his profession, and at sea affected those blunt and careless manners which endear a commander to the sailors. No officer in the service, therefore, had higher authority; and the mutineers, in the transport of their excitement and anger, which no Lord of the Admiralty could appease, at once gave utterance to expressions of joy and hope, when they heard that Black Dick, as they loved to call their renowned Commander, was coming among them to listen to their complaints, and redress their wrongs. The conduct of Lord Howe on this trying occasion was marked by judgment and temper. Knowing the

margin note: Lord Howe at Portsmouth.

strange mixture of suspicion* and generosity of which the character of the British sailor is compounded, he sought to allay the one, and to conciliate the other; at the same time that he maintained the dignity, and even under such anomalous circumstances the authority, of his station. He listened attentively while the men eagerly poured into his ear the story of their wrongs. Their specific grievances had been already redressed, but the officers by whose tyranny and petty oppression they had been so much harassed were restored to power; and they now insisted on the removal of these obnoxious officers. Lord Howe saw that to restore peace and confidence, it would be necessary to comply with this demand; but he veiled this dangerous concession so skilfully, that it assumed the form of a gracious indulgence, rather than a yielding to mutinous dictation. He told the men they had behaved very badly, that he wished to help them out of their difficulties, and to do all he could to satisfy their complaints. But he advised them, in the first place, to express contrition for their conduct, and to address a petition to himself, praying for his good offices, which he promised to employ. The men willingly came into this suggestion; and the Commander-in-Chief, on his quarter-deck, announced to the representatives of the different ships' companies, that Parliament had passed an act, confirming the promises of the Board of Admiralty, and securing to them permanently the advance of wages and the other benefits which they had sought. At the same time it was made known, that extensive changes were to be made in every grade of the officers of the fleet. An admiral, four captains, twenty-nine lieutenants, seventeen mates, and twenty-five midshipmen, besides marine and petty officers, were

---

* He described the seamen as 'the most suspicious, but most generous minds he ever met with in the same class of men.'— Barrow's *Life of Earl Howe*, p. 337.

dismissed. But while the men rigorously insisted on this proscription, it deserves to be mentioned to their credit that they desired no proceedings should be taken against the discharged officers, in respect to their alleged misconduct; and, in fact, the greater number of them were subsequently appointed to other ships.* An attempt to give a political character to the mutiny was likewise indignantly repelled; and some loose talk having been heard in one of the ships of giving her up to the French, she was threatened with destruction by the rest of the fleet, and a vigilant look-out was kept, to prevent the disaffected ship from holding any communication with the shore.

The measures proposed by the Government, in accordance with the engagements of the Admiralty to allay the discontents of the seamen, were readily agreed to by Parliament; and although the Opposition did not fail to find topics of censure, no man denied the existence of the grievances, or blamed the concessions which had been made.†

The second mutiny at Spithead lead to an outbreak in the ships at the Nore. While Lord Howe was engaged in restoring order and discipline at Portsmouth, a disturbance of a very different character broke out at the mouth of the Medway. The squadron at the Nore consisted of the 'Sandwich,' a ninety-gun ship, the 'Montague,' a seventy-four, and seventeen other ships of inferior rating. The 'Sandwich' carried the Admiral's flag; and in this ship the mutiny commenced on the 11th of May. Many of

* Barrow's *Life of Earl Howe.*
† To this, it appears, there was one characteristic exception. Some of the ministers (Windham, of course, being the foremost) consulted Burke, then within a few weeks of his death, as to the treatment of the mutiny. With the same want of judgment and temper which generally marked his public counsels, the dying statesman strongly recommended the employment of repressive measures. Had his advice been taken, the most disastrous consequences must have ensued.— Lord Stanhope's *Life of Pitt,* vol. iii. p. 50.

the other ships, at the same time, rose and overpowered their officers. Delegates were appointed, after the example of the Portsmouth mutineers, and a man named Parker, a supernumerary seaman of the 'Sandwich,' assumed the leading post. The delegates at first held their meetings at Sheerness, in open contempt of the authorities, both by sea and land, parading the town with music and banners; but they subsequently moved the ships to the Great Nore, to be out of the range of the land batteries.

The next day, Admiral Buckner's flag was hauled down by the mutineers, and the red ensign was displayed in its place. They then put forward a manifesto or statement of their grievances, which they forwarded to the Admiralty. This paper contained demands subversive of all discipline, and calculated, according to the boast of the foreign emissaries and domestic traitors, who were anxiously watching their proceedings, to convert every man-of-war into a floating Republic. But even Republics have found that men-of-war cannot be governed on their own principles; and have ever enforced a discipline not less strict than that of the navies of despotic monarchies. Parker's demands insisted, among other things, upon a revision of the Articles of War, and indemnity to deserters—the disqualification of all officers who were not agreeable to the ships' companies—and an increase of prize money. It was well observed, that this document neither contained the sentiment nor was expressed in the language of seamen.

The Admiralty, in their reply, remonstrated with the men on the impracticability and impropriety of these demands, but offered a free pardon to all who should immediately return to their duty. Buckner undertook to carry this answer to the 'Sandwich.' But the Admiral's reception was very different from that which Lord Bridport and

Lord Howe had experienced from the Channel fleet. He was allowed to go on board; but he was received with none of the honours due to his rank. The offers of the Admiralty were rejected; and the Admiral was informed by Parker, that the delegates would be content with nothing less than unconditional compliance with their demands, and the attendance of the Lords of the Admiralty at the Nore, to ratify the conditions. To show their determination, the mutineers, on the following day, hauled down the Admiral's flag, and displayed the red ensign of rebellion in its place.

That no means of bringing back the men to obedience by persuasion might be left untried, Earl Spencer, the First Lord, accompanied *Earl Spencer at the Nore.* by other members of the Board, went down to Sheerness, and had an interview with Parker and the delegates. Parker was the only spokesman on this occasion; and it was evidently his policy to prevent any accommodation between the authorities and the men. He conducted himself with great insolence, and ended by insulting the Commissioners in the grossest manner. The Board returned to London, and the delegates, throwing aside all show of moderation, proceeded to the most violent extremities. They seized and plundered two store-ships and a merchantman. They fired upon two frigates which would not join them; they blockaded the mouth of the Thames. All this they did with impunity; and their success induced other ships to join them; the 'Lancaster,' a frigate, which lay in the river, and four ships belonging to Admiral Duncan's squadron.

The mutiny at the Nore had now continued three weeks, and no attempt had as yet been made towards its suppression. The inha- *Alarm at Sheerness.* bitants of Sheerness, apprehensive of a bombardment, abandoned the town in great numbers. Fears even were entertained for the safety of the metropolis.

Parliamentary denunciation of the mutineers.

At length, the Government determined to adopt vigorous measures. They had nothing to fear from any opposition in Parliament. At the first outbreak of the mutiny at the Nore, party spirit subsided in the presence of a common danger; and Sheridan, the most uncompromising, if not the most factious opponent of the Ministry and its measures, denounced the conduct of the mutineers as unseamanlike and un-English. He proposed, in the first place, a measure of conciliation; but, at the instance of Pitt, he postponed a proposal which might embarrass the action of the Government, and subsequently supported the Government in the assertion of their authority. On the 1st of June, a message from the Crown was brought down to Parliament, recommending a more effectual provision for the prevention and punishment of sedition and mutiny in the naval service. Bills were immediately introduced to attach the highest penalties of a misdemeanour to the seduction of soldiers and sailors from their duty; and to make it felony to hold intercourse with ships which were declared, by proclamation, to be in a state of mutiny. These Bills were suffered to proceed without comment from the leading members of the Opposition, and within a week they received the royal assent. On the following day, proclamations were issued in accordance with these acts. Admiral Buckner was alone empowered to hold communications with the mutineers, and only for the purpose of receiving their submission. Adequate measures were also taken to suppress the insurrection. Ships were put in commission; gun-boats were despatched; the buoys at the entrance of the river were taken up, and batteries were erected on the shore to command the rebel fleet. The mutineers had already begun to feel alarm. While the coercion bills were passing through Parliament, the Earl of Northesk, captain of the 'Monmouth,' who had been detained a close prisoner in his cabin since the commencement of the mutiny, was taken on board the 'Sandwich,' and was charged, by Parker, with a letter to the King, containing terms which the mutineers affected to offer as their ultimatum. One of these terms was new, the most impudent and absurd that had yet been propounded. No punishment was to be inflicted without the sanction of a jury of the ship's company! Lord Northesk was enjoined to bring back an answer within fifty-four hours. He told them his errand was not very hopeful; but he executed his commission with fidelity. The letter of the delegates was laid before His Majesty, and an official answer was returned that nothing short of unconditional submission would be accepted.

Cut off from all intercourse with the shore, already suffering many privations, and seeing formidable preparations to reduce them by force, the only hope of the mutineers was in the support and co-operation of other ships at the home station. But instead of encouragement, they received addresses from the crews of the ships at Portsmouth and Plymouth, desiring them to return to their duty, and reprobating their conduct as a 'scandal to the name of British seamen.' It became known, also, that a resolution had been adopted, that no man engaged in the mutiny should be employed in the merchant service; and they found no sympathy in any class of their countrymen. But when the recent Acts of Parliament, and the King's proclamation, which the leaders of the mutiny in vain endeavoured to suppress, were promulgated through the ships, the men who had been coerced into the mutiny, or who had reluctantly joined it, loudly declared for immediate submission. Five of the ships slipped their cables, and deserted the piratical squadron. The 'Repulse' and the 'Leopard' followed the lead; but the former, a frigate

of the first rate, having grounded, was exposed to
the broadsides of the nearest ships for an hour and a
half, before she could be got off. Three other ships
made good their escape to the Medway in the night.
The remainder of the insurgents then separated into
two divisions; the one professing to hold out to the
last; the other willing to surrender upon terms.
Flags of truce were sent on shore; but the Government,
being advised that the mutiny was breaking
up, remained inflexible. The men, therefore, determined
to give way. Their first act of repentance
was to remove the blockade from the mouth of the
Thames. The revolted ships dropped off one by
one; and on the 15th of May, after the mutiny had
lasted five weeks, the 'Sandwich' herself slowly left
her moorings, and anchored under the battery of
Sheerness.

Parker, the ringleader, was taken into custody the
same day. In a few days he was tried
by court-martial, and condemned to death.
The sentence was executed at the yard-arm of the
'Sandwich.' Parker was a man of decent parentage,
and good education. He had been bred to the naval
profession, and, at the close of the American war, was
an acting lieutenant in a man-of-war. Having come
into some property, he retired from the service, and
married a Scotch girl, with whom he is said to have
received a portion. He appears, however, to have
dissipated his fortune; and, to avoid a prison, he
entered himself as a common seaman on board a
tender in Leith Roads. From thence he had been
transferred to the flag-ship at Sheerness. He was a
bold, unprincipled adventurer, full of arrogance and
conceit; but well fitted by education and address to
exercise a dangerous influence over ignorant and
discontented men. He styled himself, and was addressed
by the crews as, Admiral Parker. He fell
short, however, of those high qualities which enable

a man, without the advantage of position, or early training, to maintain authority and command. The possession of power disturbed the balance of his mind; and instead of the skilful leader of rebels, of whom he appears to be the comrade, while he is really their dictator, this man vaunted himself like any vulgar tyrant, who claims a legitimate right to the abuse of power. Parker affected to establish a discipline, not less severe than that which was hardly submitted to without murmuring when practised by an officer with a regular commission. His only notion of rule was force and terror. If a ship was suspected of disaffection to the cause, she was kept within range of the guns of the 'Sandwich,' or one of her consorts. If she attempted to return to her duty, she was fired into. On his trial, this man, who had behaved with such insolence and defiance to his superiors, endeavoured to set up a character for moderation; attempted to shift the blame of commencing the mutiny to a ship in which he had no control, insinuated that he had acted under duress, and finally asserted that it was owing to his influence the fleet was not carried into the enemy's port. He was persuaded that by this line of defence he should save his life. But the proof was too strong for such pretences; and the only effect of putting them forward was to deprive his well-merited fate of that commiseration which it would otherwise have received from his generous though misguided followers. Parker was thirty years of age when he suffered. Not more than four or five persons were capitally punished. Sentences of more or less severity were passed on other ringleaders; but the punishments were not numerous.

The disturbances in the fleet were not confined to the Channel and the mouth of the Thames. A bad spirit pervaded the whole service. We have seen that Admiral Duncan was deserted by a portion of his fleet; he was, in fact, left with only two ships to blockade the Texel. The promptitude and wise severity of Lord St. Vincent suppressed the first rising of a dangerous revolt in the squadron off Cadiz. At the Cape of Good Hope, it was necessary to point the guns of the batteries at Simon's Town, and to prepare red-hot shot for the destruction of His Majesty's ships in open mutiny. In another sea, the crew of the 'Hermione' rose, put the captain and his officers to death, and took the frigate into a Spanish port.

Convulsions like these happening almost simultaneously proved the existence of evils which demanded searching inquiry. The more palpable grievances of the service had been hastily redressed under dangerous and disgraceful pressure. But there remained behind deep-seated and wide-spread mischief, which could not be so readily removed. The decks of a man-of-war do not admit of luxury; nor does a seaman require to be pampered. But, rough as he is, he knows and feels the difference between a well and an ill-regulated ship. Generally, the health and comfort of the crew were but little regarded. The ventilation of a ship was unfit for the necessities of animal life; the food was frequently bad; the sick were often cruelly neglected. But more harassing and demoralising even than these hardships was the conduct of the officers, among whom it was a too prevalent notion, that to keep the men up to their duty, and make them smart, it was necessary to be continually cursing them, to call them foul names, never to address them without an oath, and never to let them be at rest. The lesson which these great mutinies taught was not forgotten. The Admiralty became more circumspect in their appointments. A lad, who was fit for nothing else, was no longer considered eligible for the navy. It ceased to be considered a sufficient qualification for the command of a ship, that the candidate was recommended by the proprietor of a borough, or a woman of fashion. Midshipmen were admonished, that it would be as well to treat bearded men something better than dogs; and captains and first lieutenants began to doubt, that the service would go to perdition, if the hands were not constantly turned up for exercise and drill. Even contractors for beef and rum were taught to think, that some little attention ought to be paid to the quality of the commodities which they supplied; and ships' pursers obtained an inkling that there was a limit to peculation. A more wholesome spirit was diffused throughout the service. A reform commenced in every department. Improvement, though slow, has ever since been progressive; and yet there is still room for an advance. As a proof how little the people of this country are acquainted with the interior economy of their favourite service, it is worthy of remark, that the two practices which had been always the topic of popular declamation as the two crying grievances of the seafaring race, namely — impressment and flogging — were never named in any of the ships during this year of mutiny.

The failure of the negotiations at Paris rendered it necessary to open a second budget for the service of the year. The country had now entered on the fifth year of a war, which had already added one hundred and thirty-five millions to the permanent debt, without having accomplished any of the objects for which it had been undertaken. We began with Austria, Prussia, Spain, and Holland as allies. Prussia had withdrawn into a dubious neutrality. Spain and Holland were firm on the side of the enemy. Austria had already lost her Flemish and Italian provinces; and to succour this, our last remaining ally, the financial arrangements

Increase of the national debt.

of the Chancellor of the Exchequer included a loan
of three millions and a half. But at the very moment when this further advance was proposed by the
weary and despondent minister to a reluctant House
of Commons, Austria had made her peace with the
triumphant Republic. The supplementary budget
was introduced on the 26th of April. In the previous week, the Emperor had signed the preliminaries of Leoben, by which Savoy and the Netherlands were ceded to France, and Lombardy was to
form the centre of a cluster of states to be called the
Cisalpine Republic.

The supplementary loan was eighteen millions,
Supplementary loan. which was afterwards reduced by the
amount of the subsidy destined for the
Emperor. Pitt announced, that he had been forced
to borrow this money on hard terms; the bonus and
interest being nearly eight and a half per cent. It
was not disputed that the loan was necessary, nor was
it suggested from any quarter that the money could
have been procured at an easier rate; but the House
was very uneasy at the vast and increasing expenditure. Nor were the country gentlemen indifferent
to the significant remark of Mr. Fox, that the public
debt would soon be equal to the whole rental of the
country. They found a fitting occasion for wreaking
their ill-humour on the occasion of a strange proposition which the minister, at the instigation of the
moneyed interest, was induced reluctantly to make.
The loan of eighteen millions raised by open subscription before Christmas had been vaunted as the
'Loyalty Loan,' although it is certain that every
subscriber, in addition to his patriotic motive, was
actuated by a strong opinion that he was making a
good investment of his money. But the scarcity of
specie which ensued, and the announcement of a new
loan, had so depreciated the 'loyalty' stock, that a
demand was raised for indemnity to those public

spirited persons who, according to their own account, had come forward with no other intent than to relieve the exigencies of the State. Pitt had so far committed himself to the cant which had designated this speculation as a pure ebullition of public spirit, that he was unable to resist the importunity of the subscribers, or rather of the combination of bankers, into whose hands many of these securities had passed. The indemnity claimed was fifteen shillings per cent. Long annuity; but the minister dared not undertake to propose more than half that amount. And even this proposal he did not attempt to found on any legal or equitable claim, but simply on an appeal to the generosity of the House. The House, however, was not in an indulgent mood. The motion was received with anger and derision from all sides. Mr. Dent, a subscriber to the loan, was the first to rise and disclaim all participation in this impudent and hypocritical pretence. He said that the claimants were merely speculators, who ought to abide by their bargain; and he asked if the balance had been on the other side, whether the public would have received, or would have expected to receive, the difference? There was no answer to this argument; and Pitt saw his supporters, in great numbers, quit their seats and walk out of the House. A small majority of the committee affirmed the resolution; but, on the report, it was carried by a majority of one in a bare House. Nothing more, of course, was heard of this unprecedented and discreditable proposal.

Motions for peace and for the removal of the ministers, as the great obstacle to the conclusion of peace, were made in both Houses. But if the Opposition really shared in the belief which prevailed among the partisans of the French revolution, both at home and abroad, that the war had been caused by Pitt, and

Motions for a change of Ministry.

was continued by his influence, they were wholly mistaken. It is no longer questioned, that he found himself forced into war, contrary to his expectations and his wishes. It is true, that the same want of sagacity which led him to the belief, that the distraction of their domestic affairs would render the French incapable of carrying on foreign war, likewise persuaded him that the exhaustion of their resources must certainly, within a limited period, bring the war to a successful termination. But the latter delusion was now dissipated like the former; and so great was Pitt's desire for peace, that in availing himself of the opportunity for renewing the proposal to treat, which the treaty with the Emperor seemed to afford, he declared, with questionable prudence, that no punctilio or formal difficulty should be suffered to prevent or interrupt the negotiations. The Emperor having given up the point upon which the British Government had felt bound in honour to insist in the recent treaty at Paris—the restoration of the Austrian Netherlands—the main obstacle to an arrangement seemed to have been removed. There was, however, a strong difference of opinion in the Cabinet, as to the expediency of renewing an attempt which had ended a few months before in ignominious failure. Lord Grenville and Mr. Windham were decidedly averse to making an overture which they believed would only result in subjecting the King's Government to further humiliation. But Pitt was resolved; and it became Grenville's duty, as Secretary of State, to make the proposal to the French minister. Delacroix, on the part of the Directory, professed the utmost alacrity to treat; and Lisle was fixed upon as a convenient place for the negotiation. But, with this preliminary interchange of notes, the amity of the correspondence ceased. When it was announced that Lord Malmesbury would be again accredited, Delacroix rudely replied, that another choice would have been more acceptable; and desired that the frequent communication, by courier, between the plenipotentiary and his court, which he said had prevented the recent negotiations from coming to a successful issue, should not be repeated. This impertinence Grenville retorted, by an intimation that the remark upon the appointment of Lord Malmesbury was unworthy of notice; that the plenipotentiary would despatch as many couriers as he thought proper; and that the motives and circumstances which led to the rupture of the late negotiations being known to all Europe, it would not be conducive to a discussion with a pacific object, that the recollection of these circumstances should be revived.

The Directory deputed three persons of note to conduct the negotiations at Lisle. At the head of the commission was Letourneur, some time a member of the Directory himself, Admiral Pleville le Pelley, and Maret, already well known in the diplomacy of the Revolution. *French commissioners.*

The Commissioners were civil; but it was manifest, from their instructions, that the rulers of France were prompted by a spirit very different from that which urged the advances of the British Government. The people of France were divided on the question of continuing the war. Those who inclined to peace from a desire of repose, of relief from the burden of taxation, and from republican jealousy of military influence, formed a numerous body. On the other hand, the ambitious few and the restless multitude, the children of the Revolution, who were unable or unwilling to adopt the habits of peace and order, were eager for a continuance of the war. These parties were severally represented in the Directory; and, at this moment, a struggle for the ascendency was going on between the five potentates at the Tuileries. *Divisions amongst the French.*

The British plenipotentiary proposed, as a formal

preliminary, to negotiate on the basis of former treaties. He offered to restore all the territory taken from the French during the war; retaining as conquests the island of Trinidad and the Cape of Good Hope, the former possessions of Spain and Holland respectively. The French ministers declared themselves incompetent to discuss these propositions, simple and obvious as they were, without instructions from Paris; and, in the meantime, they brought forward for discussion three points, the adjustment of which they stated to be an essential preliminary to further negotiations. These points were, first, the renunciation of the title of King of France, which had for centuries formed part of the style of the Crown of Great Britain; secondly, a restitution of the ships taken at Toulon, or an equivalent for them; thirdly, a discharge of any claim or mortgage upon the territory of the Netherlands, which the British Government might retain as a security for loans made to the Emperor. These strange propositions seem to have been advanced for the purpose of evading the real points in dispute, and were so considered by Lord Malmesbury. In vain, therefore, did he urge, with regard to the first point, that a similar objection, when mentioned, had been disposed of by a saving clause in every former treaty of peace between the two countries; that the second demand was so arrogant and unreasonable, that, if insisted on, it must interpose a serious obstacle to the progress of negotiation; and that the question involved in the proposition lastly stated was one which properly formed part of the treaty between the Emperor and the French Republic. The Commissioners only replied, that their instructions were positive. But as these points, which the French Commissioners themselves described as insulated, were not tendered, and could not be received by way of answer to the proposals which had been formally communicated by

Malmesbury to the French Government, it was necessary that those proposals should receive an official reply. In a few days, the answer of the Directory arrived. It resembled in character, though it differed in terms from the reply which had put an end to the former negotiation. In October, the French Government had declared themselves precluded from entertaining a treaty on the basis of mutual concession, because their municipal law did not admit of the cession of any territory which had been annexed to the Republic. In July they pretended that they could not be party to the surrender of Trinidad and the Cape, because they were bound by their separate treaties with Spain and Holland to maintain the respective territories of those allies. The impudence and hypocrisy of this pretext were so transparent, that Malmesbury and Grenville at once agreed that it was futile to carry the negotiation any further. The French Government had undertaken to treat with Great Britain on behalf of their allies, Spain and Holland, as well as on their own; and now they set up, as a bar to the treaty, their separate and secret engagements with those powers. The notoriety of the fact, that Spain and Holland had been coerced into the war, and that they would be thankful to be relieved from it on any terms, gave a cruel zest to the mockery which put forth the pretensions of these helpless dependencies of France as obstacles to the treaty.

The Secretary of State would at once have terminated a negotiation so unpromising, but the first minister was unwilling to withdraw while a hope remained. Some expressions which fell from the French Commissioners, in conversation with Lord Malmesbury, seemed to mitigate the rigour of their formal instructions; and, accordingly, Malmesbury was directed to answer the French note, and to require the statement of a counter proposal on the part of France. The Commissioners admitted that this demand was reasonable; but the British minister expected in vain any proposition from Paris. At length, after several weeks had been passed in communications between the plenipotentiaries, which did not advance the negotiation a single step, the contest between the rival parties at Paris was terminated by the act of violence known by the name of the revolution of the eighteenth Fructidor. The war party having obtained the mastery by the simple expedient of turning the peace party out of the executive and out of the legislature, their first measure was to put an end to the conference at Lisle. The Commissioners, who had shown a disposition to promote the ostensible object of their mission, were recalled, and two persons of very different character were accredited in their places. These men informed Lord Malmesbury, that their instructions were to demand the restitution of all conquests made by England from the Republic and its allies during the war; and to require a positive and immediate answer to this preliminary. The British plenipotentiary replied by referring to his former communications, which laid down the principle of compensation as the basis on which alone he was empowered to treat. The French envoys thereupon announced the pleasure of the Directory, that his lordship should return to his Court within twenty-four hours, in order to obtain fresh powers. Malmesbury, of course, immediately left France; while the Commissioners, either from wanton insolence, or under a flimsy pretence of moderation, remained at Lisle, affecting to await the return of the British embassy.*

* It appears that Barras made an overture through an agent whom Pitt considered credible, to bargain a peace on the terms proposed by the British Government, with the addition of Ceylon, in consideration of a payment of two millions sterling to himself and his friends in the Directory. Pitt obtained the consent of the King and the members of the Cabinet, to entertain this proposal, abating the demand to four hundred and fifty thousand pounds. Whether this or any other sum was actually offered,

Shortly after the rupture of the negotiation at Lisle, the preliminaries of Leoben were carried into effect, by the treaty of Campo Formio. The terms imposed on Austria appeared, on the whole, moderate. In exchange for the Low Countries, of which she was not unwilling to be rid,* and for Lombardy, which she could not hold, Austria was to acquire Dalmatia, the city of Venice,

Proposals to Austria.

does not appear; for the matter dropped.—EARL STANHOPE's *Life of Pitt*, vol. iii. p. 61, and Appendix vii. When he came to reflect upon it, Pitt could hardly have failed to see that nothing but disgrace and ridicule could result from such a scandalous traffic. It is difficult also to see how he could have obtained the money. The secret service fund was wholly inadequate to meet such a demand; and it would have been impossible to lay an estimate before Parliament. The very fact, however, that Pitt did not immediately reject such an overture, is a proof that, so far from pursuing the war policy, which vulgar opinion has attributed to him, he was for peace almost at any price.

A few days after Lord Malmesbury had left Lisle, three envoys arrived from America to settle difficulties which had arisen between the Government of the United States and the French Directory; for the Trans-Atlantic Republic had not less reason than the old European monarchies to complain of the overbearing insolence of the French democracy. It was in vain that the American minister attempted to open a regular negotiation; but after a time, these propositions were conveyed to them through a secret channel, as necessary preliminaries to a formal treaty. One of these propositions, which, we are told, was 'urged with scandalous pertinacity, was the gift of a large sum of money to the members of the Directory.' The Government at Washington took a much more sensible and becoming view of a proposal of this nature than the Cabinet of St. James's. 'In no event,' they said, 'is a treaty to be purchased with money, by loan or otherwise. There can be no safety in a treaty so obtained. A douceur to the men now in power might, by their successors, be urged as a reason for annulling the treaty, or as a precedent for further and repeated demands.'—TRESCOTT's *Diplomatic History of the Administrations of Washington and Adams*, pp. 187-190. Boston, 1857.

* At the commencement of the war, the Imperial Government proposed to exchange the Netherlands for Bavaria; but the English Court opposed the scheme.—*Lord Grenville to Lord Auckland*, 3rd of April, 1793.—AUCKLAND *Correspondence*, vol. iii. In fact, it was more for the interest of England than of Austria, that the latter should retain the Belgic provinces.

the command of the Adriatic, and an important military line from the Adige to the Po; and as France was not yet ready or willing to absorb the rich Italian provinces, which had been wrested from the Emperor, these territories were, for the present, consolidated under titular independence, with the title of the Cisalpine Republic. The Ionian Islands were appropriated by France. By secret articles, the Emperor engaged to use his influence with the Germanic body to obtain their confirmation of the boundary of the Rhine, including the fortress of Mentz, which the Emperor ceded to France. It was not, however, without as much resistance as they ventured to offer, that the Austrian Government consented to terms, which circumscribed its dominions on so many points. They pressed hard for a Congress of the States, hoping to obtain better terms from the support of the Germanic body; but Bonaparte peremptorily insisted on having the essential articles determined between the principals, reserving for the consideration of a Congress those points only in which the members of the Germanic Empire had a common interest.

Ionian Islands ceded to France.

The conferences at Lisle were followed by a succession of invectives, official and unofficial, by the French Directory against the British nation and its Government. The series was terminated on the 5th of November, by a proclamation, circulated through the whole of France, announcing a project of invasion and conquest of the British Isles. These rodomontades were intended to flatter the vanity of the army, to stimulate among the people the military spirit, which had begun to flag, and, above all, to appease and divert the ambition of Bonaparte, whose towering abilities and reputation were more terrible to the rulers at Paris than the enmity and power of Great Britain. The conqueror of Italy himself had the sagacity to see

French invectives against the British.

that the Republic had more to fear from England
than from all the other powers of Europe. It was
true, that she had no great army; that her statesmen seemed incapable of forming any great military
plan; and that her generals were incompetent to the
petty services with which they were charged. But
England maintained her supremacy upon the sea;
and until her hardy and skilful seamen, with such
leaders as St. Vincent, Nelson, and Duncan, could be
matched, the conquest of England was hopeless, and
the permanent aggrandisement of France impossible.
Bonaparte was as loud as Barras and Reveillere
Lepaux in his denunciation of the British Government; but, as a matter of business, he came to the
conclusion, that the military resources of the Republic were not yet adequate to such an enterprise
as the invasion and conquest of the British Isles.

The project of getting possession of the Channel,
by the junction of the Spanish and Dutch *Projects for in-*
fleets, having been frustrated by the vic- *vading England.*
tory of St. Vincent, the invasion of England was, for
the present, abandoned; but the minor plan of a
descent upon Ireland, which had long been preparing,
under the direction of Hoche, was still entertained.
The Spanish fleet, at Cadiz, being closely blockaded,
the Dutch ships in the Texel were destined to effect
a junction with the French fleet at Brest, and to land
fifteen thousand troops on the Irish coast. Admiral
Duncan had been watching the Texel during the
spring and the summer. When the Dutch had
nearly completed their preparations for sea, four of
Duncan's ships deserted to join the mutiny at the
Nore; and, at this critical period, the British Admiral
had only two ships of the line under his command;
but happily the mutineers returned to their duty
before advantage could be taken of their misconduct.
Storms and contrary winds detained the Dutch fleet
in port throughout the summer; and Duncan's squadron had, by that time, received reinforcements, which

gave it a slight superiority over that of the enemy. About the same period it was found that the fifteen thousand French troops, which had been so long waiting for transport, had nearly consumed their provisions. The season was fast approaching, when the expedition would have to encounter the periodical perils of the seas, in addition to the terrors of the British seventy-fours. In these circumstances the cautious Dutchman thought fit to inform his Irish friends, who had been eagerly watching every change of wind for the last two months, that the expedition to the Irish Channel, on the scale originally planned, must be abandoned. But the energy of Hoche was called in aid to animate the sluggish counsels of the Dutch Government; and after the termination of the conferences at Lisle, the Directory insisted on some effort being made by the fleet of their reluctant ally. At this time Duncan, having been eighteen weeks at sea, had withdrawn the greater part of his ships to Yarmouth Roads, to victual and refit. De Winter, availing himself of the opportunity, slowly moved from his anchorage, intending to sail for Brest, to effect a junction with the French fleet, and then to return to the Texel for his transports. Duncan, who had prompt information of De Winter's movements, came in sight within forty-eight hours after the Dutchman had put to sea. On the 11th of October, the English Admiral found the Dutch fleet off Camperdown, about nine miles from the land.

The ships on either side were equal, being sixteen sail of the line; the English had a slight preponderance in tonnage, and were more numerously manned; but the difference was not appreciable between two fleets well matched as they were, in seamanship, skill, and valour. The prompt decision of Duncan, and the vigorous execution of his orders by his captains, soon determined the fortune of the day. The Dutch fought with a courage

Equality of the forces.

and obstinacy which sustained their ancient reputation.* The rival flag-ships maintained a dreadful conflict for three hours, and it was not until his ship was disabled, and every officer on the quarter-deck, except himself, was either killed or wounded, that De Winter struck. His second in command, Keyntjies, in like manner, struck to Admiral Onslow, but not before he was mortally wounded. The Dutch captains, seeing their leaders vanquished, either surrendered or fled. Eight sail of the line, with three ships of inferior rate, were taken. The loss in killed and wounded on the side of the English was one thousand and forty; on that of the Dutch, one thousand one hundred and sixty. No naval action, during the war, was fought on more equal terms, or with greater obstinacy, than the battle of Camperdown. This victory, following the victory of Cape St. Vincent, put an end, for the time, to all apprehension for the safety of the British Isles. Projects of invasion were, indeed, still vaunted; a flotilla of flat-bottomed transports was to be fitted out; a new loan was proposed to be secured on the future plunder of Great Britain; a decree was passed, declaring all ships, conveying British goods, to be lawful prize. Menaces of this kind sufficiently proved that the enterprise was no longer seriously entertained.

Parliament was called together for the autumnal session a few days after the announcement of the great victory at Camperdown, and its first business was to acknowledge the achievements of that noble service, upon which the glory, the prosperity, and the safety of the nation mainly depend. On such an occasion it behoved

Factious conduct of the Opposition.

* 'The appearance of the British ships at the close of the action was very unlike what it generally is when the French or Spaniards have been the opponents of the former. Not a single lower mast, not even a top-mast, was shot away. It was at the hulls that the Dutch had directed their shot.'—James's *Naval History*, vol. ii. p. 103.

every man of mark to be in his place; yet the leaders of the Opposition in both Houses thought this a fitting occasion formally to withdraw from attendance in Parliament.

Unconstitutional conduct of the Whigs. Such conduct was as unconstitutional as it was petulant and short-sighted. It is the duty of a member of Parliament to attend the service of the House; and in the Commons, this duty is enforced. It was pretended by the principal men in opposition, or alleged on their behalf, that their continued attendance in Parliament was useless when their resistance to the arbitrary measures of the minister was futile, and when their motives were maligned. But if these men had faith in their principles, and in the constitution, which an earlier generation of Whigs steadily maintained through not less evil times, they would not have taken a step which was calculated to direct the affections of the people towards another form of Government. The session was attended by a demonstration which seemed, indeed, to imply, that Fox and his friends were prepared to recommend republican institutions, instead of the Constitution of 1688. The principal members of the Opposition assembled at a public dinner to celebrate the birthday of their leader. The Duke of Norfolk took the chair, and in proposing the health of Mr. Fox, thought proper to remind the company that Washington had no greater number of followers than were assembled in that room when he undertook the liberation of his country; and he desired them to make the application. This significant hint was received with great applause; and at a later period of the evening, His Grace proposed for a toast, 'their Sovereign—the people,' which was drunk with acclamation. For this proceeding, the Duke of Norfolk was dismissed from the lieutenancy of the West Riding, and deprived of his regiment of militia.

In the absence of Fox, the forlorn band, which still remained on the Opposition benches, was led by Mr. Tierney, a clever and accomplished barrister, who had recently entered Parliament. The first important measure of the session was a Bill to continue the restriction on cash payments by the Bank of England for the duration of the war. Tierney, having somewhat presumptuously announced, that he had a general retainer to oppose the Government, commenced by attacking the Bill; but, though his criticisms were marked by shrewdness, knowledge, and good sense, Pitt did not deign to answer him. The Bill, recommended as it was by the report of a secret committee, was agreed to.

Mr. Tierney.

The financial plan for the year was brought forward before Christmas. It was remarkable for a bold attempt to push the principle of providing by taxation for the service of the year. Hitherto the expenses of the war had, for the most part, been defrayed by loans; and, in this manner, the permanent debt had been increased by upwards of one hundred and thirty millions within the last four years. But as the prospect of an early termination of the war had vanished, Pitt determined to try the resources and public spirit of the country, by taxation equivalent to a large proportion of the estimated extraordinary expenditure. Twenty-five millions and a half were required for the service of the year. Of this amount, nearly seven millions were met by ordinary revenue, leaving about nineteen millions to be provided for. The Chancellor of the Exchequer proposed to raise twelve millions by loan, and seven millions by trebling the assessed taxes.

The budget.

The financial plan of the Government was recommended chiefly for the principle which it enunciated. A great and protracted war cannot be carried on without borrowing. There is a point beyond which taxation cannot be pushed without encroaching upon capital, and so diminishing the source from which enterprise and industry are fed. On the other hand, a nation is demoralised and discredited which shrinks from pressure, and lightly casts upon posterity burdens which the present generation should bear. A wise minister pursues the just medium between these extremes; and Pitt is entitled to the high praise which is due to such a policy. The particular measure of finance which he adopted is less to be commended. He framed a graduated scale by which the assessment was increased in proportion to the income of the person chargeable; a plan which has been often reprobated as containing the principle of confiscation. The measure, though nominally an increase of the assessed taxes, was, in fact, a disguised income tax. An assessed tax is essentially self-imposed or self-adjusted. Every man can either decline the commodity taxed, or reduce the standard of taxation. But the minister deprived the payer of this election; for he took the assessment of the preceding year as an arbitrary basis; and charged every person who had come under that assessment with an increase ascending from one-fourth to five times the amount. The sole merit of this plan was that it admitted of a tolerably accurate estimate of the sum which it would yield; and being propounded only as a temporary expedient, it was not perhaps fairly open to the criticism to which it would have been subjected had it been brought forward as part of the permanent system of finance.

Nevertheless the plan was vehemently opposed. The attempt to conciliate the favour of the multitude by heaping the burden upon the rich, was not successful. The resolutions were, however, voted in the Committee of Ways and Means by a great majority.* In matters of finance this

* 214–215.

stage is practically considered as conclusive. When the resolutions of this committee are confirmed on the report, the new duties are levied, or the repealed taxes are discontinued without waiting for the Act of Parliament which formally ratifies the resolution of the House. But when it became known that a larger sum than had ever been raised within the year was to be collected by increasing the taxes on houses, windows, and shops, as well as on carriages, horses, and servants, loud murmurs went forth from the principal cities and towns in the kingdom. The inhabitants of Westminster, always foremost in every political movement, called upon Fox to return to his place in Parliament, and denounce the odious impost. Sheridan also appeared in his place on the day appointed for the second reading of the Bill. The leader of opposition attacked the scheme in unmeasured terms, and the minority increased from fifteen to fifty. Pitt became uneasy. He had treated with contemptuous indifference the well-argued objections of Tierney, Hobhouse, and others, in the committee; but now he admitted, with unwonted candour and moderation, that many of the objections were well founded, and that, without extensive modifications, the measure would be oppressive to the industry of the country. Some modifications were accordingly introduced in the committee on the Bill; but, so far from mitigating the Opposition, the minority increased to seventy-five on the third reading. Pitt himself became, for the time, the most unpopular man in the kingdom. On the day set apart for a national thanksgiving on account of the naval victories, when the King and the two Houses of Parliament went in procession to St. Paul's, the Prime Minister was forced to take refuge from the angry populace in Doctors' Commons, and was conducted home in the evening by a troop of City Light Horse. These demonstrations, however, were but temporary, and indicated no desire to shrink from the efforts which were necessary for the honour and safety of the nation. A few months after Pitt had been hooted through the City, the commercial and trading classes, which had complained of the burden of taxation, eagerly came forward at a suggestion from one of the minister's most devoted friends, and subscribed sums amounting to more than two millions in contributions varying from a guinea to thousands of pounds.* The immediate apprehension of invasion, and not any desire to prosecute the war, prompted this prodigious addition to a taxation hitherto unparalleled.

Another proposal, which added much to Mr. Pitt's reputation as a financier, was his plan for the redemption of the Land Tax. This ancient impost, which belonged to the primitive form of taxation, when land was the principal source of the public revenue, had varied for the last century from one shilling to four shillings in the pound. The tax had remained at the maximum during later years, and the minister proposed to make it perpetual at this rate on the original valuation of 1693, giving the landowner the power of redemption at twenty years' purchase, payable in three per cent. stock. Taking the stock at the price of the day, which was about fifty, it followed that, by this arrangement, the public would benefit to the extent of one-fifth; and assuming the whole amount to be redeemed, the land-tax of two millions

---

* The idea originated with the Speaker. The greater part of this noble free-will offering was contributed by the commercial and trading classes. The Bank headed the subscriptions with two hundred thousand pounds. Among other donations of equal amount Mr. Peel (the father of the minister), a calico printer at Bury, put down ten thousand pounds, as the subscription of his firm. When he told his senior partner, Mr. Yates, not without some misgiving, what he had done, the answer was, 'You might as well have made it twenty thousand, while you were about it.'—LORD STANHOPE'S *Life of Pitt*, vol. iii. p. 92. The munificence which characterises the merchants and manufacturers of this country has never been duly appreciated.

would be converted into revenue yielding two millions four hundred thousand pounds. The arrangement was not less beneficial to the landholders than to the public; for the value of land being about thirty years' purchase, it enabled them to redeem what was really a rent-charge at little more than two-thirds of its value. The proprietors, indeed, raised a faint voice against the perpetuation of the tax at its maximum, as a measure of confiscation; but many availed themselves of terms so advantageous. The effect of the measure was to strengthen public credit, and inspire new confidence in the resources of the minister.

The probability of invasion, in the spring of 1798, was again considered so imminent as to call for prompt and extraordinary preparations. Prospect of invasion. A supplementary budget was, therefore, opened in the month of April, in order to provide for the interest of eight and a quarter per cent. upon a new loan of three millions. Taxes on salt, on tea, and on armorial bearings, were proposed, and readily assented to. The modifications of his original scheme of trebling the assessed taxes, having reduced the minister's estimate from seven millions to four millions and a half, the deficiency was made up by other imposts; the most remarkable of which was a scale of export and import duties.

The demonstrations and menaces of the French Government still continued. An army had been organised, called the army of Defence of the country. England, and distributed along the French coast, as if in readiness for embarkation. A flotilla of flat-bottomed boats was ostensibly announced as in preparation, to transport this army across the Channel. The bankers of Paris were assembled to subscribe to a loan, to be secured on English property, which was to become the prize of the invaders. Such gasconade did not indicate any serious intention to undertake an enterprise so desperate as an invasion of this island; but a contemptuous neglect of all preparation for defence on the part of Great Britain might have exposed the country to insult, and even temporary disaster. Accordingly, a royal message to Parliament, immediately after Christmas, announced that orders had been issued to call out and embody a portion of the militia.[*] A Bill was subsequently introduced, to indemnify persons whose property might be sacrificed in the event of an invasion. A Bill for manning the navy was passed through all its stages in one day. This extraordinary proceeding, though not without precedent, seemed to be an unnecessary departure from the practice of the House. Tierney, without objecting to the policy of the measure, questioned the necessity of pushing it forward with such irregular precipitation; and, considering that the object of the Bill was to extend the odious power of impressment, it was not unreasonable, in the absence of any immediate dread of invasion, to pause a little before enlarging a mode of manning the navy, which experience has shown to be as bad as it is barbarous.[†] But Pitt, assuming the air of a dictator, would not brook any opposition, and charged Tierney with a desire to obstruct the defence of the country. Tierney, instead of flinging back this wanton insult, more properly appealed to the chair for protection. The Speaker, instead of vindicating the freedom of debate, by instantly calling upon Pitt to retract an imputation, which, whether just or unjust, was a clear breach of plain parliamentary law, made an evasive response, conveying a timid suggestion

---

[*] In 1799.

[†] Lord Clarence Paget, the Secretary to the Admiralty, in opening the Navy Estimates of 1859, stated, on the authority of an Admiralty return, that, in the last three years of the impressment system (which ended in 1813), three thousand able-bodied seamen were constantly employed on shore to press twenty-nine thousand six hundred and five, of whom twenty-seven thousand three hundred deserted.—Hansard's *Debates*, 154, p. 909.

to the overbearing minister, that he should explain away the language he had used. Pitt said something which was accepted as an explanation; but reference having been afterwards made, in the course of the debate, to this supposed explanation, Pitt denied that he had given any explanation at all. 'I gave no explanation,' he said, 'because I wished to abide by the words I had used.'* The Speaker remained silent; and thus the dignity and the privilege of the House of Commons were laid prostrate at the feet of one too arrogant member. Tierney, failing to obtain from the House the redress to which he was entitled, had recourse to the alternative which the manners of the time approved. A meeting took place between the Prime Minister and the political opponent whom he had insulted. The parties exchanged shots, happily without effect, and the seconds declared the law of honour to be satisfied.

The Government persevered with varying fortune in the policy of putting down freedom of opinion in the press and on the platform by the extreme rigour of the law. Numerous minor prosecutions followed the great trials of 1794-5. The trial of Stone for high treason, in 1796, resulted in an acquittal. One Crossfield, a surgeon in the navy, and three other persons, were arraigned in the same year on a charge of a conspiracy to take away the King's life by means of a poisoned arrow blown through a tube. This was much ridiculed at the time under the name of the 'Pop-gun Plot;' and it turned out to be little more than an idle story. Crossfield was acquitted, and the other prisoners were consequently discharged. Gale Jones, a well known and active agent of the Corresponding Society, was prosecuted to conviction for a seditious speech at Birmingham. O'Coigley, an Irish priest, with

* Dean Pellow's *Life of Lord Sidmouth*, vol. i. p. 200.

Arthur O'Connor, an Irishman of good family and fortune, who was on terms of friendship with many of the leaders of Opposition, both in England and Ireland, together with three other persons of less note, were tried by a special commission for a treasonable correspondence with the French Government. The case against O'Coigley being clearly established, he was convicted and hanged. O'Connor, the principal culprit, escaped through the failure of evidence. The inferior agents of this treasonable plot, which was planned in connection with the Irish rebellion in the year 1798, were acquitted.

It appears that, about this time, the Government, which had been hitherto content with small prey, entertained the idea of prosecuting the chiefs of the Opposition. When a king's lieutenant so far forgot himself as to propose for a toast 'Our Sovereign—the majesty of the people,' accompanied with language and allusions which could not be mistaken, the Government had no alternative but to dismiss him from his office. Nor could a Privy Councillor have much reason to complain of being dismissed from the Council Chamber of the Crown for a similar offence. But the Court party were not satisfied with this reparation; and the Government was urged to take further proceedings against the eminent persons who had so rashly echoed the jargon, if they had not actually abetted the purposes of the revolutionary faction. The friends of monarchy and order were at least consistent in desiring that the Norfolks and the Foxes should be brought under the subjection of the law as well as the Hardys and the Thelwalls. It was distinctly proposed that some proceeding should be taken against Fox, who, after his dismissal from the Privy Council, had deliberately repeated at the Whig Club the offence which had been so signally reproved. But though the indignation of the Tories was in a great measure justified, the minister himself might well pause before he ventured on so bold a step as the prosecution of his great rival. The result would probably be an acquittal; and an acquittal would be a triumph such as the revolutionary party had not yet attained. Reasoning in this manner, Pitt prudently determined to refrain from the attempt to put the law in motion against the leader of Opposition.*

Had Pitt persevered in his idea of sending his rival to the Tower, or expelling him the House of Commons, he would have found that assembly pliant to his purpose; and such was the temper of the times, that it is much to be doubted whether Fox would have found half the support and sympathy out of doors which a former generation had lavished upon Wilkes. State prosecutions no longer excited public interest; and persons were acquitted or convicted according to the evidence upon charges of treason or sedition, without becoming heroes or martyrs. Erskine exerted all his eloquence and skill, as counsel for the Crown, in prosecuting to conviction a poor bookseller who had sold 'The Age of Reason.' The great champion of the liberty of the press is said, indeed, about this time, to have made an overture to the minister.† A few days before Fox's name was

* The record of this transaction, which has recently come to light, does not place Pitt's character in a pleasing point of view. Having made up his mind, that it was not expedient to prosecute the leader of the Opposition for an attempt to stir up sedition, Pitt was not ashamed to entertain a suggestion of a very different kind. He thought of having Fox reprimanded in his place, calculating on the certainty of his repeating the offence at the next meeting of the Whig Club, 'When'—to use Mr. Pitt's own words—'he (Fox) might be sent to the Tower for the remainder of the session, which would assert the authority of the House as much as an explanation, and save the inconvenience of a Westminster contest.'—*Pitt to Dundas,* 5th of May, 1798.— Lord Stanhope's *Life of Pitt.* This idea of laying a trap for the most frank and careless of men, was more worthy of the low cunning of a policeman than the generous rivalry of public life.

† Lord Stanhope's *Life of Pitt,* vol. iii.

struck out of the list of Privy Councillors, Sheridan went down to the House of Commons; and, on the occasion of a message from the Crown asking for fresh powers to suppress domestic treason, he delivered a speech so loyal and patriotic, as to call forth the applause of the great majority of the House, and high compliments from the minister himself. The minority, which had become so small since the commencement of the war, had suffered a sensible diminution during the present session; and, except on the Assessed Tax Bill, had never numbered more than fifteen. Yet the Duke of Bedford, who was considered the head of the Whig party, thought it worth while to rise in his place, and move an address to the Crown for the dismissal of His Majesty's ministers. This solemn mockery was supported by the Marquis of Lansdowne, in whose administration Pitt had first filled the office of Chancellor of the Exchequer. The Whigs, however, were in proportion stronger in the Lords than in the Commons; for the Duke's motion found thirteen supporters in a House of one hundred and twenty-six members.

The change which had taken place in the public feeling is not to be attributed to popular caprice. The war, in its origin, was regarded with disfavour by many honest friends of liberty, as a war in which this country ought not to have engaged. It was a war in which we were allied with despots who, under pretence of vindicating the rights of a brother sovereign, were intent only on objects of rapacity and ambition. At the same time, the conduct of the Government seemed designed to bring the administration of affairs at home into harmony with that which obtained at Vienna and Berlin. Because freedom had been abused at Paris, the liberties of Englishmen were assailed. The press was put under restraint; legions of spies were let loose upon the country, and no man could speak his

Changes in public opinion.

mind in safety, or even do the most harmless acts
without fear of question. It is no wonder that the
old English feeling was aroused, and that the State
trials of 1794 were regarded with an intensity of
interest which had not been equalled since the trial
of the Bishops. The public safety at that time depended on the trial by jury, and men were satisfied
that their liberties were safe, when it appeared that
the great institution which had so often sustained
them was still sound and unshaken. The Government had considered it necessary for the preservation of law and order, to institute these prosecutions.
Had they been successful, thousands of foolish people
would have thought the country was saved; but on
the day that Hardy and his fellow-prisoners suffered
at the gallows, hundreds of thousands of men who
were no friends to French principles, but who loved
the good old cause of English liberty, would have
lost their confidence in the constitution. Happily
the prosecutions failed, and from their failure was
derived that security which, but for these trials,
would not have been ascertained. Three years had
wrought a change in public feeling. The French
Revolution had become a gigantic military aggression on the independence of other nations; the
insolence with which England had been repulsed
when she almost sued for peace showed that nothing
less than the humiliation of this country would content the overbearing Republic. The menace of invasion only was wanting to rally every Englishman
in support of the Government, to suspend domestic
strife, and to separate from the rest of the community the faction, whether of fanatics or traitors, who
thought this a convenient season to agitate questions
which would cause irreconcilable divisions. The
idea that the war had been promoted by Pitt and
the aristocracy, for the purpose of suppressing parliamentary reform and popular measures, no longer

had possession of the intelligent and the well-informed. It was now pretty certain, that Pitt, at least, had been reluctantly forced into the war, and that he was sincerely desirous to bring it to a close. Meanwhile the nation felt a just pride in the exploits of that noble service which had ever been her protection against foreign foes, and the cause of her ascendency among the powers of the world. If the country could no longer find a General worthy to lead her soldiers, there was no falling off in the sister service, for the Hawkes and the Rodneys were succeeded by the St. Vincents and the Duncans; and the rising fame of one consummate captain promised to eclipse the glory of the most renowned commanders. Thus it was that the public spirit and loyalty of the people mounted high; and the danger which, for a time, threatened the monarchy no longer alarmed the existing generation.

CHAPTER XXXVIII.

IRELAND—THE REBELLION—THE UNION.

THE state of Ireland had, for some time, been a subject of anxious consideration to the Ministry. While they watched, with intense satisfaction, the rapid decay of that great army of volunteers, which had suddenly risen to a height hardly compatible with the authority of a regular Government, the French Revolution gave a new impulse to Irish discontent. The causes of Irish disaffection were manifold, and some of them were deeply seated in the social and political constitution of the country. There were also grievances which Ireland shared in common with her imperial sister. Each island had a Parliament, the representative branch of which was imperfect and corrupt. The British system, however, was capable of reform and restoration; but the Irish system was, throughout, incurable and rotten. In England, there were many close boroughs, and there were also many open boroughs. Every county comprised a numerous body of yeomen and freeholders, who returned gentlemen of the first figure and fortune. There were a few constituencies with whom men of ability and public spirit usually found favour. But in Ireland, all the boroughs were close; the counties were, for the most part, as close as the boroughs; nor was there any Middlesex or Westminster, to send up members who would speak with the voice of the people, and expose the delinquencies of power. There was, indeed, no want of loud vaunting patriotism in the

House of Commons; but there were only two men
in the Irish Parliament who could, undoubtedly, be
called disinterested and upright lovers of their country.
These were Lord Charlemont and Henry Grattan.
With the exception of the small minority composing
the ostensible opposition, every Irish member had his
price, and this price was, in each case, ascertained by a
careful appraisement, made by the principal minister
at Dublin, and communicated by him, in the shape of
a semi-official paper, to the head of the Government
in London.* Hence the country was governed, and
indeed governable only, through this corrupt agency,
and the whole patronage of the Crown in Ireland was
dispensed through the foul channel of Parliament.
Nay, so degraded had the Irish administration become,
and so contemptible in the eyes of English statesmen,
that whenever a job was too gross to bear even the imperfect light shed upon such transactions in England,
it was transferred to the Irish establishments.† Dis-
reputable men and women were placed upon the Irish
pension list, or had annuities charged upon the revenues of the Irish establishments. In more than one
instance, Irish peerages were given to persons who
would now be sufficiently rewarded by knighthood.
The standard of public morality in Ireland has never
been so high as in this country; but the Irish Parliament was a scandal, which a people with any sense
of shame must have felt to be intolerable. A theme
so fertile of declamation as parliamentary reform
was not neglected by a nation of rhetoricians. The
question was frequently discussed, with great fervour,
both within and without the walls of Parliament; and

---

* Vol. iii. 117, 118. More than one-third of the Irish House of Commons consisted of placemen and pensioners.

† I have before me a letter from the Duke of Rutland to Pitt, remonstrating against an intention to create a loan contractor on the Stock Exchange, an Irish peer, the reason being that the contractor was a proprietor of an English borough.—*Bolton Papers*.

at one time, when the debate was conducted under the bayonets of the volunteers, there seemed to be a possibility that a reform of Parliament would really take place; but this alarm passed away, and public affairs relapsed into their old routine. If the faulty state of the representation had been the only, or the principal, grievance of which Ireland had to complain, a vigorous minister might have applied a remedy. He could have remodelled the whole system; or taken the more decisive course of abolishing an assembly which never could rise above the level of a debating club, or exercise functions of much more importance than those of a provincial vestry. But the grievance which mainly affected the peace and prosperity of Ireland lay beyond the reach of any political remedy. Religious dissension had always more or less distracted that unhappy island. The English Catholics, diminished, scattered, and overwhelmed by the wealth, the power, and the dominant will of the Reformed Church, had long ceased to struggle with adverse fortune; but in Ireland the Romanists were the majority of the population, and comprised a large proportion, if not the majority, of the old nobility and landed gentry. An equal participation of civil rights with the Protestant minority, which itself was almost equally divided between the Presbyterians and the members of the Anglican Church, was not unreasonably demanded by the united Catholic body. They had extorted some small concessions from time to time; by the Act of 1793 many of the most important disabilities, which attached to them, were removed, and they were admitted to the exercise of the elective franchise. It followed, almost of necessity, that urgent efforts were made by the Catholics to complete their emancipation from civil disability. Here, however, they encountered the vehement opposition, not only of the zealous Protestants and the old exclusive ruling party, but of a large section of liberal politicians, including such men as Lord Charlemont, who voted against some parts of the Act of 1793, even as going too far. After the French Revolution, the Catholic question became complicated with the question of parliamentary and administrative reform, with the question of separation from England, with the question of expelling the English race, with the question of an Irish Republic. Several associations had been formed, after French and English fashion, for the promotion of these different objects; but the Society of the United Irishmen, founded in 1791, comprised, as its name imports, most of the floating elements of Irish mischief.

Besides the Catholic Relief Act, several other just and liberal measures were passed in the session of 1793. The odious Hearth Tax was repealed. Placemen and pensioners who had hitherto infested the House of Commons were, to a great extent, excluded. The pension list was reduced by one-third. No charge was thenceforth to be placed on the Irish revenue without the sanction of the Irish executive. Fox's libel law was adopted. Grattan and his friends, who hated democracy only less than political corruption and injustice, and who desired only to walk freely within the sphere of the British constitution, went heartily with these measures. But this wise and patriotic party was very small. The old dominant faction, whose only principles of government were Protestant ascendancy, patronage, and bribery, were necessarily opposed to every measure of concession and reform; while the revolutionists were impatient at the removal of any particular cause of discontent, and of any policy calculated to cement the union with Great Britain.

Remedial measures in Ireland.

Treasonable projects of French invasion.

The measures of 1793, therefore, were unproductive of good; and the malcontents only increased their efforts—alarmed at the prospect of humane legislation and honest administration in Ireland. The absolute and immediate emancipation of the Catholics, together with a parliamentary reform on the basis of unrestricted suffrage, were put forward as the pretexts for rebellion. The office bearers and leaders of the United Irishmen, Hamilton Rowan, Napper Tandy, and Wolfe Tone, were, meanwhile, either by action, correspondence, or personal communication, arranging with the French Directory and the French General the plan of a descent upon the island.

In 1794, the accession to office of the Duke of Portland and his friends led to an attempt towards a change of system in the administration of Ireland. It was proposed that Lord Westmoreland, who was entirely in the hands of the old corrupt Castle party, should be removed from the lieutenancy, and that a successor should be sent over to form other connections, and introduce a different policy. Pitt discouraged this proposal, even at the hazard of a breach with his new colleagues.* He was averse to any change of system; or even to a change of placemen in Ireland. Lord Westmoreland's recall, too, he insisted, must be contingent on the possibility of making an arrangement which would provide him with a suitable office to compensate him for the one of which he was to be deprived. Lord Fitzgibbon, the Irish Chancellor, though a man of great ability, was, on account of his domineering temper and intolerant policy, the most unpopular minister in Ireland. It was proposed to dismiss him. But Pitt positively refused to remove Fitzgibbon on any terms. Lord Camden, the son of Chatham's devoted friend and follower, was designated by Pitt for the new Lord Lieutenant. After much discussion, the ascendancy of the first minister was maintained; the Whig lords yielded every point but one. The Lord President,

sidenote: Duke of Portland's policy.

---

* Windham to Pitt.—LORD STANHOPE'S *Life of Pitt*, vol. ii.

Earl Fitzwilliam himself, offered to go to Ireland. Such a candidate put an end to all competition. It seemed impossible to have made a happier choice. Fitzwilliam was the heir of the Marquis of Rockingham, under whose administration the legislative independence of Ireland was achieved. He was, in respect of property, an Irishman, being in fact one of the largest landowners in the country. He was a Whig grandee, a traditional leader of that party of which Charlemont and Grattan were the representatives in Ireland.

While this important business was in progress, Lord Fitzwilliam wrote to Grattan, with whom he had no personal acquaintance, announcing the contemplated change in the viceroyalty, and intimating also, what indeed might have been inferred, the probability of important changes in the policy and administration of the Irish Government. Grattan went to London, and, soon after his arrival, was sent for by Pitt. In this interview, it has been stated on authority, that Grattan was informed, that while the Government were desirous of postponing the Catholic question, and would not bring it forward at present on their own responsibility, they would not oppose it, if brought forward by others.* Such an intimation, made at an interview of his own seeking, by the first minister to the leader of Opposition, could hardly be interpreted otherwise than as an invitation to aid in the settlement of a question

Overtures made to Grattan.

---

* It is so stated by the son and biographer of Grattan. Lord Stanhope questions the accuracy of Mr. Henry Grattan's version of what passed between his father and Mr. Pitt. But Mr. Grattan must have obtained his information from the most authentic source, and was incapable of wilfully misrepresenting what he was told. Lord Stanhope opposes no authority to Mr. H. Grattan's statement. Pitt would hardly have sent for Grattan without a purpose. His own views were notoriously favourable to the Catholic claims, and Mr. H. Grattan's statement is substantially corroborated by Lord Fitzwilliam's letters to Lord Carlisle.

which vitally affected the social, no less than the political, condition of the country. Grattan took the hint, and went back to Ireland to prepare a bill of Catholic emancipation.

Lord Fitzwilliam arrived in Dublin at the close of the year 1794. His reception was significant of the import attached to his mission. Loyal and congratulatory addresses poured in from all parts of the island; the Roman Catholics went in a large and imposing procession to the castle, and presented an address, in which they plainly expressed their hopes that their friends would be promoted to the foremost place in His Excellency's counsels. The Lord Lieutenant's reply did not discourage this expectation. The Irish Parliament was opened on the 22nd of January. Grattan moved the address; and, in a few days, he brought in a bill, repealing absolutely and immediately all the penalties and disabilities affecting the Roman Catholics. This step was taken by the desire of the Lord Lieutenant, who was apprehensive lest the subject should be taken up by some one of the many presumptuous intruders who are always ready to seize on popular questions.* The bill itself was framed in concert with the Viceroy, and by him communicated to the Cabinet, before the meeting of the Irish Parliament. It was not until the 8th of February, that the Duke of Portland, whose duty it was as Secretary of State to correspond with the Irish Government, wrote to the Lord Lieutenant, urging him, in the strongest terms, to refrain from committing himself by any engagements or even by any encouraging language to the Catholic measure. The postponement of the question, His Grace added, would be 'the means of doing a greater service to the British Empire than it has been capable of receiving since the Revolution, or at least since the

Fitzwilliam's arrival in Dublin.

---

* Lord Fitzwilliam's first letter to Lord Carlisle. *Annual Register*, 37, p. 132.

Union.' Considering that the Duke of Portland, ever since he had himself filled the Viceroyalty, and up to this moment, had held that Catholic emancipation was the cardinal point of Irish policy, Lord Fitzwilliam might well be surprised at this portentous reply to a letter, written nearly a month before, in which he had announced his intentions, subject to the immediate disapproval of the Cabinet, to give the support of the Government to Grattan's Bill. It was evident that something had occurred to convert the hesitating and languid acquiescence of the Cabinet in Lord Fitzwilliam's policy into active and peremptory disapprobation.

The cause was easily discovered. It would have been idle to remove Lord Westmoreland, and to replace him by a man of such mark as Lord Fitzwilliam, unless with the view to a change of policy which required a change of administration. It was obvious that this change could not be confined to the Lieutenancy. Pitt had only insisted that no change should take place in the Great Seal. But Fitzwilliam naturally desired to be rid of some at least of the obscure herd of placemen who had long oppressed the public service, and to confer principal offices on the distinguished men who had hitherto supported, under adverse fortune, the just and enlightened policy which he desired to adopt. Accordingly, he proposed to remove Wolfe and Toler, men of inferior parliamentary and professional standing, from the offices of Attorney and Solicitor-General, and to appoint Ponsonby and Curran, the one the first debater in the House of Commons, and the other the most eloquent advocate in the Four Courts. In England such an arrangement, under analogous circumstances, would have been a matter of course. But Wolfe and Toler thought themselves exceedingly ill-used, and demanded compensation for the loss of their offices, as if they had been vested interests. Each claimed a

Peerage, and the reversion of a Chief Justiceship; and their impudent demands were partially submitted to by the English Government. Cooke, the Secretary at War, was also dismissed, and though he was to receive one thousand two hundred pounds a year by way of compensation, this gentleman complained as loudly as if he had been deprived of his estate. But the clamours of the Wolfes, the Tolers, and the Cookes, would have died away and been forgotten, if the new ruler of Ireland could have withheld his hand from one greater than them all. It would be difficult to make the nature of Irish Government before the Union intelligible to an English reader; nor is it possible, perhaps, for an Englishman accurately to understand it. England, up to a recent period, was governed by an oligarchy; and so was Ireland; there was a corrupt House of Commons at Westminster; and there was a corrupt House of Commons at Dublin; but here the resemblance ended. There was no comparison to be made between the Whig grandees, who distributed the patronage of the Empire, and the two or three Irish families which divided among themselves and their followers the spoils of a narrow province. The Cavendishes and the Russells, the Fitzwilliams, the Pelhams and the Grenvilles, who long ruled in England, were very different persons from the Boyles and the Stones, the Shannons, the Fosters, and the Beresfords, who, during the same period, reigned supreme in the inferior island. The English statesmen were the representatives of a great policy, and whatever their private jealousies and contentions, these were ever kept subservient to the principles on which the throne of the house of Hanover was based. They governed partly by corruption, because the doubtful fortunes of the new settlement had raised a tribe of time-servers whom venal motives alone could attach to the precarious cause of civil and religious freedom. But the vile means which circumstances obliged them to employ for a noble end left little or no taint on the statesmen of the Revolution. Even Newcastle himself, who reduced bribery and corruption to a system, and who hardly knew any other mode of government, was personally unsullied; and, far from profiting by a command of political patronage which has never been equalled, a great part of his private estate was sacrificed to what he considered the public service. But the families which governed Ireland, though they adopted the party titles of Whig and Tory, regarded political power merely as a means of obtaining for themselves and their connections titles, offices, emoluments and advantages of every description at the public expense. Instances are related of regiments of militia raised for the sole object of patronage, of barracks erected to improve the property of a member or friend of the ruling family; of canals cut in the wrong direction for a similar purpose. The Irish pension list was a proverb. Jobs, which, in the days of the Walpoles and the Pelhams, could not be attempted in England, were not considered too gross for Ireland.* Political spies, foreigners whose services could not be set forth, and cast-off mistresses were placed on the Irish establishment, though not always without murmurs from the ruling families, who thought their domain unduly invaded. The Irish oligarchy had no excuse for—nor indeed did they ever pretend to excuse—

* The memoirs of Lord Chesterfield and the Duke of Bedford, both of whom were Irish viceroys, contain numerous passages illustrative of the system. The following is from the Duke's correspondence: 'As things are circumstanced, business may be easily carried on the next session; but the leading people must have donecrurs, a great many of which I must, at a proper time, lay before His Majesty. By these means he may do what he pleases with this country. The Princess of Hesse may have her pension of five thousand pounds; but other things of the like nature must be given in Ireland.' May 24, 1768.—*Bedford Correspondence*, vol. ii. p. 335.

their system of corruption. They had no disputed
succession to deal with; no party in the state actively
and avowedly engaged in behalf of the exiled family;
no double-faced friends more dangerous than open
enemies; no waiters upon providence uncertain to
which side their private interests should incline them.
All these were the cares of English statesmen, and
the justification of the means which they employed.
But what with English statesmen were means justified only by the end, were, with Irish politicians, the
end itself. Political power, on the other side of St.
George's Channel, was sought with no other object
than the advancement of private interest. Any pretence of public spirit was treated as cant and hypocrisy. 'Did I ever give an honest vote in my
life?' said an honourable member, whose family
was maintained at the public charge, and the House
rang with applauding laughter.*

Among the native families, through whose agency
this system of jobbery and corruption had *Influence of the*
from time to time been worked, the family *Beresfords.*
of Beresford had long maintained the first place. It
has been said by a well-informed writer, not prone
to exaggeration, that one-fourth of all the places in
the island were filled by this family.† In England,
the chief, or some other member of a ruling family,
held high office, or filled a conspicuous position in
public life; but in Ireland the men of influence were
seldom men who sought distinction in Parliament,
or the great offices in the State. This was remark-
ably the case with the Beresfords, none of whom ever
attained any position in the House of Commons, or
occupied a responsible place in the Government.
One of the Lord Lieutenants said that he found the
influence of the First Commissioner of Wide Streets,
who was the Beresford of the day, more powerful

* Wakefield's *Account of Ireland*, vol. ii. p. 302.
† Ibid. vol. ii. p. 364.

than his own.* Lord Fitzwilliam, on his arrival in Dublin, found the chief of the Beresfords filling the subordinate office of Commissioner of Revenue. But this man exercised such influence, that Fitzwilliam called him the King of Ireland,† and the Viceregent was not disposed to endure such rivalry. One of the earliest acts of Earl Fitzwilliam's administration was to dismiss Beresford from his employment.

This unexampled and unexpected act of power spread consternation through the whole rank and file of office. Such an alarm had not been known since the year 1782, when Lord Temple announced his intention of bringing a Government defaulter to account.‡ Beresford immediately went to London, not in terms to demand the recall of the Lord Lieutenant, but to take such measures as should secure that result.

Lord Fitzwilliam had in fact made the two most powerful men in Ireland his mortal enemies. The Chancellor, by his great ability, and still more by the force of his character, had almost the weight and influence of a Prime Minister; and Lord Fitzwilliam, it was well known, had, for a long time, insisted on the removal of the Chancellor, as a condition of his undertaking the Government of Ireland. A Beresford only could be a more formidable enemy than Lord Fitzgibbon. The precipitation with which the new lieutenant gave his sanction to a sweeping measure of Catholic relief afforded the pretext, if indeed it did not afford a sufficient reason, for appealing to the English Cabinet. But the liberality of Mr. Pitt's views on the subject of the Catholic claims made it very doubtful whether he would convict the Viceroy of an irreparable error for his hasty concession of civil rights to the great

---

* Wakefield, vol. ii. p. 364. ‡ Hardy's *Life of Lord*
† *Courts and Cabinets of*   *Charlemont*, vol. ii. p. 65.
George the Third, vol. ii. p. 331.

majority of the Irish people. It was suggested, therefore, by the prompt and daring genius of the Chancellor, that the appeal should be carried at once, and in the first resort, to the highest quarter. Fitzgibbon himself had always been an uncompromising opponent of the Catholics, and had gone so far as to declare that emancipation would be incompatible with the connection between Great Britain and Ireland. The King was known not to be favourable to the pretensions of his Romanist subjects; and if his narrow understanding could be possessed with the notion that there was an insuperable bar to these pretensions, the question would be postponed at least for the existing reign, and the wrongs of the Beresfords and the Fitzgibbons would be avenged. Accordingly, it was intimated to His Majesty that grave doubts were entertained by high authority,* whether the concession of the Catholic claims would be compatible with the coronation oath. The King, greatly disturbed, took the opinion of the Chief Justice. Kenyon, as bigoted as his master, and hardly more competent to give an opinion on a high question of constitutional law, still shrunk from committing himself at full length to the doctrine so boldly laid down by the Irish Chancellor. He gave an evasive answer, the effect of which really was that His Majesty might construe the oath in either sense, but that he would do well to follow his own inclinations, and resolve the doubt on the side of intolerance. The Chief Justice probably knew that the King had made up his mind already, and only wanted to have his opinion supported by legal authority. The idea which had been put into his head regarding the coronation oaths had already become a ruling idea,

---

* 'This idea was Lord Fitzgibbon's, and it was probably communicated, through Lord Westmoreland, to the King.'— *Auckland Correspondence*, vol. iii. p. 304. This is confirmed by a passage in Lady Harcourt's papers, MSS.

like that of rescuing the Crown from the dominion
of the Whigs, or that of suppressing American liberty.
He sent for Pitt, and insisted on the immediate recall
of Lord Fitzwilliam. Much as Pitt contemned the
reason assigned for this peremptory proceeding, he
was in truth not much disposed to resist the pressure
put upon him. In sending Fitzwilliam to Ireland,
he had, for the first time since he had been at the
head of affairs, yielded reluctantly, and with a very
bad grace, to the influence of a section of his Cabinet.
He was probably not ill pleased that his formidable
Whig colleague should have discredited himself by
want of judgment and conduct. A Cabinet was summoned, and even the Duke of Portland had nothing
to say in vindication of his friend and colleague.
The Earl Fitzwilliam was recalled, and his rival, the
Irish Chancellor, was immediately afterwards advanced in the peerage with the title of the Earl of
Clare.

Fitzwilliam, not content with vindicating his conduct in his place in Parliament, appealed
to the public, in two long and intemperate
letters addressed to his friend the Earl of Carlisle.
Both in his speeches and in his writings, he persisted
in attributing his disgrace, not to the course which
he took on the Catholic question, but to his dismissal
of Mr. Beresford. The truth is that the combination
of these two events was the ruin of his administration. All-powerful as the Beresfords were in their
own country, they had hardly sufficient credit in
Downing Street to displace a Lord Lieutenant. And
in the division of public opinion in Ireland on the
Catholic question, the tendency of the Viceroy towards
the liberal side would not in itself have been considered a sufficient reason for removing him, had not
the resentment of the old Castle party hit upon the
happy idea of alarming the prejudices of the King.
But the influence of the Beresfords, co-operating

with the authority of the Lord Chancellor, the
bigotry of the King, and the indiscretion of his Lieutenant, would have outweighed the support of the
minister himself, had he put forth all his power in
support of the Irish Viceroy. Far, however, from
attempting to uphold the great officer, for whose
appointment he had become responsible only a few
weeks before, Mr. Pitt was only too ready to sacrifice
him.

Lord Camden, whom Pitt had originally designated
for the office, was appointed Lord Lieu- <small>Lord Camden made Viceroy.</small>
tenant. Under ordinary circumstances,
this nobleman would have been welcomed as a successor to the Westmorelands and the Buckinghams.
But the people of Ireland were in no humour to be
propitiated. Their hopes had been raised high. They
had been taught to think that justice was at length
to be done to their country; that the days of public
robbery and monopoly were numbered; that all men
were to be equal before the law; and that a free
Parliament would soon sit in College Green. These
fond illusions had been in a moment rudely dissipated. Lord Fitzwilliam arrived in Dublin at the
beginning of the year. Before the end of February,
it became known that the most popular Governor
who had ever occupied the Castle, was to be hastily
removed because he was about to do justice to Ireland. The excitement throughout the country was
intense. Both Houses of Parliament passed unanimous votes of confidence in the Lord Lieutenant.
Similar resolutions were agreed to by most of the
corporate bodies, many of the counties, and numerous public assemblies. The day on which Fitzwilliam quitted Ireland was a day of gloom, and a
day of evil omen which has hardly yet been fulfilled.
On that day, the Irish people abandoned all further
hope that the policy of 1782 was to be resumed and
carried into effect. The Presbyterians of the North,

who cherished the traditions of English liberty, and the Roman Catholic body, who pined for religious freedom, were now ready to unite in a common cause against a common foe. Even that party, never very numerous in Ireland, though comprising the best friends of their country, who sought to obtain both civil and religious liberty by legal and constitutional means, began to hold different language.* But moderate counsels were no longer listened to, and popular power passed from the hands of the Grattans and the Ponsonbys to those of the Edward Fitzgeralds and the Wolfe Tones.

Lord Camden arrived in Dublin on the last day of March. His entry, instead of being attended with the noisy demonstration of welcome which the warm-hearted and thoughtless people usually lavished on their new Governor, was marked by gloomy silence. But when the officers of State went to wait upon His Excellency at the Castle, the rage of the populace had nearly proved fatal to the persons who had been chiefly instrumental in procuring the dismissal of the late Lord Lieutenant. Beresford's house was attacked by a blood-thirsty mob, which was with difficulty dispersed by a military force. The Chancellor was beset in his carriage, and escaped with life only by his undaunted courage.

Beresford's house attacked.

On the reassembling of the Irish Parliament, after the prorogation, the Catholic Relief Bill was, of course, the question of the day. The new Government, or rather the old Government restored, opposed the second reading of the bill. The debate lasted through the night, and at half-past ten in the morn-

* 'It is now the established principle of the British Cabinet that Irish jobbers and Irish jobs are sacred; and that whatever redress we may look to can only be obtained by peremptory and hostile demand.' Grattan to Burke, March 14, 1795.—*Burke's Correspondence*, vol. iv. p. 293.

ing, the bill was thrown out by a majority of nearly two to one. This result being the certain consequence of the change of Government, was regarded as a formal renunciation of the policy of justice and conciliation.

It soon became evident, that Ireland must be kept in subjection by the strong hand of power. The Protestant party, not content with defeating the attempt of the Roman Catholics to obtain an equality of civil rights, followed the example of the other parties in the country, and formed an association, the professed object of which was to maintain the ascendency of their people, and to keep the Romanists in subjection. This body took the title of Orangemen; and thousands assumed the badge of King William, under the idea that they were faithful disciples of the august champion of civil and religious liberty. The United Irishmen, on the other side, wore the national colour. It was not long before the orange and the green came into hostile collision. In the autumn of 1795, a fight took place in the county of Armagh; and the Catholics, though greatly outnumbering the Protestants, were worsted. This disastrous conflict was long celebrated in provincial warfare as the Battle of the Diamond, from a village near which it was fought. The most violent animosity thenceforth separated the adherents of the Church of England and the Church of Rome; and the former having the upper hand, the law afforded but little protection to the obnoxious religionists, who, on their part, retaliated by murder, by the destruction of property, and, above all, by the seizure and collection of arms. And now commenced that series of coercive measures which were continued, with little abatement, for half a century, and have not even yet disappeared from Irish legislation.

The Society of United Irishmen, which had hitherto

pursued lawful objects, by lawful means, at this time changed its character; and from being a public body, with an avowed policy, became a secret association, whose councils were not divulged. A large majority, consisting of men whose views were limited to Parliamentary Reform and Catholic Emancipation, consequently withdrew; and the remaining members took a new pledge 'to persevere in their endeavours to obtain an equal, full, and adequate representation of all the people in Ireland,' omitting the words in the former text, importing that the reform sought was a reform of the representation *in Parliament*. The immediate object of this new league was that which had been ultimately contemplated by the original projectors of the Irish Union, the establishment, namely, of an independent republic; and to this object all its energies were now addressed.

<small>United Irishmen change their tone.</small>

The hatred of the rival races and creeds, no longer restrained by co-operation for a common end, soon burst forth with a fury which had never been surpassed in the annals of that chronic civil war, which chiefly formed the history of this ill-fated people. Bands of marauders traversed the country, plundering and destroying houses and property. The Government, instead of repressing these outrages with firmness and moderation, aided the savage policy of retaliation, to which the exasperated Protestants were too willing to resort. Lord Carhampton, the General * commanding the forces in the disturbed districts, let loose his troops upon the wretched peasantry. It was enough for a magistrate, a squireen, or even a farmer, to point out any person as suspected, to have his habitation

<small>Disordered state of the country.</small>

---

* This was the Colonel Luttrell, who gained such unenviable notoriety as the supposititious member for Middlesex, in the famous contest between the House of Commons and the constituency.

burned down, his family turned adrift, and himself either shot or transported, without trial, without warrant, without inquiry. An Act of Indemnity was passed, by the Irish Parliament, in the Session of 1796, to protect these enormities; and the Insurrection Act gave them, for the future, the sanction of law. The suspension of the Habeas Corpus completed this barbarous code, which, in effect, outlawed the whole people of Ireland.

It would have been some mitigation of this terrible policy, had it been carried into effect by a regular military force, disciplined to the usages of civilised war, and free from the passions of an infuriated party; but the Government thought fit to place arms in the hands of thirty-seven thousand Protestant yeomanry, who admitted no Catholics into their ranks, and were suffered to assume the Orange Ribbon—the insolent badge of Protestant ascendency. The cruelties perpetrated by these men both before the rebellion, and while it was raging, and after it was suppressed, differed only in degree from the worst enormities of the French revolutionists. Under the authority to search for concealed arms, any person whom any ruffian, calling himself a Protestant and Loyalist, and either with or without a military uniform, chose to suspect or to pretend to suspect, was liable to be seized, tortured, and put to death. Hundreds of unoffending people, and people who were guilty of no other offence than professing the creed of their fathers, or of letting fall a word of discontent, were flogged until they were insensible, or made to stand upon one foot on a pointed stake. These were ordinary tortures. Sometimes the wretched victim was half hanged, or the scalp was torn from the head by a pitched cap. Catholics, and reputed malcontents of the better class, were subjected to still worse treatment. Militia and yeomanry, as well as the regular troops, were billeted on them at

[marginal note: Violence of the Protestant party.]

free quarters; and this billet appears to have been invariably construed as an unlimited licence for robbery, devastation, ravishment,* and, in case of resistance, murder. This system, if long continued, would have recoiled in its effects on the Government by which it was sanctioned or tolerated. It must have resulted in wholly demoralising the army, and converting it into an armed banditti, upon which no reliance could be placed in the event of a foreign invasion. Sir Ralph Abercromby, one of the best Generals in the British service, on assuming the command of the army in Ireland, declared, in general orders, that their habits and discipline were such as to render them 'formidable to everybody but the enemy.' For this phrase, the just severity of which was confirmed by the subsequent experience of Lord Cornwallis,† the General was forced, by the clamour of yeomanry and militia Colonels, to resign his command. But the Government profited by the opinion which they had not firmness enough to defend, and Abercromby's successor was instructed to find some other mode of discovering concealed arms than that of suffering the troops to be scattered over the country at free quarters.

These proceedings of the Loyalists mainly promoted the objects, and greatly raised the hopes of those who were really intent on effecting a revolution in Ireland. Many thousands were driven to join the United Irishmen from a de-

---

* It is admitted, by the chief apologist of the Royalists, that the rebels, though they emulated the cruelties of their adversaries, did not retaliate upon the women.—Musgrave's *History of the Rebellion*, p. 429. It was boasted by officers of rank that within certain large districts, no home had been left undefiled; and, upon its being remarked that the sex must have been very complying, the reply was 'that the bayonet removed all squeamishness.' — Plowden, p. 702, note.

† Lord Cornwallis to Mr. Pitt, 25th of September, 1798.—*Correspondence*, vol. iii. p. 413.

‡ Lord Castlereagh to General Lake, *Castlereagh Correspondence*, vol. i. p. 189.

sperate sense of self-preservation, as well as from motives of hatred and revenge. The Union, therefore, made active preparations for a general rising. Their organisation was planned with an attention to minute detail almost pedantic. A machinery was contrived by which the orders of a secret directory were to be conveyed through the whole association, and implicitly obeyed by upwards of one hundred thousand men. The military discipline was necessarily imperfect; but arms were extensively distributed; every man was instructed to provide himself, if possible, with a firelock and ammunition; and, in default of a better weapon, to carry a pike.

But the Irish insurgents did not rely on their own unassisted efforts. They opened a communication with the Government at Paris. One Lewins was sent over with the sounding title of Ambassador to the Executive Directory; and the object of his mission was to invite the aid of the French in effecting a separation between Great Britain and Ireland. But the most efficient agent of the rebels was Wolfe Tone, a young barrister, who had taken a leading part in the original organisation of the United Irishmen. Tone succeeded in satisfying the French Directory that an invasion of Ireland might be attempted with success, and remained on board the Dutch flag-ship in the Texel, while the expedition destined for that service was waiting for a favourable wind. Lord Edward Fitzgerald and Arthur O'Connor went over to France to arrange with General Hoche the terms and plan of the projected invasion. A French army was to act as an auxiliary; their expenses were to be defrayed by the future Government of Ireland; and after the work of deliverance was accomplished, they were to retire. It is certain, that neither Fitzgerald nor O'Connor meant to take their country from England, for the purpose of handing it over to France; these men were fanatics, without capacity or knowledge of affairs; and doubtless believed in the professions of the French, when they offered to aid the nations of Europe in their efforts to emancipate themselves from the tyranny of their rulers. They never anticipated the possibility that Ireland might share the fate of Belgium and Holland. The project, however, was happily defeated by the disaster at Bantry Bay.

Sir James Stuart's proceedings.

The Government manifested their alarm rather than their vigour, by the series of proclamations and orders which issued from the Castle during the year before the rebellion actually broke out. These documents were, for the most part, framed in such unmeasured terms as seemed to authorise the excesses which had been committed. Notwithstanding Lord Castlereagh's letter to General Lake, directing him to discontinue the practice of quartering troops on districts supposed to be disaffected, there issued, some days after the date of that letter, and three weeks before the rebellion, an order of Sir James Stuart, the General in command of the southern district, of the most violent and atrocious character. The order denounced a practice which had been adopted in some of the proscribed districts of subscribing to provide forage and accommodation for the soldiers quartered upon them, for the purpose of evading the burden and punishment intended to be inflicted on the inhabitants individually. It declared that wherever such a practice was adopted, the troops at free quarters should be increased double, treble, and fourfold; and that the district should not be relieved from the presence of those troops until all arms were surrendered and tranquillity perfectly restored, and until it was reported to the general officers, by the gentlemen holding landed property, and those who were employed in collecting the public revenues and tithes, that all rents, taxes, and tithes were completely paid up.

Popular assemblies being prohibited, the press attempted to supply the place of incendiary eloquence. The 'Morning Star,' a newspaper published at Belfast, was the chief organ of the revolutionary party, and though its conductors were in Newgate, under sentence for seditious libels, the paper was continued with unabated virulence. A party of soldiers marched out of the barracks, forcibly entered the office of the newspaper, and destroyed the press and types. But the 'Morning Star,' though suppressed by illegal violence which almost justified the language it had used, was immediately revived in a less regular form. Sheets printed on one side, without the name of a printer, were distributed through Dublin and various parts of the country; and notwithstanding the vigilance of the military, these occasional newspapers were frequently found on the walls of the principal thoroughfares. The new series of the 'Star' contained, in every publication, a list of persons marked for assassination as traitors, spies, and informers. Another print called 'The Press,' edited by Mr. Arthur O'Connor, one of the leaders of the United Irishmen, was written in the same sense; and when this publication was, in its turn, suppressed as a newspaper, it assumed the form of a placard.

Suppression of the 'Morning Star.'

In 1797, the Irish Parliament was dissolved. Grattan, and some other members of the Opposition following his example, refused to sit in the new Parliament. The great Irish patriot could find no place in public life amidst the furious passions which distracted his country. He equally repudiated the tyranny of the Government, and the attempt to repel tyranny by rebellion. The rebellion could succeed only by the aid of France; and the aid of France could be purchased only by the independence of the nation. Grattan took leave of his constituents in an address, written with the

Dissolution of Parliament.

warmth and vehemence of his nature. It was censured by the partisans of the Government for its inflammatory tendency; and Grattan himself, in after years, admitted that the language of this paper was ill-timed. Nevertheless, the retirement of the Irish leader had in it more of dignity and consistency than the peevish and unmeaning abstinence from regular attendance on Parliament, which Mr. Fox and his friends thought to dignify by the name of secession; and if the abandonment, by Grattan in despair, at that particular moment, of the only field in which the battle of freedom could constitutionally be fought, indirectly aided the lawless proceedings which he reprobated, it was not so much his fault as the fault of the Imperial Government, which had cruelly disappointed the expectations they had raised, and driven the people to despair.

The insurgents, far from being deterred by the failure of the attempt at Bantry Bay, renewed their importunities for aid to the French Government. But there was no common understanding between the parties. The Irish thought the French would be sufficiently repaid for such a perilous enterprise as an invasion of the British Isles, by the possibility of aiding an oppressed people to throw off the yoke of their tyrants; but the French, under the guise of a catholic zeal for liberty, concealed—if, indeed, they did conceal—a raging ambition for conquest, and an enmity to the independence of every other nation. Barras and Lepaux and Bonaparte must have smiled at the simplicity of the M'Nevins, the Fitzgeralds, and the Emmetts, the 'Executive Directory,' as they styled themselves, of the Irish people, who proposed to borrow half a million on the security of the Church lands, and who stipulated for a contingent of not less than five thousand, nor more than ten thousand, French troops— a number they said which would suffice for an auxiliary force, but would be insufficient for permanent occupation of the country. The loan was not granted; but fifteen thousand good troops were sent to Holland to be embarked, under convoy of the Dutch fleet, for the coast of Ireland. The battle of Camperdown put an end, for the time, to the hope of making Ireland a province of France.

The rebel leaders, undeterred even by this disappointment, made every effort to extend the conspiracy, and with such success, that there were few families into which it had not made way. It was dangerous to talk, without reserve, on the state of the country. Spies of the Loyalists and spies of the United Irishmen were to be found in almost every household. If a man was so rash as to let fall any expression condemnatory of the excesses of either party, even at his own table, it was all but certain that he would be denounced to the District Revolutionary Committee, or to the next magistrate. Still, the utmost precaution was taken not to hazard the success of the projected revolution by a premature outbreak. At length, in the spring of 1798, it was announced, by the military committee of the United Irishmen, that all was ready, and that they only waited for the expected movement of their French allies. They reported that the Insurrectionary League comprised nearly half a million of men. The 23rd of May was fixed for the general rising; but before that day arrived, the whole plan was disconcerted by an event to which extensive conspiracies are commonly liable.

Extent of the conspiracy.

Among the Roman Catholic members of the United Irishmen was one Reynolds, who had a small estate in the county of Kildare. This man, from his influence with the middle class of his co-religionists, had been considered an important acquisition to the cause of rebellion; and accordingly he was immediately nominated to high titular rank

Reynolds the informer.

in the Rebel Government. He was styled Treasurer and Representative of the County of Kildare, and Delegate for the Province of Leinster; he also accepted the commission of Colonel in the rebel army. Reynolds, like many other men, had originally joined the Union with no further view than that of compelling the Government to yield the two great measures of Catholic Emancipation and Parliamentary Reform; but had been carried far beyond these points by the energy and resolution of the rebel leaders. Whether actuated by remorse, or by fear, or by a still viler motive, he was induced to betray the counsels of the conspiracy. He opened his mind to a friend named Cope, a merchant in Dublin, and a friend of the Government. After some hesitation he yielded to those arguments and importunities to which his state of mind inclined him to listen; and, having obtained, through Cope, a promise of secrecy as to the source from which the information was to be supplied, Reynolds made known to his friend, that on the 12th of March the Leinster delegates would meet at the house of Oliver Bond, one of the chief conspirators, to make final arrangements for the insurrection. This disclosure led to the apprehension of Bond, together with thirteen other persons, and the seizure of papers containing a description of the plot. The leader of the rebellion, Lord Edward Fitzgerald, was still at large, and, by the influence of his family, might have effected his escape, with the connivance of the Government, had he been so disposed. For several weeks he lay hidden in the neighbourhood of Dublin; but a thousand pounds having been offered for his apprehension, Fitzgerald was traced to the house of one Murphy, a petty shopkeeper, in a back street called Thomas Street. A Secretary of State's warrant was issued, and Town-Major Sirr, accompanied by Mr. Swan, a magistrate, Captain Ryan, a yeomanry officer, and a party of soldiers, proceeded to make the arrest. Swan, the foremost of the party, seeing a woman hasten upstairs to give the alarm, pushed by her into a bedroom, where he found Lord Edward lying on the bed in his dressing-gown. The magistrate immediately announced his business, and that he was prepared to execute his warrant with a force which would render resistance useless. Fitzgerald, notwithstanding this intimation, started up, fell upon the magistrate, hacking at him with a dagger, and inflicting many wounds. At this moment, Captain Ryan entered the room, and seeing Swan engaged in a mortal struggle with his prisoner, made a lunge at the latter with a sword cane, which glanced aside. Ryan then closed with his desperate opponent, and received no less than fourteen wounds from the murderous weapon which Fitzgerald wielded with savage recklessness. Sirr, having by this time disposed his men round the house, so as to prevent an escape, went upstairs, and found his two companions on the ground weltering in their blood, but clinging to the legs of Lord Edward, who was endeavouring to break away from them up a staircase which led from his chamber to the roof of the house. Sirr immediately fired his pistol, and Fitzgerald, being wounded, was at length secured.* An attempt to rescue the prisoner on his way to the Castle was repulsed by the soldiers. Swan recovered, but Ryan's injuries proved mortal. Fitzgerald, also, after lingering a few days, died of his wound. The most exquisite lyric poet of modern times, himself an Irishman and half a rebel, has attempted to invest the character of Lord Edward Fitzgerald with heroic attributes.† But in truth this young nobleman was a rebel of the ordinary kind. A son of the Duke of Leinster, he had entered the army at an early age,

* Mr. Ryan's Narrative, Lord Castlereagh's *Correspondence*, vol. i. p. 468.

† Moore's *Life of Lord E. Fitzgerald.*

and had attained the rank of captain, when he was
dismissed the service for the violence with which he
expressed opinions hostile to the Government and
constitutions of the country. Exasperated at the
sentence which he had justly provoked, Fitzgerald
went to Paris, and became the friend of Tom Paine,
and other extreme partisans of the Revolution. At
Paris, also, he formed a connection still more remarkable. He married a beautiful and accomplished girl
called Pamela, a natural daughter of Egalité by the
celebrated Madame de Genlis. On returning to
Ireland, Lord Edward kept up a regular correspondence with his French friends; he obtained a seat in
the Irish House of Commons, and soon distinguished
himself in an assembly where words were seldom
measured, and not always wise, by the extravagance
and folly of his language. He early became implicated in the counsels of the United Irishmen, among
whom his rank and name secured him a leading position. He had the sort of sincerity in the cause
which belongs to weak and wilful minds, and the
energy which springs from unreasoning vehemence.
It was at his urgent instance, and upon his wild,
though not intentionally false representations, that
the French Government were induced to undertake
the expedition to Bantry Bay; and, up to the moment
of his apprehension, he was impatient to strike a decisive blow for Irish independence, although it was
manifest to common sense that such an attempt could
not even for the moment be successful without foreign
aid, and could not be permanently established, even
if it was for the moment achieved by such assistance.
Though by birth and nurture a gentleman, and therefore very different from the base and malignant spirits
with whom his revolutionary tastes brought him into
contact, both in France and Ireland, Lord Edward
Fitzgerald did not escape the contamination of his
associates. The ferocity with which he sought the

lives of the officers who came to capture him, when he must have known that resistance was vain, and the assassin's weapon which he used with fatal effect, showed the desperate outlaw, who would shrink from no deed of cruelty or blood, in his warfare against social order. His life being already forfeited for treason, the death which he provoked was little better than suicide; and, had he survived, his last act would have consigned him to the doom of a felon.

Several other persons were made prisoners at the same time, in every case from information supplied by spies, who had procured admittance to the counsels of the conspirators. Two brothers, named Sheares, members of the Irish bar, and foremost leaders of the rebellion, were, in this manner, betrayed to the Government. Among their papers was found the draft of a proclamation, framed after the French fashion, denouncing death and confiscation against all their opponents. This paper was to have been promulgated on the day of the insurrection, which had been fixed for the 21st of May, the day following that on which the Sheares's were arrested. The insurrection was to have commenced by the stoppage of the mails; Dublin was to have been the centre of action; and arrangements were completed for the seizure simultaneously of the Castle, the arsenal at Chapelizod, the magazine in the Phœnix Park, and the camp in the neighbourhood of the city. The houses of the principal persons were to be attacked, and the leading members of the Government were to have been put to death.*

Apprehension of the Sheares's.

By this timely discovery the capital was saved from massacre and pillage, and possibly from a temporary occupation by the insurgents. But the plans of the rebels, though seriously disconcerted, were not defeated. A partial rising took place on the appointed

* Lord Grenville to Marquis of Buckingham, 25th of May, 1798.—*Courts and Cabinets of George the Third*, vol. ii. p. 394.

day throughout the island, and though the rebels were generally repulsed, yet in some instances, the Loyalists were overpowered, and horrible atrocities were perpetrated. One party, headed by Dr. Esmonde, a man of family and fortune, surprised a detachment of militia at a place called Prosperous, seventeen miles from Dublin, and burnt the barracks in which they were quartered, murdering the men who escaped from the flames. Esmonde himself, at the time, held a commission in a corps of yeomanry; and, on the day following the attack on Prosperous, dined at the mess of his regiment. He was, however, immediately arrested, and his guilt being clearly proved, he was hanged on the 14th of June.

<small>Dr. Esmonde.</small>

On the same day, attacks were made by bands of pikemen on the towns of Naas and Kilcullen; the first attempt was defeated with great slaughter; but the rebels succeeded in occupying Kilcullen for a few days. On the 24th of May, martial law was proclaimed; and it may be mentioned, as a proof of the fierce vindictive spirit which actuated the Irish gentry, that when this proclamation was laid before the House of Commons, Colonel Maxwell, afterwards Lord Farnham, rose, in his place, and suggested that the proclamation should be made retrospective, so as to reach the prisoners in custody before the rebellion, and awaiting their trial in due course of law. The terrible powers conferred on the military were abused in the most shocking manner. The first example, in point of time, and the most conspicuous, on account of the rank and innocence of the victim, was that of Sir Edward Crosbie. At two o'clock on the morning after the proclamation, a tumultuous body of insurgents rushed into the town of Carlow. The garrison, consisting of about four hundred and fifty men, being prepared for their reception, the rebels were driven

<small>Attack on Naas and Kilcullen.</small>

back, routed, put to the sword, or burned in the
houses to which they had fled for refuge. Eight
houses were destroyed, and many hundreds of lives
were taken without the loss of a single soldier. But
this was not enough to satiate the fury of the Loyalists. It unfortunately happened that the miserable
rabble, before entering the town, had paraded in the
grounds of Sir Edward Crosbie, who resided at the
distance of a mile and a half from Carlow. There
was not a tittle of proof that this gentleman was, in
any way, connected with the rioters, or that they had
assembled on his lawn, at midnight, with his knowledge, preparatory to their lawless proceedings. He
had not accompanied them, nor did it appear that he
had held any communication with them. But Sir
Edward was a friend to parliamentary reform, and
hostile to the oppression of the tenantry by their
landlords. To be friendly to the poor and to reform
was presumptive evidence of disaffection; and presumptive evidence of disaffection was sufficient proof
of complicity in the rebellion. The day after the
attempt on Carlow, several persons were seized, tried
by court-martial, and hanged. Among others, Sir
Edward Crosbie was dragged before a set of ignorant
blood-thirsty ruffians, who styled themselves a court-
martial. There was not a particle of evidence which
could have had the least weight with a fairly constituted court, though Catholic prisoners had been, by
torture and promises of pardon, converted into witnesses against the accused. Numerous Loyalists came
forward to state, what everybody in the neighbourhood
knew, that Sir Edward was a good subject of His
Majesty, as well as one of the few humane and accomplished gentlemen that Ireland possessed. But
these witnesses were excluded from the place where
the proceedings were held, by the bayonets of the
soldiery. A gentleman of rank and fortune, who
thought that Parliament should be reformed, and

that squireens should not be permitted to grind and
insult the peasantry, was a dangerous member of
society, and must be made an example of to deter
others. Accordingly, Sir Edward Crosbie was doomed
to death by a court-martial, the president of which
was an illiterate fellow who could not spell. The
sentence was immediately put in execution at the
gallows; and the remains of the murdered gentleman were abused in a manner shocking to humanity.
Such was the insolent malignity of the faction, in
whose power the Government had placed the lives
and liberties of the people of Ireland.*

At one moment there seemed to have been an
opportunity of bringing the rebellion to a
close within a week of the first outbreak.

<small>Duff's attack on the rebels.</small>

General Dundas, having recovered the town of Kilcullen from the insurgents, two thousand of them,
posted near the Curragh of Kildare, offered to lay
down their arms, on condition of being allowed to
return to their homes. This proposal having been
accepted, another body of six hundred men offered
to come in; but while these last were marching to
the place appointed by the General, they were unfortunately met by a detachment of troops. The
officer in command, ignorant of the capitulation,
attacked the advancing rebels, who immediately fled,
and were pursued, with great slaughter, by a corps
of yeomanry called Lord Jocelyn's Foxhunters. A
timely order from General Dundas, who had foreseen the possibility of such an accident, saved these
people from utter extermination. Although the two
thousand men who first came in had actually given
up their arms and dispersed, it was still insisted, by
the Orangemen, that the offer to surrender was only
a treacherous feint to throw the Government and the
military off their guard. With more show of reason,

---

* Gordon's *History of Ireland*, vol. ii. p. 392.

the rebellious peasantry said that they had been treacherously deceived; and that their enemies would be satisfied with nothing less than their blood. Rage and despair, from that moment, took possession of their breasts, and the rebellion spread into districts which had been pronounced wholly free from disaffection.

A few months previously, when disturbances were expected, the Roman Catholics of the county of Wexford presented an address *Wexford address.* to the Lord Lieutenant, in which they declared their loyalty to the Crown, and their readiness to take up arms, if required, in defence of the country against foreign or domestic foes. The Government, relying on these assurances, corroborated, as they seemed to be, by the peace and prosperity of that part of the island, thought they might safely except the county of Wexford from the extraordinary preparations which they were making in every other county for the preservation of the peace. The priests, taking advantage of this negligence, assembled their flocks, and joined the rebellion. Father Murphy, a ferocious bigot, put himself at the head of several thousand country people, near the town of Wexford, and cut to pieces a detachment of militia which attempted to oppose them. Another party plundered and burnt the bishop's palace at Ferns. Murphy then marched his men to Enniscorthy, a town about six miles from Ferns, which was occupied only by a regiment of militia and a troop of yeomanry. After a short struggle, the military were overpowered, the greater part of the town was burnt, and almost all the Protestant inhabitants were massacred. The insurgents then entered Wexford, having dispersed a body of troops which opposed their progress. The rebel force being greatly increased by their successes were divided into three corps; one was placed under the command of Bagenal Harvey, a gentleman of fortune, who had recently been lodged in the jail at Wexford on a charge of treasonable practices. The second and third divisions were commanded by priests, of whom Murphy was the principal. Several encounters took place between the rebels and the military force, in which the latter were defeated, often through the incapacity of the commanders. Harvey marched upon the town of New Ross, and after an obstinate conflict, was driven back by General Johnson. The rebels, in their retreat, murdered three hundred prisoners whom they had taken on previous days. Harvey resigned, or was displaced from his command, after his failure at New Ross; and the rebel bands were afterwards led exclusively by priests whose cruelty and fanaticism emulated the most revolting outrages of the Orangemen. Such progress had the rebellion made at one time, that fears were entertained for the safety of Dublin. The Lord Lieutenant sent Lady Camden to England; and many other ladies left the country. The triumph of rebellion was, however, short-lived. A sufficient number of troops having been collected under competent officers, skill and discipline prevailed against tumultuous numbers. General Moore, who afterwards attained such sad distinction in the Peninsula, defeated the insurgents, with a decision which struck them with dismay. Many dispersed and returned to their homes. General Lake drove the main body from Vinegar Hill, a strong position commanding the town of Enniscorthy; and the next day, Enniscorthy itself was retaken. Wexford also was reoccupied by the King's troops, and most of the rebel leaders were taken and executed under a military commission. These severe measures were necessary. But the courts-martial, composed mainly of Protestant yeomanry and militia, grossly abused their powers to gratify revenge, and to retaliate on the enemies of their religion and race. At the time when the rebellion was at its height, the English Government thought it necessary to replace Earl Camden by a lieutenant, who should be competent to exercise supreme military authority; and the Marquis Cornwallis, who combined high reputation as a statesman and a general, was induced to accept the Viceroyalty. Lord Cornwallis arrived in Dublin the day before the occupation of Wexford by the King's troops; and his first act was to check the violence of party, and to restrain the administration of military law within due bounds. The plenary powers granted to courts-martial by the alarmed and excited government of his predecessor were withdrawn, and the sentence of every court-martial was to be submitted for approval before execution, according to ordinary practice. The order was just in time to save the life of a peasant, who had been condemned to death for having possession of arms with a treasonable purpose, on the single fact that a bullet had been found in his cottage.*

Before he had been a week in Ireland, the Viceroy thought the authority of Government had been sufficiently vindicated, and that the time was come when an effort might be made to put an end to the cruel strife. Accordingly, on the 29th of June, he proclaimed an amnesty to all who, within fourteen days, surrendered their arms and took the oath of allegiance. Many availed themselves of this offer to abandon a desperate cause; but the greater number still stood out and dispersed themselves in bands, which harassed the troops and rendered every man's house unsafe, although they were no longer formidable as a revolutionary insurrection.

The policy of Lord Cornwallis was loudly resented by the Loyalists, whose exasperated passions and raging thirst for revenge could be satiated with nothing less than the extermination of

* *Annual Register*, vol. xl. p. 136.

the Romanist party. One of the Viceroy's measures seemed indeed to go to the verge of moderation. The prisons were crowded with persons of various conditions, every one of whom was probably liable to the penalties of treason. With seventy-three of these men, the most active and intelligent of the rebel leaders, the Irish Government opened a communication; the result of which was, that the prisoners, in consideration of their lives being spared, and of the sentence of death which had been already passed upon Oliver Bond, one of their chiefs, being commuted to banishment, agreed to expatriate themselves and to make a full disclosure of the plot, with the exception of such information as would be evidence against any member of their body. The Protestants, who regarded the suppression of the revolt as the triumph of their party, did not suppress their indignant murmurs at a clemency which stinted them of their revenge. Even the Government at home thought Cornwallis had gone too far in treating with criminals on such easy terms; and Lord Grenville expressed an opinion that the Irish Government had become party to a misprision of treason in allowing the prisoners to withhold evidence against their accomplices.* This was to say that a felon who does not turn approver is guilty of misprision of felony; a doctrine which crown lawyers would have considered somewhat novel. But Cornwallis, fresh from the Government of India, and inured to habits of military command, seems to have cared as little for the opinion of the British Cabinet † on these questions as for the opinion of the Orangemen of Armagh. His object was to restore the public peace as quickly as possible,

* *Courts and Cabinets of George the Third*, vol. ii. p. 406.
† Lord Grenville repeatedly complains that he was kept in ignorance of Irish affairs, and that he knew no more than he found in the *Gazette*.—*Courts and Cabinets of George the Third*, vol. ii. p. 406.

and to give no triumph to either of the religious factions which distracted the country. Many of the State prisoners were sincere and honourable men, who, though repenting the excesses into which they had been hurried, and willing to repair the mischief they had caused, would have died rather than purchase their lives by the betrayal of their companions in guilt. What the Lord Lieutenant wanted was not blood, of which enough had been already shed, but information such as the chief actors in the rebellion could supply. Accordingly, among others, O'Connor, Emmett, Neilson, and M'Nevin, gave evidence before secret committees of the Irish Parliament, and furnished the materials for reports which gave an authentic summary of the origin and progress and character of the rebellion.* Bills of attainder were passed against Lord Edward Fitzgerald, Grogan, and Bagenal Harvey; the two latter having been taken in arms and executed after the defeat and dispersion of the principal rebel force, called the army of Wexford. After these proceedings, followed the amnesty in accordance with the Lord Lieutenant's proclamation. From this act of grace thirty persons only were excepted. These were persons who had fled the country, or who had been foremost in deeds of bloodshed and rapine.

Some weeks after the rebellion had degenerated into a scattered and fugitive banditti, the French Government tardily yielded to the urgent representations of the Irish emissaries, and fitted out an expedition for a second attempt at invasion. Bonaparte, who knew the qualities of men, had little confidence in a cause which was represented by reckless and vaunting adventurers like the Napper Tandys and the Wolfe Tones; and though well aware that Ireland was the vulnerable part of the British

margin: Bonaparte's distrust of the Irish.

---

* See Report of House of Commons, *Annual Register*, vol. xl p. 265.

Isles, he waited for an assurance that the rebellion had substantial support, before he risked, for a second time, the success of a French enterprise upon Irish co-operation. Nor was he in any degree flattered by the servility with which the Irish revolutionists imitated the French Revolution at the period of its greatest vigour. It was in vain that they burnt their enemies alive—that they tossed children upon pikes —that, in dealing with their prisoners at the camp of Vinegar Hill, they copied the precedent of the Abbaye—that they called each other citizens, and styled their Government a Directory. The proposal that the French Republicans should aid their brethren in Ireland on the footing of equals and allies was treated with almost open derision. The only question with the Directory at Paris and their Generals was, whether the force which they had assigned for the conquest and annexation of the island would meet with such efficient local aid as would make it worth their while to face the fleets and armies of Great Britain. It is probable, that the French would have made no attempt on Ireland at this time, but for the rashness of a subordinate officer who commanded a brigade of the army destined for the expedition to Ireland. General Humbert, who was quartered at Rochelle, ventured, as it appears, without orders, to embark his force, consisting of about a thousand men, in two frigates, and set sail for Ireland. He effected a landing at Killala, in the county of Mayo, on the 22nd of August; and having dispersed a corps of yeomanry which offered resistance, he marched to the town of Castlebar, where General Lake, the Commander of the forces, was stationed, with three thousand men. Humbert, having left two hundred men at Killala, to keep open his communications with the sea, advanced with only eight hundred soldiers, and a rabble of about fifteen hundred Irish, to attack the English General. His situation was so desperate, that his only alternative was to fight, or to surrender at discretion. In a regular campaign, a General, in such circumstances as Humbert found himself, would hardly have been justified in fighting a pitched battle against such odds. But the Generals of the Revolution were not bred in the regular school of war, and Humbert determined to try his fortune. His little army, more than two-thirds of which consisted of irregulars, was threatened with annihilation by the well-appointed artillery of the English; but by a rapid movement on the flank, Humbert obtained an advantage, which decided the fortune of the day. The British force was thrown into disorder, a rout ensued, the broken battalions fled, many of the militia and yeomanry deserting to the enemy, and were pursued to the town of Athlone, a distance of seventy miles from the field.* Many of the militia and yeomanry deserted to the enemy during the action. The French then marched towards Sligo; but they were held in check by Colonel Vereker, with a detachment of less than three hundred militia, until Lord Cornwallis himself came up. The French General had advanced, in the hope that he would be joined by the country people; but the accessions to his ranks were few; and with thirty thousand men before him, he could neither advance nor retreat. Humbert, therefore, laid down his arms; but as he was in no condition to exact terms for his rebel auxiliaries, these people were pursued and put to the sword. Between eight and nine hundred French soldiers, including officers, being the whole invading force, which had survived the short campaign, surrendered to the English General.

The promptitude of Lord Cornwallis prevented a revival of the insurrection in a more formidable

---

* This battle was long known by the opprobrious designation of the Castlebar Races.

shape. Three thousand rebels were already on their march to join Humbert, when they were intercepted by the English army. If the French General could have maintained his footing for a few weeks, he would have been supported by large reinforcements from France. As it was, the information of his success at Castlebar determined the hesitation of the Directory, and a seventy-four gun ship, with eight frigates, conveying three thousand troops, was despatched, under the orders of Admiral Bompart, to the coast of Ireland. About a week after Humbert's corps had laid down their arms, a French brig landed a party on the island of Rutland, near the coast of Donegal. This detachment was under the command of Napper Tandy, who now bore a commission in the French service; but, on hearing of the fate of Humbert, Tandy re-embarked, and made his escape to Norway. On the 11th of October, Bompart's squadron was pursued by a portion of the Channel fleet, of seven ships, under Sir John Borlase Warren. After a chase of twenty-four hours, in tempestuous weather, Warren came up with the enemy off Lough Swilly. The chase had been so severe, that the French ship of the line had carried away her mainmast. Bompart nevertheless immediately formed in line of battle, and, after a gallant defence of nearly four hours, the Frenchman struck. The frigates attempted to escape, but three of them were taken. Four more ships were fallen in with, and surrendered, on subsequent days, to Captain Graham Moore, Captain Martin, and Captain Durham. Thus the whole of the French expedition, with the exception of one frigate and the brig which conveyed Napper Tandy, was captured. All the ships were heavily laden with troops, arms, stores, and ammunition. Among the prisoners was Wolfe Tone, who had been foremost in organising the United Irishmen, and was indeed the only man among the

rebel leaders of any ability. Tone had taken no
active part in the insurrection, having been absent
from Ireland during the last four years, engaged in
what may be termed the diplomatic service of the
rebellion, in France and Holland. He was tried by
martial law, illegally, as it seemed, his offence being
treason, and condemned to death. He desired to
be executed as a soldier, on the ground that he bore
a commission as an officer in the French service; but
this claim being disallowed, he anticipated the ignominious fate of a felon by committing suicide in
prison.

In the disaster of the French expedition, the last
hopes of the rebellion were extinguished. *Suppression of the rebellion.*
The grievances of the Irish people were
manifold; and it must be admitted that the prospect
of redressing those grievances by lawful means had
nearly disappeared when the insurrection began.
The release from civil incapacity of the Roman
Catholic people, which had been in progress since
1782, was to have been completed by the great
measure of emancipation which was brought forward
by Ireland's most honoured statesman, with the
approval of the Irish Government, in 1794. When
this policy was suddenly and rudely reversed by the
recall of Lord Fitzwilliam, the Catholics of Ireland
felt that they must either submit to the denial of
their political claims or resort to those means of
relief which the people in all ages have attempted
under intolerable oppression and wrong. But the
Catholics, if they rose, would have to encounter not
only the British Government, but the fierce and
resolute minority of their own countrymen, who were
ready and willing to maintain Protestant ascendency
by the extermination, if possible, of the hated Romanists. They might, indeed, join the revolutionary
party, and possibly throw off the dominion of Great
Britain; but this would be to exchange the dominion

of heretic but monarchical England for infidel and republican France. And even if Ireland were to establish her independence, the Catholic Church would still languish under the shade of a Protestant democracy.* The intelligent Catholics, for the most part, held these opinions. A few days before the rebellion broke out, a paper was put forth with the signatures of the most eminent and respectable members of the Catholic body, exhorting their people to abstain from violence, and to relinquish treasonable engagements, which would only bring ruin on themselves, and disgrace on their religion. Among the leaders of the insurrection, which included several gentlemen of family and fortune, no Catholic of note was to be found. Lord Edward Fitzgerald, Arthur O'Connor, Bagenal Harvey, Colclough, and Oliver Bond were Protestants. Even the adventurers, Wolfe Tone and the brothers Sheares, who desired to revolutionise Ireland after the French model, if they belonged to any religious persuasion, were Protestants. Reynolds, the son of a bankrupt trader† in Dublin, was considered an important accession to the rebel Directory, because he was a Roman Catholic; but Reynolds, when he found that the views of the United Irishmen were not limited to reform, and the removal of religious distinctions, recoiled with horror from their plans of treason and revolution, and could find no rest until he had put the Government in possession of the conspiracy against them. In the shallow counsels of the United Irishmen, the rebellion was to accomplish a great political revolution, and Ireland was to be an independent republic; but

---

* 'There are, in this country, two sets of men who are interested in promoting a change: the Catholics of the south, the known friends of monarchy; the Presbyterians of the north, the votaries of republicanism.' - *Ponsonby's Speech on Parliamentary Reform.* —*Irish Debates,* vol. ii. p. 236.

† 'Reynolds was what was called a squireen; and, like most persons of that class, was in embarrassed circumstances.'—*Life of Thomas Reynolds.*

no sooner was the sword unsheathed, than the political character of the insurrection vanished into air; and the conflict degenerated into a provincial struggle between the rival religions and races, whose animosities had distracted the island since the time of Strongbow. The Catholic peasantry, led by priests, went out to meet Protestant yeomanry, who fought under the Orange banner, the latest of many emblems of the subjection of the Celtic race. The savage joy with which the peasantry of Leinster revelled in the unwonted luxury of English blood at Prosperous and at Wexford was inflamed by the traditions of Tredah and Wexford when Cromwell destroyed their forefathers like vermin a century and a half ago. A hundred years had nearly elapsed since the Irishry had swarmed from the cabins of Connaught and Munster to defend the cause of absolute monarchy against the revolutionary doctrines of limited and responsible power; and again they had been crushed by the master race. But whether they fought in the name of absolute monarchy, or in the cause of simple democracy, it was still the rage of Papistry against Protestantism, of the Celt against the Saxon, which animated their tumultuous ranks. Oliver, and William, and George were all alike to the Whiteboys, and the Defenders, and the Croppies, who knew no other cause than the cause of Popery and Irishry, against the heretic and the foreigner. But they ever fought in a hopeless cause. Ireland, to be Catholic, must be independent of England; and she cannot be independent of England while England herself is free. Even if the geographical position of the island left it possible that her independence, or her dependency on any other country but Great Britain, could be compatible with the British Empire, the Irish people themselves are perhaps the least qualified of any people in Europe for free institutions. They have not yet acquired the elements of political education, and appear to be as far as ever from learning the first maxim of good government, the separation of political affairs from spiritual control. While the English barons in Parliament assembled were waging war with prerogative, and winning the liberties of their country; while the English Commons were successfully asserting the great principles of representative government, the state of Ireland was much the same as that in which Britain was found by Severus, or the lieutenants of Claudius. The Celtic principalities of the Sister Isle had never been visited by those hardy missionaries from the *officina gentium* who founded the Heptarchy, and substituted for a savage license the rudiments at least of political freedom. Barbarous England had undergone this wholesome invasion; and the Teutonic settlers had been, in their turn, invaded by a superior tribe, which united with the vigour and enterprise of the north a tincture of politeness and of the arts of civilised life, to which the Saxon race were strangers. The Norman conquest of Ireland was on too small a scale to effect the subjugation of the country; and the noble race which attempted to colonise Ireland pined in provincial inactivity, or degenerated to the level of the slothful barbarians, with whom they mingled their blood. Then came the English of the pale, who occupied the Irish soil, as the English now occupy New Zealand. Yet the natives fared better under the Norman nobles, who treated them as barbarians, than under the Republican dispensation. Cromwell and his lieutenants, not satisfied with prosecuting a war of extermination against the unhappy people, drove the remnant whom the sword had spared to the savage rocks and mountains of Connaught; and forbade them to intrude on the more fertile and habitable portions of the island. More than five millions of acres of the best land were parcelled out among the puritanical adherents, and the soldiers of the Commonwealth. Despised as an inferior race, and disqualified by their religion for the privileges of citizens, the Irish for six hundred years had been ruled by a government over which they had no more control than the Hindoos or the Cingalese. Their virtues and failings were in an opposite direction to those which are found in people who flourish under free municipal institutions. Their failings were such as are bred by oppression and the denial of political rights; dissimulation and falsehood, recklessness, indolence, want of self-reliance. Their virtues were religious reverence, courage, fidelity. But their religion was a blind superstition; their courage, for want of proper training and a just direction, became wanton and mischievous; their fidelity, like that of another branch of the Celtic family, consisted in a passionate attachment to the old territorial aristocracy. These are not the qualities which make good citizens or a great people; though they have made Irishmen, when removed from the depressing influences of their native soil, brilliant adventurers, eminently successful in civil affairs, and unrivalled in the field of war.

No sooner had the rebellion been suppressed, than the Government proposed, to the Parliament of each country, the union of Great Britain and Ireland under a common legislature. This was no new idea. It had frequently been in the minds of successive generations of statesmen on both sides of the Channel; but had not yet been seriously discussed with a view to immediate action. Nothing could have been more safely predicted than that Ireland must, sooner or later, follow the precedent of Scotland, and yield her pretensions to a separate legislation. The measures of 1782, which appeared to establish the legislative independence of Ireland, really proved the vanity of such a pretension, and hastened the inevitable day when the Parliament at Dublin must

Union proposed.

merge in the Imperial Parliament of Great Britain. So long as the Irish Chambers were content to leave the initiative of their legislation to the English Government, to submit to the supremacy of English law, and to a standing army, they differed little from the old French Parliaments, and might have prolonged their harmless existence for many a year; but when they broke loose from the law of Poynings, which kept them under the control of the Crown, and demanded the repeal of the Declaratory Act of George the First, which subjected them to the Parliament of England, and claimed the right of passing an annual Mutiny Act, which secured their independence, the relations between the two kingdoms were completely changed. Canada and Australia, separated from Great Britain by vast seas, are permitted the free exercise of legislative rights, because the connection of those great dependencies with the mother-country is not necessary to her existence; but if Ireland, separated from Great Britain only by a narrow channel, was to be passing protective tariffs, while England was declaring free-trade; if Ireland was to admit universal suffrage and vote by ballot, while England was carefully guarding her parliamentary constitution from the inroads of democracy; if it was to depend on a vote of the House of Commons, in College Green, whether Ireland should send her contingents of seamen and soldiers to a war with France or America, in which Great Britain might be engaged; or, lastly, if the Parliament in Dublin was permitted to debate the question of independence, the integrity of the British Empire would be destroyed. The measures of 1782, by which the English Government acknowledged the independence of the Irish Parliament, had not yet been fatal to the Irish Parliament, only because its corruption rendered it wholly subservient to the dictation of the Crown.

On one occasion only, during the eighteen years of Irish independence, when the British Government was, for a moment, in abeyance, from the incapacity of the King, did the Irish Parliament act upon its own counsels; and on that occasion it transferred the whole power of the Crown, without restriction or condition, to the heir-apparent, while the Parliament of England had accompanied a similar offer with restrictions and conditions of the most binding quality. Here was a signal proof, if proof were wanting, that a free Parliament in Ireland could not work harmoniously with a free Parliament in England. All the energies of the Irish patriots were, nevertheless, directed to a state of affairs, which must bring about a collision fatal to the independence of the country. They demanded a reform of Parliament, which at present was a Parliament only in name, and the admission to civil privileges of the majority of the people of Ireland, who were kept without the pale of the constitution, as necessary parts of the policy of 1782. It was impossible to deny the justice of these claims, and they had always been admitted by the Whig party on either side of the Channel. Lord Fitzwilliam would have carried these measures; and had he been permitted to pursue this honest policy, the rebellion would not have taken place. But though the rebellion would have been prevented, the day of reckoning between England and Ireland would only have been postponed; and it was better that the weaker country should at once be told that two sovereign Parliaments cannot exist in the same political sphere, than that another military conquest should complete the series of wars, in which Ireland has been crushed in the attempt to achieve her independence of Great Britain.

On the assembling of the British Parliament at the commencement of the year, the question of the Union was recommended by a message from the Crown; and the address, after some opposition, was carried without a division. Pitt, at

Opening of Parliament.

this, the earliest stage, pronounced the decision at which the Government had arrived to be positive and irrevocable. 'I see the case so plainly,' said he, 'and I feel it so strongly, that there is no circumstance of apparent or probable difficulty, no apprehension of popularity, no fear of toil or labour that shall prevent me from using every exertion which remains in my power to accomplish the work that is now before us, and on which, I am persuaded, depend the internal tranquillity of Ireland, the interest of the British Empire at large, and the happiness of a great portion of the habitable globe.'

Lord Cornwallis also expressed his conviction that union was the only measure which could preserve the country.* The Chancellor Clare, the ablest of Irish statesmen, went over himself to urge upon the English Cabinet, that, unless the Union could be effected, there was little hope of maintaining the connection between the two islands.† No person of note in England, beyond the narrow circle of the regular Opposition, expressed any doubt as to the policy of the Union; but there was a very large party in both countries, who would not consent that the measure should be accompanied by any concessions of the Catholic claims.

<small>Chancellor Clare.</small>

The day before the intended Union was signified by a royal message to the English Parliament, the Irish Houses assembled; and the Viceroy's speech, of course, contained a paragraph relative to the project. The House of Lords, completely under the control of the Castle, agreed to an address, in conformity with the speech, after a short and languid debate, by a large majority; but the Commons were violently agitated. A debate pitched

<small>Royal message.</small>

---

* Lord Cornwallis to Mr. Pitt, 20th of July, 1798.—*Cornwallis Correspondence*, vol. ii. p. 364.

† Lord Cornwallis to the Duke of Portland, 8th of October, 1798. — *Cornwallis Correspondence*, vol. ii. p. 418.

in a tone of exaggerated sentiment and high-flown eloquence, was so much the ordinary key of that assembly, that a temperate discussion of an important question would have been an extraordinary occurrence; but what was remarkable, and indeed unprecedented, in the Irish House of Commons, was the result of this debate. An amendment to the address, pledging the House to maintain the Union, was lost by one vote, after the House had sat twenty-one hours;* but on the report, the amendment to omit the paragraph referring to the Union was carried by a majority of four.† That a Government, in the height of its power, should be defeated and out-voted in a House of Parliament, the great majority of whose members were registered and priced in the minister's book, was one of those events which denote a crisis in the history of a nation.

The truth is, that the project of Union had, at first, attracted little attention; and many persons of mark had, at first, yielded a half assent to a proposal of the Government which they did not believe to be seriously entertained. The Irish people, with habitual indolence and procrastination, troubled themselves little about a measure which was not of immediate moment. But when it was understood that the Government was in earnest, and that the Union was to be recommended from the Throne to the Parliaments of both countries, there was little difficulty in alarming a people, among whom the machinery of political agitation had, for some years, been extensively organised. The bar of Dublin took the lead, and it at once became evident that the policy of the Government had effected a union among Irishmen far more formidable than that which all the efforts of sedition had been able to accomplish. The meeting of the bar included not merely men of dif-

Revival of agitation in Ireland.

---

* The numbers were 105 to 106. Nearly one-third of the members absented themselves from the division.   † 109 to 105.

ferent religious persuasions, but, what was of more importance in Ireland, men of different sides in politics. Saurin, the leader of the Four Courts, a Protestant and a Tory, who subsequently became Attorney-General, summoned the meeting, in his character of Captain of the Lawyer's Corps of Yeomanry, and was with difficulty dissuaded from attending in uniform.* Nearly the whole body assembled, and, by a majority of five to one,† agreed to a resolution condemning the project of a legislative union between the two countries. In the majority, besides Saurin, were Plunket, Bushe, and Joy, with other eminent men; the minority contained hardly a name of any reputation. It was said, and probably with truth, that the leaders of the bar were opposed to the Union, because attendance in Parliament, and the regular practice of their profession, would no longer be compatible, if the seat of legislation was transferred to London. But, however conclusive the argument in favour of Union may appear to Englishmen, it was difficult for an Irishman to regard the Union in any other view than as a measure to deprive his country of her independent constitution, and to extinguish her national existence. Mr. Foster, the Speaker, took this view. It could hardly, indeed, have been otherwise. He was the last person who could consent to the final dissolution of that assembly, which had elected him as their chief. The Speaker's adhesion, however, was so important that every effort was made to conciliate him. He went to England, and had several interviews with Pitt. He was assured of high advancement under the new system, and might, indeed, have named his terms; but Foster, though hitherto a firm friend of the Government, under which he had, at one time, held high office, proved incorruptible. He returned to Ireland the declared

* Mr. Cooke (Under-Secretary of State) to Lord Castlereagh, Nov. 8, 1798.—*Memoirs of Lord Castlereagh*, vol. i. p. 127. † 166 to 32.

inveterate enemy of the Union, and was at once acknowledged the leader of the national party. Sir John Parnell, the Chancellor of the Exchequer, followed the Speaker. Mr. Fitzgerald, the Prime Serjeant, a law officer of the Crown, was on the same side. Ponsonby, the leader of the Whigs, was vehement against the scheme; so was Grattan; so was Curran. Great efforts were made, by the Government, to quiet the Protestants, and to engage the Catholics to support the Union. These efforts were so far successful that most of the Orange lodges were persuaded to refrain from expressing any opinion on the subject. The Catholic hierarchy were conciliated by the promise of a provision for the clergy, and of an adjustment of the Tithe question. Hopes were held out, if promises were not actually made, to the Catholic community, that their civil disabilities would be removed. The Catholics, as a body, therefore, were not indisposed to the project of the English Government; and even if no prospect had been held out to them, that their particular grievances would be redressed, it was not to be expected that the Catholic body should feel much interested in the maintenance of a constitution, from the benefits of which they were hopelessly excluded. The people of Ireland in general, so far as they entertained any opinion or feeling in the matter, regarded their native legislation with the contempt which it deserved. Nevertheless, the opposition with which the Government had to deal, was formidable enough to deter any Government from persisting in a measure, even of the first importance; for the Opposition combined all that was corrupt, with the little that was public-spirited, in this unhappy country. But Pitt had made up his mind to carry a measure which he considered important, if not essential, to the integrity of the Empire; a measure, too, which he had contemplated long before the recent disturbances,*

* In 1795.—*Personal Recollections of Lord Cloncurry*, p. 38.

and to which no time seemed so favourable as the present.

Address to the Crown.

If the Union was to be accomplished by constitutional means, it could be effected only by a vote of the Irish Parliament, concurring with a vote of the English Parliament; and if the Irish assembly were to pronounce an unbiassed judgment on the question of its extinction, it is certain that a very small minority, possibly not a single vote, would be found to support the measure. All the influence of the Government had failed as yet to incline the House of Commons to listen to the proposal. The vote on the address was followed, in a few days, by an address to the Crown, in which the Commons pledged themselves to maintain the constitution of 1782. The majority in favour of national independence had already increased from five to twenty, the ministerial members remaining the same, and corresponding almost exactly with the placemen and pensioners in the House.

The votes of the Irish Commons had disposed of the question for the current session; but preparations were immediately made for its future passage through the Irish Houses. The foremost men in Ireland—men whose abilities would have raised them to eminence in any country, whose eloquence would have moved any assembly, ancient or modern, and whose patriotism was sincere—had first been tempted, but had indignantly refused every offer to betray the independence of their country. Another class of leading persons * was then tried, and from these, for the

---

* 'Those who are called principal persons here are men who have been raised into consequence only by having the entire disposal of the patronage of the Crown, in return for their undertaking the management of the country; because the Lord Lieutenants were too idle or too incapable to manage it themselves. They are detested by everybody but their immediate followers, and have no influence but what is founded on the grossest corruption.' Marquis Cornwallis to General Ross, Nov. 23, 1798.— *Cornwallis Correspondence*, vol. ii. p. 442.

most part, evasive answers were received. The minister understood the meaning of these dubious utterances. There was one mode of carrying the Union, and one mode only. Bribery of every kind must be employed without hesitation and without stint.

The plan of parliamentary reform which Mr. Pitt proposed at the outset of his administration was founded on a recognition of the claims of the borough owners, and contained provisions for the compensation of those claims. If such an arrangement was just and expedient with regard to the reform of the English Parliament, it was not less just and expedient with a view to the extinction of the Irish Parliament. But this mode of meeting the difficulties of the representation, though it might have been justified by necessity, could not for a moment stand the test of argument; and Pitt probably was in no mind to revive the crude idea of his youth. The force of public opinion in 1832 swept away the great obstacle to parliamentary reform; but the public opinion of Ireland in 1799 could not be appealed to for the abolition of the Irish legislature. Yet if it was considered unreasonable or hopeless to expect that the owners of Gatton and Old Sarum should relinquish their vested interests in the abuse and decay of the representative system without an equivalent, it was at least as unjust and unreasonable to expect that the owners of the Ballyshannons and the Banaghers should offer up their rotten boroughs, not for the purpose of restoring and invigorating the parliamentary system, but as sacrifices to the common ruin. There could be no comparison between the importance of a seat in the British House of Commons and a seat in a provincial assembly, which had more resemblance to a municipal council than to an Imperial Parliament; yet the value of borough property in Ireland was equal to that of the same description of property in England. There have always been men willing to spend two or three thousand pounds for a seat, or even the attempt to obtain a seat, in the English House; and these candidates have been as often actuated by their estimate of the social position which a seat in Parliament confers as by the hope of advancing their fortunes. But when an Irish gentleman gave twenty thousand pounds for a borough, or when an Irish adventurer hired a seat for two thousand pounds, he invested his money in a speculation for which he had reason to expect a safe return. The commoner wanted a peerage; he had two votes at the service of the minister, and Irish peerages were held in higher estimation by Irish commoners than by the British minister. Pitt was always more willing to reward a political friend with a title than with a place, and he lavished Irish peerages with the profusion of contempt. He sometimes gave these titles to persons who would now be considered sufficiently honoured by knighthood, and on one occasion was only restrained by the indignant remonstrance of the Lord Lieutenant from making a London stock-jobber an Irish peer.* The offices and sinecures on the Irish establishment were a proverb and a scandal; but as every member of the Irish House of Commons who gave a vote to the Government expected to be paid for it, the offices and sinecures, numerous as they were, proved insufficient to satisfy the claims of members of Parliament, their families and followers; and a pension list of eight thousand pounds a-year afforded temporary relief to a parliamentary supporter until his services could be rewarded with a more adequate provision.

Such was the Parliament by whose vote the British minister was to effect the legislative union of the two countries. And, in the first place, he made it under-

---

* Duke of Rutland to Mr. Pitt, 1780.—*Bolton MSS.*

stood that while willing to traffic in votes after the fashion of the Walpoles, the Pelhams, and the Foxes, he would not tolerate the patriotism of persons already in the receipt of public money. Accordingly, Sir John Parnell, the Chancellor of the Exchequer, and Mr. Fitzgerald, the Prime Serjeant who had voted on the amendment to the address, were peremptorily dismissed. It was hoped that these examples might act as a warning to men like the Speaker, and Mr. John Claudius Beresford, whom the Government hardly ventured to attack, as well as to the numerous stipendiaries of the Crown, with respect to whom they were unwilling to pursue the relentless policy by which the elder Fox had terrified the opponents of the peace of Paris in 1763.*

The Duke of Portland, having officially instructed Lord Cornwallis to make known the fixed determination of the Ministry to carry the measure of the Union, and that the conduct of individuals upon the subject would be considered as the test of their disposition to support the King's Government,† the Castle of Dublin soon became a mart for parliamentary traffic, more extensive than had hitherto been known in Ireland or in England during the most critical period of the Hanover succession. It was not merely a trade in votes, but the purchase of the fee simple of corruption which the Irish Government was to undertake. Cornwallis had seen too much of courts and camps to be shocked by the selfishness and baseness which a long experience of public life reveals. In America he had seen armies led to destruction by men of fashion, and an empire lost through the influence of the back stairs. In India, he must have seen enough

_{Duke of Portland's instructions}

---

* Mr. Beresford resigned his sinecure place. The Speaker's son was subsequently deprived of his office by the express desire of Mr. Pitt.—*Cornwallis Correspondence*, vol. iii. p. 55.

† Dec. 21, 1708.—*Cornwallis Correspondence*, vol. iii. p. 20.

to lower his estimate of public virtue; but the experience of Asia and America had not prepared the able statesman and soldier for the universal dishonesty and the clamorous corruption which he encountered in Ireland. Lord Cornwallis's correspondence, both official and private, during the whole period of his viceroyalty, describes Ireland as a land of jobs, the upper classes hopelessly corrupt, and the lower orders of people animated with an impartial hatred to the English Government and their native rulers. The only class of which he speaks in terms of qualified commendation were the Roman Catholic hierarchy, and the noblemen and gentlemen of that persuasion. Long schooled in political adversity, these persons had learned to be moderate in their demands; and, excluded from all share in the public pillage, they were necessarily free from personal corruption.

Lord Cornwallis, therefore, addressed himself with a dogged disgust to the odious duties which the determination of the English Government had imposed upon him. His business lay chiefly among the political leaders, who were to be gained over by peerages and the higher description of patronage. But there was other work of a lower kind, to which the Lord Lieutenant neither could nor would put his hand. Members of the House of Commons were to be privately convinced by arguments more conclusive than those of the ministerial orators; persons of influence out of doors were to be treated with; the press was to be bought. This business, to be done effectually, must be under the immediate superintendence and direction of a person of sufficient power and station to have credit and authority, but not so highly placed as to be inaccessible to the meaner agents of corruption. In those days, there would have been little difficulty in finding among the holders of subordinate offices, in either island, an able and ambitious man, who would consider it a high responsibility, and a certain step towards advancement, to be charged with a secret service of this description. The Lord Lieutenant was so fortunate as to find in a young nobleman who had recently been appointed to the principal office in his Government a person eminently qualified for the peculiar duties which, at this juncture, the Chief Secretary was required to perform. Viscount Castlereagh was the son of an Irish gentleman who had been recently ennobled; he had been educated in Ireland, and had taken his seat in the Irish House of Commons when he became of age. Lord Castlereagh, during the earlier years of his parliamentary life, had acted with the Opposition; but during the administration of Lord Camden, to whom he was related by a family connection, he accepted a small office, and during the absence of Mr. Pelham, the Chief Secretary, Castlereagh was appointed to perform the duties of the office. The rebellion which soon after broke out afforded full scope for his energy and ability. The harsh measures which were adopted by the Lord Lieutenant were attributed to the advice of his young kinsman; and when Camden quitted Ireland, his successor continued the temporary arrangement of the Secretary's office. When Pelham finally resigned, in November, 1798, Lord Cornwallis endeavoured to obtain the services of Mr. Thomas Grenville,* who had declined the office when it had been pressed upon him by Lord Fitzwilliam, in 1794. Grenville still persisting in his refusal to connect himself with a branch of administration so little coveted as that of Ireland, several other names were mentioned, and ultimately, though not without misgiving on the part of the Home Government as to his capacity for an office which had now become

* Lord Grenville to Marquis of Buckingham.— *Courts and Cabinets of George the Third*, vol. ii. p. 410.

so arduous, Castlereagh was appointed. At this time he was in his thirtieth year.

It was a traditional rule of the Home Government that no Irishman should be appointed Chief Secretary to the Lord Lieutenant; and Cornwallis had sought to remove this objection which had been urged against Castlereagh, by assuring the Duke of Portland that his young friend was so unlike an Irishman, that an exception ought to be made in his favour. It is not easy to understand the policy which pronounced an Irishman disqualified for the principal office of business in the Irish Government. The invariable practice of sending over an Englishman to act as minister for Ireland, and to take the lead of the Irish House of Commons, always ranked among the principal grievances of the country; and as the English Secretary was usually a second-rate politician and an indifferent speaker, his position in the Irish House, which generally included men of great oratorical power, was often humiliating, and sometimes ridiculous. In the succession of secretaries to the Lord Lieutenant since Addison had gone over with Wharton, there had been none superior to Castlereagh in political ability and aptitude for affairs. Independently of his personal qualifications, it cannot be questioned that his position as an Irishman of rank and fortune, together with the knowledge of his countrymen, which he had acquired by having lived among them from his earliest years, gave him advantages in negotiating a local question of unprecedented magnitude and difficulty, which no Englishman could have possessed.

One of the earliest acts of Lord Castlereagh was to draw upon the secret service fund for five thousand pounds.* This instalment, which was readily furnished from the Secretary of State's office, was em-

---

* Lord Castlereagh to Mr. Wickham, Under-Secretary for the Home Department. Jan. 2, 1799.—*Cornwallis Correspondence*, vol. iii. p. 27.

ployed principally in engaging young barristers of the
Four Courts to write for the Union. After the failure
of the measure in the House of Commons, Lord
Castlereagh was convinced that it could be carried
only by bribery administered on a large and systematic scale;* and this view of the question was kept
before the English Government in every despatch
sent from the Castle from the beginning of 1799
until the bill was passed in June, 1800. Accordingly,
the Chief Secretary drew up a scheme by which, under
the name of compensation, a million and a half of
money was to be distributed among borough proprietors, part owners of counties, lessees of seats, and
barristers who had entered the House of Commons
to advance their professional fortunes. This latter
class consisted of fifty members. The plan also included an arrangement by which occupiers and
owners of houses in Dublin, where hostility to the
Union was most prevalent, should receive an equivalent for the estimated depreciation of their property.† The English Government were at first
startled by the proposal to carry the Union by the
simple expedient of buying up the House of Commons. But the recognition of property in the close
boroughs having formed the basis of the parliamentary reform originally proposed by Pitt, no
objection was raised on principle to that part of
Castlereagh's plan. It was determined that the
county representation should not be curtailed; and
thus the difficulty of adjusting compensation in the
numerous cases in which the two county seats were
divided between two or more predominant interests
was avoided. The claims of lawyers and other adventurers who speculated in seats were peremptorily
rejected. The tradesmen and householders of the
capital were to be conciliated as much as possible:

* *Castlereagh Correspondence*, vol. iii. p. 330.
† *Memoirs of Viscount Castlereagh*, vol. ii. p. 148.

but, at the same time, to be distinctly informed that their particular interests would not be suffered to impede the progress of the Union. Dublin was, however, to return two members to the Imperial Parliament.

<small>Resolutions moved by Pitt.</small> A week after the Irish House had refused to entertain the question, the English minister moved a series of resolutions, embodying the principal provisions of the intended Union. In opening this, the greatest and most enduring measure of his administration, Pitt delivered one of those complete arguments which, in the judgment of men of sense and candour, determine the merits of a question. There were, probably, few members of the British Parliament who cared more for the proceedings of the Irish Parliament than for those of a provincial vestry, or whose information about Irish manners and politics was much more accurate than that of an ordinary Frenchman about his country at the present day. That Ireland was very like a froward child, over which the parent country must hold a strict hand; that the Irish House of Commons was a mere debating club, capable only of cultivating flowery oratory; that the Irish gentry were a race of spendthrifts and fortune-hunters; and that the Irish people were hardly a remove from savages, were common articles of belief throughout the mass of English society. The promulgation of a United Kingdom of Great Britain and Ireland excited an interest among the British public less lively than the announcement of legislative institutions for a new colony, or the annexation of an Indian province, would cause at the present day. Pitt's speech, though ten thousand copies of it were circulated by authority throughout Ireland, was, in fact, much more calculated to satisfy the English nation, that the Union would be advantageous to them, than to reconcile the Irish people to the loss of their native legislature.

The minister proved, from recent events, what, indeed, was almost demonstrable, from the physical relation of the two islands, that their close connection was essential to the welfare of both; in other words, that the control of Great Britain over Ireland was necessary to the independence of the more powerful kingdom. He showed that this connection could be secured only by means of a common legislature; and he was aided by a willing audience, when he proceeded to argue, that the final settlement of 1782, by which the legislative independence of Ireland was recognised, was not inconsistent with a plan for absorbing the Irish legislature into the Imperial Parliament. Such a proposition was, indeed, hardly tenable; but the great orator relied, with more security, on the illustrations by which he supported his main argument, that there could be no real or safe connection between the two countries, on a footing of equality and independence. The remarkable case of the Regency in 1788, when the two legislatures differed as to powers conferred upon the Regent, was, of course, cited. Suppose, said Mr. Pitt, the independent Parliaments to have gone a step farther, and to have differed as to the person who should exercise the power of the sovereign? Suppose the Commons of England supporting the Crown in a just and necessary war, and the Commons of Ireland disapproving of the war, and refusing supplies? Was such a state of things to be tolerated? Ought the possibility of a collision, tending to anarchy, to exist? Could there be one executive in England and another executive in Ireland? Was England to be at war, and Ireland to be at peace? The settlement of 1782, so far from being final, was in its very nature finite. Ireland might have a vestry, but she could not have a Parliament. If the two kingdoms were to remain united under one Crown, they must be united under one legislature.

Not content with establishing the necessity of union on such high ground, Mr. Pitt went on to show, what might have been more debatable, the incompetency, in point of fact, of an Irish Parliament to deal with Irish questions. The Catholic question, the Tithe question, he maintained, were more likely to attain a satisfactory settlement in a united Parliament than in an assembly distracted by local jealousies and provincial faction. The Catholics, he said, could not receive the full measure of their political claims under a separate legislature. Such a concession could not be granted to a body, which formed the great majority of the inhabitants, without transferring to that class a preponderating influence, which would shake the constitution of Ireland to its centre.*

Mr. Pitt then disposed of another point which had been lightly touched by the English Opposition, but had been gravely insisted upon as an insuperable obstacle by the lawyers and patriots of the Irish Parliament. This was the incompetency of that

* Mr. Pitt should have thought of this before he suffered Lord Fitzwilliam to amuse the Irish Catholics with the hope of emancipation. Lord Fitzwilliam fancied that he was recalled for having dismissed Mr. Beresford; but he was recalled when it became apparent that his intention was to turn out all the old Protestant party, and to fill their places with the friends of Catholic emancipation. See a letter from Pitt to Lord Westmoreland, November 19, 1794, in Lord Stanhope's recently published *Miscellanies*, p. 14. Lord Clare, as well as Beresford, went over to England, for the purpose of procuring the removal of Fitzwilliam; and it was probably owing to the representations of Clare, rather than to those of Beresford, that the Cabinet as well as the King took the alarm. Clare was by far the ablest of the old ruling party in Ireland, and the only Irish minister to whom Pitt listened. It will be recollected that the one point upon which Pitt was inflexible when Fitzwilliam went to Ireland was that the Great Seal should not be disturbed. It was Lord Clare who, through the medium of the English Chancellor, Loughborough, possessed the King's mind with the idea of the coronation oath; and it is remarkable, that when important concessions were first made to the Catholics of Ireland, in 1793, Fitzgibbon used substantially the same language, as to the danger of Catholic supremacy, which Pitt uttered in the speech on the Union resolutions.

Parliament to annihilate itself, and to transfer its functions to a foreign legislature. Pitt contented himself with meeting the more limited objection which had been raised in the debate on the King's message, recommending the Union. On that occasion, Sheridan, who took the leading part, questioned only the competency of the Irish Parliament to entertain the question without a special appeal to their constituents. This argument suggested one of those rhetorical invectives against democracy, from which hardly any of Pitt's great orations, for the last ten years, had been free, but which the House was never weary of applauding. He denounced the doctrine that the representative body could not entertain a new question without returning to its constituents as a dangerous innovation, sprung from the theory of the sovereignty of the people, the favourite delusion by which Jacobites and Revolutionists misled the understandings, and inflamed the passions of the populace. None will dispute Mr. Pitt's position, that every political system must contain somewhere an absolute, unlimited power; nor that, in our system, this power is to be found in Parliament. But the wisdom of modern times, when Parliament is a far better representative of the country than it was in Pitt's days, avoids a strain even upon this, the strongest part of the constitution; and practically no change of policy takes place, and seldom is any capital measure adopted, without the immediate sanction of the constituent body.*

* This change in constitutional practice is one of the most remarkable consequences of the Reform Act. Under the system of close boroughs, and the franchise so irregularly distributed, that in some places it was so limited as to afford no scope to the sense of the inhabitants, in others so widely diffused as to drown their sense in profligacy and clamour, it was idle to appeal to the electoral body for an authentic expression of public opinion. It was only when the current set violently in one direction, as in 1784, that a minister could resort to a dissolution, for the purpose of determining a policy or settling a

Another objection raised to the great policy of the Government, was one, said the minister, entitled to respect on account of the generous source from which it sprang. It had been urged that this was a case in which a nation was called upon to surrender its independence, and that no consideration of material benefit could be allowed to compensate for a sacrifice so ignominious. But if this principle had prevailed, Europe would still be distracted by the barbarous strife of petty states. And as the doctrine of the sovereignty of the people struck at the stability of all Government, so this extreme idea of independence would ever have prevented the consolidation of an empire, and finally sent mankind back to the state of nature. Mr. Pitt treated this topic in his finest manner. It was not, he said, a proposal for subjecting Ireland to a foreign yoke, but rather the free and voluntary association of two great countries, which join, for their common benefit, in one empire, when each will retain its proportional weight and importance under the security of equal laws, reciprocal affection, and inseparable interests, and which want nothing but indissoluble connection to render both invincible.

He concluded by moving a series of resolutions, affirming the expediency of a union between the two kingdoms for the benefit of both, and for the consolidation of the monarchy. The principal articles recommended an equality of trade between the two countries, that the Union should comprise Church as well as State, that the public charge should be distributed in such proportions as should be settled by

party question. Before the Reform Act, a Parliament generally lived through the term of its legal existence. During the thirty years that have elapsed since the Reform Act, there have been eight Parliaments and eleven Administrations, of which the fates of six were determined by appeals to the constituencies. In this manner, the national will is more distinctly imposed upon the councils of the State, than if a general election was a matter of annual routine.

the Parliament of each country before the Union; that the proportion of Irish members which were to sit in the united Parliament should be determined in like manner, and that the oaths and declarations to be required from the members of the united Parliament would remain unchanged until the said Parliament *should otherwise provide*. The last words were inserted for the purpose of satisfying the Catholics that the question of their emancipation from political disability was to be kept open.

Long debates and several divisions took place on the different questions which the forms of the House required or permitted, before the resolutions were agreed to. The Opposition contended that the proposal of the Government was in violation of the settlement of 1782, the only question then reserved being the question of trade, which Mr. Pitt himself had endeavoured to settle by his commercial propositions in 1786; that Ireland had proved her readiness and ability to provide for her own defence against foreign aggression by the army of volunteers which she had raised when England was unable to afford her assistance; that the remedy for Irish misgovernment was the reform, and not the abolition of her Parliament; and that the certain consequence of a legislative union would be the impoverishment of the country by the desertion of its principal landholders. The Speaker on this occasion laid aside the dignified reserve which keeps the chair apart from the conflict of party; in committee he supported the resolution in a long and elaborate argument; nor on a high constitutional question like this was it unbecoming that the first commoner should pronounce a matured opinion; and possibly Mr. Addington might have been moved by the consideration that his Irish brother had taken the leading part on the other side. The resolutions were carried by large majorities in thin Houses. One hundred and seventy-three was the highest number that divided on a question which concerned the consolidation, if not the integrity, of the Empire. Never had so much apparent indifference been exhibited on a question of capital importance. In truth, the absence of members was attributable rather to distaste than indifference. The Union was reluctantly assented to by many as an unavoidable necessity; and others who were not convinced by the arguments of the minister yielded from habit to his will. The county members and the fine gentlemen of the House were somewhat dismayed at the prospect of an irruption of representatives from Connaught and Munster. The roof of St. Stephen's would be rent with unaccustomed eloquence; for the dialect of Kerry and Tipperary had hardly yet been heard within those walls. The genius of Burke himself had never overcome the remains of the Celtic brogue. Still it was better that a hundred Irish gentlemen should enter the House of Commons, than that a French Directory should sit at the Castle of Dublin, or a French fleet ride in the harbour of Cork.

On the other side of the Channel every effort was made to avert the odious Union. After the adverse vote on the address, a Regency Bill was brought in by Mr. Fitzgerald, who had been dismissed from his office of Prime Serjeant for taking a prominent part in opposition to the Union. It was proposed by this measure to obviate one of the most practical objections which had been made to the legislative separation of the two countries. The Government could not in decency oppose a bill brought in for the express purpose of removing an anomaly which had been referred to as a justification of their great measure; but it was not the less certain that the bill would not be suffered to pass. The bill was indeed framed so imperfectly that it appeared to have been merely put together as a convenient groundwork for an attack upon the policy of the Government, and never intended as a remedy for a particular defect. Foster, the Speaker, availed himself of the committee on the bill to deliver a carefully prepared reply to the speech of Mr. Pitt. It was not a very successful argument, even in the opinion of its partial hearers. It was no answer to a speech such as that of the first minister to call it a 'paltry performance,' and to denounce Pitt 'as the worst minister the Irish nation ever heard of.' The Speaker was answered by Lord Castlereagh. The debate, which was long and vehement, turned almost wholly on the all-absorbing question of the Union. The Regency Bill, it was found, could not by any ingenuity be so framed as to provide for harmony of action between the two Parliaments. And as the Imperial Parliament would certainly not consult a provincial Parliament in making an arrangement for the exercise of the executive power, it followed that the inferior assembly must, if intolerable confusion was to be avoided, submit implicitly to the dictation of the greater. But no security could be given for such acquiescence without infringing on that absolute legislative independence for which Irish patriotism contended. When the report of the committee on the bill was brought up, Lord Castlereagh therefore moved that the consideration be postponed to a day when the House would not be in session; and his motion was agreed to without a dissenting voice.

The Irish Houses were shortly afterwards prorogued; but not before they had, at the instance of the Government, and without opposition, passed a bill, which is in itself sufficient to load the memory of the last Irish Parliament with execration and contempt.

Irish Houses prorogued.

In the previous year an act had been passed for the protection of magistrates and other persons in authority, who, in the vigorous discharge of their duty in the suppression of the rebellion, might have overstepped the law. During a state of rebellion, it may be necessary to commit acts of power, such as arresting suspected persons, entering houses, impressing cattle; and it is not unreasonable that public servants, who have committed such irregularities, at a time when there is an insurrection against law and order, should be protected against vexatious litigation. The act of the Irish Parliament was framed upon the model of an act passed by the English Parliament, after the rising of the Jacobites in 1715. But an indemnity, which was sufficient for the protection of persons who had been compelled by the sudden exigencies of the public service to act, in some instances, without warrant of authority, proved wholly inadequate to protect the agents of a Government, which permitted a rebellion to be dealt with by means wholly unknown to the law. I have already related how the miserable peasantry were scourged, picketed, and half strangled to extort information as to concealed arms and United Irishmen. After the rebellion had been suppressed, some persons, in a higher walk of life, who had been subjected to this treatment, resolved to try the question whether it was intended, by the Act of Indemnity, to sanction the application of torture to a subject of the Crown of England. And that the experiment might be fairly tried, proceedings were taken, not against a yeomanry trooper, or a petty justice, who might have been disavowed, but against an executive officer of the highest rank and responsibility in his district.

The county of Tipperary, which has since attained an ill reputation, was not much disturbed by the rebellion. Colonel Bagwell, one of the members for the county, and Mr. Hely Hutchinson, brother of the Earl of Donoughmore, one of the principal resident landlords, declared in their places in the House of Commons, that the county was almost free from disturbance. It is admitted by a strong partisan,* that a respectable minority of the magistrates and gentlemen of the county were of the same opinion; but the majority of the landowners, either stricken by the terror of which meanness and cruelty are susceptible, or anticipating the rising of the people to revenge the cruelty and contumely to which their race and creed had long been subjected, thought fit to take such measures of prevention as their nature dictated. For their purpose, they had recourse to a small proprietor near Thurles, Thomas Judkin Fitzgerald, a man who was known to be capable of any degree of violence which could be expected from an ignorant ferocious partisan; and this man they procured to be appointed High Sheriff. Fitzgerald, eager to justify the confidence of his employers, and willing, no doubt, to earn the pay with which successful vigour would be rewarded by the frightened and distracted Government,† soon signalised his zeal. His plan was to seize persons whom he chose to suspect, often without the slightest ground, if not from sheer malice, and by dint of the lash, and threats of instant death, to extort confessions of guilt, and accusations of other persons.‡ So abject was the terror of the peasantry, abandoned as they were to the inhuman tyranny of this miscreant, that at his

* Sir Richard Musgrave.—*Hist. Rebel.*

† This applies to Lord Camden's Government and all the Irish officials at the Castle, except the Chancellor.

‡ When General Sir John Moore, on the march from Fermoy, entered the town of Clogheen, he saw with disgust a man tied up in the street, and under the lash, while the street itself was lined with country people on their knees, with their hats off; nor was that disgust repressed when he was informed that the High Sheriff, Mr. Fitzgerald, was making great discoveries, and that he had already flogged the truth out of many respectable persons. His rule was to flog each person till he told the truth. — *Castlereagh Correspondence*, vol. ii. p. 280, note. Sir R. Musgrave also mentions with approbation, that Fitzgerald made the people prostrate themselves before him.—*Hist. Rebellion*, Appendix x.

approach, they fell on their knees before him. But
this cruel persecution was not confined to the lower
orders. Confident in impunity, Fitzgerald assailed
persons in a higher rank of life. Indeed, it is owing
to this circumstance that the name of Judkin Fitzgerald has acquired a particular infamy. Had he
merely tortured peasants, this man would have been
hardly distinguished from the herd of petty Irish
gentry, who had, for generations, abused the poor,
and whose habitual outrages on decency and humanity were the primary, and, to a great extent, the
proximate cause, if not the justification, of the rebellion. But, in reviewing the acts of the last Irish
Parliament, we find its special protection extended
to proceedings such as are now to be described.

At the Tipperary Spring Assizes of 1799, one
Wright brought an action of trespass against Fitzgerald, the late Sheriff. The plaintiff was a teacher
of languages at Clonmel, but connected by kindred
with more than one Irish family of rank. Wright,
hearing that he was suspected, and knowing the fearful consequences of suspicion, hastened to deliver
himself up, in the hope that he might thus save his
character and life. But Fitzgerald was not to be
disappointed of his victim. He received Mr. Wright
with a torrent of abuse, and ordered him to fall on
his knees *to receive his sentence.* ' You are a rebel,'
said he, ' and a principal in this rebellion. You are
to receive five hundred lashes, and then to be shot.'
The poor man begged for time, and was so rash as
to ask for a trial. This aroused Fitzgerald to fury;
he railed at his prisoner for daring to open his mouth
after he was condemned. Wright was hurried to the
flogging ladders, which were erected in the main
street; and expecting immediate death, had placed
his hat before his face while he muttered a prayer.
Fitzgerald, with his own hand, tore away the hat,
trampled on it, dragged his fainting victim by the

hair, kicked him, and, finally, slashed him with a sword, drawing blood. Wright was then fastened to the ladder. Fifty lashes had been inflicted, when a Major Riall came up, and asked what Wright had done? The Sheriff answered by flinging Riall a note taken from the person of Wright, as a justification of the punishment to which he was subjected. The note was in French, a language of which Fitzgerald was wholly ignorant, and contained two lines excusing the writer for having failed in a visiting engagement. Riall assured Fitzgerald that the note was perfectly harmless; nevertheless the lash continued to descend, until the quivering entrails were visible through the flayed flesh. The hangman was then ordered to apply his thongs to a part of the body which had not yet been torn, while the Sheriff himself went to the General in command of the district for an order to put his prisoner to death. This order, however, was not granted, and Wright was ultimately set at liberty.

These facts were proved on the trial of Wright's action. The defendant attempted to justify himself by calling one of his followers *Trial of Fitzgerald.* to swear that the plaintiff had acknowledged his guilt in a written paper which he gave to the witness, and which the witness had given to the defendant. The judge called for the production of this paper. The defendant refused to produce it, on the impudent pretence that it contained secrets of State. The trial would not have been complete, had not an Orange parson been called on the part of the defendant to swear that this notorious bloodshedder, who throughout Ireland was called 'flogging Fitzgerald,' was a mild and humane man. Fitzgerald conducted his own defence with matchless effrontery. He avowed and gloried in the system of terror which he had pursued; maintaining that he was justified in taking any measures he thought fit to extort confessions

from persons whom he suspected, and that if every
other method failed, he had a right to cut off their
heads. The grotesque atrocity of this avowal is said
to have disturbed the gravity of the court. Such an
exhibition, in an English court of justice, would,
probably, have led to an inquiry into the state of the
defendant's mind. The judge told the jury that the
character of the plaintiff was unimpeached; that he
had been grossly and wantonly abused, and that he
was entitled to the whole amount of damages laid in
the declaration. Lord Yelverton, the Chief Baron,
who was also in the Commission, and sat upon the
bench during the trial, expressed, in emphatic language, his concurrence with the summing up of Mr.
Justice Chamberlain. The jury gave four hundred
pounds, the damages being laid at a thousand.

The success of this appeal to a superior court of
justice revived the spirit of the people,
and notices of other actions were served
upon the late High Sheriff. Among the suitors who
came forward to obtain legal redress for the outrages
which this man had perpetrated, was a gentleman
of family and fortune named Scott, who had been
arrested at his country house by Fitzgerald, on a
ridiculous charge of having sold timber from his
woods, which had been afterwards manufactured into
pikes. Scott positively denied the imputation—such
as it was—and bail was offered to the amount of a
hundred thousand pounds to meet any charge which
might be brought against him. Fitzgerald, however,
dragged Mr. Scott to jail; but after some days, was
forced, by the interposition of the General in command of the district, to liberate him on bail for twenty
thousand pounds. No charge was preferred against
Scott, and his repeated demand of a charge having
been treated with contempt, Scott brought his action
of false imprisonment against Fitzgerald. To such
an action there could be no answer, and as the

superior courts had shown that they meant to dispense impartial justice, it was difficult to estimate the measure of damages which might be awarded for an outrage so flagrant. Fitzgerald and his abettors became alarmed. It was represented to the Government that the man who had rendered such signal services to the cause of order was in danger of being ruined, because the judges would not give an interpretation to the Indemnity Act sufficiently liberal to cover the indiscretion of a too zealous loyalty.* The Government readily listened to this appeal; but Fitzgerald, not content with leaving his interests in the hands of his friends at the Castle, petitioned Parliament for redress against the severity of the law. Cooke, the Under-Secretary, put himself forward, or was probably put forward by Castlereagh, who did not care to appear prominently in such a business, to support the petition; in doing which, he expressed his regret that the activity manifested by Mr. Fitzgerald had not been imitated more extensively.† Mr. Yelverton, the son of the Chief Baron, who followed Cooke in the debate, took occasion to describe the services which the Under-Secretary had stamped with official approbation. Mr. Hutchinson told the story of Scott, and added an anecdote of a man, who, when nearly flogged to death by Fitzgerald, made a false accusation against another person to save his own life. It was alleged on behalf of Fitzgerald that funds were being raised by subscription for the purpose of harassing him by legal proceedings.

---

* See Lord Castlereagh's letter to the Duke of Portland, April 26, 1799.—*Castlereagh Correspondence*, vol. ii. p. 279.

† Debates in Irish House of Commons on Fitzgerald's petition, appended to report of the trial of the action *Wright* v. *Fitzgerald*.—*State Trials*, vol. xxvii. Cooke was one of the men whom Lord Fitzwilliam dismissed from office in pursuance of his plan of reforming the Irish administration. Cooke had been replaced by Lord Camden, and was the confidential agent of Lord Castlereagh.

The answer was, that Fitzgerald had maligned a regiment of yeomanry, by accusing them of disaffection; and that the men had subscribed a guinea a piece, to vindicate the character of their body in a court of justice. The Attorney-General, Toler, had the effrontery to say, that the regiment, by raising a fund in this manner to defend their professional honour against a slanderous ruffian, had been guilty of a conspiracy, for which they ought to be prosecuted. The debate grew warm; but no attempt was made to deny any one of the charges alleged against Fitzgerald, or even to hint that they had been too highly coloured; but only one voice was found to point to the conclusion, which ought to have been unanimously adopted. Dr. Browne, member for the University, said, if such conduct as Fitzgerald's was to be justified, the sooner the Irish Parliament was extinguished the better. Still, it must be recorded, that this assembly, vile as it was, fixed a limit to its career of shame. Fitzgerald had asked for a secret committee; but the House of Commons, though prepared at the bidding of the Government to indemnify all the misdeeds of all their agents, hesitated to license one homicidal slanderer secretly to attack the character and life of any person he chose. The motion for a secret committee was, therefore, suffered to drop; but leave was given to bring in a bill to amend the Act of Indemnity.

Use of torture. As the use of torture was not sanctioned by the law of Ireland, any more than by the law of England, it was difficult to understand how the ingenuity of the Irish crown lawyers could frame an act which should cover such practices as tearing the scalp off the head with pitched caps, penetrating the soles of the feet with pointed stakes, cutting with swords, and flogging to the peril of life. An act had been passed early in the session to extend the indemnity to magistrates who 'had been obliged to punish such offenders [*i. e.* 'criminals' and '*suspected* persons'] even with death.'* But this did not meet the case of torture. And as there was no Jeffries or Scroggs on the Irish bench willing to stretch the law, it was necessary that the new statute should speak in plain terms. A bill was therefore framed exactly according to the pattern required by the exigencies of Mr. Sheriff Fitzgerald. It was provided in a few simple words, which could not be misunderstood, that when the jury in an action against a magistrate, or other officer found for the plaintiff, the verdict should be set aside, and a nonsuit entered, unless the jury also found that the act was done maliciously, *and* not with intent of suppressing rebellion; so that in order to give the plaintiff the benefit of his verdict, it was not sufficient for the jury to find express malice; they must also find that such malicious act had no connection with the suppression of the rebellion. Even an honest jury—such a jury as convicted Oates, or acquitted Hardy, could not say that Fitzgerald's crimes, malignant as they were, and prompted as they also were by base and sordid motives, had nothing to do with the rebellion.† But the Orange juries who were to try the issues between the Fitzgeralds and their victims, would feel no scruples in ascribing any act of irregular zeal to the loyal vigilance against papist traitors. Mr. Scott, the gentleman who had been sent to prison without a charge, and held to excessive bail to answer nothing, was heard at the bar by his counsel against this flagitious enactment, but without any other result than to affect the House of Commons with full knowledge of the wanton, and all but incredible outrage, to which they were about to extend a special immunity. After the act was passed, the Sheriff conducted himself with an inso-

* Thirty-ninth Geo. III. c. 3.—*Irish Statutes.*   † Ibid. c. 50.

lence which the most hardened ruffian has seldom
exhibited. One Doyle, a tradesman in the town of
Carrick, was seized by Fitzgerald, and flogged until
he fainted. No charge having been brought against
him, Doyle brought an action of assault and false imprisonment. Fitzgerald pleaded the statute, and
conducted his own defence. One of the witnesses,
Captain Jephson, who commanded a troop of yeomanry, declared that the conduct of the Sheriff had
been calculated to convert loyal men into rebels, and
that he himself, had he been in any other situation,
would have been driven by such wanton cruelty as
he had witnessed to join the rebellion. Fitzgerald
addressed the jury in a speech, the like of which, it
may safely be asserted, was never before heard in a
court of justice, and such as no criminal in the dock
would now be suffered to utter without rebuke. He
was indeed more like an outlaw vaunting his exploits to his gang of cut-throats in their den than a
sane man taking a part in a transaction of civilised
life. He named several persons whom he had flogged
under circumstances more aggravated than those of
the case before the court. He mentioned one man
who had cut his throat to escape the horrors and
ignominy of torture. He admitted or boasted that,
in his search for rebels, he had flogged many persons who proved to be perfectly innocent. Lord
Avonmore, the Chief Baron who tried the cause, did
not dissemble his grief and indignation at having to
administer such a law as that which had recently
been enacted. 'Before the Indemnity Acts passed,'
he said, in summing up to the jury, 'no damages
you could give would be too great; but if, under
these acts, you believe the defendant was forced,
through imperious necessity, to commit this abomin-
able outrage against the plaintiff (a man of acknowledged loyalty) you are bound to find for him; the
information he acted on he has told you was that of

a vile, perjured, and infamous informer, and this too not upon oath. To render a verdict for the plaintiff of any avail, you must find that the defendant acted maliciously, and not with the intent of suppressing the rebellion, or of serving the State; such are the words of the Act, which places an insuperable bar between injury and redress, and sets all equity and justice at defiance.' With these words, the judge dashed the Act upon the cushion, and threw himself back on his seat. The jury found for the defendant, who thereupon sued the plaintiff for double costs under the statute, and obtained a verdict.

It remains to be mentioned with reference to this subject, that among the persons ultimately recommended for their services to the special favour of the Crown was Mr. Thomas Judkin Fitzgerald, who received a considerable pension, and, after the Union, was created a Baronet of the United Kingdom. When these murders and torturings were first alluded to in the English Parliament, they were stoutly denied; and when they could no longer be denied, it was as stoutly maintained that they had been perpetrated without the knowledge of the Government. But it was notorious that rebels, or reputed rebels, were subjected to the picket and the lash in Dublin itself under the very shadow of the Castle. Beresford's riding-house was the terror of the Catholic populace. In the old custom-house, the Royal Exchange, and many of the barracks, there were daily and hourly exhibitions of torture.*

---

* John Claudius Beresford himself afterwards admitted, in his place in Parliament, the cruel practices by which the discovery of concealed arms had been enforced. 'I fear,' he said, 'and feel a deep shame in making the avowal—I fear it is too true. I defend it not, but I trust I may be permitted to refer, as some palliation of these atrocities, to the state of my unhappy country, where rebellion and its attendant horrors had roused in both sides to the highest pitch all the strongest passions of our nature.'—*Life of Wilberforce*, vol. iii. p. 326. According to the report of

Cornwallis, when he undertook the Government of Ireland, well knew the system of cruelty that had been pursued. Pitt knew it, and gave Cornwallis full power to put a stop to it.* The despatches and private letters of Lord Cornwallis, from the commencement to the close of his Irish administration, abound in expressions of disgust at the baseness of the people who surrounded his Government, and at the cruelty, equally inhuman and impolitic, with which this vile portion of the minority abused their power. In one of his earliest letters to the Secretary of State, the Lord Lieutenant says, 'The principal persons of this country, and the members of both Houses of Parliament are, in general, averse to all acts of clemency; and although they do not express, and perhaps are too much heated to see, the ultimate effects which their violence must produce, would pursue measures that could only terminate in the extirpation of the greater number of the inhabitants, and in the utter destruction of the country. The words papists and priests are for ever in their mouths, and by their unaccountable policy, they would drive four-fifths of the community into irreconcilable rebellion.'† Again, he says, a few days later, in a private letter, 'The conversation of the principal persons of the country, all tend to encourage this system of blood, and the conversation, even at my table, when you may suppose I do all I can to

his speech in the *Parliamentary History* (debate on the Martial Law Bill, 1801) he maintained that his party were perfectly justified in the use of torture.

* Wilberforce describes Pitt in conversation with him 'resenting and spurning the bigoted fury of Irish Protestants.'—*Life of Wilberforce*, vol. ii. p. 297. He describes Pitt's conduct on another occasion, when Lord Clare undertook to defend the torture in the House of Lords, 'I shall never forget Pitt's look; he turned round to me with that high, indignant stare which sometimes marked his countenance, and stalked out of the House.'—Ibid. vol. ii. p. 326.

† Lord Cornwallis to Duke of Portland, July 8, 1798.—*Cornwallis Correspondence*, vol. ii. p. 356.

prevent it, always turns on hanging, shooting, burning, &c. &c., and if a priest has been put to death, the greatest joy is expressed by the whole company.'*
Lord Cornwallis, when a member of the Cabinet, had been the first to disapprove of the ebullition of anger in which Sir Ralph Abercromby described the Irish militia, as formidable to everybody but the enemy; but he had not been long in Ireland before he expressed a similar opinion.† After he had been a year and a half in the island, the Lord Lieutenant writes thus—'The greatest difficulty which I experience is to control the violence of our loyal friends, who would, if I did not keep the strictest hand upon them, convert the system of martial law (which, God knows, is of itself bad enough) into a more violent and intolerable tyranny than that of Robespierre. The vilest informers are hunted out from the prisons to attack, by the most barefaced perjury, the lives of all who are suspected of being, or of having been, disaffected; and, indeed, every Roman Catholic of influence is in great danger.'‡

No man of less firmness than Cornwallis, or with less weight, derived from position, character, and knowledge of affairs, could have borne up under the storm of opposition, which counsels of moderation and humanity would be sure to encounter, from a party long inured to a policy of violence and repression. Lord Cornwallis had no supporters among the Government party, except the Chancellor Clare and his own secretary Castlereagh. The Chancellor,

* Lord Cornwallis to General Ross.—*Cornwallis Correspondence,* vol. ii. p. 368.

† 'The Irish militia are totally without discipline, contemptible before the enemy, when any serious resistance is made to them, but ferocious and cruel in the extreme when any poor wretches, either with or without arms, come within their power; in short, *murder appears to be their favourite pastime.*'—*Lord Cornwallis to Duke of Portland,* July 8, 1798.

‡ *Cornwallis Correspondence,* vol. iii., Nov. 16, 1799.

though firm in his adherence to ascendency principles, was a man of cultivated intellect, and, therefore, could not quite go the whole length with the furious bigots who thought that Ireland was to be saved by hanging, shooting, and torturing papists. The secretary was a friend of the Catholics: but the factions were as corrupt as they were cruel; and the minister who had the dispensation of patronage was a privileged person. But even Lord Clare and Lord Castlereagh could not be depended on for that hearty and unreserved co-operation which the Lord Lieutenant required to defeat the intrigue, the evasion, and duplicity, as well as the open opposition, with which his policy was assailed. The English Cabinet were, with one exception, unfriendly to him; and he had been hardly six months in Ireland, when the question of his recall seems to have been discussed.* Lord Grenville declared that he should deplore to the hour of his death, the share he had in the appointment of Lord Cornwallis. The Chancellor was his most active and formidable opponent.† The Duke of Portland, the minister with whom, as Secretary of State, he was in immediate correspondence, gave him a hesitating and wavering support. But the Viceroy had one friend in the Cabinet, and that friend was, happily, the chief minister. The rash dismissal of Fitzwilliam, in 1795, would have dwindled into an insignificant event, in comparison with the removal of Cornwallis, in 1799. The revival of the rebellion, and the indefinite postponement of the Union, would have been the probable consequences of disgracing Cornwallis, and substituting in his room some Tory peer,‡ who would have been received with shouts of exultation by the Orangemen, and with the

---

* Lord Grenville to Marquis of Buckingham.— *Courts and Cabinets of George the Third*, vol. ii. p. 429.

† *Cornwallis Correspondence*, vol. iii. p. 317.

‡ Or, as Lord Grenville expressed it, 'Some old woman in

deep murmur of despair by the great mass of the population of Ireland. It was to the firmness and wisdom of Pitt, in supporting, with the single weight of his authority, the only Lieutenant who had attempted to govern Ireland with an impartial hand, and to chastise the insolence of a cabal as cruel and intolerant as any tyranny which has crushed mankind, that the salvation of the island, and perhaps the integrity of the Empire, is to be ascribed. Cornwallis himself was worthy of such confidence. The slander with which he was systematically assailed, in a country where slander was virulent, and truth was weak, still taints his fame, and the great services which he rendered to Ireland, and through Ireland to the Empire, have never been duly appreciated. From a pure sense of public duty, and without a moment's hesitation, Cornwallis, already sated with wealth and honours, accepted an office for which he felt the utmost repugnance. But while he refers to the life of a Lord Lieutenant as fulfilling his idea of 'perfect misery,' he is never deterred by weariness or disgust from the task which he had undertaken, and never shrinks from the performance of duties which, to a high-minded man, must have been odious and revolting. His political sagacity is manifest in the whole tenour of his administration. He saw that the great grievances of Ireland did not admit of topical remedies. A reform of Parliament was impracticable, there being no materials out of which a constituency could be created. Catholic emancipation and a local Parliament were incompatible with British connection. Legislative union with Great Britain was the only remedy, and he would hear of no other. He was determined to check the savage spirit of Protestant ascendency. But his resolute will was tempered with

a red riband to a post which required the civil and military talents of a Marlborough.'— *Courts and Cabinets of George the Third*, vol. ii. p. 430.

prudence and caution. Had he proceeded, after the fashion of Lord Fitzwilliam, at once to root out abuses, which had long been imbedded in the political system of Ireland, he would have experienced the fate of that rash, though well-meaning ruler. Cornwallis knew that he could not make Protestant noblemen, gentry, and yeomanry, long accustomed to domineer over the subject race, moderate, just, liberal, and conciliatory, all in a moment. He was content, therefore, to restrain them, so far as he could, from murdering and torturing people, whose only offence was their religion. He would not suffer the forms of martial law, the superintendence of which immediately concerned him, to be abused to the purposes of private malice and political rancour. He greatly mitigated, therefore, but could not wholly prevent the persecution of the Catholic people.* Nor was he strong enough to deny to the Judkin Fitzgeralds the protection which they demanded against the outraged laws. He was frequently baffled even in his efforts to keep the administration of martial law within the limits of common sense and humanity. One example may be mentioned, not because it was one of peculiar atrocity, for there were many similar cases, but as showing what Irishmen of high station, and conse-

* 'I never can permit them [the yeomanry] to take advantage of their military situation to pursue their private quarrels, and gratify their personal resentments; or to rob and murder at their discretion, any of their fellow-subjects whom they may think proper, on their own authority, to brand with the name of rebels.' Lord Cornwallis to Duke of Portland, March 1799. 'You write as if you believed that there was any foundation for all the lies and nonsensical clamour about my lenity. On my arrival in this country, I put a stop to the burning of houses and murder of the inhabitants by the yeomen, or any other person who delighted in that amusement; to the flogging for the purpose of extorting confession, and to the free quarters, which comprehended universal rape and robbery throughout the country.' Lord Cornwallis to General Ross, April 1799.—*Cornwallis Correspondence*, vol. iii. pp. 74-89.

quently of some education and knowledge of the world, were capable of in those times.

A part of the Mount Kennedy corps of yeomanry were, on an autumn night, in the year 1798, patrolling the village of Delbary, in the county of Wicklow. Two or three of the party led by Whollaghan, one of their number, entered the cottage of a labouring man named Dogherty, and demanded if there were any bloody rebels there? The only inmates of the cabin were Dogherty's wife and a sick lad, her son, who was eating his supper. Whollaghan asked if the boy was Dogherty's son; and, being told that he was—'Then, you dog,' said Whollaghan, 'you are to die here.' 'I hope not,' answered the poor lad. And he prayed, if there was any charge against him, to be taken before Mr. Latouche, a magistrate in the neighbourhood, of known humanity and justice. The fellow replied that he cared nothing for Latouche, and raised his gun. The mother entreated him, for the love of God, to take her life instead of her child's. Whollaghan, with a volley of abuse, pulled the trigger twice, but the piece missed fire. A comrade then handed him another gun; and the woman rushed at the muzzle to shield her son. In the struggle the piece went off, and the ball broke young Dogherty's arm. When the boy fell, the assassins left the cabin; but Whollaghan returned, and seeing the lad supported by his mother, cried out, 'Is not the dog dead yet?' 'O yes, sir,' said the poor woman, 'he is dead enough.' 'For fear he is not,' said Whollaghan, 'let him take this.' And with deliberate aim, he fired a fourth time, and Dogherty dropped dead out of his mother's arms.

Whollaghan was tried for murder, not by the civil tribunal, as he should have been, but by court-martial. The facts were not disputed; but the defence was that the poor boy had been a rebel, and that the prisoner was a humane and loyal subject. That the Dohertys were rebels is probable enough; as, indeed, it was hardly possible that a Catholic peasant should have been anything else. But no legal evidence of the fact was tendered; and the hearsay which was admitted was about as credible as the oaths of the Orangemen who came to give Whollaghan a character for humanity. But the real defence was, that the prisoner and his companions had been sent out with general orders from their officer to shoot anybody they pleased. The court seem to have been of opinion that such orders were neither unusual nor unreasonable; and it is difficult to collect, from their finding, that they thought the prisoner had been guilty even of an error in judgment. They found, 'that the prisoner did shoot and kill Thomas Dogherty, a rebel; but do acquit him of any malicious or wilful intention of murder.'

Now this crime was perpetrated, not in the wilds of Connaught, but in the metropolitan district. The trial took place in Dublin; and the president of the court was the Earl of Enniskillen, one of the chiefs of the Irish nobility. When the proceedings of the court were submitted to Lord Cornwallis, he signified his entire disapproval of the acquittal of a man who by the clearest evidence had been guilty of a cruel and deliberate murder. He directed the court-martial to be immediately dissolved; that Whollaghan should be dismissed from the yeomanry, and that this order should be read to the president and members of the court-martial in open court.*

Court-martial dissolved by Cornwallis.

A similar case to Whollaghan's, and one, if possible, still more flagrant, so far as the conduct of the court-martial was concerned, was that of a lieutenant and a party of militia, who were tried for another

* *Cornwallis Correspondence*, pp. 419, 420, 421. Plowden's *History*, part ii. p. 810.

act of deliberate murder. The court, sympathising with the act, and willing to shield the perpetrators, came to a conclusion, which mingled absurdity and baseness in a manner that no other country or faction could have equalled. They acquitted the officer who gave the order, and convicted the men who had committed the homicide in obedience to the order. 'But,' they added, 'it appearing that the deceased had belonged to a yeomanry corps which had been *disbanded, and that he had not joined any other*, the court are of opinion that at the time the crime was committed, the prisoners did not think they were doing an improper act, in putting a person *they thought a rebel* to death; and from their former good conduct, the court submit to His Excellency, whether they are not fit objects for mercy, and to be sent to serve in a regiment abroad for life.' Lord Cornwallis, of course, disallowed the sentence altogether as regarded the men, who were clearly entitled to their acquittal; but as regarded the lieutenant, he took the opinion of the law officers, whether a finding so manifestly perverse must be considered final. The acquitted murderer, however, could not be tried again; and all that Cornwallis could do, to repair the iniquity of this officer's accomplices on the courtmartial, was to procure his dismissal from the service.* The trials were numerous, in which the court endeavoured to adapt the evidence to their foregone conclusions, by rejecting legal, and admitting illegal, proof—thus showing a determination, at all hazards, to avoid giving a just and honest decision. Yet, for interposing whenever he could, to protect the lives of the people committed to his charge from assassination and perjury, the King's vicegerent was assailed with calumny and insult, by a faction never before thwarted, or even checked, in its cruel inso-

* *Cornwallis Correspondence*, vol. iii. p. 421.

lence and tyranny. 'Croppy Corny,' and 'Rebel,' were the epithets in which the vulgar herd of partisans railed against the Lord Lieutenant. The Orangemen made common cause with Lord Enniskillen, in the disgrace which had so justly befallen him, for the affair of Whollaghan.* Even in England, where the state of the sister island was as little known as the state of a sugar island in the Caribbean Sea, or a remote province of the continent of Asia, there was a prevalent opinion, in which the ministers themselves shared, that the Lord Lieutenant was too lenient; that he favoured the sanguinary rebels, and discouraged the brave Loyalists, and that the calamities of Ireland were to be attributed to a departure from the system adopted by his predecessor.† Cornwallis, however, was not to be moved from his purpose, either by the clamour for blood which raged around him, or by the hints, sometimes extending to remonstrances, addressed to him by the Home Office, against 'a ruinous system of lenity.' Lord Castlereagh at length ‡ furnished the Secretary of State with a return of the punishments which had been inflicted during the administration of his chief. Lord Cornwallis had decided personally on four hundred cases. Out of one hundred and thirty-one condemned to death, eighty-one had been executed; and four hundred and eighteen had been transported, or banished, in pursuance of the sentences of courts-

---

* Dr. Duigenan, the organ and champion of the Orange party, had the audacity to write to Lord Castlereagh, in these terms:— 'In truth, my Lord, I must plainly tell you that the unaccountable conduct of the present Lord Lieutenant, which has rendered him not only an object of disgust but of abhorrence to every loyal man I have conversed with since my return from England, has induced many persons to oppose a union, who, if uninfluenced by resentment against the Marquis Cornwallis, would have given no opposition, if they did not support the measure.' Dec. 20, 1798. — *Cornwallis Correspondence*, vol. iii. p. 89.

† *Cornwallis Correspondence*, pp. 13, 73, 89.

‡ April 6, 1799.

martial. After this statement, no further complaint appears to have been received from Whiteball.

The Irish Parliament was prorogued soon after the passing of the Indemnity Bill; and as it was the fixed purpose of the Government that the next session should be the last of the local legislature, the recess was employed in preparing the way for the accomplishment of the Union. The English Cabinet, in their impatience to bring the event to a conclusion, had urged upon the Lord Lieutenant the immediate proposal to the Irish Houses of resolutions similar to those which had been passed by the English Parliament. But Lord Cornwallis produced so many and such cogent reasons for delay,* that the matter was not pressed. The borough owners, finding that the Government were determined to take their property, for the most part came to terms, and made the best bargains they could, in addition to the fixed scale of compensation which they were to receive. While this traffic was going on under the superintendence of the chief secretary, the Lord Lieutenant himself made a tour through the island, with the view of ascertaining the sense of the people, both with reference to the Union, and to the possibility of a French invasion. The result of this visit was a confirmation of the opinion which he had always expressed, that the opponents of the Union were chiefly those who had an immediate interest in the maintenance of a local Parliament. These were the owners of seats whose claims were to be satisfied; a few men of political mark who were not to be purchased, and the citizens of Dublin, who must inevitably be sufferers by the removal of the legislature, but whose losses did not admit of compensation. The real grievances of the country were not to be found in the abolition of legislative insti-

Prorogation of Irish Parliament.

---

* Marquis Cornwallis to Duke of Portland, March 29, 1799. *Cornwallis Correspondence*, vol. iii. p. 82.

tutions, which had done little to recommend themselves to the respect and confidence of the people. The sullen calm which appeared to the Viceroy, in his dignified progress, to denote tranquillity and content, covered a deep-seated hatred which was ever on the watch for opportunities of revenge. Hardly had the Viceroy returned to the Castle, and sent his congratulatory despatch to London, when he was followed by reports of disturbances in the counties of Waterford and Tipperary, and brought to the melancholy conclusion, that the spirit of disaffection was so deeply rooted in the minds of the people as to require not only time, but a total change in the system and constitution of the Government, before it could be eradicated.*

The Irish Parliament reassembled on the 15th of January. The principal proprietors of the House of Commons, with the exception of the Marquis of Downshire, had been gained over to the Union. But this great nobleman, who owned seven seats, and returned one member for his county,† besides dealing largely with boroughmongers who sold their nominations, was not to be compensated for the loss of political influence so extensive, by any terms which the Government could offer. In the balanced state of the House of Commons, Lord Downshire's opposition was extremely formidable; and the Government, finding it impossible to conciliate him, were willing to take advantage of an opportunity, which he was so rash as to afford them, of making him feel the weight of their resentment. The Marquis, long accustomed to take the leading part if not to dictate his will in the north of Ireland, among other means

---

* *Cornwallis Correspondence*, vol. iii. p. 132.

† Lord Castlereagh had himself wrested the other seat for the county of Down from the Marquis's nomination, at the election in 1790. The contest cost his father sixty thousand pounds, and nearly ruined him.—*Memoirs of Lord Castlereagh*, vol. i. p. 7.

which he took of opposing the Union, sent down the draft of a petition against the measure to be signed by his regiment of militia quartered at Carlow. So flagrant a breach of military discipline was not likely to be overlooked by Lord Cornwallis. A general officer was immediately sent down to Carlow to investigate the matter, and his report, notwithstanding the earnest remonstrances of Lord Downshire, who was fully sensible of his misconduct, was transmitted to London to be laid before the King. The consequence was that Lord Downshire was removed from the command of the regiment of militia, and from the government of the county of Down. The King also directed that his name should be struck out of the list of the Privy Council. This act of vigour had a wholesome effect. In all countries, and in none more so than in Ireland, the assertion of authority is respected. People are ever ready to desert the fallen potentate, and to go over to the side of successful power.

In order to avoid risking the fate of the measure on an amendment to the address, no reference was made to the Union in the speech of the Viceroy; an amendment, nevertheless, was moved in the Commons, pledging the House to the maintenance of the local Parliament. It was moved by Sir Laurence Parsons, heir presumptive to the earldom of Rosse, and seconded by Mr. Savage, Lord Downshire's member for the county of Down. The debate was sustained with great animation during the whole night, Plunkett, Bushe, and Ponsonby, having spoken in support of the amendment. After the House had sat fifteen hours, a scene took place highly characteristic of the chief actor in it, and of the country in which it was acted. A vacancy having occurred a few days before the meeting of Parliament in the representation of Wicklow, an arrangement was made with Mr. Tighe, the patron of the borough, to return Grattan, who had retired from Parliament at the general election two years before. It was intended to take the House by surprise, and the returning officer being friendly to the scheme, the election, which was fixed for the 16th of January, was allowed to be held immediately after midnight on the 15th. Tighe himself took the return; and, riding all night, arrived in Dublin at five o'clock in the morning. Grattan, wasted by sickness, was taken out of bed, dressed, wrapped in a blanket, and conveyed in a sedan chair to College Green. At seven in the morning, when the jaded House was half asleep, the vehement declamation of an orator named Egan, was interrupted by the voice of the Speaker summoning a new member to the table to take the oaths. The House started from its slumber as the spectral figure of Grattan paced slowly up the floor, supported by Ponsonby and Arthur Moore. Few members were aware that Grattan was to be returned, as he had been substituted at the last moment for another man to whom the seat for Wicklow had been sold. The return of the writ had not been expected before the following day. The House became greatly excited, the throng of strangers in the spacious galleries, mingling, as was their custom, in the emotions which agitated the House. The scene was indeed one which might have moved a less susceptible assembly. The man of 1782, the champion of the revolution which had made Ireland a nation, was come back as from the grave to rescue the independence of his country. Nor was any accessory wanting to complete the affecting spectacle. The patriot was attired in the uniform of the volunteers, which so aptly reminded the spectators of the most glorious era in the history of their country. Many of the old friends of Irish independence pressed around him, as he moved slowly toward the table, casting a severe glance at the Treasury benches. After he had been sworn, Grattan took his seat by the side of Plunkett. It soon became known that he meant to follow the gentleman who was in possession of the House; and, to excite still more the impatience and expectation of the audience, it had been arranged, as a part of the scene, that Grattan should enter the House while some dull uninteresting speaker was wearying its patience. Mr. Egan was soon clamoured down; and amid breathless silence, Grattan rose slowly, and with pain. He asked, and obtained leave, to address the House sitting. He spoke for two hours, and his speech showed evident marks of careful preparation. He discussed every branch of the question, and these were his concluding words. 'I have heard,' said he, 'of a Parliament impeaching a minister, but here is a minister impeaching a Parliament. He does more; he impeaches the parliamentary constitution itself. The abuses in that constitution he has protected; it is only its being that he destroys. He proposes to you to substitute the British Parliament in your place; to destroy the body that restored your liberties, and restore the body which destroyed them. Against such a proposition, were I expiring on the floor, I should beg to utter my last breath, and record my dying testimony.' *

Grattan was answered by Corry, the Chancellor of the Exchequer, one of those clever and ready tools of power which the political market of the sister

---

* The reader will be struck by the resemblance between this scene, and the appearance of the elder Pitt in the English House of Commons, when he went down to oppose the Peace of Paris.—*Supra*, vol. i. p. 127. There were, indeed, many points of comparison between Chatham and Grattan. Both were men of lofty mind and ardent temper. Both were patriots of the highest order. They were the greatest actors that have appeared on the political stage. Their eloquence was of the same kind; impetuous, epigrammatic, and animated with the true fire of genius. But the range of the great Irishman's sympathies was confined within provincial limits. Chatham's magnanimous spirit could prefer freedom to the narrow and selfish interests of the country which he loved and had made so great.

kingdom could always supply. The amendment was rejected by a majority of forty-two; a result which was decisive of the question, unless the friends of independence could outbid the Government in the only means which could influence the majority of members. This was, indeed, impracticable; nevertheless, a vigorous effort was made to raise funds for the purchase of seats; Lord Downshire subscribed five thousand pounds; Lord Lismore and Mr. White three thousand pounds; the two Ponsonbys four hundred pounds each. It has been said that a hundred thousand pounds was raised for this purpose. A few days after the debate on the address, two seats, vacated by members accepting office, were won, or bought, by the Opposition; and Lord Castlereagh became urgent for a further supply from the secret service fund.* A last effort was also made to arouse public feeling out of doors, and with a degree of success in Dublin, at least, which caused the Lord Lieutenant to call for military reinforcements from England. On the 5th of February, Lord Castlereagh brought down a message from the Lord Lieutenant recommending a union. On this occasion the decisive struggle took place. The division was the largest ever known in the Irish House, two hundred and seventy-three members having voted. Cornwallis and Castlereagh both declared it to be within their knowledge that the Opposition offered four thousand pounds, ready money, for a vote.† But they name only one man who was purchased, and his vote was obtained for four thousand pounds. From the language of Lord Cornwallis, it is certain that if money was spent by the Government in this way, it was without his knowledge; but many things may

---

* Lord Castlereagh to Mr. King (the Under-Secretary for the Home Department), Jan. 25, 1800. — *Cornwallis Correspondence*, vol. iii. p. 170.

† *Cornwallis Correspondence*, vol. iii. pp. 183 and 184.

have been done by the inferior agents of the Government, and possibly by Castlereagh himself, which they would not venture to lay before the Lord Lieutenant. It appears, however, from the papers which have recently come to light, that the prevalent belief of the Union having been mainly effected by a lavish expenditure of money, is not well founded. Still it is certain that much money was expended in this way. Castlereagh's letter conclusively establishes this fact.*

The Government had a majority of forty-three; this, though numerically an increase of one, as compared with the last division, was really a falling off. Twelve members, who voted with the Government on the address, deserted them on the direct question, and great doubts were entertained of the result. The Lords affirmed the resolution for union by seventy-five votes against twenty-six. The firmness of the Government in pressing the measure, did more to discourage the Opposition than any bribery or intrigue which, at that stage, might have been practised. On the 18th of February, the first resolution, affirming the principle of a united Parliament, was carried, after a debate of eighteen hours, by a majority of forty-six. The argument having been, by this time, nearly exhausted, the debate was enlivened by a violent altercation between Corry, the Chancellor of the Exchequer, and Grattan. The quarrel was deliberately planned; Corry made the first attack, accusing his rival of encouraging rebellion, and associating with rebels. Grattan's reply

---

* To King. Private and secret. Feb. 27, 1800. 'I see no prospect of converts. The Opposition are steady to each other. I hope we shall be able to keep our friends true; a few votes might have a very injurious effect. We require *your assistance* [sic], and you *must* be prepared to enable us to fulfil the expectations which it was impossible to avoid creating at the moment of difficulty. You may be sure we have rather erred on the side of moderation.'—*Cornwallis Correspondence*, vol. iii. p. 200.

was in a strain of invective, compared with which the denunciations of Lord North by Burke and Fox were mild and moderate censures. 'He calls me,' said Grattan, 'an unimpeached traitor. I ask, why not traitor unqualified by any epithet? I will tell him; it was because he dare not. It was the act of a coward, who raises his arm to strike, but has not courage to give the blow. I will not call him villain, because it would be unparliamentary, and he is a privy councillor. I will not call him fool, because he happens to be Chancellor of the Exchequer. But I say he is one who abuses the privilege of Parliament and the freedom of debate, to the uttering language which, if spoken out of the House, would be answered only by a blow.'* The House was in committee, but the chairman took no notice of this language; no member moved that the words should be taken down; nor did it seem to occur to the Speaker, who was present, that it was his duty either to resume the chair, or to take any measure for the suppression of such language, or the prevention of the consequences to which it must lead. On the contrary, he sat by while the arrangements for a hostile meeting were made within the House, and he saw the principals and their seconds go out to settle the matter while the debate was proceeding. One of the combatants, indeed, was permitted to make use of the Speaker's chamber until there was light enough to fight.† A great multitude accompanied the parties to the ground, and the Sheriff of Dublin was present, but declined to interfere. Mr. Corry was wounded in the arm at the first fire; and it was well for him that the affair terminated in this manner; for if the fortune of the duel had been against Grattan, his antagonist would probably have been torn to pieces by the mob. To complete this scene, it was agreed, before the

* *Grattan's Speeches*, vol. iii. p. 432.
† Grattan's own narrative.— *Life of Grattan*, vol. v. p. 108.

meeting, that in the event of either of the principals being killed, or disabled, the other should be considered to have paired with him.* This precaution was said to be taken with the view of defeating a policy, which was attributed to the Government, of increasing their majority by fixing personal quarrels on their opponents, and shooting them in single combat.†

The House of Commons having thus affirmed the main resolution, 'That a legislative union of the two kingdoms was desirable,' the measure was virtually carried. The resolutions of detail were, in fact, agreed to without any serious opposition. One more trial of strength on a motion by Ponsonby, that the petitions against the Union should be laid by the Lord Lieutenant before the King, showed that the relative position of parties was not materially altered; and it was ultimately determined that the resolutions should pass without further opposition. On the 28th of March, Lord Cornwallis was enabled to transmit to the English Government the resolutions of the Irish Parliament in favour of union. The Houses were, therefore, adjourned until May, to await the concurrence of the British legislature.

The resolutions having been returned from England without any substantial modification, Lord Castlereagh, on the 12th of May, moved for leave to bring in a bill to regulate the election of the Lords and Commons of Ireland to the Parliament of the United Kingdom. After a short and spiritless debate, the motion was carried by a majority of fifty-five in a thin House. The great bill itself, for the union of Great Britain and Ireland, was subsequently brought in, by a majority of sixty.‡ It was contested in some of its stages, but the Government maintained their majority. On the 7th of June, the bill was

* *Cornwallis Correspondence*, vol. iii. p. 196, note.   † Grattan alluded to this in his speech.   ‡ 160 to 100.

passed by the Commons; and, on that occasion, several members who had hitherto opposed the measure, declared, that when it should become law, they should think it their duty, not only to obey it themselves, but to use their influence in rendering it efficient. On the 2nd of August, the Lord Lieutenant announced the royal assent to the Act of Union; and, on the same day, the Irish Parliament sat for the last time. The principal Articles of the Union were the representation of Ireland in the Imperial Parliament by four spiritual peers, sitting by rotation, and by twenty-eight peers elected for life by their own body; and by one hundred commoners, returned according to the existing mode of election, to the Lower House. Freedom of trade with some modifications was to be established between the two kingdoms. The contribution of Ireland to the Imperial revenue was to be in the proportion of two to fifteen for a period of twenty years; after which, a new arrangement was to be made; and, in the meantime, the respective debt and charge of each kingdom was to constitute a distinct consolidated fund. And, lastly, the laws of Ireland, so far as they were compatible with the Act of Union, were to continue in force until altered or repealed by the Imperial Parliament.

Early in April the Articles of Union were proposed in the English Parliament.

In opening the resolution which referred to the proposed representation of Ireland in the united House of Commons, Mr. Pitt took occasion to renounce the opinions which he had formerly professed on the subject of Parliamentary Reform. Hitherto he had resisted motions for the amendment of the representation, on the ground that the season was inopportune. But he now declared, that if anything could have thrown a doubt on the advantage to be derived from the legislative union of the two kingdoms, it would have been the necessity of disturbing the representation of England. This, he said, might not be consistent with opinions he had at one time expressed. But he thought, that a man who boasted of his consistency, without regard to time and circumstances, was a slave to the most idle vanity. Seeing the little chance of that species of reform to which he alone had looked, and which was as different from modern schemes as modern schemes were different from the Constitution; seeing also the dreadful consequences which had ensued whenever such false reform had taken place, he should feel ashamed of himself, if any former opinions induced him to think that the form of representation, which, in times like the present, had been found amply sufficient for protecting the interest and securing the happiness of the people, should be idly and wantonly disturbed, from any love of experiment, or predilection for theory.

The English manufacturers of woollen, alarmed at the prospect of Irish competition, petitioned, and were heard by counsel and witnesses, against the Sixth Article of the Union, which provided for the removal of all prohibitions and bounties on the export of articles, the growth, produce, or manufacture of either country. But this was considered in Ireland the most important part of the measure;* and Pitt, whose authority in matters of trade and commerce was supreme, would bear of no modification. The manufacturers, therefore, found little support in the House of Commons, and the resolution was passed. The opposition to the principle of the measure was faintly renewed by the

<small>Sixth Article of Union.</small>

---

* 'We are most impatiently looking to the decision of the British Parliament on the woollen business; in the event of which I think the success of our great measure entirely depends.' Marquis Cornwallis to General Ross. — *Cornwallis Correspondence*, vol. iii. p. 231.

English Whigs. Sheridan, in the absence of Fox, who had not been drawn from his retirement to express an opinion on this great question, had led the attack in the preceding session. And now Sheridan relinquished the forlorn hope to Grey. The point taken last year was, that the measure ought not to be entertained, until the consent of the Irish Parliament had been given. Now that the Irish Parliament had consented, it was urged that there should be an appeal to the people. But an appeal to such a constituency as that which returned the Irish House of Commons would have been a mere mockery. The Union was a measure of imperial policy rather than of local interest; and the formal assent of the provincial legislature having been obtained, it was far more fitting that the British Government should propose it on their own responsibility, than on the pretended suffrage of the people of Ireland. Grey's motion, for the reference of the question to the sense of the Irish people, received but little support; nor was he more successful in a crude attempt to couple a branch of the question of the reform of the English representation with the adjustment of the Irish representation in the United House of Commons. The resolutions were agreed to by the Lords after some discussion, and a few divisions, in which the minority varied from three to twelve. A bill, embodying the Articles of Union was then introduced, being the counterpart to the bill which was simultaneously making its progress through the Irish Houses. Both bills received the royal assent about the same time.

It now only remained that the Government should fulfil their part of the bargain, by paying the price at which they had agreed to purchase the Irish Parliament. One million two hundred and sixty thousand pounds were distributed among the proprietors of eighty-four disfranchised boroughs, returning one hundred and sixty-eight members; seven thousand five hundred pounds being the sum awarded for each seat. The claims were adjusted by commissioners appointed by the Crown. This compensation, though promised for the purpose of gaining support to the Union, enured to the benefit of some who had opposed the measure. Such was the case with the Marquis of Downshire, who received a larger amount of compensation than any proprietor, having established his claim to seven seats. But, in a Parliament, hardly any member of which was returned by open election, there was a great mass of floating parliamentary influence, which could not be estimated by its value in money. Much of this influence the Government had found it necessary to engage on such terms as the parties chose to exact. The ordinary patronage of the Crown was quite inadequate to meet these special demands. The pension list was largely augmented under the pretext of compensation. Some found it convenient to sell their votes for cash in hand. Others, who did not want money, stipulated for peerages. No sooner had the bill passed the Irish House of Commons, than Lord Cornwallis transmitted to the English Government the names of sixteen persons for elevation to the Irish peerage, on account of their services in the matter of the Union. The Duke of Portland demurred; but both Cornwallis and Castlereagh insisted on the list, as the result of express bargains made in pursuance of the unlimited authority which they had received from the Cabinet. Ultimately, twenty-two peerages were created; five Irish peers received English peerages, and twenty peers were advanced to higher titles. It is a curious fact that one lord, a warm supporter of the Union, refused an earldom twice offered to him, on the ground that he did not consider that he was entitled to a reward for a vote in Parliament.* No other peer or commoner who supported the measure seems to have felt any such jealous scruple.

There was no difficulty in the fulfilment of bargains which were to be transacted in titles, place, and money.† It would have been well if engagements of a more honourable character, and which conduced greatly, if not mainly, to the easy progress of the question in Ireland, could have been performed with equal punctuality. But the difficulties which impeded, and, for nearly thirty years, frustrated the attempt to satisfy the just expectations of the Catholic body, belong to a subsequent period of this narrative.

* *Cornwallis Correspondence*, vol. iii. p. 319. The nobleman so honourably distinguished was Lord Gosford. His lordship, in 1806, was advanced to an earldom, but without any disparagement of his former refusal of the dignity.

† Some of these promises, it appears, were not fulfilled. Lord Cornwallis, in February, 1804, when his retirement was in immediate contemplation, sent in a list of fifty, from unsatisfied claims for peerage, pensions, and offices. Thirty-five of the persons mentioned in this list were members of Parliament, and had voted for the Union, *and three of the pensions, though granted nominally to persons not in Parliament, were actually to be received by members.* ... Lord Hardwicke, when he assumed the government, recognised the engagements made by Lord Cornwallis, and, as far as he was able, fulfilled them; but he also resigned before all the claimants had been satisfied; and the Duke of Bedford, who succeeded him, did not consider himself bound by the antecedent promises.'— *Cornwallis Correspondence*, vol. iii. p. 340.

CHAPTER XXXIX.

FRENCH EXPEDITION TO EGYPT—BATTLE OF THE NILE—NAPLES AND ITS COURT—CAMPAIGNS IN EUROPE—EXPEDITION TO THE HELDER—SIEGE OF ACRE—FALL OF SERINGAPATAM.

THE treaty of Campo Formio, by which Austria obtained terms highly advantageous to her interests, dissolved the offensive and defensive alliance of the continental powers, and left England alone in arms. The humiliation of this country was to be the last and the greatest achievement of French ambition; and it was manifest, from the rude repulse with which the pacificatory advance of the British Government had been met, that the rulers of France believed that the time had arrived when the rival of the old monarchy and the foe of the new republic must at length yield to the irresistible will of a power which aimed at universal dominion.

During the autumn and winter of this year, preparations for a great armament were proceeding at Toulon, and other harbours in possession of the French. The army of Italy, clamorous for a promised donation of a thousand millions of francs, which the Directory were unable to pay, had been flattered by the title of the army of England, and appeased by the prospect of the plunder of this country. But whatever might be the view of the Directory, or the expectation of the army, Bonaparte had no intention of undertaking an enterprise so rash as a descent upon the coast of England, while the fleets of England kept possession of the seas. There was another quarter from which the British Empire might be menaced with a better chance of success. India could never be secure while Egypt and the great eastern port of the Mediterranean were in the possession of one of the great maritime powers. Egypt had been an object of French ambition since the time of Louis the Fourteenth; and if the country which bordered on the desert was considered worth having a hundred years before, how much more was it to be coveted when it had become the most convenient approach to a territory which offered the strongest temptations that had ever been held forth to conquest and rapine. It was for Egypt, therefore, that the great armament of Toulon was destined. The project was not indeed considered a very hopeful one at Paris; but such was the dread and hatred of the ruling faction for the great military genius which had sprung out of the anarchy of France, and of the thirty thousand creditors whom they were unable to satisfy, that the issue of the expedition which they most desired was, that it might never return from the banks of the Nile. Bonaparte himself, though he had once dreamed of being King of Jerusalem, already saw a more splendid crown within his grasp, and would have lingered at Paris to accelerate his destiny. A quarrel between the French ambassador at Vienna, and the government of the Emperor, afforded a pretext for delay of which he attempted to avail himself; but the Directory urged his departure. He offered to resign, as he had done before, when the fate of the Republic was in his hands. But his offer was now eagerly accepted. Rewbell put a pen into his hands, but Merlin dashed it to the ground. The affrighted Directory ordered their General to repair to Toulon. Napoleon, after some hesitation, obeyed. The pear, he said, was not yet ripe.

<small>Fleet sails from Toulon.</small> The fleet, consisting of thirteen ships of the line, with several frigates, smaller vessels, and transports conveying twenty-eight thousand picked troops, with the full equipment for every

kind of military service, set sail on the 14th of May. Attached to this singular expedition, destined for the invasion of a friendly country, and the destruction of an unoffending people, was a staff of professors, furnished with books, maps, and philosophical instruments for prosecuting scientific researches in a land, which to a Christian and a philosopher was the most interesting portion of the globe. The great armament commenced its career of rapine by seizing on the important island of Malta. Under the shallow pretence of taking in water for a squadron which had left its anchorage only two days, a portion of the troops were landed, and after a show of resistance, the degenerate knights, who had already been corrupted, surrendered Malta, Gozo, and Cumino, to the French Republic. A great amount of treasure and of munitions of war, besides the possession of the strongest place in the Mediterranean, were thus acquired without loss or delay. A conquest of such importance would have amply repaid and justified the expedition, if no ulterior object had been pursued. But Bonaparte suffered himself to be detained no more than twenty-four hours by this achievement; and having left a garrison of four thousand men in the island, and established a form of civil government, after the French pattern, he shaped his course direct for Alexandria. On the 1st of July, the first division of the French troops were landed at Marabou, a few miles from the city. Aboukir and Rosetta, which commanded the mouths of the Nile, were occupied without difficulty. Alexandria itself was incapable of any effectual defence, and, after a few skirmishes with the handful of Janissaries which constituted the garrison, the French entered the place; and for several hours the inhabitants were given up to an indiscriminate massacre. Bonaparte pushed forward with his usual rapidity, undeterred by the horrors of the sandy desert, and the sufferings of his troops. After two victories over the Mamelukes, one of which was obtained within sight of the Pyramids, the French advanced to Cairo; and such was the terror which they had inspired, that the capital of Egypt was surrendered without a blow. Thus in three weeks the country had been overrun. The invaders had nothing to fear from the hostility of the people; a rich and fertile country, the frontier of Asia was in their possession; but, in order to hold the possession secure, it was necessary to retain the command of the sea.

The English Government, on their side, considered the capture of the Toulon armament an object of paramount importance; and Earl St. Vincent, who was still blockading the Spanish ports, was ordered to leave Cadiz, if necessary, with his whole fleet, in search of the French; but at all events, to detach a squadron, under Sir Horatio Nelson, on that service. The selection of the junior flag-officer on the station for this most important command was naturally resented by Sir William Parker and Sir John Orde, the senior admirals; but the judgment of the Commander-in-Chief coincided with that of the Board of Admiralty; and happily, in this instance, neither a regard to the claims of seniority, nor jealousy of superior merit, were allowed to mar the fortunes of England. Nelson left Gibraltar on the 8th of May, with three ships of the line, four frigates, and a sloop, with orders to cruise off the coast of Provence; and if he should thus be enabled to ascertain what the French were doing, to rejoin the fleet at Cadiz. He failed to obtain any more particular information than Lord St. Vincent already possessed as to the movements of the French fleet; but Nelson's opinion, from the first, pointed to Egypt as the place of its destination; and he was reinforced, on the 5th of June, with ten sail of the line. His frigates had parted company with

him on the 20th of May, and never returned; a loss
which greatly retarded, and in the event almost
defeated, his operations. On the 20th of June, off
Messina, Nelson heard of the capture of Malta, and
the departure of the French fleet. On the 28th, he
arrived at Alexandria; but to his great disappointment, he there found only a Turkish line of battle
ship and four frigates. On the 20th of July, he reported to Lord St. Vincent, that after sailing six
hundred leagues, he had obtained no tidings of the
French fleet since they had left Malta. Two days
afterwards, he obtained permission, through the influence of the British Ambassador, Sir William
Hamilton, or rather through the influence of Lady
Hamilton, with the Queen, to victual and water his
fleet, at Naples. Nelson then sailed for the Morea,
and on the 29th of July, the 'Culloden,' which had
been sent forward, returned with the welcome intelligence that the French fleet had taken a southeasterly course from Candia four weeks previously.
The Admiral then formed his squadron in close order,
and steered straight for Egypt. On the 31st of July,
the 'Alexander' and the 'Swiftsure' were sent to reconnoitre; but a signal from the 'Zealous,' at four o'clock
in the afternoon of the 1st of August, announced the
French fleet, sixteen sail, at anchor in line of battle,
in the Bay of Aboukir. Nelson, having determined
to fight whenever he came up with the enemy,
whether by day or by night, immediately made the
signal for action. Although the French fleet lay in
an open roadstead, they had taken up a position so
strong as to justify their belief that they could not
be successfully attacked by a force less than double
their own. They lay close in shore, with a large
shoal in their rear; in the advance of their line was
an island, on which a formidable battery had been
erected; and their flanks were covered by numerous
gun-boats. A prudent commander might have been

well justified in hesitating to risk his squadron by an attack on an enemy in such a position. But Nelson, though his daring was remarkable even in a British seaman, was never rash. He had repeatedly discussed with his captains every possible contingency under which the enemy might be encountered, and had inspired them with entire confidence in his skill and judgment. The fortune of this great day, according to the ordinary tale, was decided by a brilliant manœuvre, which Nelson adopted upon a survey of the enemy's position. The celebrated phrase 'where the French ships have room to swing, the English ships have room to anchor,' has been always quoted, as if a great discovery, in naval tactics, had been then made by the genius of Nelson. But the importance of the movement was as well known to naval commanders, as the importance of outflanking an army in the field is known to the youngest General in the service. It was well known to Nelson that his old Commander, Lord Hood, had lately intended to attack the French in this manner; but had found the attempt, in the particular case, impracticable. Lord Duncan had executed the manœuvre with partial success at Camperdown. Nelson's merit consists, not in having made a discovery in the art of naval warfare, but in the prompt judgment which determined when a movement of the most hazardous character could be made with success. In this sense, the fine discrimination which decided that there must be sea-room along either side of a ship which swung at her anchorage, was a stroke of genius which stamped Nelson as a seaman of the highest rank. It does not appear that he issued any particular orders to his captains immediately before the engagement.*

* 'It is almost unnecessary,' says Sir Edward Berry, who was Nelson's flag captain, 'to explain his projected mode of attack at anchor, as that was minutely and precisely executed in the action which we now come to describe.' —*Nelson Despatches*, vol. iii. p. 50.

The signal for action being given, the foremost ships forged ahead, heaving the lead as they advanced. At length five ships succeeded, notwithstanding a heavy fire from the batteries and gun-boats, in casting anchor between the French line and the shoal; and these ships, damaged as they were, became instantly engaged in close action with their opponents alongside. Nelson's own ship, the 'Vanguard,' with the rest of the squadron, except the 'Culloden,' Captain Trowbridge, which struck on a shoal at the entrance of the bay, took up positions to seaward of the enemy. The general action commenced at sunset, and continued throughout the night until six o'clock the following morning, a period of nearly twelve hours. But in less than two hours, five of the enemy's ships had struck; and soon after nine o'clock, the sea and shore, for miles around, were illuminated by a fire which burst from the decks of the 'Orient,' the French flag-ship, of one hundred and twenty guns. In about half an hour she blew up, with an explosion so appalling that for some minutes the action was suspended, as if by tacit consent. At this time, the French Admiral Brueys was dead. Although thrice wounded, the brave Commander refused to leave his quarter-deck, and was killed by a chain-shot before the ship took fire. Nelson also had been carried below, with a wound which was, at first, supposed to be mortal. He had been struck in the head with a fragment of langridge shot, which tore away a part of the scalp. His friends, however, and the whole ship's company, were soon relieved by the cheering announcement of the surgeon that the wound was only superficial. But he was disabled from taking any farther part in the engagement. Faint with loss of blood, suffering from the anguish of his wound, and blinded by the lacerated membrane which hung down over his remaining eye, the heroic

Admiral remained below, content with the assurance that the victory was won. About an hour after he had been hurt, Captain Berry came below to report the conflagration of the 'Orient,' and Nelson was led on deck to witness the awful scene, as well as to observe, through the hideous glare, the condition of the fleets. He immediately gave orders to his first lieutenant to lower the only boat left in the 'Vanguard,' and, with such other boats as he could collect, to proceed to the relief of the enemy's men, beleaguered in a wall of fire; for the humanity of Nelson was not less heroic than his valour and self-devotion. He then suffered himself, though not without much persuasion, to be led to his cot. His last act that night was to sign Captain Hardy's commission to the 'Vanguard,' in the place of Berry, whom he had already determined to send home with the despatches announcing the result of that glorious day.

The victory was, indeed, won before the explosion of the 'Orient.' After that event, the French line was reduced to the six ships in rear of the squadron.* But these still maintained the combat with the desperate bravery which distinguished the service of the Republic. At three o'clock in the morning four more of the French ships were destroyed or taken. There was then an interval of two hours, during which hardly a shot was fired on either side. At ten minutes to seven another ship of the line, after a feeble attempt at resistance, hauled down her colours. The action was now over. Of the thirteen French ships of the line, nine had been taken, and two had been burnt. The English had the mortification of seeing the remaining two line-of-battle ships, with two frigates, weigh anchor in the morning, and make their escape, without the power of preventing them.

---

* 'When L'Orient blew up, the six van-ships had surrendered.' Nelson to Earl Howe, 3rd Dec.— *Nelson Despatches*, vol. iii. p. 230.

Nelson had thirteen sail of the line; but the 'Culloden,' commanded by Trowbridge, his most trusted and valued captain, from the accident already mentioned, could take no part in the engagement. None of his ships exceeded the rating of seventy-fours, and all of them, as compared with the enemy, were undermanned. Nelson had only one frigate and a brig. Including the crew of the 'Culloden, he had eight thousand and sixty-eight seamen and marines. The French had also thirteen sail of the line; one of them, the 'Orient,' carrying one hundred and twenty guns; three eighties; and nine seventy-fours. These, with four frigates, included a complement of eleven thousand two hundred and thirty men. The British killed and wounded were eight hundred and ninety-five. The loss of the French, including prisoners, was five thousand two hundred and twenty-five.

Such was the great battle of the Nile, the most brilliant, and the most important of the series of naval engagements which had sustained the reputation and assured the safety of the British Empire from the arrogance of the common enemy of Europe. The victory would have been complete, had any frigates and small craft been attached to the British squadron. With such auxiliaries, none of the French transports in the harbour of Alexandria could have escaped destruction. 'Were I to die at this moment,' writes Nelson in one of his despatches, '*want of frigates* would be found stamped on my heart.' Though suffering great anguish and prostration from the wound in his head, the Admiral forgot nothing, and omitted nothing which his duty required. At the same time that he sent his despatches home, he wrote to the Governor of Bombay, informing him that the French had invaded Egypt, with an ultimate view to the invasion of India; but that he had annihilated their fleet, and thus removed immediate danger. This communication had the effect of saving the East India Company a vast expenditure in preparations, which had been ordered for the expected approach of the French army. The 'Leander,' his only frigate, which Nelson had sent home with the despatches, was taken off Candia, on the 18th of August, by one of the French ships which escaped from Aboukir Bay; but Nelson had sent duplicate despatches by the brig 'Mutine.' The glorious news, however, which in these days would have been rung through England in forty-eight hours, did not reach London until the 2nd of October, two months after the action.* The joy and pride of the English people knew no bounds. The long and unsuccessful voyage in search of the enemy had given rise to murmurs; and wise people were heard to say, that the Government was unpardonable for having entrusted a command of such importance to a young rear-admiral.

The public were slowly and reluctantly yielding to this opinion, when a Gazette Extraordinary † announced in the concise and unadorned language of a British Commander, 'A great victory over the fleet of the enemy, at the mouth of the Nile.' The particulars were soon known. Thirteen out of seventeen ships burnt, sunk or captured. The flag of England not lowered in a single ship. The name of Nelson

---

* I have taken the account of the battle of the Nile from Nelson's despatches, and the accompanying statements of officers who were in the action. The true history of great deeds is commonly very unlike the dramatic version of them. One of the most striking particulars in Southey's narration is a dialogue which Nelson is supposed to have held with his flag captain before the action. 'Captain Berry, when he comprehended the scope of the design, exclaimed with transport, "If we succeed, what will the world say?" "There is no *if* in the case," replied the Admiral, "that we shall succeed, is certain; who may live to tell the story, is a very different question."' We are assured, however, on the authority of Captain Berry himself, that no such scene took place.—*Nelson Despatches*, vol. iii. p. 65.

† Admiral Viscount Hood to Lord Nelson, Oct. 15, 1798.

and the Nile were in every mouth; and all men
agreed that this was the greatest sea-fight England
had yet won. There were not wanting competent
judges deliberately to confirm the opinion which the
multitude uttered in the fervency of their gratitude
and joy. Lord Hood pronounced the victory 'the
most complete and splendid history records.'* Admiral Sir Roger Curtis described it as 'an unparalleled victory;'† and Collingwood, one of the noblest
of England's illustrious warriors, pronounced it 'the
most decisive, and, in its consequences, perhaps, the
most important to Europe that was ever won.'‡
Among the numerous letters of praise and homage
which Nelson received from kings and princes, down
to persons in a private and humble walk of life, some
of the most touching, and probably not the least acceptable congratulations, were those which he received from women. Englishmen, from habitual
reserve, or dislike of demonstration, commonly express less than they feel; but Englishwomen, of
whatever rank, when their sense of reverence and
admiration is deeply moved, can seldom restrain the
generous effusions of their hearts. There are two
letters in the published collection of Nelson's correspondence which contrast forcibly with the measured
and official style in which potentates, statesmen, and
commanders convey their sense of the merits and
services of the man who with just pride described
his achievement as a conquest rather than a victory.
They are letters of congratulation addressed to Nelson
by the Countess Spencer, the wife of the First Lord
of the Admiralty, and of Lady Parker, the wife of a
gallant veteran, the Port-Admiral at Portsmouth.
'Joy, joy, joy to you, brave, gallant, immortalised
Nelson!'—thus wrote Lady Spencer,—'. . . My heart
is absolutely bursting with different sensations of joy,

---

* *Nelson Despatches*, vol. iii. p. 85.
† Ibid. p. 86.
‡ Ibid. p. 87.

of gratitude, of pride; of every emotion that warmed the bosom of a British woman on hearing of her country's glory—and all produced by you, my dear, my good friend.' In this strain the letter proceeds; and the English matron fondly associates the name of her husband with the fame of the hero of his choice. 'What a fair and splendid page have you and your heroic companions added to the records of his administration of the navy! And, as wife of that excellent man, what do I not feel for you all as executors of his schemes and plans!' Lady Parker, whose husband, when commanding in the West Indies, had been one of the first to perceive and bring forward Nelson's merits, writes in a transport of maternal pride and affection: 'My dear and immortal Nelson—I am very sure that you know what I feel upon your unparalleled victory. Captain Cochrane will tell you that I am not yet come to my senses. . . . . All Europe has cause to bless the day that you were born. . . . . I am very uneasy about the wound in your head. . . . . A few months' relaxation in a cold climate will soon fit you for another enterprise; but should you continue in constant exertion of both body and mind, years, not months, will be required for your recovery. . . . . Sir Peter and I ever regarded you as a son, and are, of course, truly happy at your well-earned honours.'*

The honours and rewards which the Government thought sufficient for the services of Nelson were far from satisfying the gratitude and admiration of the country. The great Admiral was raised to the peerage by the title of Baron Nelson of the Nile, and received the pension of two thousand a year, which is generally conferred for eminent military services. Sir John Jervis had been thought worthy of an earldom for the victory of Cape St.

* *Nelson Correspondence*, vol. iii. pp. 74-83.

Vincent, in which Nelson himself bore a leading part. Duncan was made a viscount for Camperdown. Both Jervis and Duncan were well entitled to their advancement; but great as were the victories of St. Vincent and of Camperdown, the victory of the Nile was greater than either; yet Nelson was admitted only to the tail of the peerage. It is satisfactory to record that the great minister was not responsible for this ungracious parsimony. Pitt had recommended Nelson for a viscountcy;* but the King objected, on the ground that Nelson was only second in command; and the narrow formal mind could not understand how any degree of merit should weigh against a technical point of etiquette. If, however, it had been a question whether an Irish boroughmonger should be bought with a barony or an earldom, the bargain would not have been suffered to go off upon a punctilio as to the man's pretensions to this or that degree of the peerage.

All Europe rang with the fame of Nelson's victory. The great power itself which had been awed; the minor nations which had been deprived of their neutrality by that audacious democracy whose ambition was not content with ruling and domineering over one quarter of the globe, began to think the day of deliverance was at hand. Some of these could not refrain from openly expressing

Exultation on the Continent.

---

* 'Mr. Pitt told me, the day after Captain Capel arrived [with the despatches], that you would certainly be a viscount; which I made known to Lady Nelson. But it was objected to in a certain quarter, because your lordship was not a Commander-in-Chief. In my humble judgment, a more flimsy reason was never given. But, in fact, your lordship stood in the situation of Commander-in-Chief at the mouth of the Nile, and could not possibly receive any advice or assistance at the distance of near a thousand leagues from Earl St. Vincent, and conquered from your own personal zeal, ability, and judgment.' Admiral Lord Hood to Nelson, October 15, 1798.—*Nelson Despatches*, vol. iii. p. 85. In fact, Nelson had only general orders 'to use his best endeavours to take, sink, burn, or destroy' the enemy's fleet, wherever he could find it.—*Nelson Despatches*, vol. iii. p. 26.

their joy and hope. The Czar sent the British Admiral a box set in diamonds, with a complimentary letter. The grand Signior, by whose authority Bonaparte had proclaimed that he invaded Egypt to assert the authority of the Porte against the usurpation of the Beys—ordered a note to be addressed to the British plenipotentiary, with his congratulations on the joyful event, and his acknowledgment of the great service which Nelson had rendered to the Ottoman Empire. This unprecedented condescension was accompanied by a wreath of diamonds taken from the Imperial turban, and a fur pelisse, which he requested that the Admiral might be permitted to wear. The Sultan also sent a present of money to be distributed among the crew of Nelson's squadron. The Court of Naples, which had with difficulty been induced to give Nelson permission to victual and water his ships in a Sicilian port before he sailed for Alexandria, so great was their terror of the French, became delirious with joy when the great news arrived. The King of Sardinia, who had been subjected to every humiliation by the French, preparatory to his intended expulsion from his kingdom, and had been compelled to refuse the British fleet admission to his harbour, sent Nelson a letter of thanks, and a royal present.

On the 7th of September, Nelson sailed for Naples. He left a few ships, which he could ill spare, to watch the entrance to the Nile; and, before his departure, he addressed the most earnest entreaties to the Government at Constantinople to send bomb-ships and troops to destroy the French transports, and complete the destruction of the French army, already suffering severely from the climate, and the want of supplies. His primary object in returning to Naples was to obtain small craft, and to return to Alexandria to direct the destruction of the troop-ships. Had he effected this object, which seemed to be an easy undertaking, when compared with many things which he had done, Nelson had consummated a victory which would have altered the course of history, and prevented the fate of Europe.

Before Nelson could reach Naples, he was at the point of death. For nearly five years he had experienced no intermission of severe and anxious professional toil, except during the period when he was laid up with the loss of a limb. His long and anxious pursuit of the French fleet, with the eyes of Europe upon him, had excited his enfeebled frame to a dangerous pitch; and the wound which he received at the battle of the Nile would have completed his prostration, had he not been sustained by the pressure of business which necessarily followed the action. But when this pressure ceased, and the wearied frame should have enjoyed an interval of ease, fever took possession of it, and for eighteen hours, during his voyage to Naples, his life was in imminent danger. Even when the crisis had passed, he was so weak and emaciated, that he thought his end approaching. He would have died gloriously, and with unblemished fame, had his eyes been closed in the cabin of the 'Vanguard' on that ill-omened voyage. But his work was not yet done.

The conqueror of the Nile was welcomed at Naples with a passion of exultation and delight. Coerced and intimidated by Bonaparte, the Neapolitan Court had, in the first instance, refused the succours which Nelson required to enable him to proceed to Alexandria. And when they had yielded, with fear and trembling, to the influence of the British embassy, they felt they had staked their existence on Nelson's success. The Queen, a daughter of Maria Theresa, the sister of Marie Antoinette, and the wife of a Bourbon, who might well be excused for the implacable hatred which she bore towards the French, had gone off in hysterical transports of joy, when the tidings arrived of the battle of the Nile. Lady Hamilton fell on the floor as if she had been shot. And these women, day by day, and hour by hour, could talk or think of nothing but their hero, the conqueror of the French, the saviour of Italy. When the crippled 'Vanguard,' bearing the Admiral's flag, appeared at the entrance of the bay of Naples, the whole population seemed to line the shore, and a fleet of boats, led by the Ambassador's barge, put off to the flag-ship. Lady Hamilton, when she saw Nelson, sprang up the ladder, and fell into his arms mute with joy, until tears came to her relief. Presently the royal barge came alongside, and the King came on board to welcome Nelson as his deliverer and preserver. Nelson took up his abode at the British Ambassador's house, and Lady Hamilton became his nurse and devoted servant. Such homage from a woman, renowned through Europe for her talents and graces, could hardly fail to produce an impression on the least susceptible heart; and Nelson had a sailor's sensibility for beauty. It is certain, however, that at this time Nelson had no other feeling for Lady Hamilton than that of warm and grateful friendship. The most pleasing letters in his published correspondence, are those addressed to his wife shortly after his return to Naples, describing, in the most artless manner, the honours which were paid him, the emotion of Lady Hamilton on his arrival, and her unceasing kindness.* He had been

---

* 25th September, 1798. To Lady Nelson. After describing Lady Hamilton falling into his arms on the deck of the 'Vanguard,' he says, ' I hope some day to have the pleasure of introducing you to Lady Hamilton; she is one of the very best women in the world; she is an honour to her sex.' Again, on the 6th October, 'The continued kind attention of Sir William and Lady Hamilton, must ever make you and me love them.' He must have been a very pitiful fellow who could have been capable of writing in this strain to his wife about a woman to whom he had

very unwilling to return to Naples, but his orders left him no discretion; and when he did return, his mind was intent on stimulating the slothful and cowardly Government and people of Naples to take measures for their own defence. Amid the splendid festivities celebrated in his honour, and the blandishments of the Court, Nelson never for a moment failed to urge forward the stern business with which alone he was concerned. A week after his arrival, his birthday was commemorated by the most brilliant fête ever displayed even in this city of pleasure. But Nelson, though not indifferent to adulation, could not repress his contempt and impatience at the frivolity of a people, which seemed to take more interest in the success of a spectacle, than in the preservation of their country threatened with imminent danger. The day following this notable birthday celebration, Nelson wrote four lines to his friend and commanding officer, St. Vincent—'I trust, my Lord, in a week, we shall be at sea. I am very unwell; and the miserable conduct of this Court is not likely to cool my irritable temper. It is a country of fiddlers and poets, whores, and scoundrels.'* To the Neapolitan King himself, the British Admiral bluntly offered the alternative of taking up arms against France, or being kicked out of his kingdom. Nothing, indeed, but this paramount policy of resisting the ignominious thraldom which had already overspread half the Continent, and threatened the whole of Europe, could have engaged the sympathies of a free people with such a Government as that of Naples. The kingdom of the Sicilies, in 1798, was much the same as it was in 1860, when it finally ceased to exist. It was a Government of priests and of police, headed by a Spanish Bourbon,

---

transferred his affections. No letters to Lady Nelson are to be found after the 14th of October. The letters to Lady Hamilton, after that date, assume a warmer tone.

* Sept. 30.—*Nelson Despatches*, vol. iii. p. 138.

the most degraded type of a degenerate dynasty. It had neither the power of internal improvement, nor of external defence, and was tolerated already by the great despotic powers, only as a part of the system of legitimate monarchy. On the other hand, there was a large and respectable party, comprising nearly all the public spirit and intelligence of the nation, with a large proportion of the higher classes, which was prepared to accept any change rather than endure longer the dull oppressive despotism of the Bourbons. The Government, indeed, had few supporters beyond the old devotees of divine right, the sycophants of the Court, and the lazzaroni of Naples. Yet these were the allies with which an imperious exigency obliged England to co-operate.

Movement of Russia. Since the commencement of the revolutionary wars, there had never been a fairer opportunity for making a stand against French aggression. The conqueror of Italy was shut up in Egypt. The victory of the Nile had aroused Europe from despondency. The Czar was moved at length to take an active part, and an army, under the renowned Suwarrow, was about to march. The Congress of the German States which had assembled at Rastadt at the close of the preceding year, ostensibly for the purpose of settling questions of boundary with France, but really for the purpose of carrying into effect the secret articles of the treaty of Campo Formio, by which Austria and France had agreed to seize and partition the smaller German principalities between them, was virtually terminated. The French having easily obtained all they had originally demanded, advanced new claims, so exorbitant, that it became evident no peace could be obtained from concession; and, in the summer of 1798, France and Austria made preparations for a renewal of the war. The Court of Vienna sent General Mack, their famous strategist, who planned the campaign of 1793, to

organise and command the Sicilian army. Nelson
never ceased to urge the expediency of putting this
army into immediate motion, and defending the
kingdom, by marching into the Roman states, which
were prepared to rise against the French. But this
energetic advice suited neither the cowardly and
half-treacherous Italian Government, nor the German
pedant, who could not move without five carriages.*
Much precious time was, therefore, squandered.
Nelson himself sailed in the third week of October
with a portion of his squadron to expel the French
from Malta; intending to proceed from thence to
destroy their transports at Alexandria. But the importunities of the Neapolitan Court wrung from him
a promise to return to Naples in November; their
object being, as he well knew, to secure their escape
under his protection, in the probable event of their
army being scattered, and the kingdom lost. On
his arrival at Malta, Nelson had a practical proof
that the wretched Government which he had made,
and was making such efforts to preserve, was past
redemption. He had been assured that the Governor
of Syracuse had received orders to send arms and
munitions to the inhabitants of Malta, who had risen
against the French, and forced them to take refuge
in the town of Valetta. But no supplies had been
sent, and the Governor of Syracuse had received no
orders. The Neapolitan Government would do nothing which they thought the English would do for
them, and they thought the English could do everything. Had not the Maltese been supplied with a
few hundred stand of arms, and some barrels of gun-
powder from the fleet, they must have given up the
gallant struggle. Yet the King of the two Sicilies
claimed Malta as a part of his dominions, and Nelson
had gone to support and establish that claim. The
island of Gozo surrendered to Nelson's summons; and

* Southey's *Life of Nelson*, p. 180.

having left one of his best officers, Captain Hall, with a small blockading squadron, the Admiral returned to Naples. On his arrival, he was met with clamours from the Court for pecuniary aid from England, without which they declared they could make no progress; but Nelson told them plainly that until they had made every possible exertion to help themselves, they must expect no money from England. He found Mack at the head of an army of thirty thousand men, the finest army in Europe, as he called it. With this army he was to march to Rome, with the view of being ultimately supported by an Austrian force. A small expedition, under the immediate direction of Nelson himself, proceeded to Leghorn, which immediately surrendered. The port was full of French privateers, and Genoese ships laden with corn, destined for French harbours; yet the Neapolitan General hesitated to seize, or even to detain these ships, under the absurd pretence that Naples was not at war with France. After much difficulty, General Naselli was induced to lay an embargo on the vessels until he received instructions from his Government. Nelson then returned to Naples, leaving Trowbridge with three ships. Trowbridge immediately proceeded to settle the question as to the fate of the French ships in the harbour, after the fashion of his great Commander. He desired Naselli to seize the ships or to let him do it; and after trying in vain to convince 'the old fool,' as the blunt English captain described the Neapolitan Commander, that the march of the Sicilian army to Rome was an act of war against France, he at length gained his point by threatening to withdraw his squadron.*

Whatever was done under the direction of Nelson or his captains had a successful result; but no confi-

* Trowbridge to Nelson, 4th December, 1798.—*Nelson Despatches*, vol. iii. p. 182, note.

dence could be placed in operations removed from their influence. The King had accompanied his army to Rome. The right wing, consisting of nineteen thousand men, under General St. Philip, encountered three thousand French troops, near Fermi. After a little distant firing, which resulted in the loss of forty men, St. Philip went over to the enemy. Michaux, the second in command, ran away; his officers followed his example; all the infantry dispersed, and would have been cut to pieces, but for the good conduct of two regiments of cavalry, which made a stand. But all the artillery, the tents, baggage, and military chest, were abandoned to the enemy. Within a week after this infamous affair, Mack reported that he had no hope of stopping the progress of the French, and advised the royal family to abandon Naples without delay. The King, who had loudly vaunted his determination to conquer or die, quitted the army, on the first check it received, and returned to Naples. On the night of the 21st of December, the King and Queen, with their family, were conveyed on board the 'Vanguard.' Treasure, to the value of two millions and a half, had already been secretly removed to the British ships, as it was feared that the lazzaroni, who alone had displayed any public spirit or fidelity, would resist the King's departure from his capital. They did in fact raise a riot; several lives were lost, and it was with difficulty that His Majesty made his escape from his too loyal subjects. The British Ambassador and Lady Hamilton accompanied the Court. Their destination was Palermo; the island of Sicily offering a secure retreat while the English fleet had the command of the Mediterranean; and the loyalty of the Sicilians leaving no ground for apprehension of an internal revolt.

The city of Naples, thus abandoned by the King and the army, and betrayed by the sycophantic cowardice of the nobles, was defended by the rabble with so much gallantry, that it was not until after several days' hard fighting, the invaders effected an entry. The French General, Championet, immediately decreed the abolition of royalty, and proclaimed the Parthenopian republic.

Meanwhile military preparations on the most extensive scale had been made by Austria. Early in the spring, two great armies took the field. The Archduke Charles, at the head of seventy-six thousand men, advanced to attack the French, who had crossed the Rhine, seized the fortress of Mannheim, and laid siege to Philipsburg. After several obstinate engagements, the French were compelled to retreat across the river. But the expulsion of the French from Italy was the great object of the Imperial army; and the forces of the Czar were ordered to co-operate with the Austrian army of Italy. Before the Russians came up, the French General Schérer attacked the Imperial troops, and being defeated at Castel Nuovo and Magnano, was forced to retreat upon a defensive position on the Adda, and on the great fortresses of Mantua and Pizzighitone. At this juncture, fifty thousand Russians under Suwarrow pressed upon the French retreat; and the movements of the Russian General, skilful, prompt, and vigorous, inspired confidence throughout the subjugated states of Italy. Schérer, finding, as so many of his predecessors had found, that the Republic would not be served by an unsuccessful General, resigned his command to Moreau. The new General, urged by the Directory, was forced to risk a premature action, under unfavourable conditions. The result was, that he suffered a defeat, with the loss of seven thousand men and a hundred pieces of cannon. Moreau succeeded, however, in effecting a retreat on Genoa. Macdonald next attempted to arrest the victorious progress of the Russian General; and a great battle, which lasted two days, was fought on the banks of the Trebbia. The final result was that the French were driven through the passes of the Apennines, and, after a campaign of four months, Genoa alone, of all the conquests of Bonaparte in Italy, acknowledged the authority of the French Republic.

Macdonald had succeeded Championet in the government of Naples; and, by the rigour and rapacity of his administration, had exasperated the hatred of the people towards the French; when Macdonald, therefore, quitted the city to take the field against the Russians, secret preparations were made for a revolt. Cardinal Ruffo, who had recently been appointed Vicar-General, and was armed with full authority, organised a force which he called the Christian army in Calabria. About three hundred men were collected in the first instance; and the little band, having received accessions from all quarters, until it amounted to twenty-four thousand, the motley army marched to Naples. The city and the anchorage of the bay were commanded respectively by the forts of St. Elmo, Uovo, and Nuovo. It was manifestly impossible to advance, without securing at least one of these positions—the command of the sea-board or of the town. St. Elmo, which overawed the city, was garrisoned by the French; the other two forts were in the possession of native revolutionists, most of whom had taken up arms, not so much to welcome the French, as to take advantage of the only opportunity likely to happen of redressing the intolerable grievances of their Government. To these people, Ruffo addressed himself, and, knowing their quality, he proposed that they should surrender, on a guarantee for their protection in person and property. These were liberal terms; but the reduction of the forts, if it could have been accomplished by such a force as Ruffo's,

Macdonald at Naples.

would have taken time; and the French fleet might arrive to relieve the place at any moment. The terms were approved by the Russian and English Commanders, and by Captain Foote of the 'Sea-horse,' the only British man-of-war on the station. The forts were given up, and the capitulation was signed by the Cardinal, in the name of His Sicilian Majesty, and by the representatives of his allies. Nelson was at this time cruising with his squadron in search of the French fleet, which had eluded the blockade at Brest, and was returning to Naples with his fleet largely reinforced, when he was informed that an armistice had been agreed upon between Ruffo and the garrisons of Uovo and Nuovo. He arrived at Naples on the 24th of June. The capitulation had been signed on the previous day; but, as the arrangements for carrying it into effect were not yet completed, flags of truce were still flying on the Castle, and in the 'Sea-horse.' Nelson immediately signalled to terminate the truce; and, assuming that the flag merely covered a negotiation, either party had a right to take this step. But Nelson believed that he was annulling an *armistice*, which is definite in its terms, and binding like any other treaty. The only ground on which such an engagement can be set aside, is an excess of authority by the agent of the party desiring to repudiate it; and, even in such a case, a nation, jealous of its honour, would hesitate to disavow a treaty which had been concluded in good faith, and by which the position of the other contracting party had been altered for the worse. The justification of his conduct, which Nelson has himself recorded, unhappily disposes of every apology which has been or could have been urged in its extenuation. He assumed, that an armistice for twenty-one days had been agreed to, on the condition that if the place was not relieved at the expiration of that time, it should be surrendered. But he argued,

that such an armistice imported that if either party
should be reinforced before the lapse of the stipulated period, the armistice was at an end. In other
words, that the compact should be observed, unless
it suited either party to break it. No such armistice
had, in fact, taken place; nevertheless, yielding to
the infatuation which had taken possession of him,
Nelson was ready to tarnish his own hitherto unsullied honour, and the fame of the country for which
he had often risked his life. In order to gratify the
vengeance of the Neapolitan Court, Nelson was determined to trample upon treaty, truce, or armistice;
and as there could no longer be any question as to
the reduction of the three forts, with the ships of
war at his command, he peremptorily set aside the
capitulation, and summoned the forts to surrender at
discretion. It has been alleged, in apology for
Nelson, that Cardinal Ruffo exceeded his instructions; and Nelson himself asserts, in a letter to Lord
Spencer, that on his arrival at Naples, 'he found an
infamous treaty entered into with the rebels, in direct disobedience of His Sicilian Majesty's orders.'[*]
The order which Ruffo is thus charged with having
disobeyed, must have been an express order not to
treat with the French, or with the rebels; and such
an order would have been a definite limitation of
the full powers conferred upon the Cardinal by his
commission as Vicar-General of the kingdom. The
production of this order would have settled the question; but Lord Nelson's papers, though containing
many minute details with reference to the surrender
of the Neapolitan forts, do not furnish a particle of
evidence upon the only point which is material to
the Admiral's justification. On the day after the
arrival of the British squadron, Ruffo went off to
the flag-ship, to remonstrate with Nelson against the

---

[*] July 13, 1799.—*Nelson Despatches*, vol. iii. p. 406.

rejection of the treaty. The conference lasted for several hours, during which Nelson and the Hamiltons in vain endeavoured to convince the Cardinal that the King might refuse to ratify articles of capitulation which had not yet been carried into execution. In this interview the argument urged by the Court party implied no more than a disapproval of the *discretion* which the Cardinal had exercised; if his *powers* were denied, it would not have been necessary to protract the discussion for hours. Five minutes would have sufficed. But the Cardinal had never heard it questioned, until it was denied by a British officer and a British ambassador, that a general at the head of his army was not competent to conclude a purely military convention without the sanction of his Government. The Cardinal retired with an unavailing protest; and Lord Nelson, instigated by two bad women, proceeded to violate a sacred engagement,* to which one of his own captains representing the British flag had been a party, and to which the representatives of Russia and the Porte had set their hands. The garrisons of Uovo and Nuovo, unable to offer any resistance, surrendered at discretion. The French, who had been promised a free transport to Toulon, under convoy, were treated as prisoners of war. The Neapolitans, who called themselves patriots, and of whom many deserved the name, were delivered up to the vengeance of the cruel and cowardly Government unworthily restored to power.

But the whole of this sad story has not yet been told. Among the numerous persons who quitted the castles of Uovo and Nuovo, before the capitulation, was Prince Caraccioli, a Neapolitan of high rank, and an admiral in the service of His Sicilian Majesty. This man had ac-

Prince Caraccioli.

---

* Captain Foote's own words.—*Nelson Despatches*, vol. iii. p. 488.

companied the King's flight to Palermo, but had been
permitted to return to Naples to save his large
estates from the confiscation which had been decreed
by the French against the property of absentees.
Caraccioli, however, soon found, as might have been
foreseen, that he was a person of too much importance to be suffered to remain in retirement and
neutrality. He was in a manner compelled Return of Caraccioli.
to accept a commission under the new
Republic; and, in fact, he commanded some gun-
boats, which fired into the Minerva frigate. After
the re-establishment of the King's authority at
Naples, Caraccioli wrote to the Duke of Calviranno
for protection; but, not receiving a satisfactory answer, fled to the mountains. He was soon after taken
in the disguise of a peasant, and brought on board
Lord Nelson's ship, the 'Foudroyant.' It was only a
few weeks since the prince had been received on
board the same ship, with the honour due to his
rank, and welcomed by Nelson as his friend and companion in arms. The old man—he was seventy
years of age—was now hurried on board, in squalid
attire, scared, bound, and manacled. Captain Hardy,
when informed of the quality of the prisoner, personally interposed to rescue him from the insults and
threatened violence of the Neapolitan rabble who
loitered in the ship. His fetters were removed, and
he was placed in a cabin with two sentries at the
door. Stern duty would, perhaps, have justified
the British Admiral in transferring Caraccioli to the
Sicilian authorities, although such a proceeding
would have consigned the prisoner to certain death.
But Nelson, by an exercise of authority, as unnecessary as it was illegal, condescended to anticipate the
cruelty of the vile Court of which he had constituted
himself the servant and the tool. He immediately
issued an order to Count Thurn, the senior officer in
the Sicilian fleet, to hold a court-martial on Carac-

cioli, on board the British flag-ship, and to report to *him* the finding of the court. There was not a shadow of authority for such a proceeding. The British Admiral held no commission in the service of His Sicilian Majesty, nor was he empowered by his own Government to accept such a commission, if it had been offered. Lord Nelson merely commanded a squadron under the orders of Lord Keith, the Commander-in-Chief in the Mediterranean. He had power to try and punish breaches in the articles of war in the ships under his immediate orders, but he had no power, and he knew that he had no power, to interfere in the internal discipline of the auxiliary fleets which served under him for the common purposes of the war. If he could order a court-martial on an officer of His Sicilian Majesty, he could try an officer in the Russian, in the Portuguese, in the Turkish fleet.*

A court-martial composed of Neapolitan officers was not long in trying a man against whom any evidence of disloyalty could be found. It was proved that Caraccioli had held a command in the rebel fleet, and that he had fired on the Sicilian flag. His defence was that he had acted under duress, and that he had been compelled to serve as a common soldier before he accepted a command. He asked for time to produce his witnesses; but he was allowed no time. He might possibly have found it difficult to satisfy a court, before which the proceedings were

---

* In expressing his disapprobation of the conduct of Commodore Campbell for hastily destroying the Sicilian ships in the bay of Naples, to prevent their falling into the hands of the French, Nelson writes thus:—' I feel that His Sicilian Majesty has great cause for displeasure; and was Commodore Campbell an English officer, I should instantly order him to be tried by a court-martial, for the positive breach of my orders to the Marquis de Niza [the Portuguese Admiral]. *I am sorry it cannot be done by me to any auxiliary squadron.*' To Sir John Acton, the Neapolitan minister, January 15, 1799. —*Nelson Despatches*, vol. iii. p. 233.

regularly and fairly conducted, that any people would be so rash as to force a command upon an officer who was friendly to their foe; but the improbability of the defence was no ground for refusing to hear the witnesses. The court-martial—if court-martial it could be called—under the presidency of the very officer into whose ship the prisoner was charged with having fired, had no difficulty in finding the prisoner guilty, and sentencing him to death. This finding was reported to the British Admiral, two hours after he had signed the order for the trial. Nelson directed that the sentence should be carried into execution at the yard-arm of the Minerva, at five o'clock.

Caraccioli sent a message to the Admiral, through Lieutenant Parkinson, the officer who had charge of his person, requesting a new trial, on several grounds; among others, on the fact that Count Thurn, the president of the court-martial by which he had been condemned, was his personal enemy. But Nelson replied that his trial had been fair, and that he must abide the result. The prince then prayed that, in consideration of his age, rank, and former services, he might be shot. But even this mercy was refused; and the venerable nobleman, who had faithfully served his sovereign for forty years, was hanged at the yard-arm of a ship which had once been under his command. Lady Hamilton, who refused to see Caraccioli before his death, was present at his execution. A horrible incident to this painful tale is usually narrated, but is only worthy of notice as displaying a trait of sycophantic baseness on the part of the husband of the woman, whose baleful influence had tarnished Nelson's name, which in a man of English birth, is hardly to be paralleled. The body of Caraccioli had, by Nelson's orders, been taken out to sea and sunk. About three weeks after the execution, a fisherman hailed the flag-ship, and announced that the prince had arisen from the bottom

of the sea, and was swimming to Naples. This
strange tale reached the ears of the King, and, to
gratify his curiosity, the ship was steered in the
direction indicated by the fisherman. They had not
proceeded far, before the ghastly apparition was
visible, moving towards the ship. The corpse, owing
to chemical changes which take place in drowned
bodies, had risen to the surface, notwithstanding a
great weight of shot which had been attached to it.
It was considered necessary that any disagreeable
impressions which this incident might suggest to the
royal mind should be averted, and Sir William
Hamilton undertook the delicate task. He told the
King that Caraccioli could not rest until he had come
and implored pardon of His Majesty himself for his
crimes against him.[*] Such was the loathsome adulation ministered, not by a slave to an eastern despot,
but by the representative of the British Crown to a
Christian king.

The restoration of the royal authority at Naples
was celebrated by the license of the rabble, who have
ever been the most loyal subjects of the Bourbon
dynasty. After the populace had been satiated with
indiscriminate massacre, violence and rapine, justice
was executed on the rebels, or rather the vengeance
of the Court was let loose on its political opponents,
among whom were included almost all the virtue
and intelligence in the city. The fort of St. Elmo
surrendered to Captain Trowbridge, after a siege of
eight days, and the garrison marched out with the
honours of war. Capua and Gaeta shortly afterwards
capitulated on the same terms.

The kingdom of Naples being now freed from the

---

[*] Clarke and M'Arthur's *Life of Lord Nelson*, vol. ii. p. 187. These writers, though dull and incapable of exercising an independent judgment on the conduct of their hero and his friends, are nevertheless honest and painstaking. They greatly admire Sir William's tact and address on this occasion.

invaders, the Court returned to Palermo, to resume
the pleasures which had been so rudely interrupted
by the French. Rome, however, was still occupied
by the enemy; but the garrison, with an effective
strength of two thousand five hundred men, was
wholly inadequate to the defence of the city together
with the fortress of Civita Vecchia. Nelson applied
to Sir James Erskine, the Commandant at Minorca,
to aid an expedition against Rome, with twelve
hundred men; but Sir James having declined to
undertake such a responsibility without orders, Nelson
determined to send Trowbridge with a small force to
summon Civita Vecchia, while General Boucard, a
Swiss officer in the Neapolitan service, should march
with a few regiments on Rome. This daring attempt
was completely successful. The French, who knew
that an Austrian army was advancing upon Rome,
preferred surrendering to the English. Accordingly,
after some parley, Civita Vecchia was given up to
Trowbridge; and Louis, another of Nelson's captains,
took possession of the city of the Cæsars. Two days
after * the capitulation had been signed, the Austrian
General encamped under the walls of Rome, and
could with difficulty be convinced that he had been
disappointed of his plunder by the promptitude and
energy of a British commodore. It was, however, to
the military successes of the Imperial and Russian
arms, and especially to the great victory of Novi,
which had been won in August, that Italy was mainly
indebted for her deliverance from the French yoke.
The plan of the Russian General was to attack the
French in Genoa, while the Archduke pressed them
in Switzerland, and ultimately to invade France with
the united armies. But this great plan was defeated;
and the bright prospects of Europe were again ob-
scured by the differences which had arisen between

* 22nd September.

the allied powers. The Imperial Court had renewed, with views more exclusively selfish, a policy more shallow and perverse than had ruined the common cause in former campaigns. The restoration of the French monarchy, which England had originally proposed, and which Russia now proposed, was not the object which Austria desired. Neither, on the other hand, did she wish well to a Government founded on the ruins of legitimate authority. She dreaded the propagation of revolutionary principles in Italy, lest her own arbitrary Government should be endangered; and she was not less unfriendly to the establishment of the Italian States, as being adverse to the aims of her avarice and ambition. The military capacity of Russia, so signally displayed in the late campaign, excited her jealousy; and the naval ascendency of Great Britain on the seas, which she could not emulate, she could nevertheless regard with malevolence. Suwarrow, after his brilliant campaign in Italy, had hastened to effect a junction with the Austrian army in Switzerland. On his arrival, after encountering great difficulties in his march, he found that Kersakoff, his lieutenant who had been previously detached with a division of the Russian army to co-operate with the Austrians, had suffered a disastrous defeat at Zurich. A quarrel took place between Suwarrow and the Archduke Charles; and the two Generals would hold no correspondence with each other. The old Russian Marshal, finding himself in a manner deserted, and his army reduced to thirteen thousand men, was forced, for the first time after forty years of command, to make a retreat. This movement he effected with his usual skill and success; but the Czar, indignant at the conduct of the Austrians, ordered his army to return to Russia; and his faithful General was involved in the indiscriminate fury with which Paul was transported, after the manner of barbarous despots. Suwarrow, whose fame resounded through Europe, languished and died in disgrace soon after his return to St. Petersburg. The main result of the great campaign was the expulsion of the French from the Italian peninsula; that they were not driven out of Switzerland was wholly due to the mean and perverse policy of the Cabinet of Vienna. The Austrians might, but for envy of a too glorious ally, have finished the campaign in France; but they chose to forego the military advantages they had themselves gained, rather than aid the rising reputation of a rival. In October, the Imperial and the Republican armies occupied much the same situation they had occupied in April on either bank of the Rhine.

Early in the year, the British Government projected an expedition to Holland with one of the largest armies that had ever been sent from the island. Thirty thousand men were destined for the service, and the Czar undertook to furnish seventeen thousand troops. Whatever might be the military fortune of such an enterprise, it is obvious that its ultimate success in a military, as well as in a political sense, must depend upon the favour of the people, whose territory was to be invaded. But no inquiry was made whether any aid might be expected from the Dutch themselves, or whether they would be disposed to welcome their deliverers. It was intended that the army should land on the northern coast of Holland, and march to Amsterdam; but on the last occasion, when the English had attempted to defend Amsterdam against the French, the people had risen upon them, and forced them to quit the country. Since that time, the English had destroyed the Dutch fleet. It was supposed, however, that the experience of the last six years had altered the sentiments of the people. But they had made no complaint; they had not asked for the interference of England, nor of any other power at war with the

French. The English Government could not keep their secret so well as the enemy could keep his; and it was well known for what purpose preparations were making at Portsmouth. These preparations commenced early in the spring, and the summer was far advanced before the first division of the army had embarked; but, during that interval, no sign of encouragement was visible from any part of the United Provinces. The people were, no doubt, impatient under the exactions of the French; but they were accustomed to exaction, for they had long been subjected to higher taxation than any people in Europe. Holland was not one of those nations which had been suddenly and strangely forced to assume the name and forms of a republic by the Paris Propaganda. Centuries before the French Revolution, the United Provinces had been familiar with republican institutions; and, for many generations, the country had been distracted by the contentions of the party which professed to uphold the independence of the States against the ascendency of one illustrious house in which the office of chief magistrate was hereditary. The Stadtholderate of the house of Orange had been abolished mainly by the influence of Amsterdam, which was the centre of political action and power: and it was at Amsterdam that it was proposed that the banished Prince of Orange should be restored to the Stadtholderate by English and Russian bayonets. The Low Countries were, in fact, the last place in which the cause of the European powers against French democracy could be successfully fought; and of all the provinces, the great State of North Holland, of which Amsterdam was the capital, was the worst battle-ground which could have been chosen. To complete this ill-planned expedition, the General selected for the chief command was the same General who had been recalled from the same scene of action for incompetence or ill fortune five years before.

And during those five years, in which so much military experience might have been gained, the Duke of York had not been employed in active service. It has been alleged that the King insisted on his son's appointment to this arduous duty. There can be no doubt that the King urged the appointment; for it would be absurd to suppose that the minister, who had felt it his duty to remove the prince from a subordinate command in 1796, would name him to the chief command of a great army destined for a most important service in 1799. But His Majesty's pleasure could not relieve the minister from his responsibility. It was for Mr. Pitt, and not for the King, to decide who should lead a British army in the field; and if Mr. Pitt had represented to His Majesty, with the firmness that became him, and which he could maintain when he thought fit, that His Royal Highness was not the proper person to be appointed, the King would probably have given way without much pressure. George the Third had many faults; but he was not wanting in public spirit, nor was he incapable of practising self-denial.* He was tenacious of patronage, and gave away more places than any Sovereign of this country, before or since. But his object was not so much to usurp the constitutional function of his minister, as to maintain his parliamentary interest; and he was the last man in his dominions who would wilfully jeopardise their interests by jobbing and favouritism.

The first division of the British army, consisting

* 'I asked Lord Melville the truth of an anecdote which had been told me respecting his father:—That when he entertained the King at Wimbledon, His Majesty filled a glass of wine, and drank the following toast—" Here is the health of that minister who had the confidence to oppose the King's opinion as to sending our troops to Egypt, and to whom, therefore, the success of our arms in that quarter is, under God, to be attributed." Lord M. said it was perfectly true; and it was the most flattering compliment his father had ever recorded.'—*Locker MSS.*

of about twelve thousand men under Sir Ralph Abercromby, embarked for the Helder on the 13th of August, but was prevented landing by stress of weather until the 27th. They were opposed by a force of more than ten thousand men under General Daendels, and, after an obstinate conflict of ten hours, which the British sustained without artillery or cavalry, the Dutch gave way, and abandoned the Helder with one hundred pieces of cannon, to the English General. A reinforcement of five thousand men, under General Don, arrived the next day; and on the 30th of the month, the thirteen men of war in the Texel, being chiefly the remnant of De Winter's squadron which had escaped after the battle of Camperdown, surrendered without firing a shot to Admiral Mitchell, who acted under the immediate orders of Lord Duncan. According to the statement of the Dutch Admiral, his crews mutinied, and refused to fight. From the 1st to the 8th of September, Abercromby continued his advance slowly and cautiously, still gaining the advantage in several minor encounters with the Dutch. On the 14th, the Duke of York landed at the Helder with three brigades of British troops, and the first division of Russians, consisting of seven thousand good troops. The allied army now amounted to thirty thousand men; and the Duke of York determined to push forward before the Dutch should have obtained reinforcements, still calculating on the dutiful response of the people to the proclamations of the Prince of Orange.

No country in the world afforded such facilities for arresting the progress of an invading army as the Netherlands. The canals, the dykes, the banks with which the soil is traversed, render it almost impassable; and in the last resort, the ocean itself could be summoned as an ally. In addition to the difficulties created by the art of civil engineers, hardly less formidable than the works of Vauban or Cohorn, there were numerous sand-hills and villages which afforded excellent positions for a defensive force; and of these the Dutch General had not omitted to avail himself. It was not the fault of the Duke of York that he found himself in the face of difficulties which would probably have baffled an able and experienced General. The campaign had been planned in London; and the British Commander had no discretion beyond the disposition of his forces in the field. Under these disadvantages, it became necessary to risk the fate of the enterprise on a general action. The Duke disposed his army in four divisions. The left wing, under Abercromby, was to turn the enemy's right, which rested on the Zuyder Zee. Two other positions were to be forced by the central division; but the most arduous duty, upon the due performance of which the fate of the day depended, was assigned to the Russian General D'Hermann, of whom, and the force under his command, the British Commander could know nothing. These troops were destined to attack the heights of Camperdyne, to storm the villages beneath the heights, and finally to occupy the town of Bergen. The divisions of Sir Ralph Abercromby and Sir James Pulteney, consisting of disciplined troops, and guided by skilful officers, performed the duties assigned to them; and had the right wing been equally steady, the fortune of the day would have been different to what it was. But the Russians rushed forward with wild impetuosity. Impatient to be the first in the field, they would not wait till daylight. The violence of their onset carried the first positions of the enemy; but they soon became involved in confusion; amidst the mist and darkness they could not distinguish friend from foe, and they suffered more from their own guns than from the fire of the French in front of them. The

French General, when he saw the state of affairs, judiciously fell back before his barbarous assailants, who pressed forward until they became an armed mob, separated from their officers, and far in advance of their supports. Hurrying forward in this manner, though galled by an incessant flanking fire from the French infantry, which had dispersed as riflemen among the hedges and behind the banks, the Russians at length reached the town of Bergen. Here they found artillery and cavalry drawn up in such a manner as to ensure their destruction if they advanced; and after a desperate resistance, during which their General, D'Hermann, was taken prisoner, the whole division made a rapid retreat, until they halted near the position which they had quitted before dawn. In a few days, the Duke of York made a second attack on Bergen, and after a hard struggle, in which the loss on either side was nearly equal, he succeeded in obtaining possession of the town. But far from having made any material progress, the position of the army was worse than at its first landing. The inhabitants gave them no encouragement, while the levy of the French was met with alacrity. Losses in battle, with the usual casualties of an army in the field, more destructive than fire and sword, had thinned the ranks of the invaders, while the opposing armies were rapidly augmenting. The season was far advanced; a forward movement was hopeless; and even a retreat could not be effected without great loss. In these circumstances, Sir Ralph Abercromby, with the concurrence of the other Generals, advised His Royal Highness to abandon the enterprise; and their representations having been submitted to the Cabinet,* the Duke of York was ordered to make terms for the withdrawal of the army from Holland. The negotiation was not protracted. The Dutch

* Duke of Portland to Lord Cornwallis, Oct. 14, 1799.—*Cornwallis Correspondence,* vol. iii. p. 136.

were unwilling to exasperate an enemy which might open the sluices and inundate the country. The French were satisfied with the utter failure of the enterprise. The restoration of the Dutch fleet was at first demanded; but these terms being peremptorily refused, it was ultimately agreed that the British should surrender the Helder in the same condition in which they found it; that eight thousand French and Dutch prisoners should be released, and that the allied armies should evacuate the Low Countries before the end of November. Such was the end of this ill-conceived expedition, which was only redeemed from utter failure by success in a subordinate detail unconnected with the main design. The capture of the ships in the Texel, had it been a separate undertaking, would have ranked among the brilliant exploits of the war; but it was weighed down by the disaster of the great military enterprise. Fortunately, however, for the fame of England, and the safety of the British dominions, if not the British Isles, her military blunders and disasters were compensated by the irresistible prowess of her fleets, and the skill and conduct of her naval commanders.

When Nelson removed his squadron to the Bay of Naples, he left a small force to blockade the port of Alexandria; and the Government justly attached so much importance to this service, that they sent Captain Sir Sidney Smith with a broad pennant in the 'Tiger,' an eighty-four gun ship, to assume this particular command. Smith, however, soon after his arrival, ascertained that the French, instead of attempting to reach their transports, had marched into the interior with the design of overpowering St. Jean d'Acre, which would give them the command of Syria, and facilitate their progress, either to Constantinople, or to India. The Porte had invested a native chief Djezzar, lately a formidable rebel, but now actively engaged in op-

Sir Sidney Smith.

posing the common enemy, with the pachalics of
Egypt and Syria. Djezzar was prepared to defend
Acre, and the English commodore determined to
proceed in the 'Tiger' to his assistance, having previously despatched the frigate 'Theseus' on that service.
In his way, Sir Sidney Smith had the good fortune to
fall in with and capture the French flotilla of gunboats, containing the battering train for the siege of
Acre, which had eluded the blockade of Alexandria.
Bonaparte, in his march to Acre, had reduced the
forts of El Arish, Gaza, and Jaffa. At the lastmentioned place, he put the garrison to the sword,
on the pretence that they were prisoners who had
been liberated on parole at El Arish. But his attempt to justify the murder by traducing the honour
of his victims only aggravates the atrocity of his
conduct. Bonaparte was a genuine child of the
Revolution. No fear of God or man influenced his
actions. No feeling of humanity, no sense of honour
ever checked the career of his ambition, or restrained
him from any word or deed which his interest, or the
exigency of the moment seemed to require. His
proceedings in Egypt were a tissue of cruelty, blasphemy, and lying. The troops destined to march
over sands and inhospitable deserts, were told that
they were going to a land flowing with milk and
honey, and that every soldier on his return to France
would be rewarded for his services with six acres and
a half of his native soil. The people of Egypt were
told that the French were true Mussulmans, and
that they came as the allies of the Sultan, to deliver
the country from the tyranny of the Beys. The inhabitants who would not believe these professions,
and who dared to resist the invader, were given up
to plunder and massacre. The most atrocious acts
of the army of Egypt were perpetrated either with
the connivance, or at the instigation, or by the express orders of Bonaparte himself. His entrance to

Alexandria was celebrated by a general massacre of the inhabitants, without distinction of age or sex. It was Bonaparte who provoked, and afterwards punished by a like massacre the insurrection of the people of Cairo. At Jaffa, the order for the murder of nearly four thousand prisoners of war was given under his own hand, and, in person, he superintended the execution of a command which his own officers, rude and unscrupulous as they were, obeyed, with murmurs of indignation and disgust. Bonaparte was not the first conqueror, who, from a cruel policy, has put prisoners to death; but Bonaparte was the only military chief, so far as history affords an authentic record, who sought to dispose of his own disabled soldiers by putting them to death. It is a well-established fact that, after the retreat from Acre, Bonaparte proposed to the medical officers at the hospital at Jaffa to get rid of the sick by poison.

The massacre of the garrison of Jaffa had the effect of making the troops of Djezzar fight with the desperate resolution of men who fore- *Siege of Acre.* knew the fate of submission or defeat. The defences of Acre were in bad condition, and on the land side not a single gun was mounted. The place was in fact pronounced by Sir Sidney Smith not to be defensible, according to any rules of art, nor, of itself, worth defending. But the English commodore determined, nevertheless, that it must and should be defended, for the purpose of stopping the progress of French conquest, and convincing the multitude assembled on the surrounding heights that the invaders were not invincible.* Weak as the place was, the loss of the battering train greatly protracted the siege. For fifty days, a series of assaults on the one side, and of *sorties* on the other, were attended with no other result than loss of life. At length a few field-pieces

---

* See Sidney Smith to Lord Nelson, 2nd May.

which the French had brought with them effected a practicable breach in the crumbling walls; and, at the same time, a fleet of transports under Hussein Bey, which had been anxiously expected by the garrison, anchored in the roads. Bonaparte determined on storming the place before the reinforcements could be landed. An incessant cannonade was kept up by the French all the night of the 7th of May, and in the morning the storming parties advanced to the breach. The newly arrived troops had by this time nearly disembarked, and were forming on the shore; but the English commodore, who was eagerly watching the operations, seeing that they would not be in time, hastily collected a few boats' crews and led them into the breach. The appearance of a handful of sailors in the foremost post of danger inspired more confidence among the soldiers of Djezzar than all the troops of Hussein, or any other reinforcement of their countrymen could have done. The French had by this time obtained possession of a portion of the works, and the tri-coloured flag streamed from one of the towers. They pressed forward to the great breach fifty yards in width, and here a deadly struggle, hand to hand, took place. The assailants at length gave way, and ultimately retired, after repeated efforts at different points to carry the place by assault. Baffled in fair and open conflict, Bonaparte made a villanous attempt to surprise the garrison by fraud. A flag of truce was brought in, proposing a cessation of arms to bury the dead; and during the negotiations, while the flag was still flying, the French, under cover of shot and shell, rushed to the assault.* Happily, the garrison had

* It would appear hardly credible, that even Bonaparte could be guilty of such infamous conduct, were not the fact stated by Sir Sidney Smith himself in his despatch to Lord Nelson, May 30. Two attempts to assassinate the commodore had previously been made at the instigation of Bonaparte, as Sir Sidney believed, though he does not state the grounds of his belief.

not been thrown off their guard, and the murderous attempt was defeated with slaughter and disgrace. Sir Sidney Smith sent back the fraudulent messenger to the French General with a letter, expressing in unmeasured language the sentiments, with which an officer and a gentleman could not fail to regard such a flagrant breach of the laws of honour and of war.*
On the 20th of May, Bonaparte raised the siege of Acre, after remaining before the place sixty-one days. He gratified his spleen before departure by bombarding the public buildings, and destroying the palace of the Pacha.

In a despatch to the French Directory, Bonaparte affirmed that he had taken Acre, but that he had abandoned his conquest in consequence of the plague. Had he succeeded in planting the republican flag on the ruins of Acre, his position would have been untenable. The sea was commanded by English and Turkish ships and gunboats. The native chiefs who had hitherto stood aloof from dread of the invincible invader, reassured by the successful defence of Acre, came pouring in from the mountains and the plains, to stop the advance and harass the retreat of the French army. It was indeed with great difficulty that the French General, leaving behind the greater number of his wounded and his artillery, could bring off the shattered remnant of the insolent host which two months before had marched upon St. Jean d'Acre, with an assurance of easy triumph. The line of retreat was covered with corpses and blasted with ruin, the invaders laying waste the country as they marched in the wanton rage of disappointment and revenge. On the 16th of June, twenty-seven days after their repulse from

*Bonaparte's despatch.

---

* Bonaparte affected to treat this letter as a challenge; and to speak with contempt of Sir Sidney Smith as a madman unworthy of notice. Bourrienne reprobates the insolence of his patron, and does justice to the reputation of the distinguished commodore.—*Memoirs*, vol. ii. p. 295.

Acre, and five months after their departure from Egypt to effect the conquest of Syria, Bonaparte and his weary followers re-entered Cairo. They were received nevertheless with triumphal honours, their approach having been heralded as usual with bulletins of victory and unrivalled feats of arms. Bonaparte had not enjoyed many days' repose before intelligence arrived that a Turkish fleet had anchored at Aboukir, that the fort had been taken, and that Alexandria was about to be invested. With his usual rapidity and decision, the French General attacked the assailants in their intrenchments, drove them forth at the point of the bayonet, took all their cannon and field-equipments, and regained possession of the fort. But while he continued to issue bombastic proclamations, to keep the people of the country in awe, and to delude his army, which had frequently been on the point of mutiny, he could no longer conceal his desperate situation from the Government at Paris. He told them plainly, that unless they would send him large reinforcements of men and arms, the country must be given up. He did not then know the reverses which the French arms had sustained in Europe; nor that during his absence the Directory had lost almost all that his valour and conduct had won. The intelligence soon after reached him through English and French newspapers, which were said to have been sent him by Sir Sidney Smith. His resolution was immediately taken. He determined to return to France without delay. Having delegated the command of the army to Kleber, and announced his departure in general orders, Bonaparte, accompanied by Berthier, Murat, Lannes, and Marmont, quitted or rather escaped from Egypt, on the night of the 22nd of August.

The expedition had, in fact, proved a total failure. The conquest of Egypt and Syria would have enabled the French, on the one hand, to convert the dominions of the Grand Turk into a Byzantine republic, and, on the other, to threaten the British Empire in India. The victory of the Nile and the defence of Acre had frustrated both of these designs. The re-establishment of the French in India was the main object of the expedition. Long before the preparations were commenced at Toulon, French agents had been busy at Seringapatam, flattering Tippoo Sultan, who inherited the martial spirit if not the ability of Hyder Ali, with the hope of French assistance in expelling the English from Hindostan. Accordingly, in December 1797, Tippoo sent an embassy to the French Governor of the Mauritius, asking for ten thousand French soldiers and thirty thousand negroes, to co-operate with the army of Mysore in hostilities against the East India Company; and proposing that the territory of the Company should be equally divided between the Sultan and the French Republic. In the event of the Governor at the Mauritius not being empowered to conclude a treaty of this importance, the Mysorean envoys were accredited to the Directory at Paris. It was, however, the policy of Tippoo to keep this negotiation secret until he should be in a condition to defy the British forces, which lay within eight days' march of his capital. On the other hand, it seemed to the French Governor equally politic to commit the Sultan of Mysore to an irreparable breach with the Government at Fort St. George. Neither party, in fact, could trust the other. Besides the Oriental contempt for European infidels with which Tippoo was fully possessed, he had been assured by his ministers that the French were seldom true to their engagements, and that Ripaud, the principal French agent at Seringapatam, was a lying adventurer, in whom no confidence whatever could be placed. Malartie, the Governor of the Mauritius, on his side, was not ignorant that Hindostan was, beyond any other known portion of the globe, the country of fraud and falsehood. Tippoo's ambassadors were sent to the Mauritius in the guise of merchants, with instructions to observe the utmost secrecy in their communications with the French authorities; but on their arrival, they were received, in spite of their remonstrances and entreaties, with all the honours of their rank, and were publicly announced as the plenipotentiaries of the Sultan of Mysore, the ally of the French Republic. No sooner had the Mysorean ambassadors delivered their credentials, than Malartie issued a proclamation announcing the proposal of the Sultan, and inviting volunteers to enrol themselves in the service of this mighty potentate who was about to declare war against Great Britain, and to expel the English from Hindostan.

This proclamation was received at Calcutta in June, 1798. Lord Mornington, the Governor-General, at first questioned its authenticity; but, in a few days, his doubts were removed by a despatch from Lord Macartney, and by the arrival of persons who had been present at the reception of the ambassadors, and at the promulgation of their embassy. Lord Mornington was moreover informed, that the ambassadors had subsequently left the Mauritius in a French frigate with French officers and two hundred men, engaged for the service of the Sultan. On the 26th of April, this force landed at Mangalore. About the same time, Lord Mornington ascertained that Tippoo had despatched an embassy to Zemaun Shah, the ruler of Cabul, Khorassan and Cashmere, who had always been the determined enemy of the English.

The Governor-General took immediate measures to repel the expected attack. But it appeared, upon inquiry, that the forces of the Company could not be made ready for active service in less than six months; and the only native allies upon whose fidelity reli-

ance could be placed, were the Peishwa and the
Nizam; but the feeble and distracted Governments
of these princes, afforded little hope of their being
able to fulfil the conditions of the treaty of 1792,
by which the Courts of Poonah and Hyderabad were
bound in alliances offensive and defensive with the
East India Company. At the beginning of August,
Lord Mornington heard of the French preparations
in the Mediterranean; and on the last day of October,
the account of the victory at the Nile reached Calcutta. On the 8th of November, the Governor-General addressed a letter to the Sultan of Mysore,
apprising him that his correspondence with the
French was known to the Government of the Company, and proposing to send an envoy to Seringapatam with the view of detaching him from the French
connection, and restoring the friendly relations which
it had been intended to establish by the treaty of
1792. This letter had no effect; and several attempts of a similar kind to maintain peace having
been frustrated by the evasions of the Sultan, Lord
Mornington on the 3rd of February, 1799, ordered
General Harris to enter the territory of Mysore, and
to march direct upon Seringapatam. The force under
Harris consisted of about thirty thousand men besides
a contingent of twelve thousand well-appointed troops,
with a large body of cavalry, which, contrary to expectation, had been promptly furnished by the Nizam.
At the head of the 33rd British regiment was the
brother of the Governor-General, a commander who
was soon to fill India, and ultimately Europe, with
his fame. Arthur Wellesley, though he bore no
greater military rank than that of a regimental
colonel in this expedition, was nevertheless high in
the counsels of the Commander-in-Chief. He was
associated with General Harris and three other officers in a political and diplomatic commission, to
which the Governor-General had delegated all his

powers of making terms or concluding peace with the Government of the Sultan.

Meanwhile Tippoo had marched in pursuit of an army under General Stuart, which was advancing from the coast of Malabar, to effect a junction with Harris's main body. The Sultan at the head of ten or eleven thousand of his best troops came up with Stuart's advanced guard of two thousand men near Periapatam. The brigade sustained the assault of the Sultan's troops, until Stuart arrived, when the Mysoreans were compelled to retreat with heavy loss. Undaunted by this reverse, Tippoo was disposed to try his fortune in a general action, and when the main army was within a few days' march of the capital, he attacked the outposts at the village of Mallavalley. But after a sharp struggle, in which Wellesley's regiment took a prominent part, the Sultan retreated; and making no farther attempt to resist his enemy in the field, he retired within the fortifications of Seringapatam.

On the 4th of April, a week after the battle of Mallavalley, General Harris appeared before the capital of Mysore. The works were of great extent, and had recently been repaired. The defence was conducted by French engineers, and the garrison was of sufficient strength. During the progress of the siege, Tippoo endeavoured to negotiate; but at this stage of the conflict, the English General could offer only peremptory terms. These were the renunciation of the French alliance; the payment of two crores of rupees; the cession of a large territory; and the surrender of hostages for the performance of these conditions. An answer was required within forty-eight hours; and none being received at the expiration of that time, the siege proceeded. On the 3rd of May, the breach was effected, and on the following morning, the assault took place with two thousand five hundred European, and nineteen hundred native troops, under the command of General Baird. The storming party encountered a galling fire of musketry in the advance, but the breach was undefended, and the place was soon in the possession of the assailants. Tippoo Sultan himself fell, fighting to the last. The capture of Seringapatam placed the whole kingdom of Mysore at the disposal of the Company. The conquerors appropriated to themselves a portion of the coast which extended their sea-board from Coromandel to Malabar. They likewise retained the fortress and island of Seringapatam, together with some smaller districts. Portions of territory were assigned to the allies of the Company, the Nizam and the Peishwa. The territory of which Hyder had dispossessed the Hindo rajah forty years before, was restored to his heir, a child of five years old, but under such restrictions as rendered him a vassal of the Company. Colonel Wellesley was appointed Governor of Seringapatam instead of General Baird, who had led the assault with such signal success; a preference which was complained of, not without reason, by the senior officer. Treasure, to the amount of nearly a million and a half, was found in Seringapatam;* together with a mass of papers which proved that Tippoo had long been in correspondence with the French relative to designs against the British power in India. A letter from Bonaparte, announcing his arrival at the Red Sea, with an innumerable and invincible army, to rescue the Sultan from his oppressors, and requesting him to send a confidential agent to Suez or Cairo, was published among the Indian despatches after the fall of Seringapatam.

* The rapacity of General Harris, in appropriating to himself and his generals double the amount of booty to which he and they were entitled, caused a great scandal. Unsuccessful attempts were made by proceedings in the Court of Chancery to recover the share of prize-money of which the general officers had unjustly deprived the rest of the army. The opinions of the law officers on the subject, with other particulars, are to be found in the *Wellesley Despatches*.

CHAPTER XL.

INCOME TAX—BONAPARTE'S LETTER PROPOSING PEACE—HADFIELD'S ATTEMPT ON THE KING'S LIFE—SCARCITY—PROSECUTION OF THE CORN FACTORS—MEASURES OF THE GOVERNMENT.

THE Parliamentary Session of 1799 was remarkable for its financial measures. Early in the year a large subsidy had been promised to the Emperor of Russia in consideration of an army of forty-five thousand men being employed against the French. The money was readily voted by the House of Commons; Tierney, who now took the foremost part in opposition, approved the policy of cultivating continental alliances, and declared his belief in the possibility of organising a new confederacy against the French. The great victory of the British fleet, and the still more signal reverses of the French armies, had inspired new confidence in the war, and no man thought this a fitting opportunity to renew the twice rejected proposal for peace. It was now said by those who most exulted in the recent fortune of war, that the next offer of terms would come from the other side of the Channel.

The scheme of taxation by which Pitt had intended to impose the chief burden of the war upon surplus property and income, had proved a failure. The weight falling upon articles of luxury could be evaded or mitigated at the option of the sufferer; and, in the result, not only was the revenue disappointed, but trade was materially injured by the retrenchment or disuse of the luxuries, which had been selected as the criterion of taxation. The failure of the triple assessment had been supplied by a hasty and temporary expedient. It was proposed that persons who might be reluctant to submit to the inquisitorial process of an income tax, yet willing to contribute liberally to the extraordinary exigencies of the State, should be permitted, partly by way of composition, and partly by way of voluntary contribution, to subscribe certain sums. A clause to this effect was included in the **Tax Bill**. Many public bodies and persons of known wealth availed themselves of this clause, or perhaps were led by example, or forced by public opinion, to adopt it. The King gave twenty-five thousand pounds, which he said he could ill afford. Some of the ministers thought themselves obliged to give a year's salary. Pitt,* who could not pay his tradespeople, gave two thousand pounds. In this manner two millions were obtained. But an expedient so clumsy, so unfair, and so oppressive, could not be repeated. The emergency which had arisen was not one of that kind, which claims the liberality of the rich. It was not a famine, or a pestilence which had suddenly fallen upon the country, but a demand for money to carry on a great war, which was as much a part of the public service as the garrison at Portsmouth or the Court of King's Bench. Wealthy landowners and ministers of State had no greater interest in measures necessary for the defence of the country, or the vindication of the national honour, than farmers, shopkeepers, or others; and they might as reasonably have been expected to make up the deficiencies of the Customs or Excise, as to eke out the proceeds of any particular tax imposed for the extraordinary charges of the army and navy. Voluntary assessments and loyalty loans are but empirical modes of providing for the charges of a great nation.

* Lord Stanhope's *Life of Pitt.—Courts and Cabinets of George the Third.*

The estimate of expenditure for the ensuing year was twenty-nine millions; and as the ordinary sources of revenue yielded little more than six millions, adding to the estimate a million for contingencies, there would be twenty-four millions to be raised by extraordinary ways and means. Notwithstanding these vast demands, amounting to nearly five times the ordinary income, Pitt adhered to his policy of raising the war funds, partly by taxation, and partly by loan. The tax on income, though it had partially failed when applied through the medium of the assessed taxes, was an engine of such power, that it only required proper machinery to raise any amount which property could pay. And the only machinery by which it can be effectually worked, is the simple process of taking so much of every man's income, from whatever source it may be derived. To this plan, which is, in fact, a recurrence to the raw principle of taxation, Mr. Pitt now resorted. He proposed to take two shillings in the pound from every income of two hundred pounds and upwards. From that amount to sixty pounds a year, at which the tax commenced, there was to be a descending scale of assessment. Certain abatements were to be made, so as to eliminate the nett income, upon which only the impost was to attach. Computed in this way, the taxable income of the country was estimated at one hundred and two millions, upon which a levy of ten per cent. would raise, in round numbers, ten millions. The remainder of the charge, fourteen millions, was to be raised by open loan. All the objections to an income tax with which the present generation is familiar, were stated by Mr. Tierney and other opponents of the measure. The inquisitorial proceedings which it rendered necessary—the injustice of exacting the same contributions from permanent and precarious incomes—from incomes for life and incomes for years—from profits of trade, arising from a mixture of capital and industry; and profits of professions derived from industry alone;— these arguments were urged with convincing force, and were met by the only intelligible answer they have ever received, that an equitable adjustment of an income tax was impracticable. But all men felt that if the war was to go on, it had become necessary to resort to sources of supply, deeper and wider than those which sufficed for the ordinary service of the country. Hence there appeared a general disposition to submit to a hard necessity, and not to waste time in abstruse calculations, with the view of ascertaining the just proportion in which each man should contribute. To mitigate the arbitrary character of this tax, the assessment was entrusted, not to the officers of revenue, but to commissioners elected by popular suffrage. The commissioners were sworn to secrecy, and had power to administer an oath when the information afforded was not satisfactory. There could be no question as to the exact amount of liability in the cases of fundholders, mortgagees, and annuitants. There was little difficulty in ascertaining the rental of real property; but the difficulty amounted to impossibility of obtaining faithful returns of the vast incomes derived from commerce, manufactures, trades, and professions. The temptations to make fraudulent returns among this class of proprietors has always proved irresistible; in fact, they virtually assess themselves; and the consequence has been, that the revenue has been deprived of a very large proportion of the just proceeds of the tax. It is in this inherent defect, that the real injustice of an income tax consists. The tax presses with undue weight on those who are neither able nor willing to evade it, in proportion as others decline to bear their due share of the burden. The bill was passed by a large majority.

Bonaparte, on his return from Egypt, found the French people prepared to receive him as a conqueror.

On his arrival at Paris, the Directory did not venture to call their unwelcome General to account for absenting himself from the army without leave; nor did he condescend to offer a word of explanation on the subject. The pear was now ripe. The series of rapid and well-contrived manœuvres by which Bonaparte abolished the effete Directory, dispersed the legislature, and constituted himself Dictator, under the title of First Consul, proved him as great a master of politics as of war. His triumph was distinguished by a moderation unknown to the various revolutions of the last ten years. There were no proscriptions; nearly all the State prisoners, amounting to many thousands, were released; the churches were re-opened, and the priesthood was re-established. The law of hostages, the forced loans, and other revolutionary edicts, were repealed. It soon became manifest that it was the intention of the new ruler of France to restore monarchical institutions, and the people, disgusted with liberty and equality, were eager for the restitution of order, under a permanent and intelligible form of Government.

Bonaparte's reception in Paris.

One of the earliest measures of the First Consul was to propitiate foreign powers by a circular letter addressed to the diplomatic agents of the Republic at the different Courts of Europe, announcing the moderate and pacific views of the new Government. To Great Britain, Bonaparte made a direct proposal of peace, in the form of a letter to the King. Setting aside the impertinence of a mode of communication alike irregular and unnecessary, the letter was striking and plausible. 'Must the war which has ravaged the four quarters of the globe for eight years be eternal?' asked the writer. 'Why should the two most powerful and enlightened nations of Europe sacrifice their prosperity and happiness to war? Why should they

Bonaparte's letter to the King.

persevere in a war which involved all other nations?'
The note, which was very brief, contained no distinct
proposition; but it seemed to suggest a cession of
conquered territory on either side as a basis of treaty.
However this might be, the Cabinet decided on rejecting the overture. The despatch in which Lord
Grenville conveyed this decision was calculated to
repel the advances of the First Consul, even if those
advances had been sincere. A paper so sarcastic,
contemptuous, and dictatorial, is not to be found in
the records of diplomacy. 'His Majesty,' said the
Secretary of State, 'was not engaged in any contest
for a vain or false glory; but for the defence of his
dominions against unprovoked attack; nor could he
hope for any satisfactory result from a negotiation
entered into with those whom a fresh revolution had
so recently placed in the exercise of power.' The
minister went on to inveigh, in unmeasured terms,
against the indiscriminate spirit of destruction which
actuated the French Government, against the ravages
and anarchy which they had carried into unoffending
countries; against their habitual violation of solemn
treaties by fresh aggressions.

The concluding paragraphs of this memorable
despatch were conceived in a spirit of dictatorial
insolence, which seemed to have been caught from
the diplomacy of the French Revolution. His
Majesty was made to say, that although he did not
insist on the restoration of the legitimate monarchy
as affording the only possible security for peace, yet
that such an event would not only remove all obstacles to negotiation, but would ensure that tranquillity and security which the nations of Europe were
compelled to seek by arms. Finally it was intimated,
that the King had no confidence in the stability of
the Government with which he was invited to negotiate, and that a period of probation must be undergone before such confidence could be created.

It appears, from the letters of Pitt and Grenville, that the leading members of the Cabinet determined at once, and without deliberation, on rejecting the overture of the First Consul.* Bonaparte, however, was so desirous of obtaining a character for moderation, that he renewed his proposal in a formal manner, through Talleyrand, the Minister for Foreign Affairs. In this paper, the accomplished diplomatist, with the serene assurance which distinguished him through his long and varied life, reminded the English Secretary of State, that France, from the commencement of her revolution, had solemnly proclaimed her love of peace, her disinclination to conquest, and her respect for the independence of all governments. It was to the aggression of Europe in entering into a league to suppress her rising liberties, and not any offensive disposition on the part of France, that the war was to be attributed; France had only made use of the means she possessed for the maintenance of her independence, and had always resumed her pacific inclinations, when the powers of Europe desisted from invading her territory. Such assertions as these required no answer. The aggression of the German powers, in 1792, might have justified the occupation of Belgium, and the passage of the Rhine. The invasion of the Milanese and the other Italian possessions of Austria

* Pitt to Dundas, December 31 (the day on which the French despatch reached London).—*Cornwallis Correspondence*, vol. iii. p. 155. Lord Grenville, in writing to the Marquis of Buckingham, the day following, says, 'I need hardly tell you we shall say No. I am occupied in studying how to say it in the manner the least shocking to the numerous tribe of those who hate the French and the Jacobins, but would to-morrow sign a peace that would put us at the mercy of both.' He certainly did not succeed in this attempt, for moderate men were generally dissatisfied with the tone of the letter to Talleyrand. When the draft was sent to the King for his approval, it was returned with this observation written on the margin: 'In my opinion much too strong, but I suppose it must go.'—*Locker MSS.*, ex. rel. Hon. Henry Legge.

was justifiable by the subsequent war with that power. But what justification could be pleaded for the invasion and spoliation of the independent states of Italy? for the seizure of Switzerland, for the occupation of Egypt, and the massacre of an unoffending people? The French minister was more successful, when he censured the presumption of the English Court in offering to dictate, not only the form of government which the French nation should adopt, but the family which they should re-instate as their rulers. 'As well,' said he, 'might the Government of the Republic recommend England to return to the Commonwealth, which she had adopted in the last century, and to restore to the throne the legitimate race whom a revolution had removed from it.' Talleyrand did not fail to remind the Cabinet of London that they had twice, within a recent period, offered to treat with a Government which was certainly not entitled to a greater degree of confidence than the Government which had succeeded to power. This note, so plausible in many parts, and so unanswerable in some, produced a great impression in this country, and led men to hope that this weary war was drawing to a close. But the Government hastened to dissipate this delusion. In a short reply, Lord Grenville peremptorily refused to treat, and reiterated the most offensive passages of his former despatch. The French Government was treated like a culprit, whose professions of penitence and amendment were to be subjected to the test of experience. And it was plainly intimated that the only test which would prove satisfactory, was the abdication of the present ruler of France, and the unconditional restoration of the old dynasty.

It is known to the present generation, if the subsequent admission of Bonaparte himself is to be believed, that the proposal of peace at this time was altogether false and illusory. Bonaparte had never any regard to truth or honour; and no engagement which it was his interest to break would have bound him for a moment. His loose assertion many years after the transaction, that, in proposing peace on his accession to power, he merely meant to amuse the English Government, is entitled to very little credit. He would rather admit that his advances were fraudulent, than that they had been defeated by a contumelious repulse. If it was his interest, in 1801, to conclude a temporary peace with Great Britain, that he might have time to confirm his power, and prepare for the renewal of war on a scale of increased magnitude and efficiency, it was still more his interest to obtain a respite from warfare in 1800, when the consular chair, which he had set up on the first stage of his progress to the throne, was surrounded by foes and traitors. His object was to dissolve the confederacy which the naval triumphs, the influence and the wealth of England had arrayed against France. A peace must have been attended with that immmediate consequence, and a peace would cost nothing; for whatever the terms might be, they would be respected so long only as it suited the French ruler to respect them.

The overtures of the Consular Government, which
<small>Lord Grenville's speech.</small> had already agitated the country with a conflict of opinion, were discussed in Parliament with a vigour which had seldom animated the debates of either House since the earlier days of the French Revolution. Lord Grenville, in a speech of great length, reviewed the history of the war from its commencement, for the purpose of showing, that on the part of France it had been a series of aggressions on the independence of other nations, and that the policy of Bonaparte in particular was that of unscrupulous conquest, and perfidious contempt of those countries which had sought to conciliate his forbearance. These assertions were, in the main, indis-

putable. They had been repeatedly made, and their reiteration now could only point to the conclusion that no peace could be made with Bonaparte; and as Bonaparte had only pursued with greater vigour and success than his predecessors the unvarying policy of the Revolution, it seemed to follow, that, in the contemplation of the King's Government, there was no security for peace with France but the restoration of the monarchy. Lord Grenville's audience, however, needed no persuasion to support the prosecution of a war which they had always favoured, and which now, for the first time, showed a promise of success.

In the Commons the question was debated with all the power of the House. Dundas, Whitbread, and Canning, who now aspired to the foremost rank in Parliament; together with Erskine, who on this occasion spoke with an effect which his parliamentary efforts seldom attained, successively addressed the House. Pitt himself followed, and, like his colleagues in the Upper House, laboured to prove that the French had always been the aggressors. In reply to the obvious remark, that this was as true in 1796 and in 1797, as it was in 1799, and yet we had twice proposed peace to the ambitious and faithless Government of the Republic, the minister said that the people were in those years staggering under a weight of debt produced by the war, and that before they could be persuaded to bear new burdens, it was necessary to convince them that terms could not be obtained. This was very much the ground on which the Directory had repulsed the first mission of Lord Malmesbury. They said, that the only object of the British Government, in proposing terms of peace, was to deceive their own people, and by pretending to demonstrate that negotiation was impracticable, to extort further supplies for continuing the war. A great part of the speech consisted of a long and bitter invective against

[margin: Debate in the Commons.]

Bonaparte; and it wound up with the usual prediction that the exhausted condition of the enemy, and the failure of his resources, must soon terminate the war. The minister had been urged to make one of his highest oratorical efforts by the presence of his great antagonist, who had on this occasion quitted his retirement, at St. Ann's Hill, to support the cause of peace, of which he had, from the commencement of the war, been the consistent champion. Fox, invigorated by abstinence from political conflict, and from the still more wearying excitement of play, threw himself upon his rival with all the force and fire of earlier days. In a few rapid sentences he held up to just derision the shallow confidence with which the minister, untaught by the repeated failures of his prognostications, still persevered in assigning a period, within which the enemy must certainly come to the end of his resources. He was not so successful in his attempt to extenuate the outrages of the French democracy. He admitted that their successive rulers had been as bad as the worst despots the world had seen. But they had only followed the evil traditions of the old Government. 'If,' he said, 'they had overrun countries and ravaged them; if they had ruined and dethroned sovereigns; if they had even fraternised with the people of foreign nations—they had acted upon Bourbon principles, and accomplished their exploits in the Bourbon manner.' He argued with more point, that if former acts of injustice and rapine were sufficient reasons for rejecting all friendly overtures from guilty nations, how could we justify our alliances with Russia and Austria, whose spoliation of Poland had been justly stigmatised as the highest public crime of modern times. 'But,' said Fox, 'I am arguing before an assembly which is prepared to vote for the address as proposed by the minister; and which would have been prepared with equal submission, but far more alacrity, to support

an address which should have approved an opposite
policy.' Few of his hearers could have disputed this
assertion; but the address was, nevertheless, carried
by a majority of more than four to one.*

An argument against the good faith of a proposal
may be inferred from the terms of the proposal in
itself; but it is impossible to conceive of any circumstances in which a belligerent is justified in refusing to listen to the proposal of his enemy on the
assumption that he is not in earnest. The truth
appears to have been that the ministers, elated by the
signal and unwonted success of the allied arms, believed that the fortune of war had at length taken a
turn; and looking at the domestic changes in France,
had hurried to the conclusion that democracy had
run its course. England was already mistress of the
seas; and another campaign, it was hoped, would enable the military powers of the Continent to recover
their strength; would repair the shaken thrones and
principalities, and reconcile the French to the restoration of their monarchy. It was thought by some
that Bonaparte's rule would be as transitory as the
rule of the ordinary men whom the Revolution had
hitherto raised to the surface; by others, that he
was only preparing the way for the restoration of
legitimate monarchy. While the English ministers
were rejecting the advances of Bonaparte as a
person with whom they could not deign to treat, the
exiled heir of the French throne was opening a cor-

---

* 262 against 64. 'About this time the Count d'Artois came up secretly, and had a long audience with Pitt, and next night with the King for two hours, and expressed himself delighted with the sterling intelligence, morals and benevolence of the King and his ministers. He dined at Lord Grenville's to meet Pitt, Windham, and Wickham. Pitt said he hoped to see the day when England should have the honour to [restore] Louis the Eighteenth to the throne of France—that though future wars might happen, we should have the satisfaction of having done our duty.'—Lady Harcourt's *Diary*, 1798. MSS.

respondence with him, as the potent and trustworthy instrument through whom the restoration of the monarchy might be effected.

The Government, so prompt in refusing to entertain any proposal for peace, had no military project of their own, and had no other present view in carrying on the war than the grant of a subsidy to Austria. On the 13th of February, a message from the Crown announced that treaties were in progress with the princes of the German Empire; and five hundred thousand pounds were demanded as an immediate advance upon a subsidy of two millions and a half for the several powers which had engaged to perform the military duties of the alliance. England reserved no voice in the conduct or particular object of the war. It was enough for her that war was to be waged against the French. She would prefer that Europe should never lay down arms until the Bourbons were brought back to Paris; but if that could not be done, English money was well laid out in paying the Emperor of Austria to defend his own territory, or even to extend his dominions. Such was the sum and substance of the triumphant answer with which Mr. Pitt silenced those who ventured to ask what benefit this country could derive from aiding the imperial court in the pursuit of those selfish objects which had caused the rupture of the last alliance, and the failure of its common purpose? The security of England against Jacobinism, according to Mr. Pitt, was involved in an Austrian campaign on the Rhine, and the restoration of Austrian rule in Italy. The vaunt of Chatham that he conquered America in Germany was no rhetorical flight. It was the exposition of a great plan by a statesman who was master of the policy of war. The elder Pitt knew the use of money in war, and was never backward in employing the resources of this country in aid of an ally, when such aid was required for a definite object; but he invariably denounced the practice of carrying on a great war by a system of subsidies. He saw this country reduced to a state of military impotence by a perseverance in that system; and the defence of the island itself against imminent invasion entrusted to foreign mercenaries. The English millions lavished on foreign armies since the commencement of the revolutionary war had been wholly wasted; in no single instance had any intelligible object been proposed, or any advantage, however momentary, obtained by this expenditure. It seemed to be asserted and accepted as a sufficient reason for this outlay that the country could afford it. In this very year, a year of scarcity, and the seventh of the war, a loan of eighteen millions was readily subscribed at an interest of four and three-quarters per cent. In addition to this, the Bank of England advanced a sum of three millions for six years, without interest, in consideration of the renewal of their charter for twenty-one years; a remarkable proof of the increasing wealth and commercial enterprise of the country.

One of those attempts which are so frequently made, but so rarely with success, on the lives of kings and rulers, called forth a new demonstration of loyalty and personal regard for the Sovereign, which was not without significance and value at this season. The King, in accordance with many good English customs, his observance of which went far to endear him to the people, frequently attended the two great theatres, where the matchless productions of the English stage were represented by actors worthy of their vocation. On the 15th of May, their Majesties went to Drury Lane Theatre. The King had no sooner entered the box, and advanced to acknowledge the welcome with which he was usually received, than a pistol was discharged at him by a man who sprang up on a

Attempt to shoot the King.

bench in the pit. Happily a person near had seen the movement in time to catch the assassin's arm, just as the trigger was pulled. It thus happened that of two large balls with which the pistol was charged, one struck the wainscot a foot and a half above the King's head, and the other passed through the curtain some inches higher. The King, who saw the flash and heard the report, turned to Lord Chesterfield, the Master of the Horse, and said, 'There is a pistol fired; there may be another; stop the Queen.' He himself stood firm, and looked round the house with a composure very different from the hurry which usually marked his demeanour. When the Queen advanced in alarm, he desired her to stay a moment—'there was a squib.' 'A squib,' said Her Majesty, 'I heard the word pistol, and the report.' 'Squib or pistol,' answered the King, 'the danger is now over, and you may come forward and make your courtesy.' For a few seconds there was an awful silence, until the audience were assured that the King was unhurt. Then burst forth cries of 'Seize the traitor; tear him to pieces!' In the midst of the uproar, the stage-manager came forward and announced that the man who had fired the shot was in custody. He had been dragged over the barrier which separated the orchestra from the pit, and hurried to the back of the stage, to protect him from the rage of the spectators. The curtain then drew up; but the performance was not suffered to commence, until the loyal anthem had been sung in chorus by the whole company.

James Hadfield, who made this attempt on the King's life, was a working silversmith, and a discharged trooper from the Fifteenth Light Dragoons. On his examination before the magistrate, and, subsequently, before the Privy Council, on the charge of treason, it appeared that he had served under the Duke of York, in Belgium; and that he had been severely wounded in the head at Lincelles. He denied that he had fired at the King, and maintained that he had fired, by design, over the King's head. He said that his object was his own death; that he was tired of life, but had not resolution enough to commit suicide. On further investigation, his former comrades in the regiment, as well as his fellow-workmen in trade, came forward to prove that Hadfield was considered insane. He was committed for trial on the capital charge, and notwithstanding the evidence as to his insanity, few persons were disposed to believe that Hadfield was not a responsible agent.

The trial was one of extraordinary solemnity. It was a trial at *bar*—that is, before the full Court of King's Bench, instead of a single judge, according to the regular administration of the criminal law. The facts were not disputed, the defence being that the prisoner was insane. Erskine defended the prisoner; and the case is remarkable as constituting the leading precedent in this branch of criminal law. At this time, the doctrine of exemption from responsibility for criminal actions, though not altogether novel, was obscure and ill-defined. Judges and juries were not informed either as to the kind or the degree of mental unsoundness which should entitle a man to impunity, who had killed or maimed a fellow-creature; and the opinion, even, was widely prevalent, that the protection of life and limb from murderous assaults, did not admit of madness as an excuse * for the commission of such outrages. The argument of

---

* Lady Harcourt, in reference to the case of Hadfield, makes these observations: 'Madmen are deterred by terror, and, at least, the executing him would prevent future pretence to madness; and, at any rate, why save a man whose crime deserves punishment, if sane, *and, if mad, is a nuisance to society.*'—MSS. This may seem the extreme opinion of a Court lady, transported with resentment at an attack on the Sovereign; but when the Bill of the Attorney-General (suggested by Hadfield's case), for providing for the custody of persons acquitted on the ground of insanity, was debated in the Commons, Windham expressed a doubt whether an offender, if insane, should not be punished for the sake of example.

Erskine was the first to place this question on the high ground of reason and humanity, from which it has never since been shaken. He contended, not that general evidence of insanity was a sufficient answer to the charge, but that if he rebutted the presumption of motive, which the law would infer from an unprovoked assault, by proof of the absence of express malice, and the existence of a delusion which probably extended to the act charged in the indictment, the prisoner was not guilty. In support of this proposition, to which the Court assented, Erskine proved by the evidence of Mr. Cline, one of the first surgeons of the day, that the prisoner's brain had been permanently injured by a sabre-cut in the head, the certain effect of which would be the derangement of his intellect. To confirm this theory, it was shown, by abundant proof, that the prisoner laboured under delusions. His mind wandered in the mazes of religion. At one time he fancied that his life was to be taken as a propitiatory sacrifice for mankind. At another he uttered horrible blasphemies, although habitually his thoughts took the direction of extreme piety and reverence. A few days before he shot at the King's box, he attempted the life of his infant child; and, about the same time, being at a public-house, when His Majesty's name was indecently mentioned, he left the house with loud expressions of indignation, crying, 'God save the King!' The Court had been very unfavourable to the prisoner during the case for the prosecution; but when they heard Erskine's argument, and the evidence in support of it, the Chief Justice interposed, and said he was satisfied of the prisoner's insanity at the time the act was committed. The Attorney-General, upon this intimation, readily consented to an acquittal; and soon after introduced the act under which prisoners acquitted on the ground of insanity are detained in custody.

The attempt on the King's life called forth a general expression of loyalty and attachment to his person, such as had not been witnessed since his recovery in 1789. The secondary reasons which had contributed to the demonstration of joy and relief on that occasion, were not diminished in force by the lapse of time. Whatever difference of opinion might exist as to the positive claims of George the Third upon the affections of his subjects, all friends of the monarchy were agreed in praying that the day might be far distant, when the heir-apparent should take his place. At the birthday drawing-room on the 4th of June, the principal members of the Opposition, who had rarely attended at Court since the dismissal of the Coalition, came to offer their respects and congratulations.* {Public expression of loyalty.}

Committees of both Houses were engaged during the session in devising means for the mitigation of distress, owing to a partial failure of the wheat crop in the past and the present years. Many persons were found to recommend sumptuary laws; restrictions in the use of wheat in distilleries and other processes; interference with the trade of millers, and other rude remedies which, if they have any effect at all, have only a mischievous effect. Parliament had the good sense to reject all these schemes. The only measure of legislation which they adopted was an act to prevent the sales of fine wheaten bread†—a measure, which was deemed of such importance, that it was passed through all its stages in both Houses at one sitting. The folly of some of the judges did more than all the acts of incendiaries to create popular discontent, and to increase the scarcity.

---

* Fox did not appear; but even his absence, according to Lady Harcourt, appears to have been caused by accident.—MSS.

† It was said that in consequence of this act, the consumption of bread in the metropolis was reduced by one-sixth.—*Second Report of the Commons' Committee*.

Some informers took advantage of the obsolete laws against forestalling, to prosecute the corn factors, a useful body of tradesmen, through whose agency the foreign trade in corn was chiefly carried on. Mr. Rusby, a partner in one of the principal corn houses in the City, was tried before Lord Kenyon, for having, in the course of his business, bought and re-sold wheat in the same market, an act, which, under an old statute of Edward the Sixth, constituted the offence of *regrating*. He was convicted under the eager direction of the Chief Justice, who told the jury that by their verdict they had conferred almost the greatest benefit upon the country that ever was conferred by any jury. The act of Edward, which included forestalling and engrossing as well as regrating, had been repealed early in the present reign.* But the legislature, while intending to abolish an offence, which could only be considered an offence in a state of primitive society, hardly removed from a state of barter, omitted to enact in the usual form, that no person should in future be prosecuted on such charges. And it was afterwards held in Westminster Hall, that two of the offences named in the statute of Edward, namely, forestalling and engrossing, were still indictable at common law. On the question of regrating, the definition of which is simply the difference between wholesale and retail trade, Kenyon could get only one of the puisne judges of his court to support his opinion, that re-selling a commodity for a profit in the market where it had been bought, was a misdemeanour. The Court of King's Bench being thus equally divided on the point of law, judgment in the case of Rusby was arrested. But the effects of Kenyon's ignorance and folly were not easily repaired. Corn factors were for a long time deterred from following their useful

* 12 Geo. III. c. 71.

business; and the starving multitude were taught by authority to add one other delusion to the creations of ignorance and want.

The session which had commenced with a haughty rejection of the pacific overtures of the French Government, was not brought to a close before the English Ministry had learned to alter their tone. Disappointed in his hope of peace, if he seriously entertained it, Bonaparte made immediate preparations for such a prosecution of the war, as was little expected. Moreau, next to Bonaparte himself, the best General which the Revolution had produced, retained his command upon the Rhine. The French army succeeded once more in crossing the river on the 25th of April, and, before the end of June, had overrun Bavaria, occupied Munich, and driven the Austrian General behind the Inn. On the other hand, Genoa, the last possession of the French in Italy, after a close investment by sea and land for nearly two months, was surrendered by Massena. Bonaparte himself, with an army of reserve, had watched the campaign in Germany and Italy. The course of events determined him upon making a great effort for the recovery of Italy, the first of his conquests. He made a feint as if it had been his intention to assemble an army at Dijon for the relief of Genoa; his real purpose never was suspected; nor was it likely to enter into the calculations of an enemy, however well-informed. Bonaparte's intention was to cross the Alps by the Great St. Bernard Mountain, and so descend upon the plains in the rear of the Austrian army before Genoa. This great enterprise was accomplished in four days; and the Imperialists, who, up to that time, had derided the idea of the French army of reserve as an impossibility and an empty vaunt, were startled by the appearance of the corps of Lannes before Ivria. Even then, the Imperial Generals regarded this as a detached

movement to divert them from the great operation in
which they were engaged. They would not believe
that a French army fully equipped, under Bonaparte
himself, had passed the Alps. The fall of Ivria even
failed to convince Melas that the French force in his
rear consisted of more than a single division, which
he could easily crush. The Austrian Commander-in-
Chief, however, removed his head-quarters to Turin,
when he heard that Bonaparte, reinforced by twenty
thousand men from the army of the Rhine, was
making rapid advances. Melas then sent orders to
Ott to raise the siege of Genoa, and to move by forced
marches with all his strength upon Pavia. But when
the order arrived, Ott was engaged in negotiating
the terms of the capitulation under which Genoa was
to be surrendered to him. Ott, without knowledge
of the urgency which had dictated the peremptory
order of his chief, delayed obedience until he had
completed the great work in which the military
energies of Austria had been so long engaged. By
this delay, not only was the garrison of Genoa,
amounting to eight thousand men, enabled to join
the French army, but the chance which might have
remained of arresting their triumphant progress was
lost. Bonaparte, having defeated an Austrian corps
which disputed his passage of the Ticino, entered
Milan on the 2nd of June, and re-established the
Cisalpine Republic. After remaining six days in the
capital of Lombardy, and having supplied the deficiencies of his army from the Austrian magazines in
the city, Bonaparte resumed his march. The time
had now arrived when the fate of Italy must be
decided by a pitched battle. Melas, satisfied that
Piedmont was no longer defensible, determined upon
holding the line between the Po and the Apennines,
making a stand at Alessandria, and ultimately falling
back upon Mantua, if Alessandria should not be
tenable. Ott, after some sharp skirmishes, and an

engagement with Lannes at Montebello, effected a junction with Melas, whose force was thus increased to forty thousand men, including seven thousand cavalry. They were encamped before Alessandria, which was separated from the great plain of Marengo by the River Bormida. At daybreak on the 14th of June, the Austrians crossed the river, and attacked in force the village of Marengo, occupied by Victor's division, which, after an obstinate conflict, was dislodged and driven in confusion across the plain. The corps of Lannes next gave way, and, at three o'clock in the afternoon, the whole French army had fallen back upon their reserve five or six miles from the field of battle. Melas, far advanced in years, exhausted by the fatigues of the day, during which two horses had been killed under him, and believing the victory secured, retired from the field. Meanwhile, the French General had observed an important position, which the Austrian had overlooked. There the shattered battalions of the French army were reformed, and sent once more to the charge under the guidance of Dessaix, who had come up with his reserve. The French made a desperate effort to retrieve the fortune of the day. General Zach, who commanded in the absence of Melas, in the heat of pursuit, had pressed forward too far in advance of his supports; and the Austrian line staggered before the tremendous onset of the French led by Dessaix. Dessaix was killed at the head of his column; but the French rushed on, and, in a few minutes, the Austrian victory was changed into a hopeless rout. Zach surrendered with five thousand men, the remains of his division. Lannes was equally successful in another part of the field; and Victor, at the close of the day, re-occupied the village of Marengo, from which he had been driven headlong in the morning.

Melas, during the night, passed the Bormida with the remains of his army, and encamped once more before Alessandria. Bonaparte, on the following day, prepared to attack him, and his advanced guard crossed the river at dawn. The Austrian General saw the French army under the First Consul before him; in his rear was Suchet with a body of fresh troops, including the liberated garrison of Genoa. The old General's decision was soon taken. He sent a flag to the French camp; and in a few hours, a convention was signed. All the territory and fortified places of Northern Italy, with the exception of the country between the Mincio, Fosca Mestre, and the Po, which included Mantua, Peschiera, and Borgoforte, were ceded to the French. This treaty was ratified by the Court of Vienna.

It was Bonaparte's policy to detach Austria from the English alliance; and, with that view, he proposed to Melas a separate peace, on the basis of the treaty of Campo Formio, before the Imperial Government had approved the Convention of Alessandria. The Court of Vienna behaved with great duplicity on this occasion. Unwilling, on the one hand, to provoke the French dictator, they sent a diplomatic agent to Paris, whither Bonaparte had returned after the Convention of Alessandria; and this agent, the Count St. Julien, a general officer in the Austrian service, was the bearer of a letter from the Emperor, as his credential. But a few days before the battle of Marengo, Thugut, the Austrian minister, had concluded a convention with Lord Minto, by which, in consideration of a further advance of two millions by Great Britain, to be paid in instalments before the end of the year, the Austrian Government engaged to continue the war, and to enter into no separate treaty with France before the ensuing February. If, therefore, the treaty with France was hurried forward, they would lose the English money; whereas, if the negotiations could be delayed until the subsidy, or the greater part of it had been paid, they would

combine all the benefits which they ever expected to
derive from the English connection with the peace
which must eventually be concluded with France.
Meanwhile St. Julien, in pursuance of the power
conferred upon him by the Emperor's private letter,
had arranged the preliminaries of a peace at Paris,
and General Duroc was despatched to Vienna by the
Consular Government. But the bargain which had
been concluded with the British minister rendered it
necessary that the negotiation at Paris should be
disavowed; and accordingly, St. Julien, notwithstanding the Emperor's letter, was put under arrest
for acting without instructions, and Duroc was turned
back from the Austrian frontier. Baron Thugut at
the same time obtained the consent of Lord Minto to
a proposal which he addressed to the First Consul,
that Great Britain should be included in the negotiations for peace. In accordance with this intimation,
Otto, the French commissioner in London, for the
exchange of prisoners, was instructed to open a communication with the English Government. Lord
Grenville expressed his readiness to send a plenipotentiary to the Congress about to sit, and named his
brother, Mr. Thomas Grenville,* as the person designated to represent the interests of Great Britain.
But the Frenchman demanded certain preliminaries
before the treaty should be opened. He required a
naval armistice analogous to the military armistice
which had been made with Austria. The blockade
of the French forts was to be raised, or at least suspended; the seas were to be free to the commerce as
well as to the armed ships of the belligerents; French
ships were to be permitted to furnish supplies to the
starving garrison of Malta; and, lastly, six frigates

---

* Pitt had applied, in the first instance, to Lord Malmesbury to undertake the mission; but it seems, that Malmesbury was not disposed to be sent for the third time on a fruitless errand.—*Malmesbury Correspondence,* vol. iv. p. 1.

were to be admitted into the port of Alexandria. A long correspondence ensued, and ultimately all the terms were agreed to by the English Government, except the last. But the right of sending relief to the army in Egypt was insisted on as a condition *sine quâ non*; and upon this point the negotiation was broken off.

It is difficult to understand how the most sanguine diplomatist could have hoped for any other result from a negotiation commenced in such a spirit. But the English Government, which, in January, would not for a moment listen to a proposal from the First Consul, was content, in August, to discuss for several weeks a proposition, the illusory character of which was sufficiently apparent. Even the tone of the French correspondence seemed to deride the credulous or the pusillanimous eagerness for peace, which could seriously entertain such unreasonable demands. The progress of this negotiation—if it can be called a negotiation—developed a strong difference of opinion in the Cabinet as to the policy of the war. A few days before the correspondence was closed, a representation in writing as to the views of his colleagues was laid before the First Minister by Mr. Dundas, the Secretary of State, who had the chief management of the war.

This remarkable paper stated, that, in the opinion of some members of the Government, the only solid hope of peace was in the restoration of the Bourbons. Others, without going that extreme length, nevertheless, maintained that no peace should be made with a revolutionary Government, and that the existing Government of France was of that character. A third section were for treating with the Consular Government, but only in conjunction with the Emperor. And there was still another division of a Cabinet comprising only eleven members, which desired that England should make a separate treaty.

These differences, Dundas added, were not theoretical, but practical, presenting themselves in every discussion, either on the prosecution of war, or the prospect of peace; and his paper concluded by an earnest hope that Mr. Pitt would take the representation into his most serious consideration before it is too late. There were almost as many opinions as there were men; and if the fact that such a paper was drawn up and presented to the head of the Government by one of its members did not rest on undoubted authority,* it would have seemed incredible that such a representation should be needed. Did the Cabinet Council ever deliberate on the conduct of the war, or the question of peace? Did the Cabinet ministers reserve their opinions in the presence of their chief, and disclose them only to each other? Strange as it may appear, the truth was that, although there were meetings of the Cabinet, Pitt rarely consulted his colleagues, and his colleagues rarely communicated with each other.† Grenville was the only member of the Cabinet who asserted himself, and Grenville, by his general ability, decision of character, and force of will, for some time exercised a power second only to that of Pitt himself. The other ministers were little more than heads of departments. The Whig lords kept very much to themselves, and were always in an attitude of semi-opposition. The Chancellor was so notoriously false and time-serving that nobody trusted him. Windham, with many great qualities, lacked common sense. Dundas, though an active and useful minister,

---

* Earl Stanhope's *Life of Pitt*, vol. iii. p. 242.

† 'Pitt and Dundas are most allied; Portland, Loughborough, Spencer, who came over together, are distinct; while probably Lord Liverpool (mistakably supposed the King's man) stands alone. To prove how little intimacy there is, he (Lord L.) asked General H. the other day, who was that pretty woman speaking to the Queen? He said, "My Lord, do you not know Lady Grenville?"' — COUNTESS HARCOURT's *Diary*. MSS.

derived his influence from the personal friendship of Pitt.

The paper drawn up by Dundas, for the information of his chief, if it meant anything, meant that no peace could be concluded by the Ministry as then constituted. Pitt himself appears to have adhered to neither of the four parties in the Cabinet. He had by turns favoured every opinion; but he always regarded the termination of the war as preferable to either. A fortnight before the date of Dundas's paper, he had expressed his willingness to concede the naval armistice, although the benefit of such a measure must be wholly on the side of France. But he said the alternative was a renewal of the war between France and Austria, with the probable result of new military disasters terminating in the ruin of our only ally.*

Before the correspondence with Otto was brought to a close, Malta, after a siege of two years, surrendered to the English. A vigorous attempt had been made early in the year to relieve the garrison; but Nelson, anticipating such an attempt, took it upon himself, according to his practice, when he thought any great service was to be performed, to quit his station without orders, and cruise in search of the expected squadron. The result was that he fell in with the 'Généreux,' one of the French ships of the line, which had escaped from the Nile, convoying three frigates, and a corvette laden with troops and supplies for Malta. After a short engagement, the line-of-battle ship and one of the frigates were taken; the other ships escaped to Toulon. The 'Guillaume Tell,' the last of the French seventy-fours, which had fought in the bay of Aboukir, was captured by three English frigates, in attempting an escape from the harbour of Malta.

* Letter to the Chancellor, 5th September, 1800.—Lord Stanhope's *Life*, vol. iii. p. 240.

The armistice of Alessandria had expired on the 7th of September; but the Austrians, not being prepared to resume the campaign, and still hoping that the necessity for a renewal of hostilities might be averted, were content to purchase an extension of the truce for forty-five days by the surrender of the great fortresses of Ulm, Philipsburgh, and Ingoldstadt. As a further earnest of his desire for peace, the Emperor dismissed Baron Thugut, the minister whose counsel had always been for war, and appointed in his place the Count Cobentzel, who had negotiated the treaty of Campo Formio. Cobentzel himself went to Paris, and, after having been subjected to an ebullition of the insolence and ill-humour which the ruler of France frequently vented on the representatives of foreign powers who would not readily submit to his dictation, was referred to Joseph Bonaparte at Luneville, where the formalities of a conference had for some time been observed. The policy of the First Consul, with regard to negotiation, was the same as that which commended itself to the most prudent and practical section of the English Cabinet. Each desired to treat on a separate basis: Bonaparte, because he thought he could impose his own terms on Austria unsupported by Great Britain; the English ministers, because they had little faith either in the resources or the stability of their ally, and were, moreover, of opinion that England could obtain better terms than if her claims were connected with German interests. The Court of Vienna, on the other hand, were sensible of the advantage to be derived from the support of England at the conference, as well as of the impolicy of giving offence to their best friend by a breach of the recent compact, which precluded either party from making a peace, or even accepting an overture without the concurrence of the other. Above all things, the Emperor desired peace; and if peace could be purchased by the sacrifice of British connection, he was content; but he was not so rash as to make the sacrifice, until he had secured his object. Cobentzel, therefore, proposed a joint negotiation; and when this was refused, he was instructed to propose a secret negotiation, but that a British minister should be present at Luneville. But this mean and shallow subterfuge was rejected with contempt; and the Austrian minister, being prepared with no other offer, the conference lingered in suspense until the 20th of November, when the armistice expired.

The military power of France was very different to what it had been in the preceding year under the incompetent administration of the Directory. Armies, estimated from four hundred thousand to nearly half a million of men, well found, and well commanded, were actually in the field. The grand army of the Rhine under the renowned Moreau, mustered one hundred and forty thousand. In Italy, Brune commanded ninety thousand. Other corps under Augereau, Macdonald, Suchet, and Murat, were detached in different parts. Austria had a disposable force of nearly equal amount; but none of her Generals were men of repute. The great army of one hundred and thirty thousand men opposed to Moreau was led by a youth, who had neither reputation nor experience, the Archduke John, whose only qualification for command was royal birth. Bellegarde, an old Marshal of the Empire, was at the head of one hundred and twenty thousand men in Italy. Among the minor corps was a well-appointed army of twenty thousand British troops under Sir Ralph Abercromby, which had left England in June, and had been kept mostly on board their transports in the Mediterranean, ready to act upon any point when their services might be needed.

Notwithstanding the advanced season, the French armies were in motion a few days after the termina-

tion of the armistice. The army of Italy and the
army of the Rhine were to march on Vienna by
different routes. The one was to cross the Mincio
and the Adige, proceeding by the Alps; the other
was to cross the Inn, and proceed by the valley of the
Danube. Moreau marched towards the Inn on the
28th of November, driving the advanced posts of the
Austrians before him. It was, however, the intention
of the Austrians to defend the line of the river, and
to stop the progress of the French. On the 3rd of
December, in a heavy fall of snow, the Austrian
columns advanced with a heavy train of artillery,
which, with the baggage, had to be conveyed along
a single road through the dense forest of Hohenlinden.
Before they could emerge from this perilous position,
General Richepanse, with a body of infantry, dashed
into the forest, and attacked the guard of the train,
consisting of three battalions of Hungarian Grena-
diers. After a short struggle the guard gave way,
and a scene of irretrievable confusion immediately
took place. A panic seized upon the artillerymen.
The drivers cut the traces of the carriages, and fled.
Eighty-seven pieces of cannon and three hundred
waggons were abandoned. The artillery being some
distance in advance of the march, the effect of their
flight was, that they fell back upon the central
columns which were defiling through the forest,
throwing them into disorder, which soon ended in a
tumultuous retreat. Meanwhile, the left wing of the
Austrian army was held in check; and the right, after
maintaining for some time an obstinate struggle with
several French divisions, likewise retreated when they
found that the disaster of the main body rendered
their efforts useless. After a loss of twenty-five
thousand men and a hundred guns, the Austrians
effected their retreat across the Inn, and fell back
to cover Vienna. The Archduke Charles, who had
led the Austrian army on the Rhine in the former

campaign with so much ability and success, was hastily recalled to the command. But it was too late. Though, in several minor affairs since the battle of Hohenlinden, the advantage had been on the side of the Archduke, it was hopeless to withstand the triumphant progress of the French armies. To save his capital, the Emperor was compelled to sue for peace; and on the 25th of December an armistice was concluded at Steyar, by which the fortified places in the Tyrol, in Franconia, and Bavaria, with all their military stores, were surrendered to the French. On the 16th of January, the army of Italy under Marshal Bellegarde also obtained a suspension of arms, by the cession of all the strongholds except Mantua, which was subsequently given up at the peremptory demand of Bonaparte. By the treaty of Luneville signed on the 9th of February, the boundary of the Rhine was again yielded to France; and the Adige was assigned as the limit of the Austrian dominions in Italy. The Emperor apologised, in a letter addressed to the King, for negotiating a separate peace;* but it was readily admitted that, in this instance, no imputations of bad faith could fairly attach to the conduct of the Court of Vienna.

England was thus, once more, left alone, for she was encumbered, rather than aided, by such helpless allies as Portugal, Naples, and Turkey. Her precarious alliance with Russia had been already changed into avowed hostility. Bonaparte had found little difficulty in gaining over the wayward barbarian who ruled at St. Petersburg. Paul had been much incensed at the result of the expedition to Holland, and was easily persuaded that his troops had been sacrificed by the jealousy or incapacity of the British Commanders. He would not

Isolation of England.

* T. Grenville to Marquis of Buckingham.—*Courts and Cabinets of George the Third*, vol. iii. p. 117.

take any part in the ensuing campaign. Since the battle of Marengo, the autocrat had regarded the First Consul with feelings of admiration, not unmixed, perhaps, with fear. Bonaparte had agents at St. Petersburgh, well instructed, to foster these sentiments. He sent back the Russian prisoners taken in Holland. He flattered Paul with a promise of the island of Malta, to which the Czar preferred a claim as Grand Master of the Order of St. John of Jerusalem—a claim, which he alleged, not without reason, to have been admitted by the English Government.* While the Russian autocrat was in this temper, events took place, which either inflamed his anger, or furnished him with a pretext for hostile demonstrations against England. Since the commencement of the war, the right of searching neutral ships, either for the property of the enemy, or for contraband of war, had been rigorously enforced by the English cruisers. Some of the maritime nations, and especially the Baltic powers, contended for the qualification, that the neutral flag should cover the cargo, except contraband of war. This was the principle of the famous Armed Neutrality of 1780; a league intended to humble the naval superiority of Great Britain, but never carried into effect, and at length formally abandoned. The maxims of the Armed Neutrality were, nevertheless, just and reasonable, and have lately been adopted in their integrity by all the maritime powers of Europe, at the suggestion of England, France, and Russia. But, though the right of the belligerent to visit a neutral private ship on the high seas was the undoubted law of nations, the exercise of that right, with regard to a ship sailing

---

* We said that a convention to that effect had been signed. This was not the fact; but it seems clear, that he was promised the island; and that the promise would have been fulfilled, if he had not quarrelled with this country.—*Courts and Cabinets of George the Third*, vol. iii. pp. 101–3.

under a convoy, without the consent of the convoy, had frequently been disputed. On the only occasion on which this claim had been practically asserted by Great Britain, it was immediately resisted by force, and eventually led to a rupture with the neutral flag.* At the close of the year 1799, the captain of an English frigate stopped several merchantmen sailing under convoy of a Danish man-of-war. The Danish captain fired on one of the boats sent to examine the ship's papers. The English officer then desisted from his attempt, upon the understanding that Captain Van Dockum, the Dane, would proceed to Gibraltar, and report what had happened to Lord Keith, the English Admiral on the station. Van Dockum, having declared that he acted by the orders of his Court in refusing to permit his convoy to be visited, and declining to submit the question to the English Admiralty Court, the matter was referred by Lord Keith to his Government. The British minister at Copenhagen was instructed to demand an apology for the violence offered to the English flag, and a disavowal of the officer who had committed it. The Danish Government, however, justified the act of their officer, on the ground that the right of search did not extend to ships under convoy. While this affair was pending, another collision took place. The captain of the 'Freya,' another Danish frigate, having resisted an attempt to search some merchant ships under his convoy, an engagement took place, in which several men on both sides were killed. The Danish ships were captured and carried into the Downs. Lord Grenville having in vain demanded reparation for what he thought proper to term, 'a wanton and unprovoked attack on His Majesty's flag,' Lord Whitworth was despatched on a special mission to Copenhagen, and a fleet was at the same time

---

* The detention and capture of the Dutch merchantmen under the convoy of Admiral Byland. Ante, vol. ii. p. 391.

sent to threaten the Danish capital. The British envoy declared, that if the demands of his Court were not fully satisfied within a week, he should quit Copenhagen. But the Danes were not intimidated. Lord Whitworth had sought to demonstrate the absurdity of the Danish doctrine, with regard to the inviolability of convoy, by the argument, that any insignificant power which had any pretension to a flag might thus cover the whole commerce of the enemy. Count Bernstorff replied, that a fraudulent use of the flag would be a breach of neutrality; but that the possibility of an abuse of his right by a neutral, could not justify the belligerent in asserting his right of visit, when the merchantman was under the protection of a ship of the State. The Count, however, with real or affected moderation, proposed to refer the question to a mediator, and he named the Emperor of Russia, a potentate who was notoriously incapable of forming a sound opinion on any subject, and who made no secret at that time of his anger against England. The Danish minister, in his reply to the Ambassador, had only repeated the argument with which he had met the former application for redress by Mr. Merry, the British Chargé d'Affaires. Nevertheless, Lord Whitworth changed his tone, and, instead of leaving Copenhagen, he made a conciliatory reply. He declined, indeed, the mediation of Paul; but he expressed his belief that a candid and friendly discussion would remove all the causes of misunderstanding. Two days after the date of this note, a convention was signed, by which the question, as to the right of searching ships under convoy, was indefinitely postponed. The 'Freya,' and the vessels under her convoy, were to be immediately restored; and the damage done to the Danish frigate was to be repaired in an English port. The Danish convoys were to be discontinued until the question in dispute should be decided by a definitive treaty. Such was the strange termination of this dispute. An envoy of the first rank, backed by a powerful squadron, had been sent to exact immediate satisfaction for an outrage alleged to have been offered to the British flag; and, after a short correspondence, in which the facts remained unchanged, the envoy, instead of obtaining satisfaction, makes reparation to the offending party, and the real question at issue is evaded by mutual consent.

The Emperor Paul, far from regarding these transactions with the equanimity of a mediator, resented the conduct of England as an attack on the independence and neutrality of the Baltic powers. On the 29th of August, the same day on which the convention had been signed at Copenhagen by the plenipotentiaries of England and Denmark, Paul, in violation of an express article in the treaty of 1793, laid an embargo on all English property within his dominions. He subsequently ordered the crews of three hundred British merchant ships to be made prisoners, and marched into the interior. This was followed by a renewal of the Armed Neutrality on the principles of 1780, with the additional term, that ships under convoy were exempted from the right of search. Sweden, whose merchant flag had lately been abused in the grossest manner by British cruisers,[*] entered into a convention with Russia on these terms.

Denmark, which at this time had an extensive carrying trade, was unwilling to risk the neutrality of

---

[*] Some officers and men belonging to the blockading squadron off Barcelona had stopped a Swedish galliot called the 'Hoffnung,' and compelled the crew to carry them and their boats under the neutral flag into the harbour, where they cut out and captured two Spanish frigates lying at anchor. This lawless act had nearly embroiled the Swedes with the Court of Spain, which sought (contrary to the well-established principles of international law) to hold them responsible for the treachery of which they had been the helpless instruments.

her flag, but was ultimately compelled by the pressure
of the Courts of Petersburg and Berlin, to accede to
this treaty. Prussia herself was not a party to the
league; but her hostility to Great Britain had been
sufficiently manifest on a recent occasion. A British
cruiser had captured, at the mouth of the Texel, a
Prussian merchantman, containing contraband, and,
forced by stress of weather, had carried her into the
neutral port of Cuxhaven. The Government of
Hamburgh, having, in these circumstances, hesitated to deliver up the ship at the requisition of the
Prussian authorities, a Prussian force immediately
occupied Cuxhaven. The ship was then restored,
and Lord Carysfort, the English Ambassador at
Berlin, remonstrated strongly against the presence
of a Prussian army in a territory, which he plainly
intimated could have been entered only with a view
to the occupation of Hanover. The Prussian minister made a haughty reply, and refused to withdraw
the troops.

The British Government, on being informed of the
league of the Baltic, immediately retali- British
ated, by an Order in Council, laying an embargo.
embargo on all the ships of Russia, Sweden, and
Denmark, in the ports of the United Kingdom.

A few weeks before the formation of the Northern
League, in immediate subserviency to the interests
of France, the Consular Government had accom-
modated the long-standing differences between the
French Republic and the United States of America,
by a treaty based on the principle of free ships, free
goods; a doctrine highly favourable to a maritime
neutral, but one which Great Britain had always resisted as contrary to the law of nations, and dero-
gatory to her belligerent rights. Thus, by a policy
which showed him to be not less a statesman than a
general, the First Consul made France once more
appear as the generous ally of the young Republic,

of which she had been the earliest friend and benefactor; while England was exhibited in the invidious light of an arrogant and selfish monopolist, who could not carry on war without encroaching to the uttermost on the commerce and navigation of neutral states.

But France, the military dictator of Europe, combined with the confederated rivals and enemies of England to reduce her maritime supremacy, was not so terrible to the great minister of England, as a domestic misfortune which had befallen the country, and for which he saw no adequate remedy.* He was under the apprehension that the country was about to be visited by famine. Such a fear could hardly have taken possession of his mind, had not his health been broken, and his nerves relaxed. There was, indeed, no sufficient ground for such alarm. A partial deficiency in two succeeding harvests could not fail to be felt under a restricted trade in corn. The price of wheat had risen to upwards of six pounds a quarter, a price with which the people became familiar during the long succeeding years of war and protective duties, but which had never yet been attained. In 1795-6, a year of scarcity, corn was seventy-seven shillings a quarter, and importation was largely resorted to. But the prevalent opinion was, that nothing could be more dangerous than trusting to the foreign market, to supply the deficiency of the home; and the monetary disturbances of 1797, which led to the suspension of cash payments, was attributed, in a great degree, to the export of bullion in exchange for foreign corn in the preceding year. The pressure on the home market, therefore, far from suggesting the expediency of lowering the barriers against foreign produce, seemed to show the necessity of raising and strengthening them. By the

* Pitt to Addington, 8th Oct., 1800.—EARL STANHOPE's *Life of Pitt*, vol. iii. p. 244.

Act of 1773, the ports were opened to foreign corn, when the price was forty-eight shillings. But in 1791, when the increase of population rendered it the more necessary to enlarge the area of produce, the standard of protection was raised to fifty-four shillings; and so steady was the progress of perverse legislation with reference to the question, that in 1814, the last year but one of the war, the prohibition upon foreign wheat was continued until the quotation of the home market was eighty shillings. The capacity of the soil for increased production had not yet been developed in proportion to the increase of population. Until the beginning of the present century, when the first census of the people was taken, the only authentic records of the population were the parish registers. These are very imperfect; but the growing pressure on the means of subsistence during the reign of George the Third, caused mainly by the rapid progress of manufactures, is shown by the enormous multiplication of Inclosure Acts. In the year 1710, Parliament, for the first time, sanctioned the cultivation of common land. Only one other act of this description was solicited in the reign of Anne. In the thirteen years of George the First, sixteen acts only were passed; in the thirty-three years of George the Second, there were two hundred and twenty-six. But from 1760 to 1796, no less than fifteen hundred and thirty-two Inclosure Acts had been passed. The extent of land thus inclosed is not ascertained; but it is estimated, in round numbers, at three hundred and forty thousand acres in the half century before the accession of George the Third; and at nearly three millions in the thirty-six succeeding years.* But a small portion

---

* *First Report of Commons' Committee on Waste Land,* 1797. They recommend the immediate addition of one hundred and fifty to three hundred thousand acres 'to the land now in cultivation, as the only effectual means of preventing that importation of

of the land so reclaimed could be adapted to the cultivation of wheat without an outlay which high prices only could remunerate. A large proportion of it was suited only for the lower cereal growths. The creation of a new class of labourers, the offspring of the manufacturing system, receiving far higher wages than ploughmen and carters, had caused a demand for an increased supply of animal food; and it was found more profitable to inclose the vast tracts of open down and upland, which had hitherto been used as sheep-walks, and to convert them into stock farms, than to prepare the heavier soils adapted for the production of wheat. Thus it came to pass that the staple of English food was not much benefited by taking in the wastes; and, indeed, it may be doubted whether the inclosure of common lands had as yet increased to an appreciable extent the breadth of acreage available for the cultivation of the wheat crop.

Every reason but the true one was assigned for the scarcity which subjected every class below the opulent to different degrees of privation, and depressed the most numerous class which, in ordinary times, can hardly keep above the level of subsistence, to absolute want. A philosophic writer had lately demonstrated, with alarming force of reasoning, that while the tendency of the population to increase was unalterable and incessant, the power of adding to the means of subsistence was limited.* It followed, therefore, that instead of encouraging the propagation of mankind, which had been the policy of this, as well as of every other country, it was the duty of the moralist and the lawgiver to check the multipli-

---

corn, and disadvantages there from, by which this country had already so deeply suffered.' The high prices obtained during the war and under the protection of the old Corn Laws, made it worth while to break up very inferior soils, as well as rich old pastures.

* The celebrated work of Malthus, on Populations, was published in 1798.

cation of the human race. The author of this doctrine was assailed with ignorant clamour, as if he had set himself up against the law of God and nature, and sought to contaminate the morals of the people. But the practice of encouraging early marriages, and of giving bounties on the production of the human species in the shape of rewards to the parents of large families, which country gentlemen and parish clergymen thought the highest offices of patriotism, did, in fact, depress the moral, as well as the physical condition of the poor. They were thus taught that the prudence and restraint which, in regard to marriage, are prescribed to the higher ranks of society, are virtues with which the lower orders had no concern; that they fulfilled the end of their creation by perpetuating their kind; and that such of their offspring as were not required for the service of the Commonwealth, had a right to be maintained by its charity.* It followed, that a peasantry, bred and nurtured under such a system as this, should be, for the most part, devoid of the independence and self-reliance which distinguish free labourers from serfs. They were oppressed by paternal Government in its most degrading form. Employment was found for them; their children were apprenticed without consulting them; and if they sought to better their condition by seeking their fortune abroad, the law of settlement proved an effectual obstacle.

To maintain this system in the agricultural districts, it was necessary that artificial prices for his produce should be secured to the farmer, by protecting him against the competition of the foreign producer. The result was, that when a bad harvest

* The principle of paying wages to surplus labourers out of the rates, *in proportion to their families*, has been extirpated from the poor-law only within the last quarter of a century. It had lasted nearly long enough to complete the demoralisation of the labouring classes, and was fast undermining property itself.

raised the price of provisions beyond the ordinary standard, the pressure fell not upon the villages, where the people lived upon the rates, but upon the towns and manufacturing districts, where the employment of the working people was regulated by the demand of the general market for labour; and as a rise in the price of the necessaries of life diminishes the demand for manufactures, the pressure of laws which impede the supply of food ultimately falls with intolerable weight upon the small shopkeepers, and on the more intelligent and industrious classes of the labouring population.

The political opponents of the war—both Whigs and Jacobins—sought to turn the discontent of the people to account by persuading them that their privations were owing to the war. This was the truth, but not the whole truth, nor even a considerable part of the truth. But the explanation of the distress which found most favour, was one which had no truth whatever, yet was put forth with perfect honesty and the conviction of profound ignorance. This was the doctrine of the Lord Chief Justice. The corn-factors were the evil-doers; it was they who had tampered with the food of the people, and intercepted the stream of plenty which flowed from the barns and granaries of the farmers. The judges on their Circuits, following the example of their chief, harangued the grand juries on the crimes of forestallers, engrossers, and regraters, by which uncouth and antiquated names they stigmatised the corn-dealers, whose trade, in times of scarcity, so far as it extends, alleviates distress. The grand juries, accustomed to look up to the judges as authorities on political matters, as well as upon law, were too willing to believe that neither they, nor their tenants were in fault.

The populace did not fail to profit by these lessons. Disturbances took place in London and in various

parts of the country; but the riots instigated by the
judges, were the most formidable. Large bodies of
men went about to the farmhouses, compelling the
farmers to bring their produce to market, and to sell
it at a low price. Associations were formed to fix a
maximum price for articles of consumption. The
corn-dealers, who had especially been held up to
popular odium, were in great danger. They were
not suffered to carry on their business; their persons
were threatened; their houses were attacked; and,
in many instances, their property was demolished.
Mr. Rusby, whom Lord Kenyon had caused to be
convicted contrary to law, was marked out for signal
vengeance. He himself escaped; but an excited
mob broke into his house at midnight, destroyed all
its contents, and as much of the building itself as
they could pull to pieces. The Corn Exchange was
threatened with demolition; but the promptitude
and firmness of the Lord Mayor checked the career of
the rioters. He read the Riot Act, and a body of
volunteers and constables, after some resistance, dispersed the crowd.

In these circumstances, Mr. Pitt wisely determined
to assemble Parliament; not from any expectation
that they could devise a remedy for the distress; but
because it was desirable that the mischievous delusions which had been propagated should be dissipated without further delay. Pitt, however, was of
opinion that the exigency might require some temporary measures, such as a guaranteed price for importations of corn and rice, the prohibition of the
manufacture of starch, and the suspension of the
distilleries.[*] Lord Grenville, on the other hand, a
stern disciple of the school of the Economists, would
admit of no paltering with the doctrine of free trade.[†]
'I am confident,' he says, in a letter to Pitt at this

---

[*] Pitt to Addington, 9th October, 1800. — EARL STANHOPE's *Life of Pitt*, vol. iii. p. 244.
[†] Ibid., p. 248.

time, 'that provisions, like every other article of commerce, if left to themselves, will and must find their level; and that every attempt to disturb that level by artificial contrivances has a necessary tendency to increase the evil it seeks to remedy. In all the discussions with which we are overwhelmed on this subject, one view of it is wholly overlooked. Every one takes it for granted, that the present price of corn is in itself undue, and such as ought not to exist, and then they dispute whether it is to be ascribed to combinations, which they wish to remedy by such means as will destroy all commerce, or to an unusual scarcity which they propose to supply by obliging the grower to contend in the home market, not with the natural rivalship of such importation as the demand might and would produce of itself, but with an artificial supply poured in at the expense of I know not how many millions to the State.'

This was true so far as it went; but it did not go far enough; and, stopping at an intermediate point, Grenville's argument was practically unsound. The law of supply and demand is a universal law, which cannot act, except in a free and open market. One hundred and twenty-seven shillings a quarter was, probably, not more remunerative to the English farmer in the year 1800, than fifty-four shillings in 1798. But it was a mockery to tell the consumer, who was compelled to eat the bread of monopoly, that it was unreasonable to complain of high prices. Lord Grenville, fifteen years later, embraced the doctrine of Free Trade, so far at least as corn is concerned, in its integrity.* But, at this time, neither he, nor any other public man of credit, was prepared to go that length. Pitt, certainly, was not so advanced in his opinions; and, if he had been convinced himself, all his powers of persuasion, and all his authority,

* The celebrated protest of ten lords against the Corn Act of 1815 was drawn by Grenville.— Lords' Journal.

would have been insufficient to convince the country that a free importation of the necessaries of life was the true policy for a great and populous nation. He might, indeed, as well have attempted to pass the Duke of Richmond's Reform Bill, as to repeal the Corn Laws. Lord Grenville accused Pitt of departing from the doctrine of Free Trade, and of forsaking the precepts of Adam Smith, for the teaching of Lord Liverpool.* But the rule of Free Trade was inapplicable to a market founded on protection. All the ministers except Grenville were agreed, that extraordinary measures were required to meet the distress.

Parliament met on the 11th of November; and the royal speech was made the appropriate vehicle for the deliberate censure of His Majesty's Government upon this mischievous nonsense, which the judges, and other persons of station and authority, had been spreading during the recess. 'If it shall appear,' the King was made to say, 'that the evil, necessarily arising from unfavourable seasons, has been increased by any undue combinations, or fraudulent practices, for the sake of adding unfairly to the price, you will feel an earnest desire of effectually preventing such abuses; but you will, I am sure, be careful to distinguish any practices of this nature from that regular and long-established course of trade, which experience has shown to be indispensable in the present state of society, for the supply of the markets, and for the subsistence of the people.' Many petitions were presented from the populous districts of London, and from the large towns, complaining of the scarcity under which the labouring classes were perishing, and the middle classes were becoming pauperised. These petitions, which, for the most part, were headed by the rector and churchwardens, or the mayor and corporation, in almost every case attributed the dis-

* Letter above quoted.

tress to forestallers, engrossers, and regraters. Some of them added large farmers, whose capital enabled them to withhold their produce until they could obtain their price; while the small occupiers were forced to sell their produce for what it would fetch. The House, however, was all but unanimous in reprobation of such ignorant prejudices; and, though the distress continued with little abatement during the following year, and recurred at intervals in subsequent years, no more was heard of re-enacting the laws against forestalling, nor of passing acts, to restrict the investment of capital in agriculture. The occasional measures adopted by Parliament were such as the exigency seemed to suggest. Bounties were readily granted on the motion of the Government, on the importation of corn, of wheaten flour, of Indian rice and pulse. Acts were also passed, prohibiting, for a limited time, the use of corn in distillation, and the manufacture of starch. The exportation of corn, and provisions of every kind, was also prohibited. The curing of fish was encouraged by several enactments. Some of these temporary expedients were adopted on the recommendation of a committee, which had been appointed on the first day of the session. Many of their suggestions were sensible; some were frivolous. And one of these measures, to which they seemed to attach the greatest importance, proved so mischievous, that it was hastily repealed after a trial of a few weeks. This was the act, to prohibit the making of bread solely from fine flour, commonly called the Brown Bread Act. It was thought that this would effect a great saving in the raw material. But it was found, that the prejudices of the people against lowering the standard of food were insurmountable; and the attempt was resented with so much indignation, that it was wisely determined not to persevere with the experiment. Finally, upon the addresses of both Houses, a royal proclamation enjoined economy in the use of grain, and the substitution of other articles of consumption, so far as was practicable. This advice had been already anticipated by the higher classes, and was soon adopted generally by householders. There are never wanting representatives in Parliament of any folly or fallacy which may be prevalent out-of-doors; and members were, therefore, ready to propose specific remedies for the distress, in the shape of a minimum wage of labour, and a maximum price of food. The first-mentioned remedy—which, as Lord Grenville truly observed, drew after it the second—found an advocate in the Marquis of Buckingham, who had the obstinacy and querulousness, without the capacity of the Grenvilles. The head of the family was followed in this antiquated error, by his brother Thomas, better versed in diplomatic than domestic affairs. And it required all the authority of Lord Grenville,[*] to restrain his elder brother from taking the lead in an agitation, which would have been far more mischievous than the clamour against the corn-factors. Grenville, however, thought that the employers of labour might be urged by example to give better wages. And in the agricultural districts, where the farmers, in accordance with the spirit in which they administered the poor laws, kept wages down to the level of subsistence, such an example might have been beneficial. But the colleagues of Grenville in the Government were of opinion, that even this qualified

---

[*] In a letter to the Marquis, he says, 'My steady persuasion is, that example, and (at the very utmost) the execution of the subsisting laws can alone remedy the evil, *which laws and the introduction of an artificial system have created*, and which new laws and a system still more forced can only increase.'—*Courts and Cabinets of George the Third*, vol. iii. p. 100. It is remarkable that, while there was a dearth in England, the produce on the Continent of Europe and in America had been *unusually abundant*. This fact was stated by Pitt himself in the House of Commons. Hence, under a system of free imports, the deficiency of this country would have been compensated by the foreign trade.

interference with the labour-market was not desirable. They were willing to enforce the laws of supply and demand as regarded the servant, but not as regarded the master.

In addition to the measures taken by the legislature, every effort was made by private benevolence to alleviate the distress. But the people were sullen and discontented. They accepted, as of necessity, the relief provided for them, but they seemed carefully to avoid any expression of gratitude for the care which was taken of their want. They felt, as if by instinct, that their sufferings were more the act of man than the act of God; but bewildered as they were by the counsels of ignorance and malignity, they had but an imperfect perception of the real cause of their privation. Many believed that the corn was carried out of the country to feed the garrisons abroad; others complained that the oats consumed by the cavalry horses had displaced the growth of wheat for the people. Not a few roundly asserted, that there was in reality no dearth at all; but that an artificial scarcity had been created by the machinations of the corn-dealers. These gross delusions passed away; but the close of the eighteenth century marked an era, when the poor were alienated from the rich, when a sense of injustice and oppression rankled among the inferior orders of society, and when doctrines were taught which tended to the dissolution of society itself. The causes of dissension went on striking deeper and spreading wider for nearly thirty years. But, at the same time, knowledge was being diffused among the upper, as well as the lower ranks of the community. At the time of the greatest gloom, a change took place. In 1828, the Test and Corporation Acts suddenly gave way. In the following year, the Catholic bulwarks were hastily removed. Thus the first burst of the storm carried away the rotten outworks of intolerance,

Extent of private benevolence.

which had been so long guarded with superstitious care, and the cause of religious liberty was, in a moment, and for ever after, triumphant. The crisis immediately followed. The Revolution of 1830 saved the State from the perils of democracy by which it was in danger of being overwhelmed, and fulfilled the scheme of the British constitution. Then the barriers of commercial monopoly were broken down; and, finally, the Corn Law fell. And thus was completed the harmonious system of religious toleration, of representative Government, and commercial freedom. To this happy combination, attained by peaceful and lawful means, is to be ascribed in chief the prosperity of the nation, the utter disappearance of that sinister discontent among the great mass of the people which alarmed our forefathers, and the unshaken stability of our institutions, amid the shocks which have rent asunder ancient monarchies and modern republics.

CHAPTER XLI.

FIRST PARLIAMENT OF THE UNITED KINGDOM—CATHOLIC QUESTION—CHANGE OF MINISTRY—KING'S ILLNESS—ADDINGTON SUCCEEDS PITT—PROCEEDINGS IN PARLIAMENT—BATTLE OF ALEXANDRIA—EXPEDITION TO THE BALTIC—PEACE OF AMIENS.

THE session of Parliament which terminated on the last day of the eighteenth century, was the last session of the Parliament of Great Britain. The Parliament which was next to assemble was, in consequence of the Act of Union, to be styled 'The Parliament of the United Kingdom of Great Britain and Ireland.' Corresponding alterations in the royal style, in forms, ceremonies, and heraldic devices, were also rendered necessary by this event. Advantage was taken of the opportunity thus afforded to omit the title of King of France, which the Crown of England had assumed since the time of Edward the Third; and to remove the lilies of France from the royal shield. The French monarchy had been too magnanimous to remonstrate seriously against the continued assumption of a title which had long ceased to have any practical meaning; but the French Republic had thought it worth while to insist on the renunciation of this empty title as an article in a treaty of peace; and as it was improbable that in a future negotiation, this demand would be withdrawn, it was thought more consistent with the dignity of the Crown voluntarily to renounce a pretension, however worthless, than to relinquish it on the dictation of the French Government, when at the height of military power.

The United Parliament was opened by commission on the 22nd of January. A question was raised that the Act of Union had put an end to the Parliament of Great Britain, as well as the Parliament of Ireland, and that the Parliament of the United Kingdom must be constituted by a general election. Such a doubt was expressed by Lord Eldon and other lawyers. But the better opinion was, that there was no reason to depart from the precedent of the union with Scotland, and that the Act of Union had not altered the constitution of the Parliament of Great Britain with Ireland, but had provided only for the addition to that Parliament of representatives for the kingdom of Ireland. The composition of the House of Commons, however, was so far changed by the transfer of the Irish representation, that it was thought fit to proceed to a new election for Speaker, and as the form of the oath was slightly altered, all the members were re-sworn. The business of the session was commenced on the 2nd of February, by a royal speech, which contained no indication of any change in the administration of public affairs. It contained few topics. The Union was referred to in general terms. The confederacy of the Baltic powers to introduce a new code of maritime law hostile to the interests of this country was duly reprobated; and the usual assurance of a desire to terminate the war on grounds consistent with the security and honour of the country was repeated. Yet three days after the speech had been delivered, the great minister, who had ruled with all but absolute power for seventeen years, was forced to yield to the same stubborn will, before which the elder Pitt, and Grenville, and Rockingham, and the Coalition had, in turn, given way.

On the 28th of January, the King held one of his ordinary levees, at which it seems to have happened that Mr. Dundas was the only Cabinet minister present. The King, in the presence of the whole circle, addressed Dundas in these terms:—'What is it that this young lord has brought over that they are going to throw at my head? The most Jacobinical thing I ever heard of.'* 'And,' he added, according to his former fashion, when he did not approve of any particular policy recommended by his minister—'I shall reckon any man my personal enemy who proposes any such measure.' This he repeated so loud as to be heard by the persons standing near. Dundas answered with spirit, 'Your Majesty will find among those who are friendly to that measure some whom you never supposed to be your enemies.' †

The report of this brief dialogue soon flew all over London. It soon became known also what was the measure to which this astounding allusion referred. The measure was the relief of the Roman Catholics from civil disabilities; and Lord Castlereagh had been for some weeks past in London negotiating the progress of this measure with His Majesty's Government.

In a letter from Castlereagh to Pitt, dated the 1st of January, the connection of this policy with that of the Legislative Union is fully and clearly recapitulated.‡ In the autumn of 1799, Lord Castlereagh, on the part of the Irish Government, represented to Mr. Pitt that the project of Union could not be carried through the Irish Parliament without the support of the Roman Catholic interest; and that the Catholics could not be conciliated without an assurance that the proposed

---

* Rose's *Diaries*, vol. i. p. 303. He alluded to Lord Castlereagh.

† Life of Wilberforce, vol. iii. p. 7. Quoted also by Earl Stanhope.—*Life of Pitt*, vol. iii. p. 274.

‡ *Cornwallis Correspondence*, vol. iii. p. 326.

measure would be conducive to the settlement of their
claims. In consequence of this communication, a
Cabinet was summoned to consider this question, and
Lord Castlereagh was invited to assist at its deliberations. The result was 'that the opinion of the
Cabinet was favourable to the principle of the measure; that some doubts were entertained as to the
possibility of admitting Catholics into some of the
higher offices; and that ministers apprehended considerable repugnance to the measure in many quarters, and particularly in the *highest*; but that, as far
as the sentiments of the Cabinet were concerned, the
Lord Lieutenant need not hesitate in calling forth
the Catholic support in whatever degree he found it
practicable to obtain it.' Lord Castlereagh proceeds,
' I certainly did not then hear any direct objections
stated against the principle of the measure by any
one of the ministers then present. You will, I have
no doubt, recollect that, so far from any serious hesitation being entertained in respect to the principle,
it was even discussed whether an immediate declaration on the subject to the Catholics would not be
advisable, and whether an assurance should not be
distinctly given them in the event of the Union being
accomplished, of their objects being submitted with
the countenance of Government, to the United Parliament upon a peace. This idea was laid aside
principally upon a consideration that such a declaration might alienate the Protestants in both countries
from the Union, in a greater degree than it was calculated to assist the measure through the Catholics;
and accordingly, the instructions I was directed to
convey to Lord Cornwallis were to the following
effect; that His Excellency was fully warranted in
soliciting every support the Catholics could afford
. . . . that it was not thought expedient at that time
to give any direct assurance to the Catholics, but
that, should circumstances so far alter as to induce

His Excellency to consider such an explanation necessary, he was at liberty to state the grounds on which his opinion was formed for the consideration of the Cabinet. In consequence of this communication, the Irish Government omitted no exertion to call forth the Catholics in favour of the Union. Lord Castlereagh went on to state, that the Lord Lieutenant was thus enabled to remove a difficulty which would have prevented the accomplishment of the Union; and that the leaders of the Catholic body with whom he entered into correspondence, were dissuaded by him from insisting on an express promise, for the reason that it was not fitting to make the removal of civil disabilities, and the accompanying measures of relief, a subject of bargain between the Catholics and the Government.

According to this statement, the correctness of which has never been impeached, a positive promise was made for a valuable consideration. Castlereagh himself, who had concluded so many bargains on account of the Union, had never negotiated a contract more plain and binding than this, which was ratified by the immediate authority of the Cabinet. Some supporters of the Union had bartered their votes for titles, some for places, and some for money; but the Catholic community, without whose aid the great measure could not have been carried, and in the face of whose hostility it would not have been attempted, demanded only honourable terms. They asked for an equality of civil rights with the rest of their fellow-subjects. Their terms were granted, and their part of the engagement was punctually fulfilled. It only remained for the Government of the Crown to perform their promise, and, at the same time, to ensure the stability, and complete the noble proportions of the great work they had accomplished. The tools, and sycophants, and hirelings of the Government had been satisfied.

No sooner was the work done, than they clamoured for their reward. So the peerages were created; the places were conferred; and the money bribes were paid. But Catholic Emancipation was not yet granted. Indeed, no time had been fixed; and the Catholics were far from any inclination to embarrass the Government, by pressing for the settlement of their claims. Something had been said at the Cabinet about waiting for a time of peace. But the war might last until the friends of religious liberty were no longer in a condition to perform their promise. And no reason had been given, why a time of peace should be more convenient than a time of war, for entertaining the question. Lord Grenville was of opinion, that there could be no more fitting time to promote domestic harmony and to do an act of justice and grace to the majority of the Irish people, than when England was wrestling with a foreign foe, and when Ireland was threatened with invasion. The Viceroy urged, that the question could not be postponed, and that, if it was not soon brought forward by the Government, it would be taken up by the Opposition.

Mr. Pitt yielded to these arguments; and, immediately after the Act of Union had been passed, the principal members of the Government prepared the outline of a measure, or of a series of measures, worthy the great and generous minds by which they were conceived. *Proposed measures for Catholic relief.* The sacramental test was to be abolished; and, in its stead, was to be substituted a political declaration, applicable to members of Parliament, office-bearers, ministers of religion of every denomination, and teachers of schools. A provision for the Catholic clergy, with the view of rendering them, to use the words of Grenville, 'more respectable in station; more independent of their flocks; and better disposed to the support of the established

Government,' formed part of the plan. The tithe system, the sorest of the practical grievances of which the Irish Catholics complained, was to be adjusted in such a manner as to render it less oppressive to the great bulk of the people, Protestant as well as Catholic, who dissented from the Establishment. The details of this great scheme of pacification and Union were never drawn out. But such were the conceptions of Pitt and Grenville.* In the autumn of 1800, Lord Castlereagh was again in attendance on the Cabinet, to aid them by his particular information in framing the Irish measures, which were to be submitted to Parliament in the ensuing session.

Thus far the business had proceeded; and the two statesmen, intent on the elaboration of their plan, saw no danger from any quarter, except possibly from the old party of Protestant ascendency on either side of the Channel. At length, it was thought time to assemble the Cabinet, in order that the Irish measures might be finally determined. And, on the 25th of September, Pitt wrote to the Chancellor, who was at Weymouth, informing him of the project in contemplation; referring him to some explanatory papers which he was to receive from Lord Grenville; and requesting his attendance in London, for the meeting of the Cabinet, on an early day.

<small>The Cabinet assembled.</small>

The King was at Weymouth when Lord Loughborough received this letter; and, though not in official attendance on His Majesty, the Chancellor appears to have cultivated the opportunity thus offered, to ingratiate himself with the King. He was now fully informed of the King's views on the Catholic question; and he was careful not to repeat the mistake which he had made in 1795; when, from ignorance of the strong bias of

<small>Loughborough's breach of confidence.</small>

---

* Lord Grenville to Marquis of Buckingham, Feb. 2, 1801.— *Courts and Cabinets of George the Third*, vol. iii. p. 128.

the royal mind, he had answered the written questions which the King put to him on the Coronation Oath, in a manner far from agreeable to his client's wishes.* The crafty and supple lawyer knew that the surest road to His Majesty's favour was by flattering his prejudices; and as he desired above all things to recommend himself to the King, he was ready to follow that road whenever an opening should present itself. Fortune seemed to have favoured his highest hopes, when he received, at a moment when none other of the ministers was near the King's person, the announcement of the measure which had been concerted between the Prime Minister and the foremost of his colleagues. He had it now in his power to give the most signal proof of devotion to his royal master, by revealing the counsels of the head of the Government, and by defeating his policy. Loughborough himself admitted, that he showed Pitt's letter to the King. And there can be no doubt, that the whole plan communicated to him by Pitt and Grenville was by him communicated to His Majesty.†

The Lord Chancellor having thus secured, as he supposed, the confidence and gratitude of the King, went to London to attend a Cabinet Council on the last day of the month. He examined Lord Castlereagh, who was present on this day, as he had been at former meetings of the Cabinet, when the affairs of Ireland were discussed. The Irish Secretary appears to have been exceedingly reserved in his answers, and to have denied that any promise had been made to the Catholics, and even that encouragement had been given them to hope for immediate relief. The Chancellor raised many ob-

<small>Loughborough and Castlereagh.</small>

---

* He complained of the 'abruptness' with which the questions had been put to him by the King, and thought an unfair advantage was taken of him.—

Rose's *Correspondence*, vol. i. p. 300.
† Lord Campbell's *Lives of the Chancellors*, vol. vi. p. 326.

jections to the measure. Considerable doubt was manifested by other members. Pitt, disappointed at the turn the discussion had taken, postponed the further consideration of the question to a future day.

The strange part of the story, so far, is that the Chancellor should have derived his first information of this most important business from the letter of Mr. Pitt, on the 25th of September, 1801, when the whole matter had been fully discussed, and the faith of the Government pledged at a meeting of. the Cabinet twelve months before. The last-mentioned Cabinet was summoned for the special purpose. It appears, from Lord Castlereagh's account, that it was attended by several members;[*] yet the Lord Chancellor never received any report of the proceedings of that Cabinet, either from the first minister, or any of his colleagues who were present. The whole transaction appears inexplicable upon the modern theory and practice of the joint and several responsibility of the leading members of administration for measures determined in Cabinet Council. And this omission seems the more remarkable, when we find that two persons, high in office indeed, but not members of the Cabinet, thought themselves entitled to complain that they had not been apprised of a project of such importance as a scheme for the settlement of the Catholic question. Lord Clare, the Irish Chancellor, reproached the Lord Lieutenant and the Secretary in bitter terms for withholding from him the intentions of the Government. Clare, having been deep in the counsels of the Union, might well feel slighted, at being kept in ignorance of a matter so intimately connected with that great transaction. But there was a reason for this reserve. The Chancellor of Ireland was the most uncompromising, and by far the ablest and most influential among the opponents of

[*] Letter to Mr. Pitt, quoted above.

the Catholic claims. He was not a man to be conciliated, corrupted, or silenced; he was deeply committed against any further concession to the Catholics; his conduct on the Maynooth Bill, in 1799, was not forgotten. The object of that bill was to provide for the education in Ireland of students intended for the Catholic priesthood; and it formed part of the measure for the endowment of the Romish clergy, a branch of the great scheme of conciliation by which the Government sought to effect the substantial union of the two kingdoms. The Maynooth Bill had passed the Irish House of Commons as a Government Bill; but when it went up to the Lords, the Chancellor broke out into an invective against the Catholic priesthood, denounced the policy of supporting institutions for the education of the priests, and would not suffer the bill to go into committee. It is probable, therefore, that Lord Clare would have made use of any information which might have been imparted to him as to the views of the Cabinet on the Catholic question, to raise a Protestant alarm in Ireland, and ensure the defeat of the whole policy. Another person, who felt himself aggrieved by the reserve of the Government, was Lord Auckland. This busy, mischievous politician, presuming partly on Pitt's friendship, and partly on an overweening conceit of his own importance, thought proper to write a long letter to Pitt, reproaching him as if he had been guilty of treacherous dissimulation, condemning the supposed measures, and intimating very plainly his expectation, that, in consequence of his disapproval, they would be abandoned. Pitt answered this ebullition of impertinence and vanity with half a dozen caustic lines, which put a summary end to the correspondence.

The removal of the Test was not proposed, nor, as it would seem, even incidentally discussed, at the subsequent meetings of the Cabinet. At a Cabinet, on the 9th of October, probably the next meeting of the ministers after the memorable Cabinet of the 13th of September, Pitt gave Lord Liverpool to understand that he was against the measure.* Shortly before the opening of Parliament, the King asked the Chancellor whether anything was in contemplation? and Loughborough replied, nothing but a Tithe Bill, which he was himself preparing, and a scheme for pensioning the Catholic and Dissenting clergy.† About the same time Loughborough drew up an elaborate paper, in which all the arguments against the Catholic claims were summed up with great ability, but not containing a word either for or against the one objection, which the King considered insuperable—his Coronation Oath. This paper appears to have been laid before His Majesty on the 13th of December.‡ On the 20th of January, the Archbishop of Canterbury, instigated probably by his brother-in-law, Lord Auckland, obtained an audience of the King to warn him against the measure of Catholic emancipation, which his ministers were about to bring forward. A few days after this interview, the King brought the matter to a crisis, by his conversation with Dundas at the levee. On the 31st of January, Pitt addressed a letter to His Majesty, announcing that a majority of the Cabinet, including himself, were of opinion, that the admission of the Catholics and Dissenters to offices, and of the Catholics, as well as Dissenters, to Parliament, would, under certain conditions, be highly advisable, with a view to the tranquillity and improvement of Ireland, and to the general interest of the United Kingdom.

---

* So Lord Liverpool told General Harcourt on the 1st of March following.—LADY HARCOURT's *MS. Diary*. The old lord complained that his colleagues had been accustomed to pay little attention to him.

† Lord Loughborough's defence of his conduct.—LORD CAMPBELL's *Lives of the Chancellors*, vol. vi.

‡ PELLEW's *Life of Lord Sidmouth*, Appendix, vol. i. LADY HARCOURT's *MS. Diary*.

The minister then proceeded to recite the various reasons which had determined him in this opinion. He declared that opinion to be unalterable; and he concluded by distinctly intimating that his continuance in office must depend on His Majesty's consent to the proposed measures.

The next day the King answered this letter. He said that, according to his view, the Coronation Oath absolutely precluded him from entertaining any proposition inconsistent with the maintenance of the Protestant establishment, which expressly disqualified Papists from holding any employment in the State. He added that Mr. Pitt's proposition was not only one of this character, but that it tended to the overthrow of the whole fabric. The King, unwilling, however, to part with his minister, proposed what he seemed to consider a compromise; namely, that if Mr. Pitt would refrain from pressing the question, His Majesty would say nothing more against the pretensions of his Catholic subjects. *The King's reply to Pitt.*

Pitt's reply was an absolute tender of his resignation, which the King could no longer refuse to accept. *Pitt's offer to resign.*

Pitt has been censured for committing himself to the policy of Catholic emancipation, knowing as he did, in common with every other man engaged in public life, the strong repugnance of the King to any material concession of the Catholic claims. And he was supposed by some to have failed in his duty to the King, in withholding from His Majesty all information as to the measures which the Government contemplated proposing to Parliament with reference to this important question. But I do not understand that the minister is under any obligation, either of duty or of courtesy, to confer with the Sovereign on any question of policy which may be under the consideration of the Cabinet. In former times, when the council deliberated in the presence of the

Sovereign, he was the chief of his ministers; but the modern system of parliamentary Government, which involves the absolute and exclusive responsibility of the ministers of the Crown, is incompatible with the participation of the Sovereign in the counsels of the Cabinet. If he disapproves of its policy, he has an appeal to the great council of the nation, and ultimately to the nation itself. But he cannot also have a voice in the policy against which he has the power of appeal. Mr. Pitt was therefore under no obligation to take the King's pleasure, with reference to any measure which he proposed to lay before Parliament, until the counsels of his Cabinet were fully matured. It is another question, whether Mr. Pitt, knowing as he did, since 1795, the King's strong repugnance to the Catholic claims, should have committed himself irretrievably to the policy of concession, without taking any pains to ascertain how far it was probable that this obstacle might be overcome. But Pitt's conduct in this respect also seems to be free from blame. He had undertaken, on the part of the Government, to carry forward a measure for the relief of the Catholics; he had not undertaken to do so immediately, or even to make the measure a capital question; but he did bring it forward without delay; and when he found an insurmountable obstacle in the highest quarter, he took the step which public duty and personal honour dictated. He resigned his office, and voluntarily surrendered power, such as no minister of this country had ever possessed. It was said at the time, and was believed by many who were not influenced by envy or detraction, that Pitt had either sought for a pretext, or willingly availed himself of a fair excuse to retire from a situation, which his failing health and the disappointment of his war policy had rendered irksome. But the real causes of great events are seldom accurately known or understood at the time when they take place. At the distance of more than half a century, every person who thinks it worth while to inquire can learn more about the fall of Pitt's administration than was accessible to any but the best contemporary information. It is probable that Pitt quitted office for the reason publicly assigned, and for no other; and that, far from wishing to retire, he gave up power with as much reluctance as Sir Robert Walpole or the Duke of Newcastle. There is every reason to believe that, had Pitt been left to himself, he would have postponed the Catholic question to a more propitious opportunity. After the Cabinet of the 13th of September, the discussion of the subject was never formally resumed, and Lord Castlereagh was instructed to inform the head of the Irish Government, that in consequence of the adverse opinion of the highest law authority, the Cabinet did not think themselves warranted, in His Majesty's absence, and without information as to the opinions entertained in other quarters, in coming to a final decision on a business of such moment.* The further consideration of the subject appears to have been thenceforth confined to Pitt, Grenville, and Dundas. But the arguments urged by Grenville were unanswerable. 1. The Government were committed to the measure. 2. It was necessary to complete the scheme of Legislative Union. 3. It was of pressing necessity in the view of a descent on Ireland by the French. 4. The measure would certainly be proposed by the Opposition in Parliament, if Government hesitated. Lastly, the public expression of his opinion by the King had precipitated the time of action. The business of the session was to commence on the 2nd of February. On the previous day, Pitt wrote to the King the letter above mentioned, which was drawn up in concert with Grenville.†

* Lord Castlereagh's letter to Mr. Pitt, 1st January, 1801.

† Lord Grenville to Marquis of Buckingham, 2nd February.—

The reports of the spies and sycophants who had
access to the King, were, to a certain extent, corroborated by what he had learned
from Grenville and Dundas. His Majesty
had therefore anticipated the formal communication
which he expected to receive from Pitt. On the
29th of January, he wrote to the Speaker, stating that
he had been informed of Lord Castlereagh's intention
to bring forward a measure to render Roman Catholics eligible to Parliament, and to office; and that
this measure was, according to their own admissions
to himself, favoured by Grenville and Dundas, and,
as he had been credibly assured, by Pitt. His
Majesty, therefore, desired the Speaker to see Mr.
Pitt, and to dissuade him, if possible, from a proceeding to which the King could never consent. In
obedience to these commands, Addington hurried
off to Pitt's house; and the result of his interview
appears to have encouraged a hope which he conveyed to the King the same day, that the great
minister would yield. But Addington must either
have misunderstood Pitt's language and demeanour,
or, which is more probable, Pitt was not disposed to
accept Addington as the medium of communication
with the King; for at the very moment of Addington's visit,* he must have had in his pocket the draft
of the letter, which, on the day following, he sent to

Sidenote: Attempt of Addington to dissuade Pitt from resigning.

Courts and Cabinets of George the Third, vol. iii. p. 128. Grenville was as little inclined as Pitt, at that time, to shrink from the responsibilities of office. Writing to Lord Buckingham, on the 2nd of February, he says, 'There could be no doubt of the line we were to follow in this unpleasant and unhappy state of things. I could heartily wish that the necessity of the thing itself had not brought the point to issue precisely at the present moment. My sense of the public difficulties is certainly much less than that which the public itself entertains; but still there is difficulty enough to make one wish *not* to quit one's post; but there seems to be no alternative, and so I flatter myself you will think.' —Ibid.

* 31st January.—*Lord Sidmouth's Life* by Dean Pellew, vol. i. p. 297.

the King. When Addington waited on the King the
same evening, he received His Majesty's commands
to form a new administration. Addington made, or
pretended to make, another effort to persuade Pitt;
but Pitt told him he entirely approved of the course
which the King had taken; the expression he is reported to have used was, 'I see nothing but ruin,
Addington, if you hesitate.'*

On the 5th of February, Addington undertook the
arduous task which had been imposed *The new
upon him. As Pitt had resigned without Cabinet.*
calling his colleagues together, and upon a question
which had never been determined by the Cabinet, the
retirement of the chief minister did not necessarily
involve that of the whole administration. Nevertheless, every man of mark, with one exception, both
in and out of the Cabinet, refused to serve under the
new chief. Grenville, and Dundas, and Windham,
and Spencer, followed their illustrious leader. The
Duke of Portland, the Earl of Westmoreland, the
Earl of Chatham, remained. The one man of ability
in Pitt's Cabinet, who was willing to serve under Addington, was the Chancellor. But the Chancellor, who
had steadily pursued his own advancement through
all the changes and chances of public life, had, in
this instance, played too deep a game. Whether he
had really hoped, according to one opinion, that he
might supplant Pitt; or, whether he merely obeyed
the instinct of a base nature, in flattering the bigotry
and obstinacy of the King, Loughborough was equally
unsuccessful. So little was he concerned in the
events which his intrigues had mainly contributed to
produce, that, on the 4th of February, when Addington was actually Prime Minister, Lord Loughborough
talked to Dundas, at the levee, of the foolish reports
in circulation as to changes in the Ministry; and

* Dean Pellew's *Life of Lord Sidmouth*, vol. i. p. 288.

was astounded, when Dundas informed him, that Pitt, Grenville, and himself, were out of office.* The next day his own successor was named without his knowledge; the King himself having expressly desired that Lord Eldon should have the Great Seal. Lord Loughborough had no doubt thought it an easy matter to cajole a man of such mean capacity as the King. But His Majesty was not deficient in that perception of character, which peculiar experience generally enables princes to acquire. During a reign of forty years, in which he had been accustomed to attend to every detail of public business, His Majesty had been served by a great variety of ministers; and he seems to have formed a tolerably accurate estimate of two generations of statesmen. Some of them he hated and feared—some he disliked and respected —some he used for his purposes—some he bore with for a time. He dissembled with many—he gave his entire confidence to none. Loughborough was one of those shameless self-seekers and time-servers, who could deceive none but the most guileless and inexperienced. And the King was not, for a moment, deceived by him.†

George the Third has been loaded with the obloquy of defeating a policy, to which the time was eminently propitious; and which, if adopted at that time, would, it is said, have averted great evils. Pitt himself has been blamed for having mismanaged the question. If he had given the King timely warning of his intention, it has been said, all would have been well.

* Rose's *Diary*, vol. i. p. 304.

† When the Archbishop had an audience to warn him of the new Popish plot, it is stated that 'the King, though he perfectly agreed with His Grace, yet made to the Duke of Gloucester a remark that showed his knowledge of human nature, and his suspicion of design and interest ever lurking under, or joining to, other motives; for he said that the Archbishop meant to bring forward his brother-in-law, Lord Auckland, as one of the new ministers, but that he (the King) meant no such thing.'—LADY HARCOURT's *Diary, MSS.*

George the Third had yielded his opinion, on former
occasions, to the representations of his ministers,
when properly submitted to him. It is true that he
had frequently yielded his opinions; and unless he
could always have commanded an indolent minister
like North, or an obsequious minister like Addington,
he could not always have his own way. During the
long years that he had been served by Pitt, whenever
the King's opinion had prevailed over the will of his
minister, it was the exception, not the rule. But
there were points on which His Majesty was immov-
able; and the Catholic question was one of them.
Whatever the time, or the circumstances, it is certain that the King would have resisted; and that he
would have parted with Pitt, or any other minister,
rather than break his coronation vow. It is unfair,
also, to blame George the Third, as if he had been
the only obstacle at the time to the admission of
Catholics and Dissenters to a footing of equality with
the members of the Establishment. The King was
supported in his opposition to this great change, by
the Primate of England, and the Primate of Ireland;
by the Lord Chancellor of England, and the Lord
Chancellor of Ireland; by the Chief Justice of England; by the Chief Justice of the Common Pleas;
and by nearly half the Cabinet. The old friends of
civil and religious liberty, who had been foremost in
the exclusion of the Papists, when they were dangerous to civil and religious liberty, now, consistently
with their principles, would have removed exceptional
and temporary restraints, which were no longer
necessary. But the friends of civil and religious
freedom were, at this time, a small minority. The
prejudices against the Romanists had survived the
causes by which they had been originally justified.
The Church of England was bitterly hostile to her
fallen rival. The Dissenting congregations were, for
the most part, equally intolerant. In no class did

the hatred of Popery prevail more widely than among the bulk of the people. The genius of Rome is repugnant to the character of the Anglo-Saxon race. Her arrogant pretensions—her arbitrary rule—her shameless corruption—her cruelty, luxury, and pride, had for nearly three hundred years been the constant theme of scorn and invective, wherever freedom of speech and of conscience were endured. There was no reason for believing, that the prejudice against Popery, which had been rooted in the minds of succeeding generations of the English people, had lately given way to more liberal views. On the contrary, if the attempt had been made at the beginning of this century, to admit the Catholics to an equality of civil privileges, it is probable that the old alarm would have been revived, and that not all the weight and authority of Mr. Pitt, supported by a united Cabinet, and an assenting Sovereign, would have reconciled the people to so great and sudden an innovation.

Nevertheless, Pitt might, had he been bent upon it, have forced the measure through Parliament; but, in doing so, he would have split up his party as Peel did in 1829, and afterwards in 1846. But Pitt was under no such stress of circumstances as compelled Peel to surrender the Protestant Tests, and to abolish the Corn Laws. Pitt, in fact, treated the question of Catholic emancipation very much as he had treated the question of Parliamentary Reform. He considered each of these measures as right in itself, and as one which must eventually be carried; but he saw that the times were not favourable to either. As regarded Catholic emancipation, he had been drawn into an engagement which must be in some sort disposed of. The whole tenour of his conduct on this occasion, and his offer to withdraw the question at the last moment,* sufficiently prove that Pitt was

* EARL STANHOPE's *Life of Pitt*, vol. iii. p. 303.

never really in earnest, as Grenville was, on Catholic emancipation; indeed, it is very doubtful whether he would have pressed the matter to the extent of a colourable support, had he not been urged forward by the strong will and sincerity of his principal colleague.

The nomination of Addington as his successor was an arrangement which exactly agreed with Pitt's view of a temporary retirement from office. His object was, in the first place, to hold together the compact party which for seventeen years had supported his administration; and, in the second place, to keep out the Whigs.* It was necessary, therefore, that the provisional minister should be a man without any quality which might make him dangerous as a rival. Addington fully satisfied this condition. He was, indeed, a man of high respectability, and had filled with fair reputation an office of great dignity, the duties of which could be creditably discharged by any member of Parliament who possessed firmness, prudence, and patience. But he had no experience of public affairs beyond that which may be acquired by the clerk at the table, or the serjeant-at-arms. He was not a man of ability. He was not a man of family. His father had been Lord Chatham's physician; and to this happy accident he was indebted for his political fortunes. Addington, in a word, was the creature of the Pitts. The elevation of Addington to the chair was submitted to, because such was the will of the all-powerful minister. Nobody could raise any objection to him, because

---

* On the 9th of February, Lord Castlereagh begins a long letter to Lord Cornwallis with these words: 'Mr. Pitt, from a conviction, I conclude, that the King's mind, could not give way, and seeing the danger of the State falling into the hands of Opposition, has used his utmost influence with his friends to lend themselves to the new arrangements.' He adds in a postscript, 'Mr. Pitt has seen the first part of this letter.'— *Cornwallis's Correspondence*, vol. iii. p. 335.

nobody knew anything about him. Many men envied, and all men admired his singular fortune. But that such a man should be Prime Minister of England, and at such a time, seemed absolutely preposterous. By some the appointment was considered as a premonitory symptom of the mental disease with which the King was again afflicted, while the new arrangements were in the course of formation. By the leader of Opposition the arrangement was pronounced 'a notorious juggle'[*]—an opinion which was not far from the truth, so far as the retiring minister was concerned. Dundas, the private friend and confidential colleague of Pitt throughout his administration, though, perhaps, of all the late Cabinet, the least unwilling to be released from the cares of office, could not flatter his chief that a Cabinet directed by Addington would hold together, even as a temporary expedient.[†] From the commencement to the close of its miserable existence, the head of the administration was assailed with a pitiless and unceasing storm of ridicule, which reminded old Parliament men of the stories their fathers used to tell of Sir Spencer Compton, Sir Thomas Robinson, and the Duke of Newcastle. Addington himself furnished the cue by which the popular contempt of his pretensions was condensed in a single phrase. During the King's illness, the principal obstacle to his recovery was want of sleep. The new minister recommended the trial of a hop pillow, which his father had prescribed in similar cases. The hop pillow was used, it is said, with success, and contributed mainly to the restoration of His Majesty's health.

[*] Fox's *Correspondence*.
[†] 'Our friends who, as an act of friendship and attachment to you, agree to remain in office, do it with the utmost chagrin and unwillingness; and, among the other considerations which operate upon them, is the feeling that they are embarking in an administration under a head totally incapable to carry it on.' Dundas to Pitt, 7th February, 1801.—EARL STANHOPE's *Life of Pitt*, vol. iii. p. 279.

When this anecdote was spread abroad, the Prime Minister became known by the title of the Doctor, and was seldom spoken of by any other name.

The derangement of the King's mind, to which reference has been made, became apparent a few days after Pitt's resignation. The pain and anxiety attendant upon the dismissal of a minister who had served him for seventeen years, coupled with the agitation caused by the attempt to make him violate what he believed to be an irrevocable and unalterable engagement, had thrown his infirm mind once more off its balance. On the 18th of February, the King closed the correspondence which had so much troubled him, by a short note, in which his late minister was, for the first time, addressed as 'My dear Pitt.'* At this time he was under medical treatment for a feverish cold. On the 21st he became delirious, raved about the Catholic Bill, and spoke of Pitt, Grenville, and Dundas with imprecations. The Willises were then called in, and it was found necessary to put him under restraint. The presence of the Willises, though perhaps necessary, increased his irritation. He declared that he was not mad, and that if the elder Willis was sent

Health of the King.

---

* EARL STANHOPE's *Life of Pitt*, vol. iii. App. xxxii. The King parted from his illustrious servant without any of the ill-feeling which, on his part, had marked the retirement or dismissal of former ministers who had thwarted or attempted to thwart his will. But he could not trust himself to see Mr. Pitt. 'I thought,' he said to General Harcourt, 'we should both, perhaps, say something we should be sorry for; we might both be warm in argument, and therefore I thought it much better that we should put our thoughts on paper, and I sent for the Speaker as the friend of both.' He repeatedly said that his motives were conscientious, and that he held the oath so sacred, he could not give way. He spoke highly of Mr. Pitt, and he said 'the Speaker had told him that Mr. Pitt, though he regretted the thing, could not but revere the King for his steadiness and conscientiousness.' — LADY HARCOURT's *Diary*, MSS. For other particulars relative to the King's illness, not before published, I quote the same authority.

for, there would be a Regency; in which event, he repeated what he had often said in his former illness, that he would never resume the functions of sovereignty. Meanwhile, public business, much of which was urgent, could not proceed. The bill for the repeal of the Brown Bread Act of last session, which had given so much offence to the people, that it was thought necessary to hurry a repealing enactment through both Houses in a single day, awaited the royal assent; and it was thought a measure of such urgency that the royal assent was obtained at a time when the King was not a responsible agent. The Chancellor took the commission for the bill to the Queen's house; but the physicians would not permit him to see the King. Dr. Willis, however, undertook to get the commission signed, and the Chancellor suffered this very questionable proceeding to take place. The physician told His Majesty that his signature was required to something for the comfort and happiness of his people; upon which, according to Willis's statement, the afflicted Sovereign made a touching reply: 'Is it,' said he, 'for the happiness of my people?' Then I will sign my best George R.'[*]

On the 22nd of February, Mr. Addington thought it right to inform the Prince of Wales, the Duke of

---

[*] Lady Harcourt's *Diary*. It is recorded by Lord Malmesbury that the Chancellor said, when he returned from the palace, that His Majesty was in the perfect possession of his understanding. —*Diary*, vol. iv. p. 17, *Correspondence*. But according to Lord Colchester, the Chancellor told Lord Hardwicke he had not seen the King.—*Life of Lord Colchester*, v. i. p. 245. He told Fox the same thing.—Fox's *Correspondence*, vol. iii. p. 336; and Rose's *Diary*, vol. i. p. 315. According to Rose, Loughborough said, that Willis, when he came out of the King's room, told him that there would be no difficulty in obtaining the royal signature to a dozen papers respecting which no detailed statements were necessary. And this professional opinion, reaching Lord Malmesbury by hearsay, is magnified into an imputation on the Chancellor of making a statement wilfully false upon a subject of the gravest importance. Lord Malmesbury's accuracy, when relating the political gossip of the day, is not to be relied on.

York, and his own colleagues, together with Mr. Pitt
and Lord Grenville, of the King's insanity. The
Prince, on the following day, sent for Pitt, to consult
him, as he said, on the present distressing occasion.
Pitt said, he presumed that His Royal Highness had
sent for him as one of His Majesty's ministers. The
Prince replied, that he had done so, and that he
wished to know, in case of the continuance of the
King's illness, what were the steps he meant to take?
Pitt said, that he would answer his question, and
give him his best opinion, on the express condition,
that His Royal Highness would refrain from advising
with those who were in opposition to His Majesty's
Government. The Prince acquiesced, reserving only
the liberty of maintaining his confidential intercourse
with his friend, Lord Moira. At this point, Pitt
seems to have terminated the interview, in order that
he might consult his colleagues of the Cabinet *de
facto*. On the 25th, he saw the Prince again, and
informed him that he had determined, should the
necessity arise, to propose a restricted regency, precisely similar to that which he proposed in 1788;
and that, in this view of his duty, he was supported
by all the Cabinet, including the Duke of Portland,
Lord Loughborough, and Earl Spencer, who, on the
former occasion, had differed from him on this point.
He reminded the Prince, that the sense of Parliament had been clearly expressed in favour of restriction; and that His Royal Highness, with every
one concerned, would do well to assent to it. The
Prince gave utterance to some expressions of discontent, but he knew that it was vain to resist. If
Parliament had consented to restrictions in 1788, it
is pretty certain that, with the experience which had
been acquired in the last twelve years, of the character
of the person who was destined to exercise the power
of the Crown, both Parliament and the country would

be all but unanimous in providing such safeguards as were practicable against its abuse.*

The two Prime Ministers—the minister in fact, and the minister elect—were in constant communication on this difficult state of affairs. It was the opinion of the Willises, that the King's illness was different from the illness of 1788, and that his recovery was probable. With this view, it was of course desired to postpone a Regency Bill until the latest possible period. That period was fixed by Pitt for the 12th of March, as the public service would not admit of a longer delay. Parliament, in the meantime, was content to leave the matter in the hands of Pitt, who, under this sudden and unforeseen change of circumstances, was regarded as the real minister. Men of sense were agreed that to set aside a statesman of supreme ability and long experience at such a juncture as this, and to supply his place with a political nonentity, was the height of folly; and some were of opinion that it was a case for the intervention of the House of Commons.†

The opinion of Dr. Willis

---

* It is remarkable that, even on this occasion, the Prince of Wales could not conduct himself with common decency. No man of any feeling, and few men with any regard to outward appearances, would care to appear in public, while a father was lying bereft of reason on a bed of sickness. But the Prince of Wales, whom base adulation described as 'the finest gentleman in Europe,' was seen at this time in public places oftener than usual. Lord Malmesbury mentions his being present at a concert on the Sunday after the King was taken ill, at the notorious Lady Hamilton's, and accosting Calonne, the 'rascally' French minister, in these terms, 'Savez-vous M. de Calonne, que mon père est aussi fou que jamais.' This would seem hardly credible, even when told of this Prince; but the anecdote is corroborated by Lady Harcourt, who relates it thus, 'The Prince had been visiting Lady Hamilton, when, meeting M. de Calonne, who asked him how the King did, he answered, "Plus fou que jamais."'—MSS.

† 'Sir Robert Peel told me, he had been urged by many independent men to state to the House of Commons the necessity of Mr. Pitt remaining in a responsible situation, and not abandoning the country. He referred plainly to the total want of confidence in Mr. Addington, and stated that to be general in and out of Parliament.'—Rose's *Diary*.

Addington's position at this time was, indeed, somewhat ridiculous. He had vacated the chair, and Sir John Mitford, the Attorney-General, had become his successor. He had taken the Chiltern Hundreds, leaving Mr. Pitt as Chancellor of the Exchequer, to bring forward the Budget. On the 27th of February, when the King's malady had wholly incapacitated him, Addington was returned to the House of Commons and took his seat on the Treasury bench, while Pitt, from a back bench, directed as usual the proceedings of the House, allayed the public anxiety about the state of the King's health, and assured the House that before any public business of importance was transacted, the state of His Majesty's health should be ascertained.

On the 1st and 2nd of March, the King's life was in imminent danger. On the 3rd, his bodily ailment yielded to the strong remedies which had been applied. On the 6th, his pulse, which had been at fever-heat, subsided; he talked rationally, asked how long he had been ill, and expressed anxiety lest the public business should have been interrupted by his illness. He inquired about the state of the Ministry, and was satisfied when he learned that Pitt, not having given up the seals of office, had continued at the head of affairs. He was very particular in his inquiries as to any allusions to his illness that had been made in Parliament. Willis told him exactly what had passed. 'One member alone moved an inquiry into the state of your Majesty's health; and Sheridan, in the handsomest manner, got up and spoke against it, and in the highest terms of your Majesty.' On which the King said, 'It is very odd, but ever since that attack of Hadfield's in the play-house, Sheridan has shown a personal attention to me.' He then asked who made the motion, and when he was told Mr. Nicholls, and that it was universally reprobated, he only observed

The King's inquiries.

'that he was always an odd man.'* From this time the King made gradual, though irregular progress, towards recovery. On the same day that he held the conversation above referred to, being the 6th of March, he desired Willis to communicate the fact of his convalescence to Mr. Addington, to Lord Eldon, and to Mr. Pitt. With respect to Pitt, he added these words, which appear to have been duly reported to his late minister, 'Tell him I am now quite well —quite recovered from my illness; but what has *he* not to answer for, who is the cause of my having been ill at all?'† It appears, that, in consequence of this message, Mr. Pitt caused it to be intimated to His Majesty that he would never, during the King's life, bring forward the Catholic question. The retiring minister made a similar announcement to his friends; upon which the question naturally suggested itself, why should he retire at all, when the only obstacle to his remaining in office, was thus, by his own act, wholly removed? Pitt himself seems to have taken this view of his position, and even to have canvassed the mode of providing for Addington.‡ He could not, with decency, make a direct offer to remain in office; but he spoke of the matter without reserve among his friends, who took measures, with his tacit concurrence, to bring about a result so much to be desired. If Pitt could not move in the matter, it was still less to be expected that the King should put such an affront on the man whom he had summoned from an office of dignity and security, as to reinstate his former minister merely because he had postponed a measure of the first importance, from deference to His Majesty's will. It was obvious that Addington, and Addington alone, could solve the difficulty. A proposal was accordingly

* Lady Harcourt's *Diary*, MSS.
† Earl Stanhope's *Life of Pitt*, vol. iii. p. 303
‡ Rose's *Diary*, 6th March.

made to the expectant minister, that he should withdraw his pretensions in favour of the minister who was not yet out of office, of whom he never pretended to be the rival, and of whom he could hardly fail to consider himself, as every body else considered him, the temporary substitute. But Addington was not prepared for the disappointment of his hopes, when, after an interval of painful suspense, they were on the point of being fulfilled. He listened coldly to the proposal of the half-accredited deputation which had waited on him. He said, that it had not been his wish to quit his former situation; that the late minister had declared his irrevocable determination to resign, and had advised his accepting the Government, as the only thing that could stand between the Crown and ruin. Finally, he referred them to the King, warning them, at the same time, of the effect which their proposal might have on His Majesty's health.* This answer was, of course, conclusive; and Pitt, seeing that the matter could not with propriety be carried any further, desired that it might be dropped. He immediately announced his intention of supporting the new Ministry, and his wish that his friends would follow his example.

Pitt's conduct throughout this transaction is open to grave observation. His readiness in March to make the most ample concession to the King's prejudice, or infirmity, upon a point to which, in February, he attached paramount importance, is not explained by any disclosures which have yet seen the light. Nothing had happened in this short interval to justify so great a change in Mr. Pitt's conduct. The King's illness was a circumstance wholly irrelevant. In February, when the King was well, Mr. Pitt announced his deliberate determination to resign, unless he was permitted to bring forward the

---

* Pellew's *Life of Lord Sidmouth*, quoting Mr. Abbot's *Diary*.

Catholic question, with His Majesty's 'full concurrence, and with the whole weight of Government.'*
He did resign, in consequence of this permission having been withheld; his successor was named; and the new Cabinet was in the course of formation when the King fell ill. But, in three weeks the King was well again—as well, at least, so far as his mind was affected, as he had been in February, or at any time since 1789. Yet Mr. Pitt was now ready to give up absolutely, and for ever, the Catholic question; and proposed to annul arrangements which had been made in consequence of his own act, and with his entire approval. Nothing had happened to diminish the force of the Catholic claims. What then was Pitt's position with regard to the Catholic question? It has already been shown that, in the autumn of 1799, the Irish minister was authorised to '*solicit*' every support the Catholics could afford, to the great measure of the Legislative Union; that the Cabinet was favourable to these pretensions; and that, if no assurance was distinctly given them, in the event of the Union being accomplished, of these objects being submitted with the countenance of the Government to the United Parliament, it was only from the consideration that a positive pledge might offend the Protestants.† Yet Mr. Pitt seems to have been of opinion, that this engagement, of which he had received the full benefit, was satisfied, so far as he was concerned, by the formal resignation of his office when the King refused to sanction the promised measure; and that he was at liberty to resume office the next day, with or without his colleagues, and upon a positive pledge, to renounce the policy which he had, only a few short weeks before, declared to his Sovereign, to be dictated by 'his unalterable

* Letter to the King, 31st January.
† Lord Castlereagh's letter to Mr. Pitt, 1st January, 1800.

sense of public duty.'* If such conduct as this is to be justified, on the ground that Mr. Pitt was under no express compact with the Catholics, I know not what species of engagement is binding upon public men. A minister cannot make a contract like a broker; and his performance should be judged with candour and liberality. But when he seeks to avail himself of a colourable pretext, to get rid of an obligation, of which all the benefit has been received, and the burden only remains, it is difficult to understand how his conduct can be reconciled with morality and good faith. Had Pitt adhered to his resignation, he might, at some future period, have resumed office unembarrassed by the Catholic question. He had not undertaken to bring forward the question at any particular time. The Catholics were not impatient. Relying on the sincerity of their powerful friend, to whose word they had given implicit confidence, they left it to him to choose the opportunity, the means, and even the terms, of their emancipation. If it had been found in 1804, that the difficulty which had disappointed their hopes in 1801, was still in existence, and undiminished; that the attempt to advance their claims at that time, would cause a regency, if not a demise of the Crown; that the country had become decidedly adverse to them; in a word, that no minister, however powerful, could hope to urge the question forward with a chance of success; the Catholics were not so perverse as to expect that their friends should stay out, and that their enemies should be kept in, by a useless perseverance in an untimely policy. Whatever might have been the prospects of the Catholic question in 1801, if the King had not interposed an obstacle, it is certain that it could not have been carried in 1804; and, therefore, Pitt might have returned to office in

* Letter to the King, 3rd February.—EARL STANHOPE's *Life of Pitt*, App. XXX.

that year, absolved from the engagement which had attached to his former administration. But, to break up a Government in February, because Catholic emancipation was indispensable, and to offer to reconstruct it in March, on the principle of Catholic exclusion, was to trifle with the King, to trifle with public men, and to trifle with a great question.

Addington, then, having declined to be made a minister one day and to be unmade the next at the caprice of Mr. Pitt, it only remained that the new arrangements should be formally completed. On the 14th of March a council was held, at which Mr. Pitt resigned the seals of office, and they were delivered by His Majesty to Mr. Addington, who thus became First Lord of the Treasury, and Chancellor of the Exchequer. Lord Hawkesbury succeeded Lord Grenville at the Foreign Office. Lord Hobart was appointed to the War Department in the room of Windham. Lord Lewisham replaced Dundas at the India Board, Earl St. Vincent succeeded Earl Spencer at the Admiralty. The Duke of Portland, Lord Chatham, and Lord Westmoreland remained in office. Lord Eldon was Chancellor. Loughborough's fate is remarkable enough to point a moral. The last thing which this deep politician could have anticipated as the result of his own intrigues, was his own exclusion from office. He thought he had certainly made the King his friend for life by betraying the counsels of his colleagues, and by making himself the tool of a prejudice, which he despised alike for its honesty and its folly. When he found that he was not consulted in the new arrangements, he had the assurance to write to the King, urging him to continue Pitt in office, and 'to rely upon the generosity of Mr. Pitt's mind.' When the regency was imminent, Loughborough hurried off to Fox, with whom he had long ceased to have any but casual communication. In

Addington Premier.

any event, therefore, he had made provision for his own safety. The manner of his dismissal was mortifying in the extreme. Addington informed him, that the arrangements which he proposed to make with reference to the legal appointments rendered it necessary that His Lordship should give up the Great Seal. To be dismissed by Addington was humiliation enough. But to be told that his services were not required in a Cabinet which contained no man of half his ability, was a significant intimation that, in the opinion of the respectable gentlemen who constituted His Majesty's Government, no attainments and no experience in affairs could compensate for the want of honesty and plain dealing. But Loughborough was not content until he had drained the last drop in the cup of degradation. The Seal had been taken away from him; but he had not been turned out of the Cabinet. He continued, therefore, to attend the meetings of the Cabinet, until he received a letter from Addington, reminding him that he was not one of His Majesty's confidential advisers, and that his presence at a Cabinet Council, already sufficiently large, was not desired.* It is said, that Addington had intended, at one time, to make Loughborough President of the Council; but if such an intention was ever entertained, it was soon abandoned. At length, his banishment was alleviated by an earldom; but his dignity was not accepted as an adequate compensation for the power and emoluments of office. Auckland, also, kindred to Loughborough in ambition and intrigue, but greatly his inferior in ability, was doomed to disappointment. Auckland, according to a contemporary statesman, who was not in rivalship with any pretender to power, had named *himself* as minister.† There was a deeper shade in the treachery of Lord Auckland than in

* Campbell's *Lives of the Chancellors*, vol. vi. p. 327.
† Lord Malmesbury's *Diary* vol. iv.

that of the Earl of Rosslyn. Auckland owed everything to the patronage of Pitt; his employments, his pensions, his peerage. He was the intimate friend of the great minister, who had admitted him to a confidence without reserve. If there was one man who should have blindly followed the fortunes of Pitt, Auckland was that man. Yet Auckland conspired with Loughborough to betray his friend and patron. And when the resignation of the late Ministry, which had been mainly caused by the intrigues of their professed friends, became the subject of discussion, Auckland was one of the first to stand up in his place in Parliament, and to attribute that resignation to some secret and unworthy motive.* It is satisfactory to record that this baseness was not rewarded. Lord Auckland had sought, by covert intrigues, and by open slander, to ruin his benefactor, because he had been refused promotion to the Cabinet. This promotion was still denied him. He had held the lucrative office of joint Postmaster-General under Pitt's administration; and he was permitted, by the contemptuous neglect of the new minister, to retain his office.

Lord Cornwallis resigned the Irish Viceroyalty,† and was succeeded by the Earl of Hardwicke. Lord Castlereagh also retired. The new Secretary was Mr. Abbot, one of the most uncom-

Resignation of Cornwallis.

---

* On this occasion, Rose wrote Lord Auckland a letter which, if he was susceptible of shame or compunction, must have wrung his soul.—See the letter in LORD STANHOPE's *Life of Pitt*, vol. iii. p. 326. Lord Stanhope adds, 'Pitt himself viewed the affair in nearly the same light. He was too proud to make any complaint. But he broke off all intercourse with Lord Auckland; and, as I believe, never again exchanged a word with him.'

† 'No consideration could induce me to take a responsible part with any administration which can be so blind to the interest, and indeed to the immediate security, of their country, as to persevere in the old system of proscription and exclusion in Ireland.'—Lord Cornwallis to General Ross, 15th February, 1801. *Correspondence*, vol. iii. p. 337.

promising of the opponents of the Catholic claims. The minor political offices were filled by some two dozen gentlemen, none of whom were of any note. Two of these gentlemen, Mr. Spencer Perceval, the Solicitor-General, and Mr. Vansittart, one of the joint secretaries of the Treasury, afterwards attained distinction. Mr. Perceval was destined to prove, that Mr. Addington was not the weakest possible minister. And Mr. Vansittart afterwards became the worst Chancellor of the Exchequer that had been known since Sir Francis Dashwood.*

Addington, personally, throughout these transactions, stands in favourable contrast, not only to such men as Loughborough and Auckland, but even to Pitt himself. He had been no party to the intrigues which had undermined the late administration. He had no knowledge of them. He had given no insidious advice to his illustrious friend and patron. When he received the first letter from the King, on the 30th of January, he went immediately to Pitt, and urged him, with so much earnestness, to desist from pressing the Catholic question, that he believed for the moment that he had prevailed. When he received His Majesty's commands on the following day, to form a new administration, he desired, and, I am persuaded, with perfect sincerity, to be excused. But when it was put to him by the agitated monarch, 'Where am I to turn, if you forsake me?' and when Pitt followed this up by saying—'I see nothing but ruin if you hesitate,' what was Addington to do? He might have obeyed the dictate of prudence, and persisted in his refusal. But an English gentleman is not accustomed to weigh personal considerations, when the line of duty is pointed out to him; and Addington might well be excused for thinking that he was

Personal character of Addington.

---

* See supra, vol. l. p. 214.

not wholly unfit for an office which his Sovereign pressed upon him, and, which the statesman, who had held it for seventeen years, told him, he alone was competent to fill. It has been mentioned, indeed, by a contemporary statesman, whose accuracy, when he does not relate facts within his personal knowledge, is very doubtful, that Addington spoke of himself merely as a temporary substitute for Pitt. That he said something of the kind is not improbable, for he relied avowedly on Pitt's support, to enable him to carry on Government.* He acted on Pitt's advice as long as Pitt was willing to advise him; and he must have felt, that he could not hope to persevere, if Pitt's protection should be withdrawn. There can be no doubt that Pitt considered Addington more as his substitute than his successor. But that there was no understanding of the kind, either express or implied, between the outgoing and the incoming minister, is manifest, from the conduct of Addington on the King's recovery, when he rejected a distinct overture from Pitt, to give way to him. Any such understanding, indeed, would have been highly discreditable to both parties.

The personal friends and followers of Pitt, the most prominent of whom were Rose and Canning, bitterly complained of the unbending pride, which would not permit their patron to tender the withdrawal of his resignation, when he caused it to be intimated to the King that he had abandoned the Catholic question. But, what appeared inflexible pride to men eager for office, was little more than common decency. Mr. Pitt's intimation to the King, that the sole cause of his retirement was removed, in itself afforded His Majesty an opening to reinstate his former minister had he been so disposed. A more direct tender of his services could hardly have

Complaint of Pitt's friends.

---

* Lord Malmesbury's *Journal*.

been made. But George the Third was a gentleman, and would have been incapable of putting such an indignity on Addington, as was involved in the proposal, which seemed so easy to Mr. Canning. The King in his reign had played many times a double part with his ministers; but those were ministers which had been forced on him. His Majesty had never deserted any man who had served him faithfully; nor was it likely that he would now, for the first time, cast aside a man, whose loyalty and fidelity had been interposed to shield his honour. If Pitt had offered to resume his office, without the full and hearty concurrence of Addington, the King could hardly have done otherwise than refuse his offer; and, a proceeding, so strange, so perplexing on the part of his late minister, would have been calculated cruelly to disturb a mind still dangerously excitable from recent disease.

When they found that the appointment of Addington was inevitable, the clever men who followed the fortunes of Pitt, were fain to console themselves with the belief, that such a minister could have but a short existence. Pitt himself seems to have partaken of this consolation. But Pitt and his friends were much mistaken, if they supposed that the country would demand their immediate restoration to power. The feeling prevalent abroad was not so much a feeling of impatience at the breaking up of a powerful administration, as of anger against the minister for distracting the mind of the good old King, by attempting to force on him a measure so objectionable as Catholic emancipation. The old English dread and dislike of the Papists began to revive; and there were many more who applauded George the Third, for his scrupulous regard to his Coronation Oath, than the friends of religious equality. Moreover, the country gentlemen, who had submitted to Pitt for so

Popular dissatisfaction with Pitt.

many long years, were getting a little weary of their master. Oppressed by the weight of his genius and authority, they were sensible of relief in the accession of a minister who was not exalted so far above their heads, and whose range of thought was not much more extensive than their own. The wits and fine gentlemen might laugh at the son of a country doctor sitting in the seat of the son of Chatham; but the wits and fine gentlemen were a small minority. The Tory squires and baronets who filled three-fourths of the House of Commons, found in Addington a minister after their own hearts.* He was a minister whom they might venture to approach; who would listen to them—who would talk to them—who would not treat them as so many heads to be counted in the lobbies. A kindred feeling pervaded the bulk of the middle classes. The natural state of public opinion in this country is a dislike of change. Hence a demand for mediocrity, equal, but not superior, to the ordinary administration of affairs. Men of parts and education in vain contend against this prejudice by argument, invective, and ridicule, in every form. All their attacks are met by passive resistance. A plain man, who does not much outrun the average intelligence of the country, will be the favoured minister in ordinary times. A prudent man, who says as little as possible, who is no orator, and not a very good speaker, is the best leader of the House of Commons. Addington was rather below the standard of mediocrity; but he was more popular with the Tories than his predecessor had ever been. And the Tories comprised all the clergy, most of the gentry, and a large majority of the middle classes.

---

* The King represented this feeling, when he addressed the new minister the day after he had been sworn as '*his own Chancellor of the Exchequer.*'—Letter to Addington, 15th March. Pellew's *Life of Lord Sidmouth*, vol. i. p. 353.

On the resignation of Pitt and his colleagues, who had agreed with him in the expediency of an immediate measure for the removal of the remaining disabilities of the Roman Catholics, Lord Cornwallis had thought it right to make a communication to that body, with reference to the disappointment of the expectations they had been taught to entertain. Accordingly, the Lord-Lieutenant drew up two papers; the one, embodying what he considered a fair representation of Mr. Pitt's sentiments on the subject; the other, framed upon his own interpretation of the opinions and views held generally by the friends of the Catholic cause. The first and most important paper contained a distinct avowal, that the leading members of the late administration had retired from office, because they found themselves unable to carry their policy in favour of the Catholics into effect; and were of opinion, that their retirement would be conducive to its ultimate success. The Catholics were assured that no opportunity would be neglected, and no effort would be spared by their friends who had quitted office, and by those who remained to advance their interests; and they were warned to give no advantage to their opponents by any want of patience, loyalty, and moderation. In the second paper, which contained only two paragraphs, the Catholics were more expressly enjoined to refrain from violent measures, and, above all, to form no connection with Jacobinical associations. In the second paragraph, it was implied that their friends would not return to office, except on the terms of concession to the Catholic claims. These minutes were communicated by Lord Cornwallis himself, or with his authority, in the first instance, to Lord Fingall and Dr. Troy, and by them circulated among the principal members of the Romanist party.

These papers, though not officially drawn, nor intended for publication, soon found their way into the newspapers on both sides of the Channel. Cornwallis maintained that they had produced the beneficial effect which had been intended; and that, with the exception of the last paragraph of the second paper, which implied an engagement on the part of the retiring ministers not to return to office without making the Catholic claims a Cabinet question, that they committed no man farther than he had committed himself.* The statements of these half-official minutes, with the exception referred to, were not disputed by Pitt or his colleagues; though their publication could hardly be very agreeable to a minister who had thought proper to renounce the policy which they so emphatically affirmed.

When the new ministers had taken their seats, general attacks were made in both Houses on the conduct of the war, the policy of the late administration, and the composition of the new. Lord Grenville made a powerful defence of himself and his friends; while the Earl of Westmoreland was the appropriate mouthpiece in the Lords, of a Cabinet, of which Mr. Addington was the head. In the Commons, the defence of the old, and the apology for the new administration, were left to Dundas and Pitt, the minister making only a few observations at the close of the debate. Pitt alluded, with a touch of feeling, seldom apparent in his public displays, to his disappointment at leaving office without having conducted the war to a satisfactory conclusion. 'Events,' he said, 'have happened which disappointed my warmest wishes, and frustrated the most favourite hopes of my heart; for I could have desired to pursue the objects of such hopes and wishes to the end of that struggle which I had worked for with anxiety and care.' But when he went on to speak of the new administration, the

<small>Grenville's defence of the late Ministry.</small>

---

* *Cornwallis Correspondence*, vol. iii. p. 345.

finer critics of the House thought they could detect the old manner—the keen irony and sarcasm with which they were so familiar,—in the high eulogistic strain which he affected. 'Are these gentlemen,' said he, 'called to a situation that is new to them? Are they new to the public?' None of their friends certainly had yet ventured to say that they were otherwise; but Pitt boldly maintained that ample experience of their principles and talents had already recommended them to the confidence of the House and the public. He singled out Lord Hawkesbury, compared him to Fox, and challenged the House to produce any man superior to him. After this, he had only mitigated praise to bestow on Lord Eldon and Lord St. Vincent, the only two men who could vindicate their pretensions to the offices which they filled. It is hardly to be supposed that, at this early stage, Pitt desired to hold up the new Ministry to ridicule;* but it is difficult to believe that such an assembly as the House of Commons could listen with gravity when they were told that his successors were distinguished by their talents and their experience; and that Lord Hawkesbury was one of the first orators and statesmen in the country.

These things were said in the presence of Fox and Sheridan; but Pitt, having referred to Fox with questionable raillery as a 'new member' in reference to his long absence from the House, Fox immediately rose. He admitted that no change in the counsels of the Government could be for the worse, and therefore the present administration must be an improvement on its predecessor; but he treated with ridicule, not less just than bitter, the absurd and hypocritical

---

* 'Canning told me Pitt had made him promise *not to laugh* at the Speaker's appointment to the Treasury.'—LORD MALMESBURY's *Diary*, vol. iv. p. 5. Canning seems to have taken this injunction in much the same sense as the people who were told by their orator not to use brick-bats and cabbage-stalks.

eulogies which Pitt had pronounced upon Addington and Hawkesbury. These personal topics, however, formed a very small part of Fox's speech, which was one of great power, and ranged over the whole field of political discussion. Pitt, according to his practice for the last ten years of denouncing everything at variance with the views of his Government as Jacobinical, a practice which had become wearisome and unmeaning—had described the declaration of the Northern powers on the question of the rights of neutrals as Jacobinical. Fox was never more happy in vigorous and pointed language, than when he stigmatised a phrase which, under the authority of Pitt, had become the common cant of Toryism, the excuse for every arbitrary and coercive measure, and the argument against every measure of enlightened progress and constitutional freedom. The few words to which Addington gave utterance on this night were remarkable only for the formal renunciation which they expressed of any reference to the form of Government in France in any future negotiations with that country. In this respect the new administration showed more sense than its predecessor, which always hampered its attempts at a treaty by offensive and impertinent allusions to the domestic institutions of the rival power. The motion for a committee was rejected by a majority of nearly three to one.[*] The division was merely a trial of strength, and excited much interest, not only as being the first party-division after the change of administration, but the first division after the change in the composition of the House of Commons effected by the Legislative Union. The minority was unusually large; but was mainly swollen beyond its usual proportions by the votes of Irish members who were dissatisfied, or were obliged to simulate dissatisfaction, with the policy

[*] 291 to 105.

upon which the new administration had come into power.

This debate which concerned the past more than the present administration, having been concluded, and the budget having been disposed of by his predecessor, Addington had no difficulty to encounter during the remainder of the session; and the sudden turn of good fortune in the war, though in no wise attributable to him, nevertheless redounded to the credit of his administration. There was only one question of a novel and curious character which gave rise to some discussion, but to no serious difference of opinion. Lord Camelford, the proprietor of the borough of Old Sarum, a man who was hardly responsible for his actions, had, in a freak of caprice, returned Horne Tooke to fill a vacancy for this borough. It was objected that a clerk in holy orders was ineligible; and a committee was appointed, on the motion of Lord Temple, to search for precedents. The report of the committee by no means sustained the objection. Up to the Restoration, the precedents were for exclusion on the plain ground that a clergyman might be elected to sit in Convocation; but when Convocation ceased to tax the body which they represented, and ceased, indeed, to sit for despatch of business, it seemed to have been assumed that the only ground of exclusion was removed, and that clerks in orders were not disqualified to serve in Parliament. In fact, several clergymen had sat in the House of Commons, and their competency had never been questioned.* The only case in modern times in which a member had been petitioned against on the ground of his being disqualified by holy orders was Mr. Rushworth, member for Newport, in the Isle of Wight. The Committee which tried this petition sat in 1785,

---

* Hatsell, vol. ii. p. 16.

after the passing of the Grenville Act. They declared Mr. Rushworth duly elected; but their decision was of no value as a precedent, because it proceeded on an unsound distinction as regarded eligibility between the order of a deacon and the order of a priest. Nevertheless, it was proposed by Lord Temple, on the report of this committee, that a new writ should be ordered in the room of Horne Tooke. The House, however, with a wholesome recollection of their encounter with Wilkes and the Middlesex electors, were not disposed to provoke a conflict with such antagonists as Lord Camelford * and Horne Tooke. Addington, with the assistance of Abbot, who was already designated as the successor to the chair, prepared a bill to remove doubts as to the eligibility of persons in holy orders to sit in Parliament, by declaring them disqualified. The bill passed without much opposition, a clause proposed by Horne Tooke to limit its operation to beneficed clergymen having been rejected by a large majority. Horne Tooke was in his sixty-fifth year when he entered the House of Commons. His first speech was listened to with eager curiosity; but the members who had thronged to hear him, soon returned to their clubs, the library, and Bellamy's. Few men, however gifted, succeed in the House of Commons who have not learned to adapt themselves to its tastes before their intellectual habits have been formed. Tooke had taken great pains to prepare himself for that fastidious and infallible audience. Looking round the crowded benches, he probably had a thorough contempt for the great majority,

---

* He is said to have threatened that, in the event of Horne Tooke being disqualified, he would return his black footman. But he did not live to carry this purpose into execution. This is the sort of practical proof which hastens and ensures the reform of a long-standing abuse. But the time was not yet come; and the close boroughs had hitherto refuted the reformers by returning some of the best members in the House.

and he saw no man of whom he was afraid. He had
rallied Fox on the hustings at Covent Garden with
great success. He had repeatedly attacked Pitt and
Sheridan. He had on one occasion insulted the
Speaker himself, and had afterwards bullied the
Commons at their own bar until they were fain to
give up the unequal contest.* Yet this man, whose
coolness and effrontery were proverbial; who had
seen the world on every side, a wit, a scholar, and a
cynic, was seized with unknown tremors, when he
stood on the floor of the House of Commons.† He
recovered, however, his self-possession sufficiently to
proceed with his speech. He gave a sketch of his
life, and told the House how his hopes and prospects
had been destroyed by the profession which he had
rashly adopted in youth, and had renounced for
thirty years. The tale was one which might have
commanded the respectful sympathy even of those
who would have refused to give relief. But the
scoffing spirit in which he spoke conveyed the impression that he made his personal wrong a pretext
for holding up the church, and even religion itself,
to ridicule and scorn. He affected to treat the disqualification for other employments worked by holy
orders, as if they were a brand of infamy. 'Cannot
a quarantine,' he said, 'of thirty years be a sufficient
guard against the infection of my original character?'
Sarcasm of this kind grated on the ear of the House.
The disputatious temper of Tooke, which delighted
in levelling authority and in trampling on pretension,
soon brought him into collision with the House, which
suffers no man to overstep his position. He criti-
cised the report of the committee with the pedantry
of a grammarian. He questioned the decision of the
Speaker on a point of practice, and argued the matter
at length in utter ignorance or contempt of the im-

* Ante, vol. ii. p. 164 et seq.
† 'I hardly knew,' he said, 'whether I stood on my head or on my heels.'

plicit deference which long usage has yielded to the decision of the chair. He was called to order for violating another well-established rule, which forbids any member to attribute motives to another. This point he disputed likewise, seeking to prove that the rule of the House was inconsistent with reason, and the freedom of debate. Any man who knows the House of Commons, which, in its essential characteristics, was the same assembly fifty or a hundred years ago as that which now sits at Westminster, will easily understand that Horne Tooke was soon set down as an outlaw, a failure and a bore. It would be difficult to produce any good reason why a clergyman, without cure of souls, should not sit in the House of Commons; nor indeed was any reason, founded either on principle or expediency, urged in favour of the bill. Nevertheless, it passed with only an ineffectual and somewhat faint opposition from the Whigs. The Lords make no objection to clergymen sitting as lay peers, nevertheless they agreed to the bill excluding clergymen from the House of Commons with hardly a dissentient voice. The bill, as originally drawn, was retrospective in its operation, its primary object being to expel one obnoxious member, but it was impossible to defend such legislation; and, when it was pointed out that such would be the effect of the enactment, Addington agreed that the bill should be framed in the usual manner.

The new Ministry made a laudable attempt to return to the old laws of England, from which their predecessors had been so willing to depart. They suffered the act for the suspension of the Habeas Corpus to expire; and, during some weeks, the people of this country were once more under the protection of the great law of English liberty. Many persons, detained under the arbitrary powers of the Suspension Act, were liberated on their own recognisances. But this good disposition was soon checked, and gave place to a fury against freedom of speech and action, such as had not been equalled when the emissaries of the Rule of Terror had been busy in London and the great towns. Committees of both Houses, listening with credulous ears to stories of plots and conspiracies, which sprang from the dregs of the Irish rebellion, and the expiring throes of the old Corresponding Society, reported in favour of a further suspension of the Habeas, and of a renewal of the Act for the prevention of seditious meetings. The country was at this time in a state of profound tranquillity; the Bread Riots of the preceding year, which had alone disturbed the public peace, and which had been mainly instigated by the judges, having entirely subsided. Nevertheless, the report of the committee was immediately followed by the presentation of a bill for taking away once more the writ of Habeas; and, as if England must perish if the liberty of the subject was endured for a moment longer, the bill was, with shameful precipitation, hurried through all its stages in a single sitting. The bill for the prevention of seditious meetings, was not suffered to pass with quite so much expedition; but it was forced through in a few days. An Indemnity Bill, for the protection of persons who had been concerned in the practice of arbitrary imprisonment since 1793, was, for the first time, brought forward. No practical necessity was urged in support of this measure. It did not appear, that any agent of the Government had been sued for false imprisonment since 1793; nor was any reason shown, why a man should be protected from punishment who had wantonly or maliciously abused the license of those times. But the arguments and protests of opposition were of no avail; and rather seemed to increase the majorities by which every measure for the curtailment of liberty and the repression of opinion was sanctioned. One of the earliest acts of legislation which the United Parliament gave to Ireland, was an act for the renewal of martial law, although there was no pretext for saying that the rebellion had not ceased; there being in fact only three or four districts in a state of disturbance. But the Irish representatives—if they were to be called representatives—were unanimous for arbitrary government. It was in the debates on this bill, that Mr. John Claudius Beresford, in the Commons, and the Chancellor Clare, in the Lords, avowed and defended the practice of torture.*

While Parliament was employed in this manner, and while gloomy apprehensions for the fate of this country, both at home and abroad, were spreading widely through all classes, the cloud which threatened the maritime power of England was suddenly dispersed; and, at the same time, an unexpected military success in an opposite quarter, restored the faded lustre of her arms.

After Bonaparte's departure from Egypt in 1799, the army which he had abandoned fell into rapid decay. Reduced to half its original strength, hopeless of reinforcement—without money —without supplies, and daily diminishing from disease and want—the proud army of Italy, whose fierce onslaught had so easily crushed the barbarous chivalry of the desert a few short months before, was now beset by new and formidable enemies. Besides the Mamelukes, who, though always beaten, and apparently annihilated, still swarmed around the French columns, a well-disciplined force of eighty thousand Turks, under the Grand Vizier, was on its march. A Russian contingent of five or six thousand men was expected to follow. To meet these armaments, the invaders had only eight thousand five hundred men. Such was the report which the French General sent to his Government. The ship containing

Affairs of Egypt

* Ante, pp. 163, 164. Notes.

his despatches was taken by the British cruisers; and the King's Government, acting immediately on the information thus obtained, issued orders to Lord Keith, to consent to no convention, which did not stipulate for the surrender of the French army as prisoners of war. These orders were sent from London on the 17th of December. Meanwhile, Sir Sidney Smith, who was guarding the entrance of the Nile with a single ship, knowing that the French army was in a desperate state, but not being informed of all which was known in London on that subject, foresaw the probability that the French General might be disposed to treat. Accordingly, with a promptitude which did him credit, Smith forbade the Turkish Commander to enter into a separate negotiation with the enemy; but desired, that any proposition which Kleber might make, should be submitted to himself and the representatives of Russia, in conjunction with the Grand Vizier. The British captain had no authority to treat beyond the power of making a military convention, which was incident to his position as commanding officer on the station. Nor did he formally become a party to the treaty which was concluded on this 21st of December, between the French General and the representative of the Porte. But the treaty was negotiated on board Sir Sidney Smith's ship, and was understood by both the contracting powers, to have been concluded with the sanction of the representative of Great Britain. The eleventh and twelfth articles of the treaty, indeed, expressly stipulated, that safe conducts and passports should be provided for the French army, not only by the Porte, but by its allies—Great Britain and Russia; and that its safe return to France should not be disturbed in any manner. It is clear, therefore, that this was a convention to which the honour of England was pledged as much as that of Turkey.

The treaty of El Arish, as it was called, was signed on the 24th of January. A few days afterwards, Sir Sidney Smith received a despatch from Lord Keith, transmitting the orders of the Cabinet of the 17th of December. This unpleasant intelligence was immediately communicated to the French General. Kleber was indignant, and not without cause. The high-spirited Frenchman published Lord Keith's despatch in general orders, accompanied by this comment:—'Soldiers,—The only answer to such insolence is victory. Prepare for battle.' Kleber soon justified this magnanimous vaunt. On the 20th of March, he routed and dispersed the army of the Vizier, eighty thousand strong, at Heliopolis. After some days a body of twelve thousand men, a remnant of the great Turkish army, was rallied at Damietta, but was again defeated. Kleber then marched to Cairo, whither a portion of the fugitive army of the Vizier had retreated after the battle of Heliopolis, and by false accounts of the battle had persuaded the people to rise and massacre the French. Cairo was taken after a desperate and sanguinary struggle; and before the end of April, the French were once more in possession of the whole of Egypt.

The British Government, when informed of the convention of El Arish, sent orders to Lord Keith to permit the French army to embark, in pursuance of the treaty concluded with the sanction of Sir Sidney Smith. This decision was communicated by the Admiral to the French minister in Egypt on the 25th of April. But the position of the French army was very different at that date to what it had been when the convention of El Arish was signed; and the offer of the British Government was peremptorily rejected.

The conduct of England in this transaction was censured by the enemy as a breach of faith; while the British Commander was blamed by his Government alike for exceeding his authority, and for the discretion which he exercised in pursuance of the authority which he assumed. But the first-mentioned charge is disposed of by a reference to dates. The despatch, forbidding Lord Keith to enter into any treaty with the French except on the footing of the surrender of their army as prisoners of war, was sent from London four days before the negotiation with Kleber was opened on board Sir Sidney Smith's ship. On receiving information of the convention of El Arish, Lord Keith lost no time in making Kleber acquainted with the orders of his Government. It is true, that when Keith wrote that letter, another arrangement had been made, with the concurrence of the officer representing the British flag. But he knew also, that Smith had no authority to conclude a treaty of such importance; and that he himself had no such authority while Lord Elgin, the British plenipotentiary, was resident at Constantinople. Besides, his orders were positive; and though they were issued before it was known that the Turks had actually treated with the French, yet they had been issued in full contemplation of such an event.

Sir Sidney Smith, on the other hand, was unjustly blamed by his Government and by his country. It is easy to say, that he should not have taken upon himself to sanction such favourable terms of capitulation without referring to his superior officer, or to the Ambassador at the Porte. But Sir Sidney thought that the evacuation of Egypt by the French was in itself the object of first importance; the communication with Constantinople or Gibraltar was tedious, and the golden opportunity might be lost before definite instructions could be obtained. If the hero of Acre had known all that the ministers in London knew, he would not have consented to let the French depart on such easy conditions; and if the English Cabinet had not been possessed of the information which they obtained from the intercepted despatches of the French General, they would have applauded Sir Sidney Smith for the exercise of a prompt and wise discretion. As the event turned out, the captain of the 'Tiger' had formed a better judgment of the policy which the situation required than the ministers in London.

The French, though elated by the great victory of Heliopolis, which relieved them from any fear of farther molestation on the side of Turkey, were, nevertheless, in a precarious condition. Cut off from all communication with Europe, and from all means of retreat, and surrounded on all sides by the vigilant and implacable hostility of the people whom they had so wantonly invaded and ruthlessly conquered, the remnant of the French army could not hope to hold the country for any lengthened period. Their recent military successes had indeed brought over some of the native chiefs, but no dependence was to be placed on such allies. The loss of General Kleber, who fell by the hand of an assassin, a few weeks after the re-occupation of Cairo, was irreparable. Kleber was one of the ablest of the many able men whom the Revolution had produced. A soldier, a statesman, and an observer of mankind, he was also a humane and honourable man. His commanding intellect and high moral qualities had gained an influence and an ascendency over the wild people of the East, which Bonaparte himself had never attained. Menou, who succeeded Kleber in command, was an officer of inferior capacity. He was a man of noble birth, and had obtained employment, and perhaps saved his life by flattering the vilest excesses of the Revolution. When he joined the army of Egypt, he hastened to incur the contempt of the Mussulmans, and of all that was decent in the French army, by the gross artifice of assuming the turban. The departure of Dessaix, who had promptly availed himself of the convention of El Arish to leave Egypt, had left this man second in command.

After they had refused to renew the convention of El Arish, the French were for many months left unmolested. Late in the autumn, it was determined by the English Cabinet that an attempt should be made to dislodge them. The troops, under the command of Sir Ralph Abercromby, which had been tossing idly in the Mediterranean all the summer, were destined to this service. The earlier fortunes of this expedition had been singularly perverse; and no army sent from England since the war began had met with such signal and discreditable failures, as the army which was ultimately to redeem the military credit of the nation. At the beginning of the year a plan had been proposed to the Government by Sir Charles Stuart, with the approval of Lord Cornwallis, to co-operate with the Austrians in Italy by sending a force of twenty thousand men to intercept the communication between France and Italy by way of the Maritime Alps, and to afford a basis for an insurrection of the Royalists in the South, upon which the Government were advised to rely; but the execution of this plan was delayed until it became impracticable, in consequence of the rapid advance of the French army. Stuart, who had been appointed to lead the expedition, resigned in disgust when his plan was frustrated; but a well-appointed army of twenty thousand men having been collected, it was determined that an attempt should still be made to co-operate with the Austrians in staying the farther progress of the French in Italy. Accordingly Sir Ralph Abercromby was summoned from Scotland to take the command of this force; and on the 3rd of July, three weeks after the battle of Marengo, and the armistice of Alessandria, by which the Austrians had ceded their Italian provinces, the British transports appeared off Leghorn. The fleet consequently returned to Minorca, where the troops were re-landed to await further orders from England.

After a delay of several weeks, an expedition, consisting of fifteen thousand men, under Sir James Pulteney, was sent from England, to co-operate with Abercromby. Pulteney was ordered to make an attack on the Spanish port of Ferrol, on the coast of Gallicia. The order to attack Ferrol seems to have been issued in utter ignorance of the place; and it was executed in a manner which brought ridicule on the army, or rather on those who directed its movements. Eleven thousand men were landed without opposition; and, after a slight resistance, took possession of the heights which commanded the town. The General, however, with the concurrence of his principal officers, except the chief engineer, who was of a different opinion, decided that the place, though not strongly fortified, could not be taken by assault; and, as no preparations had been made for a siege, the troops were sent back to their ships, and the project was abandoned. The expedition to the Spanish coast was intended to effect a diversion for the protection of Portugal, which was threatened by Spain; and likewise to prevent the Spanish fleet in the harbour of Ferrol from co-operating with the Northern Confederation. Mr. Pitt asserted, that the information upon which the Government had acted had been satisfactory, both to Lord St. Vincent and to the General in command.* But the information, which satisfied Lord St. Vincent and Sir James Pulteney, must have been strangely deficient; for it did not comprise any plan of the works, nor any account of the force available for the defence. When the General ascended the hill, it seems that he discovered, for the first time, that Ferrol was defended on three sides by the sea, and that the land defences,

---

* *Parl. Hist.*, vol. xxxv. p. 990.

extending for more than a mile, consisted of masonry with seven bastions, and other works of the best construction.

After this failure the expedition was ordered to Cadiz, where it was intended to renew the experiments which had been abandoned at Ferrol. The attempt on Cadiz was a more signal failure than the attempt on Ferrol. On this occasion, Sir Ralph Abercromby, having been joined by Pulteney's force, took the command of an army consisting of twenty thousand men. Abercromby's orders were to land and destroy the arsenal of Cadiz, if he could keep open his communication with the great fleet under the command of Lord Keith, which was to supply his army with provisions and stores. But the anchorage was found to be unsafe; the harbour had been blocked up with sunken ships in anticipation of the attack, and it was ascertained that the communication with the shore was extremely hazardous when the wind was in the south-west. The wind was then blowing from that quarter. Nevertheless, an attempt was made to disembark a detachment on the 6th of October. But this attempt was frustrated by the mismanagement of Lord Keith, the Admiral in command of the fleet.* Boats were required for five thousand men; and, after a delay of several hours, means of transport were provided for no more than three thousand. A force so small, if landed, would probably have been cut off before the main body could reach the shore. The landing was therefore postponed; and on the following day, upon a consideration of the unexpected difficulties which presented themselves, one of which was a pestilence then raging at Cadiz, it was determined to abandon the enterprise altogether.

The fortunes of these expeditions had been hitherto one unbroken series of shameful and ridiculous

* *Life of Sir John Moore.* Letter to his father, vol. I. p. 264.

failures. Sir James Pulteney had been despatched in July with eight thousand men to attack Belleisle; but a glance at the place was sufficient, and the expedition sailed away. Ferrol, defended only by four thousand troops, was also considered too strong. Abercromby's force, which had been sent to the relief of Genoa, arrived just after the city had capitulated. The combined forces of Pulteney and Abercromby, accompanied by a fleet of twenty sail of the line and twenty-seven frigates, then summoned Cadiz; but Cadiz refused to surrender, and the great armament sailed away without striking a blow. For several weeks after this last inglorious attempt, the transports sailed about the Mediterranean without an object and without orders. Sickness and discontent broke out among the men; and an army, which had been organised with great pains under the able direction of General Moore, was rapidly falling away.

After several weeks of this demoralising inaction, orders arrived from England for the departure of the expedition to the coast of Egypt. After short delays at Minorca and at Malta, to recruit the health of the men who were debilitated by long confinement in their transports, twelve thousand troops, under Sir Ralph Abercromby, departed for Marmarice Bay, a harbour on the shore of Asia Minor, where the final arrangements were to be made for the descent on Egypt. Five thousand men, under Pulteney, were left at Malta to keep open the communications.

This expedition had been ordered on the same information which had led to the rupture of the convention of El Arish. It was believed in London, on the authority of Kleber's intercepted despatches, that the French army in Egypt was reduced to eight thousand men. But Kleber's despatch, written in September, 1799, did not represent the state of the French force in December, 1800; and greatly understated the numerical force of the French army at the time when it was written. It did not include Dessaix's division in Upper Egypt, nor the detachments posted at various points on the course of the Nile. The truth was, that the French General wrote, under the influence of indignant feelings at the recent desertion of the army by Bonaparte, and was willing to put everything in the worst aspect before the Directory. Six months after the date of the intercepted despatch, which described the remains of his army as perishing from disease and want, Kleber mustered twelve thousand French troops before Heliopolis. A few ships had indeed eluded the English squadrons, and thrown some reinforcements into Alexandria; but these had probably been no more than sufficient to replace the losses occasioned by the usual casualties of service. When Abercromby landed in Egypt, instead of finding the skeleton of an army, he had to encounter a well-appointed force of more than twenty-seven thousand men.

The Indian Government had been ordered to despatch a force from Bombay by the passage of the Red Sea, to support Abercromby; and the army of the Vizier was to cross from Syria, to co-operate with the British expedition. But it was uncertain when the reinforcement from India would arrive; and experience proved that a Turkish or Egyptian army, however numerous, could make no stand against the French. Abercromby, though well aware of the strength of the enemy, determined to land without waiting either for the Indian contingent, or the Turkish battalions. Accordingly, on the 2nd of March, the fleet anchored in Aboukir Bay, on the spot where Nelson's action had been fought. The state of the weather delayed the debarkation until the 8th. The enemy, therefore, had full time to prepare for the reception of the invaders. He was drawn up in force on the crest of a hill not far removed from the shore, his flanks covered with cavalry, and the Castle of Aboukir on his right. The first division, being the reserve under Moore, and the brigade of guards, was the first to disembark; so complete had been the arrangements, and so perfect was the discipline of this noble corps, that though the approach to the shore, and the landing were effected under a heavy fire of shell, grape, and musketry, which the gun-boats were unable to check, the men formed as soon as they left the boats, and each regiment was immediately engaged with the French, who rushed down to the shore, scattering their skirmishers before them. Notwithstanding, the twenty-third and some portion of the fortieth regiment charged up the hill, a loose sandy precipice, drove the French from their position at the point of the bayonet, and took seven pieces of cannon. The remainder of the British force was thus enabled to land without molestation. The whole army then rapidly advanced, and after a sharp encounter with the enemy on the 12th of March, forced him to retreat under the fortified heights of Alexandria.

The decisive action took place on the 21st. Up to this time, the French trusting to the strength of their position, and filled with an overweening confidence in the superiority of their military prowess, had not thought it worth while to oppose an equal force to the British army. Menou had left the expulsion of the invaders to his lieutenants; but he now took the command in person. Abercromby, also finding himself in front of a position of great strength, delayed an attack until he had gathered to his support all the force which he could command. He had been informed by a friendly native, that the enemy meant to surprise him. Abercromby was too prudent to disregard this information, though he did not believe that the French General would be so rash as to quit a position almost impregnable to risk the chances of the field. But the warning proved to be well founded. The French General thought it advisable to act on the offensive, before the English army should be joined by the Turks and the reinforcement from India. Accordingly, an hour before daybreak, on the 21st of March, the attack was made. The British were already under arms; and, though it was still dark, they received the impetuous charge of the French with their usual firmness. By a daring movement, Menou succeeded in turning the right of the English position; but the English regiments wheeled about, and by unexpectedly fronting the enemy, frustrated an attempt, which, if successful, would probably have decided the fortune of the day. Menou then ordered a charge of cavalry; but the ground was unfavourable to the action of this force, and the attack utterly failed. The French infantry, however, maintained the conflict with desperate courage; the British squares were repeatedly broken by their impetuous assaults, and the battle raged for some time after the ammunition on both sides had been exhausted. At length, after fighting for seven hours, with the loss of nearly half his army and without having gained a foot of ground, Menou ordered a retreat. The Turkish Government, having failed to provide horses for the cavalry, the British were unable to complete the victory by a pursuit.* The loss of the French was computed at about four thousand, including four generals; that of the English, nearly fifteen hundred. Only one English general fell, but that general was the brave and devoted Abercromby. He received two severe wounds during the action, but refused to quit the field. After the battle was won, the heroic Commander was carried, mortally hurt, to the flag-ship, where after lingering seven days in agony, he died. Other general officers, Moore, Hope, Oakes, and Lawson, were wounded, but not

---

* Sir John Moore's description of the battle in which he bore so prominent a part is to be found in his life, vol. L p. 294.

dangerously; as was Sir Sidney Smith, who had borne a conspicuous part on this glorious day.

The victory of Aboukir was, however, valuable for its moral effect, even more than for the substantial advantages gained by it. General Hutchinson, who succeeded to the command on the death of Abercromby, found himself in no condition to make an attack on Alexandria. Cairo also was in the possession of the French. But the British force was not inactive; and gained the advantage in several affairs of posts. The Turkish troops, inspired with confidence by their allies, harassed the French detachments; and the Grand Vizier actually defeated a division of eight thousand men. Hutchinson was reinforced by a thousand men from England, and having effected a junction of a portion of his army with thirty thousand Turks and Arabs under the Vizier, the siege of Cairo was formed. The place was capable of protracted resistance; but after twenty days, terms of capitulation were offered and accepted. The French garrison of thirteen thousand men marched out, with their arms, artillery, and baggage. They were conducted to Aboukir, and from thence conveyed in English transports to the coast of France. These terms were censured as too favourable; but the English General, situated as he found himself, thought it desirable to get rid of so large a force, and to obtain possession of Cairo on any terms.

The Convention of Cairo took place in the last week of June. Early in August, Sir David Baird arrived with the first detachment of Sepoys, after a toilsome march across the desert. The remainder of the force, amounting in the whole to upwards of seven thousand, arrived soon after, but not in time to engage in active operations against the enemy. The fall of Cairo, the reinforcements which the British army had received, and the arrival of the Indian contingent, rendered it hopeless for

the French to maintain their position in Egypt. On
the 30th of August, after a short siege, Alexandria
surrendered; and the garrison of eleven thousand
four hundred men were suffered to depart on terms
similar to those which had been granted to the
French at Cairo. The ships in the harbour were,
however, taken as prizes; half of them being given
up to the Ottoman Porte, and half being retained by
the British Admiral. All the monuments of antiquity
and art which had been collected by the men of
science who had accompanied the French army, were
likewise detained. Many of these works were afterwards
sent to England, and deposited in the British
Museum.

It is to be observed that his hard-fought campaign
in which the British arms were invariably
successful, resulted in terms not more unfavourable to the enemy, than those which *Negotiations for peace accelerated.*
he had been willing to accept before a British regiment
had landed in Egypt. The circumstances,
perhaps, justified the Convention of Cairo; but there
can be little doubt that Alexandria, closely invested
by sea and land, must have surrendered at discretion,
or fallen before the besiegers, if the English Commanders
had been less indulgent. The expulsion of
the French from Egypt was, nevertheless, an event
of the greatest importance. It showed to all Europe,
that England had not ceased to be a military power
—it assured the integrity of the British Empire in
India—it saved the Turkish Empire from becoming
a dependency of France. Menou had stipulated for
permission to send a despatch ship to Toulon on the
evacuation of Egypt; and this intelligence accelerated
the negotiations for peace which had long been
lingering in London, but which were thenceforth
conducted in a very different spirit to that which had
marked the Conferences at Paris and at Lisle.

A few days after the decisive battle before Alexandria, the Northern enemies of Great Britain, or rather, the Northern agents of the French, whose enmity alone had ever been formidable to this country, sustained a signal and wholesome chastisement.

The confederacy of the Baltic Powers planned at Paris, and consummated at Petersburg, was another proof that the political capacity of Bonaparte was not inferior to his military genius. The only great continental power which he had not overawed, and whose arms had checked the career of French ambition, was Russia; and, from a menacing foe of the first rank, the policy of the First Consul had converted Russia into an ally and a tool. Denmark and Sweden were gained through the agency of Russia; and thus a triple league had been formed of the only powers which could make a stand against the naval supremacy of England. It was necessary that a danger so imminent should be promptly met. It was not a question of international law, although the quarrel intended to be forced upon England assumed that form. The revival of the exploded policy of Catherine was merely a feint; yet the English Cabinet treated the Russian manifesto as if it were really a question of belligerent and neutral rights, which might be settled by negotiation. A fleet was, indeed, sent to the Northern seas; but an ambassador was sent before the fleet. And the Ministry had more confidence in the diplomacy of Mr. Vansittart than in Nelson and his broadsides. The Ministry, indeed, did all that well-meaning men could do, to thwart and frustrate the enterprise on which the maritime ascendency of England was staked. The expedition was destined for Copenhagen, the stronghold of the Baltic Confederation. But Copenhagen, though defended by a powerful fleet, as well as by the difficulties of the navigation through which it was

Subserviency of Russia to French interests.

approached, was otherwise unprepared for defence.
Promptitude, therefore, became an important element
of success;—but, instead of promptitude, there was
delay. At the moment when this new and unexpected danger threatened the power and prosperity
of Great Britain, the statesmen of Great Britain were
engaged in a political crisis. The Ministry had been
broken up—the King had been driven out of his
mind about a domestic question, which, though one
of great importance, was not, even in the opinion of
the parties principally interested in it, a question of
urgency. While the management of public affairs
was in a state of abeyance, or in a state of transition
from the hands of Mr. Pitt and Lord Grenville, to
the hands of Mr. Addington and Lord Hawkesbury,
the British fleet lay in Yarmouth Roads waiting for
orders. When at length the orders were made
known, they filled all England with surprise and
disappointment. It seemed incredible that there
could be any hesitation in fixing on the man to
command the expedition. Of the senior admirals,
St. Vincent and Duncan alone could prefer a claim
to a command of this supreme importance. But St.
Vincent was designated as the Chief Minister for
Naval Affairs; and Duncan having passed his seventieth year, was understood to have retired from active
service.

These veteran officers being out of the question,
Nelson's pretensions were without a rival. Nelson
was indeed nearly at the bottom of the list of flag-officers; but he was foremost in the estimation of his
country, and of his country's foes. He had seen more
of active service than any officer of his rank, probably
more than any officer in the navy. He had taken
part in upwards of one hundred actions. His great
qualities had been distinguished in numerous affairs.
He had mainly contributed to the victory of St.
Vincent. He had won the greatest battle of the

eighteenth century. Yet Nelson was not thought worthy of the chief command of the Baltic fleet. To the astonishment of all men, Nelson of the Nile was appointed second to Sir Hyde Parker, a respectable officer, but quite unfit for the arduous task entrusted to him. And this was done with the consent, if not by the advice, of Lord St. Vincent, who had, when Nelson was untried in chief command, appointed him, over the heads of the senior officers on the station, to attack the French fleet. But Nelson was not in favour at Court. The King could not entrust the command of his fleets to a man who was a bad husband; and the Admiralty were not indisposed to humble an officer who was wanting in the first quality of deference to his official superiors. Nelson felt bitterly the slight which had been put upon him by placing over his head an old admiral, who had no other claim than that of seniority. He said that this was probably the last service which he should render to his country; but this service he knew was one of extreme difficulty and danger; and therefore he did not hesitate to undertake it.

Sailing of the fleet. The fleet sailed from Yarmouth Roads on the 12th of March. It consisted of fifty sail, including sixteen ships of the line, one of which, containing the ordnance and ammunition for the gun-boats, foundered and sunk off the coast of Norfolk. The rest of the fleet reached the Cattegat on the 18th; but instead of pressing forward to Copenhagen, as Nelson would have done, Admiral Parker anchored off Cronenburg Castle, and sent Captain Hammond to Copenhagen with instructions to Mr. Vansittart, the special envoy,* and Sir William

---

* Southey, who is not very accurate in dates and details, states that Vansittart accompanied the fleet from England, and was sent from the Cattegat in the 'Blanche' frigate. The fact was, that Vansittart had left England in a packet-boat long before the squadron sailed; and the 'Blanche' was sent to Copenhagen to fetch him and Drummond away. See Lord Bexley's own account.—*Life of Sidmouth*, vol. i. p. 370.

Drummond, the resident minister, to present an ultimatum to the Danish Government. Vansittart, whose mission had wholly failed, in consequence of the Danes insisting, as a preliminary, on the removal of the embargo, immediately embarked with his colleague, the ultimatum having been peremptorily rejected.

Meanwhile, the Admiral pondered in his own mind the future course of operations, in the event of Mr. Vansittart's diplomacy being unsuccessful. Up to this time, Nelson had not been taken into the counsels of his chief, and knew no more than the youngest midshipman in his ship what was intended to be done. The anchorage off Cronenburg Castle made him fret with scorn and impatience. He was of opinion that the negotiation should have been conducted in the presence of the fleet, and that 'the Dane should see our flag waving every moment he lifted up his head.' Such indeed was the construction which Nelson put upon the orders of the Admiralty;* but he was not consulted by Parker until the arrival of Vansittart's despatch announcing the determination of the Danish Government to resist, and the great preparations they had made, and were making, to defend Copenhagen. Nelson proposed alternative plans of attack; the one by the passage of the Sound; the other by the passage of the Belt; but he urged immediate action as of more importance than the choice of either. The Admiral, determined by the advice of the pilots, sailed for the Belt; but, on the earnest remonstrance of Domett, the flag-captain, who represented the danger of attempting a channel so little known, the fleet returned to its anchorage. Nelson was sent for, and, as he agreed with Domett, it was ultimately decided that the attempt should be made by the direct course, the passage of the Sound.

* Letter to Sir Hyde Parker, 24th March, 1801.—*Nelson Despatches*, vol. iv. p. 296.

Ten precious days had now been wasted in doubts and deliberations; but twenty-four hours more were sacrificed to a frivolous and absurd punctilio. Not satisfied with the dismissal or return of Vansittart, whichever it might be called, from the Court of Copenhagen, Admiral Parker thought it necessary to send a flag to the Governor of Cronenburg Castle, to inquire if he had orders to fire upon the British fleet on their passage into the Sound? To this absurd question, the Dane replied that he could not suffer a fleet to pass his guns without being informed of its destination. This answer the British Admiral treated as a declaration of war. On the 29th of March, therefore, the decisive movement was at length made; and the British fleet, led by Nelson, sailed into the narrow channel, which the natural policy of the Danish Government has always interdicted to vessels of war. The English fleet expected to be swept by the batteries of Helsingburg, on the left side of the strait, as well as by the guns of Cronenburg on the right; but finding no offensive demonstrations made from the Swedish side, the fleet stood away towards the Swedish coast; and though the strait was only three miles wide, the ships were thus placed beyond the range of the Danish guns. A discharge from upwards of a hundred pieces was wholly ineffectual. Not a ship was touched, nor a man hurt;—so weak was the ordnance of those days, when compared with the power of modern gunnery. The passage of the Sound having been safely effected, the fleet appeared within sight of Copenhagen, a distance of twenty miles, about noon. Nelson, leaving the fleet at anchor, went forward in a schooner with two or three of his captains, and some artillery officers, to reconnoitre. It soon became manifest that the enemy had profited by the tardiness of the English Commander to make formidable preparations for his defence. A flotilla of ships, gun-boats, and every other known vessel of war, together with several floating batteries, were ranged in front of the harbour and arsenal, in a line extending four miles. Immediately in advance of the line, was a sand-bank called the Middle Ground. On the western flank, and in the rear of the Danish fleet, were formidable works erected on two artificial islands, guarding the mouth of the harbour, and called the Crown batteries. Another tremendous battery, called the Trekroner, had been put in repair, and fully mounted, while the English fleet was lying at anchor off Cronenburg.

An anxious council of war was held on board the Admiral's ship. Besides the formidable enterprise which lay before them, it was urged that the Swedish and Russian fleets remained to be encountered. To all these representations, Nelson impatiently observed, 'The more numerous the better; I wish they were twice as many; the easier the victory, depend on it.' He understood and contemned the tactics of the Swedes and Russians; and had no doubt that the plan of attack which he had formed, in the event of his meeting the fleet of either of these nations, would be successful. 'Close with a Frenchman,' he said, 'but outmanœuvre a Russian.' He offered to attack the Danish fleet with ten sail of the line and small craft. Sir Hyde Parker, reassured or overborne by the energy of his vice-admiral, accepted the offer, and gave him twelve ships of the line. The next two days were occupied in taking soundings and laying down buoys in the place of those which the Danes had removed. The wind being southerly, it was resolved to make the attack from the south, instead of from the east, as had been at first proposed. While Nelson was thus employed, it was arranged that Sir Hyde Parker should menace the Crown batteries, and the ships which lay at the entrance of the harbour.

Council of war.

At one o'clock in the morning of the 2nd of April, the signal to weigh was thrown out from Nelson's ship, and was hailed with reiterated shouts of joy through the division.

The night was passed in making detailed arrangements for the action on the following morning. Soon after nine o'clock, the leading ship weighed anchor. This was the 'Edgar,' Captain Murray. The next ship, the 'Agamemnon,' grounded in the attempt to weather the shoal. The 'Edgar' was thus for some time exposed alone to the enemy's fire. The 'Bellona' and the 'Russell' also went on shore at the entrance of the King's Channel. Thus two of the twelve ships were unable to take up the stations assigned to them; and one was rendered useless. Only one of the gunboats could get into the channel. Captain Riou, of the 'Amazon,' an officer of great ability, to whom Nelson had given a special discretionary command, took up his position opposite the Crown batteries, with two small frigates, two sloops, and two fire-ships. At ten o'clock, the action commenced, the British fleet having anchored in line of battle a cable's length from the Danish line. The enemy's fleet was inferior in strength and weight of metal to the British. But this inferiority was more than compensated by the addition of several floating batteries, and the cannon of the forts. After the battle had raged more than three hours with unabated violence, Sir Hyde Parker, who was prevented by the state of the wind and tide from giving any assistance to his vice-admiral, thought proper to signal an order for discontinuing the action. The Admiral was of opinion, that Nelson's squadron must be destroyed by the fire to which it was exposed. 'I will make the signal,' he said to his flag-captain, who remonstrated against it. 'If Nelson is in a condition to continue the action he will disregard it; if he is not, it will be an excuse for his retreat.' The Admiral did not consider that the signal was known to every ship engaged, as well as to the flag-ship; and that fatal confusion might be caused by the order of the Commander-in-Chief being partially obeyed. When the signal was reported to Nelson, he was pacing the deck in the full excitement of battle. 'This is warm work,' he said to one of his officers. 'And this day may be last of any of us in a moment;—but, mark you! I would not be elsewhere for thousands.' His answer to the Admiral's signal was a simple acknowledgment, and an order to keep his own signal for close action flying. Fortunately, Admiral Graves misunderstood the signal of the Commander-in-Chief; and the other captains looked only to Nelson's ship. The order, however, saved Captain Riou's flotilla from destruction, although that brave Commander himself lost his life. About an hour after the Admiral's well-meant, but ill-judged signal had been thrown out, the fire slackened along the greater part of the Danish line; but, as the ships were continuously reinforced from the shore, every ship which was not disabled, continued to fight. It was said, that some ships which had struck, recommenced firing, after having been supplied with fresh crews. But there seems to be no ground for imputing an intentional violation of the usages of war to the brave Danes. Some of the English boats, however, which had been sent to take possession of the prizes, were fired upon. Nelson, when informed of this fact, determined to take a step very unusual in such circumstances, and one which has been attributed, by unfriendly critics, to motives very different from those which actuated him. He sent a flag of truce to the Crown Prince, with a letter, in the following terms:—' Vice-Admiral Lord Nelson has been commanded to spare Denmark, when she no longer resists. The line of defence which covered her shores has struck to the British flag; but, if the firing is continued on the part of Denmark, he must

set on fire all the prizes that he has taken, without
having the power of saving the men who have so
nobly defended them. The brave Danes are the
brothers, and should never be the enemies of the
English.' The Prince naturally desired to know the
precise object of a communication, which, on the
face of it, was not very intelligible. Nelson replied,
that his object was humanity, and that he consented
to a truce while the prisoners and the wounded were
taken out of the prizes. He added, in highly conciliatory terms, his hope, that the truce might be the
forerunner of peace and amity between the two
Crowns. Sir Hyde Parker, to whom the Danish
envoy was referred, agreed to a suspension of hostilities for twenty-four hours; during which all the
prizes should be given up, and the wounded Danes
who were unprovided with surgical aid in their ships,
should be removed to the shore. Nelson took advantage of the truce, thus hastily concluded, to
remove his shattered fleet from the channel, and to
effect a junction with Parker; an operation, which
was not accomplished without great difficulty.

Nelson himself, accompanied by two of his captains, went on shore, to negotiate an armistice with the Crown Prince. Neither party
being in a condition to renew the conflict immediately, there was no question about the prolongation of
the truce. The only difference was, as to the term
of its duration. The Danes, under the apprehension
of the displeasure of the Czar, proposed a short term;
but Nelson, with the avowed object of attacking the
Russian fleet, insisted on fourteen weeks. The conferences had nearly broken off upon this point; but
Nelson, declaring that he would bombard the city
that very night, if his terms were not assented to, the
negotiation was soon brought to a close. It was
agreed that the armistice should continue for fourteen
weeks, with fourteen days' notice of resumption of

hostilities, and that during the armistice, the treaty of Armed Neutrality, so far as Denmark was concerned, should be suspended.

Nelson's flag of truce had been dictated not less by sound policy than humanity. This great seaman, whose enthusiasm in action was always tempered by the prudence of a wise commander, was satisfied with an incomplete victory, if the object of the war could be gained without further risk and bloodshed. At the time when he sent his celebrated letter to the Crown Prince, that part of the Danish fleet which lay astern of Nelson's ship, the 'Elephant,' and consisting of one-third of their line, with the formidable Crown batteries in the rear, had not been materially injured. Most of Nelson's ships were crippled, and, though Sir Hyde Parker was working up to his assistance, the Danes might still have hoped to turn the fortune of the day. Had a French fleet been before him, this consideration would not have influenced the English Vice-Admiral for a moment. In that case, he would have been satisfied with nothing short of the destruction of his antagonist—the implacable enemy of England, and the disturber of Europe. But the destruction of the Danish power was, as he truly said, no part of his orders. Denmark was in no sense an implacable foe. She was under duress of a power which was itself the tool and dupe of the universal military dictator. The Dane might have thought with reason that England asserted her maritime rights somewhat too broadly; but the particular question at issue between the two powers had already been referred to negotiation; and with friendly dispositions on either side, there could have been no difficulty in settling such a question as that of the immunity of Convoy by convention,* if it could not

*Nelson's letter to the Crown Prince.

---

* Nelson himself suggested, as a compromise, that no convoys should be granted to vessels bound to ports at war with this

be determined upon the ascertained principles of public law.

The loss of the Danes in this battle, the hardest fought, as Nelson said, of the hundred battles in which he had been engaged, was nearly six thousand in killed, wounded, and prisoners. The English loss was under a thousand. The Danish Admiral, with needless want of candour, attempted to excuse his defeat by misstating the relative strength of the opposing forces. Nelson replied to the official report of Commodore Fischer in terms of asperity which were unworthy of him; but Captain Lindholm, the Danish Adjutant-General, writing with the authority of the Crown Prince, made ample reparation. He fully admitted the defeat which the Danes had sustained; nor has Nelson's victory,* or his motive for sending a flag of truce in the midst of the engagement been questioned by any impartial writer.

Conclusion of an armistice. The armistice was concluded on the 9th of April, seven days after the battle; and Nelson was already chafing at the tardiness of the Commander-in-Chief, who would neither send a squadron, nor go himself in search of the Russian fleet at Revel. At length Sir Hyde sailed on the 12th of the month. On the 19th, Nelson received a letter from the Admiral, informing him that the Swedish fleet was at sea. Without a moment's hesitation he ordered a boat to be launched; and at a late hour in the evening, without even a cloak to

country.—*Correspondence*, vol. iv. p. 341.

* 'I do not conceive,' writes Captain Lindholm, 'that Commodore Fischer had the least idea of claiming as a victory, what, to every intent and purpose, was a defeat. He has only thought that the defeat was not an inglorious one, and that our officers and men displayed much bravery and firmness against a force so superior in every respect. . . . As to your lordship's motive for sending a flag of truce to our Government, it can never be misconstrued;—and your subsequent conduct has sufficiently shown that humanity is always the companion of true valour.'—*Correspondence*, vol. iv. p. 347.

protect his frail body from the piercing cold, Nelson hurried away in an open six-oared boat to row against wind and tide for twenty-four miles. His only anxiety was, lest the squadron should have sailed. 'If they have,' he said, 'we will follow them to Carlscrona in the boat.' His invincible energy was rewarded. At midnight, after having been six hours at sea, Lord Nelson came up with the fleet at Bornholm, and stepped on board the 'Elephant,' the ship in which he had fought at Copenhagen.

The Swedish fleet, when the English squadron appeared in sight, retired behind the guns of Carlscrona. Sir Hyde Parker sent a flag to inform the Swedish Admiral of the armistice with Denmark, and to demand an explicit answer as to the intentions of Sweden. The reply, so far from being explicit, was of the most evasive and temporising character; but Sir Hyde was satisfied, and the fleet sailed for the Gulf of Finland. It had not proceeded far, when a despatch arrived from the Russian Ambassador at Copenhagen, announcing the death of the Emperor Paul, and that his successor Alexander had assented to the proposal of the English Government to settle the difference between the two countries by a convention. Upon this information, Sir Hyde Parker considered that hostilities were virtually at an end, and accordingly he retired to his original anchorage in Kioge Bay, there to await instructions from England.

Evasive conduct of the Swedes.

Paul, whose rule had long been intolerable to his subjects, had fallen a victim to a conspiracy hatched within the walls of his palace a week before the battle of Copenhagen. Alexander immediately reversed the cruel and oppressive acts of his father. He removed the embargo from British shipping, and released the seamen who had been thrown into prison. The treaty of the Armed Neutrality, however, the capital grievance of

Change of Russian policy.

the British Government, was not yet formally renounced by the Court of St. Petersburg; and while that treaty remained even nominally in force, the English fleet must remain in the Baltic. If Nelson could have had his way, he would have intercepted the Russian fleet before they reached Cronstadt, and terminated the Armed Neutrality by the summary process of seizing or destroying the imperial navy in the Bay of Revel.* But the Commander-in-Chief was one of those ordinary men, who in ordinary times, and by ordinary people, are considered safe and prudent directors of human affairs. Such men are born to frustrate great opportunities, and to commit blunders more fatal than those of foolish temerity. Sir Hyde Parker's well-meaning incapacity did more to mar the fortunes of the expedition under his orders than all the efforts of the enemy; and the success of his fleet lasted only so long as his authority was overborne by the energy and ability of his subordinate officer. An examination of Nelson's plans, and a comparison of those plans with the events, leave little room for doubt that, if the expedition had been placed under his orders from the time it left Yarmouth Roads, the triple league of the Baltic powers would have been dissolved at the cannon's mouth, and with less effusion of blood than had been shed at Copenhagen.†

---

* 'Nothing,' he said, 'if it had been right to make the attack, could have saved one ship of them in two hours after our entering the bay.'—*To Earl Vincent*, 10th May.

† 'On the 2nd of April we could have been at Revel, and I know nothing at present which could have prevented our destroying the whole Russian force at that port.... The difficulty was to get our Commander-in-Chief to either go past Cronenburg, or through the Belt, because what Sir Hyde thought best, and what I believe was settled before I came on board the 'London,' was to stay in the Cattegat, and there wait the time when the whole naval force of the Baltic might choose to come out and fight.' Lord Nelson to Mr. Vansittart, 12th May, 1801.—*Correspondence*, vol. v. p. 368.

On the 5th of May, orders arrived from England recalling Sir Hyde Parker, and appointing Nelson to the chief command. This measure, though a virtual acknowledgment by the Government of the error into which they had perversely fallen when they suffered the pretension of seniority, or professional jealousy, to overbear the claims of unrivalled merit, was too late to be of practical importance. Nelson, however, though sinking from bodily exhaustion now that the excitement of stirring action had ceased, soon diffused a new spirit through the fleet. The first signal which he made as Commander-in-Chief, was hailed with acclamations of joy and exultation. It was the signal to weigh anchor; and in forty-eight hours after his appointment, the Admiral was at sea. It was his intention to prevent, if it was not too late, the junction of the Swedish and the Russian fleets; to require from Russia the immediate release of the English shipping, and the restitution of English property; —not permitting these concessions to be involved in any questions which England might have to discuss with Denmark or Sweden. He thought this business would be concluded in a fortnight; and he desired, therefore, that some person might be sent out immediately to relieve him of his command. The despatches and letters from England, though gratifying in the main, as they could not fail to be, contained much that caused irritation to Nelson's sensitive mind. The armistice of Copenhagen was coldly and hesitatingly approved in the official communication, and had been the subject of unfavourable comment in the course of public discussion at home. Nelson, therefore, thought it necessary to write a private letter to Mr. Addington, fully explaining his reasons for sending the flag of truce, and afterwards concluding a military convention. The flag of truce was simply an act of humanity. By the armistice,

'Great Britain was left the power of taking Danish possessions and ships in all parts of the world, whilst we had locked up the Danish navy, and put the key in our pockets.' Such was the summary of Nelson's vindication of his policy. And he was well justified in concluding, 'I consider it as a wise measure, and I wish my reputation to stand upon its merits.' *

Nelson having left a small force at Bornholm to watch the Swedes, proceeded with ten sail of the line to Revel. But the friendly disposition of the Court of St. Petersburg rendered any further demonstration of power on the part of Great Britain unnecessary, and therefore offensive. On the 24th of May, Lord St. Helens, who had been sent out to conclude a pacification with the Baltic powers, arrived at Kioge Bay; on the 19th of June, Nelson having been superseded at his own request, resigned his command to Admiral Sir Charles Pole, and returned to England. For his services in the Baltic, Nelson was advanced a step in the peerage, but received no other reward. Admiral Graves, the rear-admiral, who served under him in the action, received the Order of the Bath; but no honour beyond the customary vote of thanks from both Houses of Parliament was conferred on Sir Hyde Parker.

The victory of Copenhagen, while it sustained the naval reputation of England, lost much of its political importance by the death of the Emperor Paul. It was to that event, that the dissolution of the Northern Confederacy must, in the first instance, be attributed, even if the policy of the new reign was finally determined by the fate of Denmark and the intimidation of Sweden. The decree of the Emperor Alexander liberating the English seamen who had been arrested by his predecessor, was published before information of the battle of Copenhagen could have

* Letter to Addington, 8th May, 1801.—*Correspondence*, vol. iv. p. 361.

reached St. Petersburg; and it is probable, that the
rash and servile policy of the Confederation would
have been abandoned if the British fleet had never
passed the Sound. However this may be, the Court
of St. Petersburg, after a decent protest against the
violence which England had employed to detach
Denmark from the triple alliance, proceeded to use
its authority with the Court of Berlin, to procure the
withdrawal of the Prussian troops from Hanover,
from Hamburg, and from Bremen, as well as to re-
open the navigation of the Elbe. Negotiations commenced in this spirit were not likely to be protracted.
On the 17th of June a treaty of peace, on terms which
comprised a renunciation of the principles of the
Armed Neutrality, was signed at St. Petersburg, by
the ministers of Russia and of Great Britain. The
immunity from visit of neutral ships under convoy
—the new term which had been introduced into the
recent revival of the Northern version of maritime
law,—was no longer insisted on. The cardinal
maxim of neutrals, that the flag covers the cargo,
was formally abandoned. On the other hand, some
concessions were made to neutrals. Contraband of
war, which, according to some expositors of the law
of nations, might include almost anything the belligerent thought fit to claim, was strictly defined. The
right of search was confined to ships with a regular
commission, and denied to privateers.* Paper blockades were abolished, and no blockade was to be respected unless it was actual and efficient. To this
treaty, Denmark and Sweden afterwards acceded.

* 'Respecting privateers,' said Nelson, 'I am decidedly of opinion that, with very few excep-
tions, they are a disgrace to our
country; and it would be truly
honourable never to permit one
after this war.'—*Correspondence*,
vol. iv. p. 395. All the civilised
nations of the world, with the
exception of the United States of
America, have by treaty at length
abandoned the use of this infamous arm.

The dissolution of the Northern League put an end to Bonaparte's hope of resisting the naval ascendency of England. He sought, by compelling Naples and Portugal to accept terms of peace unfavourable to this country, to deprive England of her only remaining allies; but, in fact, he only relieved her of burdens from which she could not with honour disengage herself. The standing menace of invasion was then revived; and formidable demonstrations were made in the French ports. But preparations for defence, far more efficient than those for attack, were rapidly completed. Though no serious apprehensions could be entertained of an invading army, which was to be conveyed across the channel on rafts and in gun-boats, the genius and resources of Bonaparte rendered it hazardous to calculate on the impracticability of any enterprise which he might think fit to undertake. It was determined, therefore, that in addition to the Channel fleet, a flying squadron should be placed under the orders of Nelson. Boulogne was the point from which it was supposed the invasion might be attempted; but a glance at Boulogne satisfied Nelson that a flotilla would not venture to leave that port. He approached near enough in a frigate to destroy two floating batteries and some gun-boats. He proposed that the squadron should be sent to take possession of Flushing, from which quarter, if from any, he thought danger might be apprehended. But the Government, yielding to public opinion in England, urged him to make an attack on Boulogne. This was an affair of boats, a service not quite worthy an officer of Nelson's rank and reputation. Nelson, however, though seeking the repose which his shattered health required, readily undertook the duty. It was enough for him that the country required his services. An attempt was made to board the flotilla by night; but the enemy were prepared. The

vessels were protected by iron spikes; their decks
were covered with soldiers, and the batteries on shore
were fully manned. Some of the vessels were,
nevertheless, taken possession of; but the attack
generally was a failure; and the boats ultimately
withdrew after losing nearly two hundred men.
Nelson himself was not, of course, present at this
affair; while the French, unaccustomed to the advantage in naval encounters, magnified the repulse
of the attempt on Boulogne into a victory which
balanced their defeat at Aboukir.

Various minor engagements took place in the
spring and summer of this year in the West Indies,
and in the Atlantic, all adding to the reputation of
the Britsh navy for skill and gallantry; but none of
them attended with any important political result.
In the Mediterranean, an attempt was made by the
French and Spanish fleets to raise the blockade of
Cadiz. Sir James Saumarez sailed from Gibraltar
with five ships of the line to prevent this movement,
but was compelled by adverse winds, after a severe
engagement near Algesiras Bay, to retreat, leaving
one of his ships, the 'Hannibal,' which took the
ground, in the hands of the enemy. This reverse,
however, was repaired in a few days. Saumarez,
having refitted at Gibraltar, returned to Cadiz with
five sail, and, in a partial engagement, defeated a
French and Spanish squadron of six sail. Two
Spanish ships of one hundred and twelve guns blew
up, and one seventy-four was taken. The remainder
of the squadron, some of them disabled, returned to
the harbour of Cadiz. On the other hand, two British
ships, the 'Success' frigate and the 'Swiftsure,'
seventy-four, were taken off Malta by Admiral Gan-
theaume's squadron, which had escaped from Brest
in the early part of the year.

But these were no more than the embers of the
great war. For some months past, negotiations had

been proceeding, though languidly, on both sides, towards a termination of hostilities. At length, after the expulsion of the French from Egypt, and the signal defeat of their northern policy, M. Otto, the French minister at London, was instructed to renew the correspondence which had been for some time suspended. These overtures were readily encouraged by the English Government; and, as both parties were now for the first time intent on peace, the terms were settled without much difficulty. England relinquished all the conquests of the war with the exceptions of Trinidad and Ceylon. The Cape of Good Hope was to become a free port. Malta was to be restored to the Knights of St. John, under the guarantee of one of the great powers. Porto Ferrajo was to be evacuated. On the other side, the Republic of the Seven Islands was to be acknowledged; the French were to withdraw from Naples and the Roman States. The integrity of Portugal was to be secured. Egypt was to be restored to the Porte. The Newfoundland fisheries were to be replaced on the same footing as before the war. The usual stipulations were added with regard to prisoners, as well as for the protection and indemnity of the inhabitants of ceded territories.

The preliminaries were signed at London on the 1st of October, and in a few days afterwards at Paris. The peace was hailed with every demonstration of joy in both capitals. General Lauriston, the messenger who brought over the ratification of the preliminary treaty, was received in a manner which gave just offence to those who respected the honour and dignity of the country. The horses were taken from the Frenchman's carriage, which was dragged through the streets by the populace to the house of M. Otto, the French envoy. The revolutionary faction was supposed to have taken the leading part in this unseemly demonstration; but the people who had been taught to attribute the suffering and privation they had long endured in a great measure to the taxation and high prices of the war, welcomed the messenger of peace as bearing the glad tidings of cheapness and plenty. The populace of London, however, though in a coarse and clamorous form, represented a feeling which was prevalent throughout the country. The people of England had been, from the beginning, consistent in their repugnance to this war. For the first time in the history of the nation, a war with France had not been a popular war. Every class, except a small class of fanatical haters of the French Revolution, inspired by the Sibylline eloquence of Burke, had been averse to the war. The English people, though their nature revolted from the wanton excesses of the French Revolution, were little inclined to join a league of despots in arms against liberty, and seeking to interfere in the domestic concerns of an independent nation. The Whigs, consistently with their principles, were opposed to such a policy. The Tories, though they would gladly have seen the Revolution suppressed, were not willing to pay the price of war. But the spirit of aggression against the rights of other nations which the Revolution assumed, and the decree of the 19th of November, 1792, which aimed at converting all the states of Europe into affiliated republics, made it apparent that war was no longer a choice, but a necessity. So late as the autumn of 1792, none but the devoted followers of Burke were for war; but at the beginning of 1793, none but the avowed Republicans contended that it was possible to maintain peace. During the nine weary years of its existence, the war had been generally regarded as a burden which must be endured. The want of military success disheartened the nation; and even the great achievements of the navy seemed to be welcome only as they revived the hope of making peace without national dishonour.

Hence it was, that the announcement of peace, after the war had long ceased to have any definite object, was greeted with demonstrations of joy, such as had never been equalled after the most signal triumphs of our arms.

The nation, being in this temper, was not very critical in scanning the terms which the Government had agreed to. At the meeting of Parliament, on the 29th of October, the address, in answer to the King's speech, announcing the convention with the Northern Powers, and the preliminary treaty with France, was voted without opposition, after short debates. The old War party, never considerable in regard to numbers, led by Grenville and Windham, denounced the treaty as a mere armed truce, entered upon without necessity, negotiated without wisdom, and concluded without honour. England, they said, was a conquered country, and Bonaparte as much its master as he was of Spain or Prussia. But it was not the *treaty*, which these statesmen censured so much as the *peace*. According to their views England should have continued the war until its original objects were accomplished; until the spirit of Jacobinism was extirpated, and until the military ambition of France was restrained within fixed limits.

On the other hand, the old opposition, as insignificant in point of following as the War party, but still more distinguished by the quality of its leaders, applauded both the peace and the treaty, because they had failed to accomplish the objects of the war. Those objects, they said, were the restoration of an odious despotism, and a guarantee to kings against the liberties of their people. Public opinion lay between these extremes, and was, on the whole, well expressed by Mr. Pitt. He said, that whatever views might have been entertained at different periods of this protracted war, all thinking men were now agreed that after the dissolution of the European

alliance, and the conclusion of peace between France
and the several Continental Powers, this country
could not fairly be expected to entertain any other
object than the termination of the war upon such
terms as should not be dishonourable to herself, or
disadvantageous to her remaining allies. He did
not describe it as a glorious peace; nor did he venture
to predict that it would be durable. Whatever treaty
we might make with the French people, whether
ruled by a Bonaparte or a Bourbon, its stipulations
would be observed only so long as they considered it
beneficial to their interest to do so. An epigrammatic phrase which Sheridan let fall in one of the
debates, was taken up and passed from mouth to
mouth. 'It was a peace,' he said, 'which everybody would be glad of, but which nobody could be
proud of.'

The convention with Russia and the Baltic powers,
which recognised substantially all the *Grenville's attack on the Northern Convention.* principles of maritime law for which this
country had ever contended, seemed hardly
to present any topic for unfavourable criticism, even
to the most captious opponent; yet Lord Grenville,
who was certainly not actuated by a personal or party
opposition to the Government, thought fit to make a
deliberate attack on this compact, as if it had surrendered the most cherished rights and privileges of
the flag. In a speech still referred to * for the great
knowledge and ability which it displayed, the late
Minister for Foreign Affairs sustained the pretensions
of the belligerent flag at their highest point, and
contended that the slight concessions made by England were a serious derogation from her maritime
rights. He went so far as to assert, that if the stipulations of the treaty remained unaltered, our system
of maritime law, instead of having been confirmed

---

* 13th November, 1801.—*Parliamentary History.*

by the issue of a successful contest, would be found to have been, in all its parts, essentially impaired; its principles shaken, its exercise embarrassed, and its clearest regulations made matter of eternal dissension and contest. But this sweeping condemnation was ill-sustained by the cavils which Grenville urged against the several articles. He complained that the first article did not, in terms sufficiently explicit, prohibit neutrals from taking up the French, or any other coasting trade in time of war; and that the colonial trade was absolutely surrendered. On these points, the Lord Chancellor replied that such concessions had not been intended, and did not result from the construction of the terms. With regard to the great principle, that free ships make free goods, which had been the foundation of the Armed Neutrality, Lord Grenville admitted that this was given up; but he thought the restricted definition of contraband, and the reduction of the number of native seamen required to entitle a ship to the privilege of neutrality, were dangerous relaxations of the existing law. The article, which abolished loose or paper blockades and substituted actual blockades was substantially adopted from the maritime code of 1780, and this, therefore, gave great offence to a statesman, who was persuaded that the belligerent interests of this country were incompatible with any independent exercise of their commercial rights by neutrals. The article, which removed the more offensive incidents to the right of search, and restricted it as a general rule to the papers of the ship subject to visit, was represented as a virtual abandonment of the right. Lord Grenville's elaborate attack upon the convention received no support, and in answer to an eloquent appeal, which he had made to the great naval commanders who had been ennobled for their services, Nelson declared that he entirely approved of the convention, which he considered just and satisfactory.

The Marquis Cornwallis was sent to Paris to conclude the definitive treaty with the French Government. The English ambassador was treated with every mark of distinction; and his reception formed a striking contrast to that which Lord Malmesbury had experienced three years before. But the vain, incapable Directory, giddy with sudden elevation, had been swept away, and in their place was a ruler who knew how to respect the power which had been exhibited at the Nile, at Alexandria, and at Copenhagen. Bonaparte himself, who had been accustomed to treat the representatives of the European states with an insolence measured by his sense of his own ability compared with their weakness, behaved with scrupulous civility and respect to the ambassador of Great Britain. While he assumed the tone of an absolute ruler with reference to the policy of France, he affected a frank, liberal, and conciliatory spirit in dealing with the demands of the English Government. He said that he was desirous of peace, because France had entirely lost her commerce, and her pecuniary resources were almost exhausted. With reference to a formidable expedition which he had lately sent to the West Indies, with the avowed object of subduing the black populations of St. Domingo and Guadaloupe, the First Consul went so far as to say, that had he been informed of the objections entertained by the British Government to that expedition, it should have been abandoned. He expressed also, in very obliging terms, his willingness to consent to a provision in the treaty for an indemnity to the Prince of Orange, since His Britannic Majesty felt a personal interest in the matter. These civilities were important only as showing the estimation in which England was held, and that French diplomacy had resumed the tone and temper which became a civilised power. But the British plenipotentiary would have been greatly misled, if he had interpreted the frankness and courtesy of the First Consul as meaning anything more.*

Difficulties in adjusting the terms.

Lord Cornwallis's instructions were to adhere to the preliminaries, adding only the demand for compensation to the Prince of Orange for the loss of his property. But great difficulty was experienced in adjusting the terms comprised in the preliminary articles; and the utmost vigilance and firmness were needed in holding the French Government to the letter and the spirit of their engagements.

After Lord Cornwallis's interview with the head of the French Government, the formal conferences were transferred to Amiens, Joseph Bonaparte being accredited as the French plenipotentiary; the Chevalier d'Azara and M. Schimmelpenninck were, after some hesitation on the part of France, admitted as the representatives of Spain and Holland. The negotiations were protracted to such a length by the evasion and duplicity of the French Government, that great doubts were entertained at home of their reaching a satisfactory termination. More than once they were, in fact, on the point of breaking off; but it was the policy of Bonaparte to make a temporary peace, and when he found that the English Government were neither to be intimidated nor cajoled, their just demands were yielded. At length, after the Congress had sat during four months, the definitive treaty was signed. It was substantially a faithful confirmation of the preliminary articles. Malta, the position of which had been left to be determined by the Congress, was placed under the protectorate of the principal European powers, with a garrison composed half of Maltese and half of troops furnished by the King of the Two Sicilies. The only additional article was that which provided for compensation to the

* Marquis Cornwallis to Lord Hawkesbury, 3rd December, 1801.—*Correspondence*, vol. iii. p. 399.

house of Nassau, in respect of their private property. The treaty was signed at Amiens, on the 28th of March, 1802.

It had been the practice in former treaties to take the opinion of Parliament on the preliminary articles. But the old War party, which had already taken the foremost ground of opposition to the new Ministry, insisted on debating, although they admitted they could neither alter nor reject the definitive treaty. Lord Grenville said, there were two grounds on which a treaty of peace might be based, the *status ante bellum*, or the *uti possidetis*; and with the usual sacrifice of truth to epigrammatic point, he described the peace of Amiens as partaking of both grounds. As regarded England, the *status ante bellum* had been adopted, by giving up all she had taken during the war; and, as regarded France, the *uti possidetis* had been resorted to, by leaving her in possession of all she had acquired. Malta, however, the principal conquest of the war, was not given up to France, but restored to its former possessors, under the guarantee of the European powers. The Cape of Good Hope, though restored to Holland, was constituted an open port. Ceylon, the richest island in the Indian Ocean, with one of the finest harbours in the world, and an invaluable adjunct to our Indian Empire, was retained. It was an absurd exaggeration to assert, as Lord Grenville did, that the definitive treaty was infinitely more prejudicial to this country than the preliminary treaty. The one treaty was, in fact, the confirmation of the other; and all that could be fairly urged was, that, in negotiating the details which had been reserved for the final treaty, Lord Hawkesbury and Lord Cornwallis were no match for Bonaparte and Talleyrand. The indemnity to the Prince of Orange, not being founded on an express stipulation by Holland, proved, in the event, to be valueless. But, it is to be observed, that the question of indemnity formed no part of the preliminaries. The arrangements, with regard to prisoners, were not so advantageous to England as they were to France; and the interests of the humble allies of England were not so carefully provided for as they might have been. Lord Grenville, when he dwelt upon these minor points, and sought to persuade the House that the treaty should have been broken off and hostilities resumed, had no more weight and authority than Lord Stanhope, or Lord Abingdon. On a division, he was left in a small minority.[*] In the Commons, the debates were protracted to a great length; but the peace was ultimately approved by a majority far larger, after allowing for the addition which had lately been made to the numbers of the House, than had ever supported the war.[†]

Thus ended the first stage of the Great Revolution, which had shaken Europe to its centre. England alone had sustained the shock with firmness;—but England sought repose before the renewal of the struggle, which all men felt to be inevitable, and which many foresaw would be a struggle for existence.

---

[*] 16 to 122.
[†] 276 to 20. Windham, who led the opposition to the treaty, is said to have acknowledged to Lord Sidmouth some years afterwards, that if it had not been for the peace of Amiens, the country could not have maintained the second war.—Pellew's *Life of Lord Sidmouth*, vol. ii. p. 53.

INDEX.

ABDUCTION

ABDUCTION of females in the middle ages and in modern times, ii. 2
Abercrombie, General, sent to reduce the forts of Ticonderago and Crown Point, i. 32. Failure of the expedition, 32
Abercromby, Sir Ralph, lands in Holland, iv. 222. Commands an expedition to Spain, 335. And to Egypt, 338. Lands, 339. Gains the battle of Alexandria, 340. Where he falls, 341
Abraham, heights of, i. 37. Wolfe's victory and death at the, 39
Acre, besieged by the French, iv. 227. The siege raised, 229
Adams, John, advocates the cause of the English soldiers at Boston, i. 349. At the Congress at Philadelphia, ii. 154. His interview with Lord Howe, 217. His account of the affair, 217.
Adams, Mr., his duel with Mr. Fox, ii. 340
Addington, Mr., proposed as Speaker, iii. 222. His antecedents, 230. Forms an administration, iv. 299, 314. Unequal to his position, 303. General contempt for him, 304. Overtures to him to resign, 311. His ministry, 317. His personal character, 317. His popularity with the Tories, 321. His parliamentary success, 325. Proceedings of the ministry, 329
Admiralty, attack of the Opposition on the, ii. 314, 316
Agriculture, state of, in the last century, ii. 47. Distinction between the urban and rural classes, 58. Manners of

AMERICAN

the farmers, 59. Slow progress of the agricultural classes, 59
Albemarle, Lord, his unsuccessful mission to Pitt, i. 176
Alexandria, convention of, iv. 258
Alexandria, battle of, iv. 340
Alien Bill, the, of Lord Grenville, iii. 294, 295
Allen, Ethan, his invasion of Canada, ii. 183
Almack's, ii. 52
Almon, the bookseller, prosecution of, i. 375
America, affairs in, in 1757, i. 26. Loss of the fort of Oswego, 26. Expedition sent from England to, against France, 31, 32
American colonies, character of the contraband trade of the, i. 140. Beneficial effects of their trade, 140. Suppression of their commerce by the home Government, 141. Indignation and measures of the colonists, 141. Customs duties imposed by the imperial Government, 142. A metallic substituted for a paper currency, 143. The Stamp Act, 143, 144. Disputes with, and French influences on, the Indians, 143. Despair and passive resistance of the colonies, 147. Innocence of Grenville's intentions, 148. His mitigatory measures, 149. Arguments in vindication of the right of Great Britain to tax her colonies, 149. The colonies neglected by England, 150. The prosperity of the colonies entirely due to the colonists them-

B B 2

AMERICAN

selves, 150. True view of the equity of extending imperial taxation to the colonies, for the purpose of providing for their defence, 151. Bill for taxing them passed by the House of Commons, 157. And becomes law, 157. Reception of the Stamp Act in America, 192. Assembly of Congress, 193. Resolutions of Congress, 193. Proceedings of the home Government, 194. The question agitated in Parliament, 196. Indecision of the Cabinet, 196. Pitt's speech, 198. And Grenville's reply, 200. Pitt's eloquent answer, 201. His advice, 205. Measures resolved on in consequence by the Government, 206. Franklin's examination at the bar of the House, 207. The Declaratory Bill, 208, 210. Repeal of the Stamp Act, 211. Conciliatory measures of the administration, 214. The wound with America reopened by Charles Townshend, 242. Unsettled state of the colonies in 1767, 248. Their resistance to parliamentary authority, 249. Suspension of the New York Assembly, 250. Disastrous policy of the home Government, 291. Suppression of the Massachusetts Assembly, 293. Views of the home Government as to America, 294. Disputes with the colonies, 294. Seizure of the sloop 'Liberty,' 295. Attempts to prohibit importation from England, 295, 296. Public excitement at Boston, 295, 296. Convention at Boston, 297. Indiscretion of the Government, 298. Boston garrisoned by General Gage, 299. State of opinion in Massachusetts, 300. Assemblies of Massachusetts and Virginia, 301. Retention of the duty on tea, 302. Change in the tone of Government, 302. Adoption of measures of conciliation, 303. Appearance of Washington and Jefferson in the Virginia Assembly, 304. Crisis of the American dispute, 304, 305. Neglect of American affairs, 344. Proposed repeal of Townshend's act,

AMERICAN

and injudicious conduct of Lord North, 345. American opposition to the tea duty, 346. Party feeling in the House of Commons, 346. Breaking out of the Revolution in Boston, 347. Successful resistance of the people, ii. 137. Attempt to revive the customs' duties, 138. Tea thrown overboard at Boston, 139. Disclosure of the correspondence between Hutchinson and Whately, 139, 140. Mischievous publication of the correspondence, 142. Resolutions of the House of Assembly and petitions of the Governor and Lieutenant-Governor of Boston, 143. Reference to the Privy Council, 143. Scene at the Privy Council, 144. Partiality and final decision of the Council, 146, 147. The quarrel inflamed, 147. Alteration of the charter of Massachusetts, 148. General Gage appointed governor of Massachusetts, 149. State of opinion as to the colonies, 150. Washington's offer to raise a thousand men, 150. The solemn league and covenant, 151. General contempt for the colonies, 152. General Gage's preparations for military defence, 153. Formation of armed confederacies, 153. Assembly of the great Congress of the States at Philadelphia, 154. Papers of the Congress, 155. Commencement of the American war, 171. Battle of Lexington, 173. The colonists emboldened, 173. Party strife in England on the American question, 173. Resolution of the Congress of Philadelphia, 175. Arrival of reinforcements from England, 175. Martial law proclaimed by General Gage, 175. Battle of Bunker's Hill, 176. Military organisation of the Americans, 177. George Washington placed in command of the American army, 178. Embarrassment of Congress, 179. Its address to the army, 180. Want of military stores, 181. Invasion of Canada by Arnold and Allen, 182. Discussions on the right to tax the colonies reopened by

AMERICAN

Parliament, 189. Lord Chatham's plan of pacification rejected, 190. Unsatisfactory nature of the ministerial propositions, 193, 194. Burke's resolutions, 195. Coercive measures popular in England, 195. Proceedings of the Americans, 196. Debates in Congress. 196. Petition to the King from Congress, 196, 197. Mr. Penn's statement to the House of Commons, 197. Lord Dunmore's wanton and vindicative proceedings, 199. Alienation of the southern states, 200. Employment of foreign mercenaries against the colonies, 200–202. Letters of marque issued by Congress, 202. The first campaign, 203. Evacuation of Boston by General Howe, 205. Expulsion of the Americans from Canada, 205. Failure of the attempts of the British on the southern provinces, 205. Reverence for the mother country, 206. Subsequent prevalence of democracy, 207. Washington commissioned to exercise sovereignty, 208. Provisional governments established, 208. Debate on Lee's motion, 209. Declaration of Independence, 209. Vigorous preparations for hostilities, 212. New York occupied by Washington, 212. Who intrenches Brooklyn, 213. Defeat of the Americans at Brooklyn, 214. Pacific overtures, 212, 215. Rejection of the terms of pacification, 219. New York taken by the English, 220. State of the American army, 221. Dilatory proceedings of General Howe, 222. General Lee taken prisoner, 223. Trenton taken by Washington, 224. Surrender of Hessian mercenaries at, 225. Capture of Princeton, 225. Debates in Parliament on American affairs, 227. Lord Cavendish's motion, 228. Military disasters in America, 242. Determination of Congress to negotiate a treaty with France, 243. Absolute powers granted to Washington, 245. The oath of allegiance to the United

AMERICAN

States, 246. Fresh levies raised, 246. Defeat of Washington at Delaware, and capture of Philadelphia, 247. Battles of Brandywine and Germantown, 247, 249. Removal of Sir Guy Carleton, 250, 251. Who is replaced by General Burgoyne, 251. Burgoyne's surrender at Saratoga, 258. Results of the convention of Saratoga, 261. Employment of mercenaries and Indians by the British, 263. Lord North's Conciliation Bills, 269. The Bills objected to as being too late, 269. Impossibility of treating with the colonies as independent, 269. Appointment of Commissioners, 271. Party for concluding peace at any price, 281. Defeat of the Duke of Richmond's motion in Parliament, 282. The British army at Philadelphia, 294. Arrival of the British Commissioners at Philadelphia, 295. Failure of the attempt to negotiate with Congress, 297. Proclamations of the British envoys and of Congress, 298. Evasion by Congress of the convention of Saratoga, 299. Defeat of the Americans at Monmouth Court House, 301. Failure of the enterprise against Rhode Island, 301. The massacre at Wyoming, 304. Remainder of the campaign of 1778, 304. The French disliked in America, 305, 325. State of affairs in America in 1780, 360. Clinton's siege of Charlestown, 360. Condition of the American army, 360, 363. Arrival of French troops, under the Count de Rochambeau, 366. Hesitation of Admiral Arbuthnot, 366. Treason of Arnold and execution of André, 367–375. Occupation of South Carolina by the Royalists, 377. General Gates sent against Lord Cornwallis, 377. American attack on Cornwallis's cantonments at Camden, 377. Defeat of Gates, 378. Cornwallis's severity towards the people of South Carolina, 378.

INDEX.

AMHERST

Close of the campaign of 1780, 379. Successes of the British, 399. Meeting at Morristown, 400. Dissensions between Clinton and Cornwallis, 400. New York menaced by Washington, 400. General Greene, 401. Action at Cowpens, 402. Siege and surrender of York Town, 405, 406. End of the struggle, and freedom of America, 407. Affairs in 1782, iii. 1. Reprisals, 2. Washington's apprehensions, 2. Negotiations for peace, 16. Question of compensation, 17. Claims of the loyalists, 18. Provisional treaty, 19. American treatment of the French, 20. Defection of America from the common cause, 22. Termination of the War of Independence, 39. Marvellous prosperity of America since this struggle, 40. The cotton trade, 41. Causes of the War of Independence, 41. Popular notions as to the resistance of the colonies, 42. English indifference to American affairs, 42. Negligence of the royal troops, 44. Institution of Congress, 45

Amherst, General, appointed to the command of the army sent to North America, i. 31, 33. His difficulties, 34. Completes the conquest of Canada, 40. Appointed to the government of Virginia, 268. Overreaches his position, 269

Amiens, peace of, iv. 368

Amusements of the last century in London, ii. 49

André, Major, conducts the correspondence between Generals Clinton and Arnold, ii. 368. His arrest, 370. Efforts to save him, 372. Illegality of his proceedings, 373. Sentenced to death, 374. His execution, 374. His burial, 375

Apprentices, the city, in the last century, ii. 67

Arbuthnot, Admiral, his hesitation, ii. 368. Joined by Admiral Graves, 368

Architecture, ecclesiastical and domestic, of the middle ages, ii. 13

BARRÉ

Aristocracy, power of the, in the last century, i. 403. In former and in modern times, ii. 3. Ignorance of the, in the middle ages, 12. Improved education of the lesser nobility in the reign of Elizabeth, 12. Condition of baronial residences, 13. Henry VII.'s repression of the barons, 15

Armed Neutrality, maxims of the, iv. 262. Dissolution of the, iv. 360

Arnold, Benedict, American General, his invasion of Canada, ii. 183. His attempt on Quebec, 186. Raises the siege of Quebec, 205. Expelled from Canada, 205. His gallant conduct on Lake Champlain, 251. Enters Philadelphia, 300. His treason, 367. His escape, 371. His intemperate conduct, 374

Artois, Count d', joins the British force at L'Isle Dieu, iv. 12

Auckland, Lord, his treachery, iv. 315

Augsburg, proposed treaty of, i. 59. Conditions of the treaty, 60

Augustus III., King of Poland, his death, ii. 125

Austria enters into an offensive alliance with France against Prussia, i. 19. Commencement of the Seven Years' War, 20. End of the Seven Years' War, 86, 90. Narrow escape of the Emperor of, iii. 398. His proclamation, 400. Secret terms between Austria and France, iv. 70. Movements against the French, 208. Selfish conduct of Austria, 218. Battle of Marengo, 257. Concessions of Austria to France, 258, 263

BACON, LORD, his works in advance of his time, ii. 12

Bahamas, the, taken by the Spaniards, iii. 16

Bank of England, suspension of cash payments at the, iv. 37. The Bank Restriction Acts, 38, 75

Barré, Colonel, dismissed from the army by order of the King, i. 137. In

INDEX. 375

BARRINGTON

Lord Chatham's administration, 224.
His speech on the scene in the Lords,
385, 417. On the printing of the
debates, ii. 78. His quarrel with
Fox in the House, 82. His parliamentary defamation, 168. Made
Clerk of the Pells, iii. 105

Barrington, Lord, succeeds Legge as
Chancellor of the Exchequer, i. 57.
Moves the expulsion of Wilkes from
Parliament, 271. His unfitness for
office, 372. His answer to the House
of Commons as to the appointment of
a Commander-in-Chief, 372, 373.
His apology, 373. His subserviency
to the King, 373

Bathurst, Lord, becomes Lord Chancellor, ii. 72. Made President of the
Council, ii. 337

Beaufort, Wolfe's repulse at, i. 35, 36

Beckford, Alderman, his speech on the
Order in Council restricting the exportation of corn, i. 238. Moves for
papers connected with the East
India Company, 239. Lord Mayor
of London, 336. His speech on a
proposed address to the Crown, i.
336. Presents the address, 338.
Challenges the censure of the House
of Commons, 340. His reply to the
King, 357. His death, 358. His
position and influence, ii. 95

Bedford, John, Duke of, endeavour to
secure him to the Court party, i.
120. Pitt's refusal to act with
him, 119, 121. The King's mode of
gaining him over, 121. Appointed
President of the Council, 122. His
claim for patronage contested by
Mr. Grenville, 123. Opposes the
pretensions of the Princess Dowager
to the regency, 161. His culpable
conduct, 163, 164. Opposes the Silk
Bill, 174. Assailed by the silk
weavers and his house threatened,
175. His interview and remonstrance with the King, 183. Attempt to form a coalition between
Lord Bute and the Tories, 218.
Overtures of the Earl of Chatham to
the Bedford party, 232. Failure of

BONAPARTE

the negotiation, 233. Renews his
correspondence with the Grenvilles,
246. His efforts to restore his party
to power,' 246. Junius's attack on,
282. His suggestion for depriving
the American colonists of trial by
jury, 296, 300. His death, 363.
His character, 363, 366. His go-
between Rigby, 404

Belgium, occupied by France, iii. 302,
310. Fall of the fortifications to the
French, 401

Belleisle, Hawke's naval victory at, i.
41. Capture of, 59. Restored to
France, 89

Benares, Hastings' transactions respecting, iii. 147

Beresfords, their influence in Ireland,
iv. 97. Mr. Beresford's house attacked, 102

Bergen taken by the Duke of York, iv.
224

Berlin capitulates to the Austrians and
Russians, i. 43

Bernard, Governor of Massachusetts Bay,
his quarrels with the House of Assembly, i. 292. Recalled, 303

Birmingham, riots at, in 1791, iii.
268

Blakeney, Admiral, his unsuccessful
efforts to retain Minorca, i. 18

Blood, Colonel, his exploits, ii. 28

Bolingbroke, Dr. Johnson's remark on,
i. 411 note.

Bonaparte, Napoleon, his command of
the artillery of the Republic, iii. 312.
His abilities and reputation, iv. 70.
His animosity to Britain, 71. His
distrust of the Irish, 122. Commands
the expedition to Egypt, 188. Seizes
Malta, 189. Overruns Egypt, 190.
His fleet destroyed at the battle of
the Nile, 192. His massacre at Jaffa,
226. Puts his sick to death, 227.
Lays siege to Acre, 227. His flagrant
conduct there, 228. Raises the siege,
229. Escapes from Egypt, 230. His
reception in Paris, 240. His letter
to the King of England, 240. His
treacherous character, 244. His
movements on the Continent, 255.

BOROUGHS

Enters Italy, 256. Gains the battle of Marengo, 257. His reception of Lord Cornwallis, 367

Boroughs, close, in 1768, i. 258. Influence of boroughs, 259

Boscawen, Admiral, commands the fleet sent to North America, i. 31. Routs the Toulon fleet, 33

Boston, in America, public excitement at, i. 295, 296. Convention at, 297. Its dissolution, 297. No precedent for it, 297. Indiscretion of the Government, 298. Garrison of Boston by General Gage, 299. Two of his regiments ordered back to Halifax, 303. Rejection of the tea duty, 303. Breaking out of the Revolution in, 347. The populace fired upon by Captain Preston's men, 348. Trial and sentence of the soldiers, 349. Successful resistance of the people of Boston, ii. 137. The tea thrown overboard, 139. Act for closing the port of Boston, 142. General Gage's preparations at Boston for military defence, 153, 172. Invested by twenty thousand insurgents, 173. Evacuated by General Howe, 204

Boston, Lord, and the 'No Popery' mobs, ii. 348

Botetort, Lord, appointed Governor of Virginia, i. 303. His address, 304

Boulogne, attack on, iv. 360

Bourbon, Family Compact of the house of, i. 63, 78. Humiliation of the house of, 86

Brandywine, battle of, ii. 247

Brest blockaded by Admiral Hawke, i. 33

Breton, Cape, taken from the French, i. 32

Bridgewater canal, opening of the, i. 94 note

Bristol, Earl of, ambassador at Madrid, imposed upon by the Spanish Court, i. 63. Ordered to leave Madrid, 75. His visits to the Earl of Chatham, 245. Becomes Privy Seal, 271. Petition from, to Parliament on American affairs, ii. 190. Defends Admiral Keppel in Parliament, 308

BURKE

Brittany, plan for invading, iv. 2. Its failure, 2

Brookes's Club, ii. 45

Bunker's Hill, battle of, ii. 176

Burgoyne, General, appointed to supersede General Carleton, ii. 251. His character, 252. Composition of his army, 253. Besieges Ticonderoga, 253. Which is captured, 254. Follows St. Clair, 255. Burgoyne's position, 256. His retreat, 257. His surrender at Saratoga, 257, 258. His return to England, 288. His charges against the Government, 385

Burke, Edmund, his eloquence compared with that of Chatham, i. 6. note. His 'Thoughts on the Cause of the present Discontents,' 54. Becomes Private Secretary to Lord Rockingham, 198. His maiden speech in the House, 198. His part in the debate on the Civil List in 1769, 290. Takes part in the debate on Almon's prosecution, 381. His compliment to Lord Chatham, 385. Employed by the Marquis of Rockingham, 404. His remarks in the House on Lord North, 417. And on a son of Speaker Onslow, ii. 77. Defends the printers of the debates, 77, 78. His contest with Luttrell, 83. His ridicule of the report of a committee, 90. His speech on a motion for the repeal of the tea duty, 157. His character as an orator, 158. His conciliatory resolutions on American affairs, 195, 198. His economical Reform Bill, 333, 337. His great speech on the subject, 338. Object of his Bill, 390. His speech on the capture of St. Eustatia, 397. His defects, and causes of his non-admission into the Cabinet, 421. His views as to freedom of trade and reform, 422. Accepts the office of Paymaster with a seat in the Privy Council, 423. His Reform Bill, 429. His bad taste, 429 His virulent opposition to Government, iii. 31. His opinions on Indian affairs, 64. His speech on Fox's India Bill, 69. His sincerity, 82.

INDEX. 377

BURKE

His intemperate conduct as to Powell and Bembridge, 103. Collects materials for the indictment of Hastings, 144. His motion for impeaching Hastings, 144. Decay of his faculties, 152. His oration on the trial of Hastings, 171. His attack on Pitt on the Regency question, 186. His virulence against Thurlow, 196. His hostility to the Regency Bill, 204. His speech on the French Revolution, 237. His revived popularity, 254. His breach with Fox, 256. His violent speech on the Quebec Bill, 257. Called to order, 258. His reply to Fox, 259. His severance from Fox's party, 261. His dagger speech, 297. His reply to Fox, 309. His language on the French Revolution, 314. His retirement from public life, 429

Bussy, M. de, envoy from France for the negotiation of peace, i. 59. Dismissed by Pitt, 65

Bute, Earl of, co-operates with Lord Chesterfield in endeavouring to promote an alliance between Newcastle and Pitt, i. 24. His conduct on the accession of George III., 54. The King's treatment of him, 55. His unpopularity, 55, 56,'83. His connection with Scotland, 56, 83. Considered as an orator, 57. Becomes Secretary of State in the room of Lord Holdernesse, 57. His peace policy, 58. His misgivings as to the policy of dismissing Pitt, 71. Places himself at the head of the Government, 83. Accepts the Blue Ribbon of the Garter, 83. His policy, 84. Makes overtures for peace to France and Spain, 87. Rage of the people against him, 95. His reply to Hardwick and Mansfield on their criticism on the peace of Paris, 101. Extension of his corrupt policy, 106. His resignation, and the reason assigned by him, 107. His wealth, 108. His influence with the King, 108. His interference with public affairs, 109. Duration of his administration, 109.

CANADA

His intrigues with Pitt, 115. His retractation of the counsel given by him to the King, 119. Burnt in effigy by the mob in London, 135. Determines upon taxing the American colonies, 156. Retires from public affairs, 158. His return to power opposed by the Duke of Bedford, 161. His windows broken by the mob, 264

Byng, Admiral, loses Minorca, I. 18. Sentenced to death and shot, 19.

CADIZ, failure of the expedition to, iv. 337

Camden, Earl, Chief Justice Pratt created, i. 190. His views as to self-taxation, 205, 208. Receives the Great Seal, 222. His remark on Orders in Council, 238. His resignation, 310. His speech in support of Lord Chatham, 311. His conduct, 312. His anomalous position, 314. His want of delicate feeling, 315. His desertion of his colleagues, 322 note. His speech on the Middlesex elections, 343. His defence of Chatham's doctrine, 378

Camden, Lord (son of the preceding), becomes Viceroy of Ireland, iv. 101. His reception in Dublin, 102. Recalled, 121

Camden, defeat of the Americans at, ii. 378

Camperdown, battle of, iv. 72

Canada, Pitt's plan for the conquest of, I. 33. Formation of the expedition against, 33. Amherst's difficulties, 33. The siege of Quebec left to the resources of Wolfe, 33, 34. Quebec taken, 39. Montreal surrendered, 40. The conquest of Canada completed, 40. Invasion of Canada by Arnold and Allen, 182, 183. Ticonderoga and Crown Point seized by them, 184. Forces sent to Canada by Congress, 184. Difficulties of General Carleton, 184. Indifference of the Canadians, 185. Capitulation of St. John's, 185. Flight of General Carleton to Quebec, 185. Defeat of

CAPITAL

the Americans under Montgomery at Quebec, 186. Expulsion of the Americans from Canada, 205. Bill of 1774 for the better government of Canada, 160. The French population, 160. The Canada Bill of 1791, iii. 254

Capital punishments in the last century, ii. 238

Caraccioli, Prince, case of, iv. 212. His shameful execution, 214

Carhampton, Lord, his conduct in Ireland, iv. 104

Carleton, General, his difficulties in Canada, ii. 184. Flies to Quebec, 185. Defeats the attack on Quebec, 186. His military ability, 250. His operations on the American lakes, 250, 251. Superseded by General Burgoyne, 251. Rewarded by the King, 290

Carlisle, Earl of, one of the Commissioners to America, ii. 295. His resignation of the Viceroyalty, ii. 426. Indignity offered to him, 426

Carolina, affairs in, in 1781, ii. 401

Caroline, Princess, her marriage with the Prince of Wales, iii. 414, 415. Her reception by the Prince, 416. Her imprudence, 417. Separation of them, 417

Caroline, Queen, consort of George II., her hatred of her son Frederick Prince of Wales, i. 4. Her character of him, 4 note. Her amiability, 105. Her last moments, 105

Cassel, besieged and taken from the French by Ferdinand, i. 86

Castlebar, battle of, iv. 125

Castlereagh, Lord, becomes Chief Secretary of Ireland, iv. 143. His acts, 144. His plan of carrying the Union, 145, 178. His motion in the Irish Parliament, 153. His views on Catholic emancipation, 287. Breach of his promise, 288

Catherine, Empress of Russia, her part in the partition of Poland, ii. 127

Catholic emancipation agitated in 1778, ii. 283. Complications of the question in 1794, iv. 90

CHATHAM

Catholics and the 'No Popery' riots in Scotland, ii. 344, 345. And in London, 346. English dislike of Romanism, iii. 165. Severity of their treatment in Ireland, iv. 106. Discussions in the Cabinet as to emancipation, 286. Lord Castlereagh's promise, 288. Proposed measures of relief, 289. Catholic emancipation premature at this time, 302

Cavendish, Lord George, resigns the office of Comptroller of the Household, i. 100

Cavendish, Lord John, his motion on American affairs, ii. 228. His resolutions condemnatory of ministers on the conduct of the American war, 414

Cawdor, Lord, his preparations for receiving the French invaders in Wales, iv. 42

Ceylon taken from the Dutch, iv. 14

Charette, his peace with the French Republic, iv. 10. Again in arms in Poitou, 12. His bravery, 13

Charlemont, Lord, his disinterestedness and patriotism, iv. 88

Charles Edward, the young Pretender, supported by Frederick the Great, i. 20. His cause extinguished in Scotland, 23

Charles I., service of the Church for him as a martyr, ii. 116

Charles II., depraved character of the Court of, ii. 28. Open profligacy of the favourites of, 29

Charlotte, Queen, her marriage with George III., i. 94. Her personal appearance and understanding, 95. Her character, ii. 103. Conduct of her sons during the King's illness, iii. 201. Charge brought against her, 201. Pitt's defence of her, 202

Chatham, William Pitt, Earl of (see also Pitt), outcry in consequence of his elevation to the peerage, i. 222. Materials of which his administration was composed, 224. Objections taken to his ministry, 225. His principles of action, 226. His conduct towards his colleagues, 227. His proposal

CHAUVELIN

Northern Alliance, 228. His project defeated, 230. His imperious proceedings, 230, 231. Resignation of the whole of the Rockingham party, 231, 232. Chatham's overtures to the Bedford party, 232. His vacillating conduct towards Lord Gower, 232. False policy of his government, 233. His Indian policy, 234. The Order in Council forbidding the exportation of corn, 236. His inquiry into the affairs of the East India Company, 239. His mouthpiece Alderman Beckford, 240. His India Bill passed, 241. His behaviour in the House of Peers, 241. His illness and conduct at Bath, 242. Anarchy of his government, 242. Lord Chatham's illness and seclusion, 244, 245. The Duke of Grafton's interview with him, 245. His physical prostration, 252. The King's confidence in him, 252. Effect of his retirement, 253. Withdraws himself from the administration, 268-270. Causes of his withdrawal, 268. Anxiety of the Ministry to retain him, 270. Review of his rump administration, 306. His reappearance in public, 308. His coolness and neglect of Grafton, 308. His speeches in 1770, 311. And on parliamentary reform, 321. Sanctions the popular movements respecting elections, 342. Brings in a Bill regarding the Middlesex elections, 342. His speech on the subject, 343. Lord Mansfield and Camden's speech, 343. Moves an address to the Crown for a dissolution of Parliament, 344. His contempt for the views and moderation of the Whig aristocracy, 356. His remarks on the 'modern doctrine' laid down by Lord Mansfield, and Lord Mansfield's reply, 377. Clamour against him in the House of Lords, 383. Burke's compliments to him, 385. His rudeness and insults in debate, 416. His Bill for reforming Parliament, ii. 97, 98. Persists in his motion for a dissolution of Parliament, 101. His

CHURCH

speeches on American affairs, 159, 174. His plan of American pacification rejected, 190. His view of American affairs, 228. His reappearance in the House, and motion on America, 229. Called for to retrieve the fortunes of his country, 262, 267, 274. His speeches on the employment of mercenaries and Indians in the American war, 263. The King's resentment against him, 275. His reappearance in the House, 276. His last appearance in Parliament and last speech, 276, 277. His death, 278. His public funeral, 278. Possible results had he lived, 279-281

Chauvelin, M., the French ambassador, his note to Lord Grenville, iii. 274. His non-recognition, 298. Lord Grenville's reply to him, 299. Leaves London, 300

Chesterfield, Earl of, attempts to effect an alliance between Newcastle and Pitt, i. 24. His remarks on parliamentary eloquence, 414

Chivalry, principles recognised by members of the orders of, ii. 3. Influence of chivalry on modern manners, 5. Chivalric gallantry, 5. Its influence on the female character, 6. Chivalric notions of honour, 7. Conservative influence of chivalry, 8. Results of the War of the Roses on chivalry, 9. Attempts of Henry VIII. to revive chivalry, 15

Church, assumption of authority by the, ii. 17. Dissensions as to Church government, 17. Peculiar influence of the Reformation, 19. Uselessness of striving after uniformity, 19. State of the Church after the Reformation, 30. Effect of Queen Anne's Bounty and other acts, 32. Abuses of patronage, 33. The educated clergy, 33. Church service for Charles the Martyr, 116. Attacks on the Church in 1772, 117. Proceedings as to subscribing the Thirty-nine Articles, 118. Relief of Protestant Dissenters, 119

CHURCHILL

Churchill, his satires, i. 411
Cider, tax upon, i. 107. Alterations in the Act, 214
Civil List, debate on the deficiency in the, in 1769, i. 288. Motion for inquiry into the, ii. 339, 342. Object of Burke's Bill, 390. Debate on the, 431
Clare, Chancellor, his opinion on the Irish Union, iv. 134
Clarkson, Mr., and the slave trade, iii. 277
Clavering, Sir Thomas, moves for a copy of the City address, i. 340
Clergy, state of the, at the time of Wickliffe, ii. 22. Immorality of the, after the Reformation, 31. The educated clergy, 33. Their proceedings in 1772 as to subscribing the Thirty-nine Articles, 118. Bill to exclude clergymen from Parliament, iv. 328
Clinton, General Sir Henry, at New York, ii. 247. His rumoured advance to join Burgoyne, 258. His reinforcements from England, 259. Appointed to the command-in-chief of the British armies in America, 294. Estimation in which he was held by the enemy, 294. Evacuates Philadelphia, 300. His siege of Charlestown, 360. Which surrenders, 361. Returns to New York, 362. Dissensions between him and Lord Cornwallis, 400, 403, 404
Clive, Lord, bribery and plunder attributed to him, iii. 427
Clostersever, convention of, i. 26, 28. Refusal of the King to ratify it, 29
Clubs, establishment of, in London, ii. 42
Coalition ministry, formation of the, iii. 32. Rupture of the, 35. Its unpopularity, 65. The King's dislike of it, 66. Break-up of the Coalition, 75, 79. Attempt to form a new Coalition, 81
Code, penal, in the last century, ii. 238
Colonies, right of the home Government of, of taxing, denied by Pitt, i. 192. The question considered, 204

CONWAY

Commerce, progress of, in the middle of the last century, i. 89
Commons, former condition of the, in England, ii. 2. Disagreements between the Commons and the Crown, 16. See Parliament.
Conflans, M. de, defeated by Admiral Hawke at Belleisle, i. 41
Congress of the States of America, meeting of, i. 193. Resolutions of, 193. Assembled at Philadelphia, ii. 154. Papers of the Congress, 155. Mr. Galloway's proposal, 156. Commencement of the war, 171. Embarrassment of Congress, 179. Its address to the army, 180. Invades Canada, 184. Debates in Congress, 196. Petition to the King, 196. Letters of marque issued by Congress, 202. Proceedings of Congress, 206. Debate on Lee's motion, 209. Declaration of Independence, 209. Pacific proposals, 212, 215. Delegates deputed to meet the British commissioners, 216. Rejection of the British terms, 219. Eighty-eight battalions voted by Congress, 221. Grants Washington absolute powers, 243. Commissioners sent from England to negotiate with Congress, 295. Failure of the attempt, 297. Evasion by Congress of the convention of Saratoga, 299. Approbation of Congress given to a project for invading Canada, 326. Apathy of Congress to the state of their troops, 327, 364. Their treatment of Washington, 364. Contempt into which it sank, ii. 399. Vigour of its earlier conduct, iii. 46. Decline of its influence, 47
Constitution, the British, its theory and practice, i. 392
Contractors, disqualified from sitting in Parliament, ii. 430
Conway, General, dismissed from the army by order of the King, i. 137. Appointed Secretary of State and leader of the House of Commons, 188. His military and political character, 188. His letter to the Governor of Virginia, 195. Acquiesces in Pitt's

COPENHAGEN

sentiments, 200. Retains office in the Chatham ministry, 222. His remark on Lord Chatham's treatment of his colleagues, 227. His conduct on Beckford's motion as to the affairs of the East India Company, 240, 243. Retires from office, 253. Attacked by Burke in the House, ii. 78. Resigns his post of Secretary of the Northern Department, 198. His desire for peace with America, 281. His motion on the American war, 412

Copenhagen, plan of attack of, iv. 350. Nelson's conduct, 351. The bombardment, 353. Conclusion of an armistice, 354

Corbet, Lieutenant-Governor of Jersey, his conduct, ii. 395

Corn, restriction of the exportation of, i. 236. Order in Council, 237. Discussion of the question in the House of Lords, 237. And in the Commons, 238

Cornelys, Mrs., her assembly in Soho Square, ii. 52. Indictment against her, 58

Cornwall, Mr., elected Speaker in 1780, ii. 385

Cornwallis, Lord, left to carry on the war in North Carolina and Virginia, ii. 362, 377. Attack on his cantonments at Camden, 377. His defeat of General Gates at Camden, 378. His severe treatment of the people of South Carolina, 378. His expedition into North Carolina, 379. Thanks of Parliament voted to him, 387. Dissensions between him and General Clinton, 400, 403, 404. His retreat into Virginia, 403. Besieged in York Town, 405. Surrenders to Washington, 406. His opinion of the charges against Warren Hastings, iii. 427. Becomes Viceroy of Ireland, iv. 121. His policy, 121. Takes Humbert prisoner, 125. His opinion as to the Irish Union, 134. His disgust at the duties required of him, 142. His letters and dispatches, 144. His government of

CUMBERLAND

Ireland, 164. Pitt's support of him, 166. Dissolves a court martial, 170. His firmness, 172. His tour through the island, 173. His resignation, 316. His address to the Catholics, 321. Napoleon's reception of him in Paris, iv. 367

Corresponding Society, their meeting at Copenhagen Fields, iv. 15

Corry, Mr., his reply to Grattan on the Union question, iv. 179. Duel between Grattan and him, 180.

Corsica, French designs on, in 1768, i. 367

Corsica taken by the English, iii. 403

Coterie, the, ii. 52

Country houses, mode of life in, in the last century, ii. 46. Want of taste in country mansions, 48

Court party, condition of the, in 1761, i. 96. Its triumph, 104

Court, arbitrary conduct of the, on the matter of the debate on general warrants, i. 137. Hired writers for the Court, 406-410. The stage made instrumental to Court policy, 410. Ascendancy of the Court in 1771, ii. 70. Its parliamentary influence in 1777, 268. See George III.

Council, Privy, hesitation of the, to deal with the Gordon riots, ii. 352

Cowpens, defeat of Tarleton at, ii. 402

Crosbie, Sir Edward, his death, iv. 117

Crossfield, trial of, for the 'pop-gun' plot, iv. 81

Crown Point fort attacked unsuccessfully by Abercrombie, i. 32

Crown, causes of the increased power of the, under the Tudors, ii. 16. Disagreements between the, and the Commons, 16. Mr. Dunning's motion for diminishing the power of the Crown, 342

Cumberland, Duke of (uncle of George III.), defeated in Hanover, i. 26. Concludes the convention of Closterseven, 26. His military incapacity, 28. Retires from public life, 29. Enters into close correspondence with Devonshire and Rockingham, 95. His annoyance with Fox, 97. Sent

CUST

for by the King as to the regency question, 162. Put by the King into communication with Mr. Pitt, 170. Offered the command of the military force intended to suppress the riot of the silk weavers, 176. Waits himself on Mr. Pitt, 177. Failure of the negotiation, 179. Again consulted by the King, 184. His death, 190. His character, 191. His profligacy, ii. 108

Cust, Sir John, Speaker of the Commons, Rigby's insolence to, i. 418

Customs' duties, origin of, according to the opinion of Lord Coke, i. 145

DARBY, Admiral, at Torbay, ii. 396
Dartmouth, Lord, becomes Lord Privy Seal, ii. 198

Dashwood, Sir Francis, appointed Chancellor of the Exchequer, i. 83. His financial measures, 106. Joins in the orgies at Medmenham Abbey, 124 note; ii. 41. His acknowledgment of his own incapacity, i. 214 note

Daun, Marshal, defeated by Frederick the Great in Saxony, i. 43

Debating Clubs, formation of, iii. 365

De Crillon, his attempts to take Gibraltar, iii. 12

Delaval, Sir Francis, Lord Chatham's sneer at, in the House, i. 416

Dempster, Mr., his amendment on the Regency Bill, iii. 196

Denmark, Queen of, question of her criminality, ii. 108

Denmark, misunderstanding between England and, iv. 268. Expedition to, 350

Derry, Bishop of, his unaccountable disloyalty, iii. 121, 123

D'Estaing, Count, his conduct off the coast of America, ii. 300, 301. Defeated at St. Lucie, 303. His exploit before Savannah, 324

Devonshire, William, fourth Duke of, applied to by the Duke of Cumberland, i. 95. Refuses to work with Fox, 97. Insults offered to him, 98. His offices, 99. His resignation of the

DRESDEN

gold key of Lord Chamberlain, 100. His name struck from the Privy Council Book, 100. His death, 158

Devonshire, Duke of (son of the preceding), introduced at Court, and treated with marked distinction by the King, i. 183

D'Hervilly, his obstinacy and imbecility, iv. 4, 5

Dickinson, at the Congress at Philadelphia, ii. 154

Dingley, his appearance at the hustings at Brentford, i. 275. Attempts to get up a loyal address to the King, 278

Dissenters, Bill for the relief of Protestant, ii. 219. Their claims to the repeal of the Test Act, iii. 243

Dockyards, attempts to burn the, ii. 236. Bill introduced for the better security of, 237

Dodd, Dr., case of, ii. 239

Dodington, G. Bubb, refuses the Chancellorship of the Exchequer, i. 24. Offers to fill the office of Secretary of State, 71

Dogger Bank, engagement with the Dutch off the, ii. 396

Dolben, Sir W., his Slave Trade Bill, iii. 179

Domingo, St., attack of the British on, iii. 403

Dowager, the Princess, proposed nomination of, to the regency, i. 161

Dowdeswell, Mr., appointed Chancellor of the Exchequer, i. 182. His part in the debate on the Civil List in 1769, 289. His motion as to elections, 329. His motion to disfranchise revenue officers, 330. His Bill to amend the law of libel, ii. 100

Downie, case of, iii. 371

Downshire, Marquis of, his conduct and disgrace, iv. 175

Drama, licentiousness of the, in the seventeenth century, ii. 19

Draper, Sir William, takes the Philippine Islands from Spain, i. 85. His hostility to Junius, i. 282

Dresden, Frederick the Great's bombardment of, i. 43

DRUNKENNESS

Drunkenness, prevalence of, in the last century, ii. 60, 63
Du Barri, Madame, i. 369. Her friendship for England, 369
Dublin, disturbances in, in 1779, ii. 331
Duffin, prosecution of, iii. 343
Dumourier, General, his defection, iii. 311
Duncan, Admiral, his victory off Camperdown, iv. 72
Dundas, Mr., his proposed India Bill, iii. 56. Takes office under Pitt, 85. Probably prepares Pitt's new India Bill, 112. His character and position, 216. His report of the views of his colleagues, iv. 260
Dunkirk, fortifications of, reduced by treaty, i. 89. Besieged by the Duke of York, 317, 318. The siege raised, 319, 324
Dunmore, Lord, driven out of Virginia, ii. 188. His wanton and vindictive proceedings, 199
Dunning, John, his argument before the Court of King's Bench against general warrants, i. 126. Resigns office, 320. Supports Serjeant Glynn's motion, 379. His charge against Lord Mansfield, 380. His consistency, ii. 71. Resigns the Solicitor-Generalship, 71. Retained for the Assembly of Massachusetts, 144. His proposal in Parliament to diminish the power of the Crown, 342. And for the correction of abuses in the Civil List, 343
Dyson, Mr., his insubordination, i. 217 note. Disparages Mr. Grenville's Elections Bill, 333. His defence of the unmannerly conduct of the Lords, 385. Manages the business of the Court in Parliament, 404

EAST India Company, affairs of the, brought before Parliament by Lord Chatham, 239. His India Bill passed, 241. A provisional measure passed in 1767, 248. Sovereign power of the Company, iii. 52. Difficulties of governing India, 52. Consequences of oppression of the natives, 53. The

ELECTIONS

Regulating Act of 1773, 54. Exposure of malpractices in India, 55. Dundas's proposed Bill, 56. Importance of India to England, 57. Mr. Fox's Bill, 59. Proposed transfer of power to the Crown, 61. Provisions of the Bill, 62. Defects of the measure, 63. Debate in Parliament, 66. The Bill carried, 71. But rejected by the Lords, 72, 79. Principles of, and objections to, the Bill, 79–82. Pitt's India Bill, 82. Conduct of the Opposition, 82. Fox's third India Bill, 90. Pitt's new Bill, 111. Hastings's reception on his return to England, 143. Intrigues of Tippoo Sultan with the French, iv. 231. Measures of the Governor-General, 232. Seringapatam besieged and taken, 234, 235. See also India.
Eaton, trial of, iii. 342
Eden, Mr., appointed a commissioner to negotiate with Congress, ii. 295. His escape in Dublin, 426. His motion in the House, 427
Education, influence of the Reformation on, ii. 10
Edward's Island, Prince, taken from the French, i. 32
Egmont, Lord, failure of his negotiation with the Duke of Newcastle, i. 22. Becomes first lord of the Admiralty, 122.
Egremont, Lord, appointed Secretary of State in the room of Pitt, i. 75. Reproves the insolence of the Spanish ambassador, 76. Becomes Secretary of State, 115. Sent by the King to Lord Hardwicke, 117. His sudden death, 117
Egypt, the French driven out of, iv. 342
Elections, corrupt practices at, in the last century, i. 257. Close boroughs, 258. Venality and debauchery exhibited, 258. Mr. Dowdeswell's motion, 329. Mr. Grenville's Bill on controverted elections, 331. Mode of getting up petitions of undue return, 332. Operation of Grenville's Act, 387. The people unrepresented, 400.

ELLIOT

Character of the lower class of voters in the last century, ii. 61. Opposition to the Bill of 1774 for determining controverted elections, 162. Debasement of the constituencies, 435. Refusal of the high bailiff of Westminster to make a return of the poll, iii. 108

Elliot, Sir Gilbert, rebukes Colonel Barré in the House, i. 417. Supports the Court against the City, ii. 80. His defence of Gibraltar, 324, 395

Ellis, Welbore, undertakes the contest against the City of London, ii. 80.

Eloquence, parliamentary, i. 411, 412. Decay of, 412. Rhetoric distinguished from, 414. Chesterfield on, 414. Parliamentary nothingness of rant, 415. Length of modern debates, 419. Burke's character as an orator, ii. 158. Characteristics of Erskine's oratory, iii. 379–381

England, state of, at the close of the reign of George II., i. 3. Military strength of the nation at this period, 17. War with France, 18. Increase of the defences of the kingdom, 22. Electoral corruption at this time, 26. National prosperity at the accession of George III., 45. Attempts to conclude a treaty of peace with France, 52. Our Spanish policy, 64. Pitt's remedy for the prostrate state of the nation, 67. War between England and Spain declared, 76. Hopelessness of peace, 77. Dislike of the public to Hanover, 77. Treaty of peace with France and Spain signed at Fontainebleau, 88. Domestic events from 1757-62, 92. Increase of the national debt, 92. Progress of commerce, 93. Domestic policy in 1761, 95. The gross corruption and ruthless civil persecutions in 1762, 101. Jealousy of France of the increasing maritime power of England, 152. System upon which that power was founded, 152. Contemplated invasion of England by France in 1760,

ENGLAND

228. The country without a government, 243. Popular want of political intelligence, and its causes, in 1768, 259. Corrupt state of the government, 260. The popular party aroused, 261. Disturbances and conflicts between the Government and the people, 266, 267. Aggravation of public discontent, in 1769, 291, 310. Attack on the Falkland Islands by France, 367. Satisfaction demanded by England, 368. Popular discontent at the conduct of the ministry regarding Spanish aggression in 1768, 370. Theory and practice of the British constitution, 392. Former loyalty of the people, 393. Effects of popular clamour, 399. The people unrepresented, 400. Debasement of political literature, 405. Parliamentary eloquence, 414. Improvement in parliamentary departments, 416. Sketch of the development of modern manners in England, ii. 1. Former condition of the Commons, 2. Power of the aristocracy, 3. Religion and morals in the middle ages, 4. Chivalry and its influence, 5–9. Influence of the Reformation on education, 10. Learning of the sixteenth century, 11. Ecclesiastical and domestic architecture of the middle ages, 13. Baronial residences, 13. Houses of the gentry, 14. Elizabethan mansions, 14. Repression of the Barons, 15. Causes of the increased power of the Crown under the Tudors, 16. Assumption of authority by the church; 17. Dissensions as to church government, 17. Conflicts of the Royalists and Puritans, 18. Licentiousness of the drama, 19. Rise of religious freedom, 21. State of the clergy at the time of Wickliffe, 22. Monasteries before the Reformation, 22. Religious bias of the northern counties, 23. Influence of laws on the popular character, 24. The Papacy opposed to freedom, 24. Social progress of England, 25. Royal edicts

ENGLAND

against the increase of the metropolis, 26. Beginning of civil and religious freedom, 27. State of manners at the Restoration, 27. Spread of infidelity, 28. Condition of the church, 30. Immorality of the clergy, 31. Queen Anne's bounty, 32. Popular contempt for religion, 34. Power of the Commons and destruction of arbitrary power, 35. Walpole's introduction of parliamentary corruption, 36. Evil results of irreligion, 37. Immorality of the people, 38. Effeminacy and profligacy of men of fashion, 39. Ministerial and royal levees, 42, 43. Prevalence of gambling, 44. Manners and education of women in the last century, 45. Mode of life in the country, 46. Establishment of clubs, 49. Places of amusement, 50. Fashionable assemblies, 52. Relaxation of moral and religious restraint, 52, 53. Effects of the unsettled state of the marriage law, 54. Religion and morality of the middle classes, 57. Distinction between the urban and rural classes, 58. Manners of the farmers, 59. Slow progress of the agricultural classes, 59. Prevalence of intemperance, 60, 61. Luxury of the London middle classes, 61. Education of the tradespeople, 63. Insolence and ferocity of the people, 64. Condition of London, 64 et seq. Rigour of the criminal law, 68. Improvements during the last forty years, 69. Popular dislike of parliamentary privilege, 87. Prevalence of slander and libel in the middle of the last century, 167. Commencement of the American war, 171. Severity of the penal code in the last century, 238. News of Burgoyne's disaster in America, 264, 265. Growing desire for peace, 265. Position of England as to the American question after the declaration of July, 1776, 269. Rupture with France, 273. Consequences of the death of Chatham, 279. Warlike preparations of

ENGLAND

England. 306. The Channel fleet under Keppel, 306. Rejoicings on the acquittal of Admiral Keppel, 309. Naval and military affairs in 1778, 315. Rupture with Spain, 316. Alarm of the country, 317. Peril of the kingdom from the combined navies of France and Spain, 322. Vigorous effort to organise a patriotic party in the country, 333. County meetings, 333 et seq. Maritime ascendancy of England threatened, 379. The right of search, 380. Formation of the Armed Neutrality, 382. War declared against Holland, 382. Weakness of the ministry, 383. Threatened by the combined fleets of France and Spain, 396. State of public opinion at the close of the American war, 408. Operations at sea, 410. Precarious condition of affairs at this time, 419. Rise of the cotton trade, 419. Exultation on Rodney's victory, iii. 5. Results of the victory, 6. Public astonishment at Rodney's recall, 9. Conclusion of peace with France, Spain, and America, 38. State of public offices in England in 1784, 105, 136, 137. General thanksgiving on the King's recovery, 221. Feelings with which the French Revolution was regarded in England, 235. Rupture with Spain, 241 The Revolution Society, 265. Riots at Birmingham, 268. A surplus revenue, 270. Formation of the Corresponding Society, 282. Measures taken against sedition, 284. Embodiment of the militia, 284, 290. War declared against England by the French Republic, 300, 304. State of opinion as to the French Revolution, 332. Indiscriminate prosecutions of the press, 339. Employment of spies and informers, 340. Severity of provincial courts, 341. Commercial distress in 1793, 357. Issue of Exchequer Bills, 358. Importation of foreign mercenaries, 361. Enrolment of volunteers, 361. Eu-

VOL. IV.   C C

ERSKINE

listment of French refugees, 364.
Renewed proceedings against seditious writings, 364. Debating clubs, 365. Suspension of habeas corpus, 367. Impolitic measures, 368. Country prosecutions, 368. Prosecution of Walker and others, 369. And of Horne Tooke and others, 371. Beneficial results of these trials, 392. Public opinion of the trials, 394. Progress of the war with France, 396. Pressure of taxation in England in 1794, 407. General desire for peace, 408. Determination to continue the war, 409. Vacillation of the ministry in the affairs of the French royalists, iv. 11. Domestic condition of the country in 1795, 14. Political meetings and riots, 15. Coercive measures, 17. Political pamphlets, 21. Censure on the Government as to the erection of new barracks, 23. War declared by Spain against England, 32. An open loan raised in 1796, 34. Drain of specie, 36. Suspension of cash payments at the Bank of England, 37. The Bank Restriction Act, 38. Dangers of an invasion in 1796, 39. Landing of the French in Wales, 40. The mutiny in the fleet at Spithead, 45. At St. Helen's, 50. And at the Nore, 53. Increase of the national debt, 61. Claims of the subscribers to the indemnity loan, 63. French invectives against the British, 70. Projects for invading England, 71. Increase of assessed taxes, 76. Prospect of invasion, 79. Defence of the country, 79. State prosecutions, 81. Indifference of the people at this period, 83. Causes of the changes in public opinion, 84. Battle of the Nile, 192. Public enthusiasm, 197. Expedition to Holland, 219. Act to prevent the sale of fine bread, 251. Isolation of England, 266. Misunderstanding with Denmark, 268, 269. And with the Northern League, 271. Apprehensions of famine, 272. State of the population, 273. Corn riots, 277.

FITZGERALD

Proclamation as to the use of grain, 281. Extent of private benevolence, 282. Discontent of the people, 282. Expedition sent to Spain, 335. Battle of Alexandria, 340. Battle of Copenhagen, 353. Honoured invasion of England by France, 360. Terms of peace, 362. Popular dislike of the war, 363. Definitive treaty of peace signed, 367, 368
Erskine, failure of his speech on the India Bill of Fox, iii. 71. Defends Paine, 293. His skilful defence of Hardy, 376. His speech, 378. Defends Hadfield, 251
Esmonde, Dr., his execution, iv. 116
Eustatia, St., captured by Rodney, ii. 396. Burke's speech on, 397. Malpractices at, 397-399. Bad results of the capture, 399
Exchequer Bills, issue of, in 1793, iii. 358
Executions, public, in the last century, ii. 67

FALKLAND ISLANDS, attacked and occupied by Spain, i. 367, 368. Ceded to Great Britain, 369
Family Compact, conclusion of the, i. 62. Its stipulations, 62. Its endeavours to strengthen its position, 78. Designs for provoking a new war, i. 367
Farmers, manners of, ii. 50. Slow progress of the agricultural classes, 52
Fashion, men of, in the reign of Anne and George I., ii. 39
Ferdinand of Brunswick, Prince, placed in command of the reconstructed army of Hanover, i. 31. Which he recovers, 31. Keeps the French in check, 44. His successes against the French in Germany, 86
Ferrol, failure of the attack on, iv. 336.
Fitzgerald, Lord Edward, his part in the Irish rebellion, iv. 107. Taken into custody, 112. His conduct, 113. His character, 114
Fitzgerald, Thomas Judkin, made high sheriff of Tipperary, iv. 135. His

FITZHERBERT

cruelties, 155. His trial, and verdict against him, 157. His petition to Parliament, 159. Act of indemnity to screen him, 161. His hardy impudence, 162. Created a baronet, 163
Fitzherbert, Mrs., iii. 156, 157. Her marriage with the Prince of Wales, 157, 160. Her dislike of Fox, 166
Fitzwilliam, Lord, becomes Viceroy of Ireland, iv. 91, 92. His overtures to Grattan, 92. His acts, 98. Animosity against him, 98. Recalled, 100
Flanders occupied by the French, iii. 310. The Duke of York in, 313
Flood, Henry, his speech on the India Bill, iii. 67
Floyd, the Papist, case of, ii. 53
Foote, opens the Haymarket Theatre without a license, ii. 62
Forbes, captures Ducsqne, i. 32
Formio, Campo, treaty of, iv. 69
Fox, Harry (afterwards Lord Holland), his character, i. 5. Terms offered to him by the Duke of Newcastle, 11. Accepts the seals of Secretary of State, 11. Which he resigns the next day, 12. Turns the leader of the House of Commons into ridicule, 12. Gained over by the Government, 13. Becomes Secretary of State, 16. Resigns, 21. Excluded from the Duke of Devonshire's administration, 22. Applied to by the Court party, 96. Disliked at Court, 97. His wholesale bribery of members of parliament, 99, 100, 101. His excuses to the Duke of Devonshire, 101. His management of Parliament, 103. His mercenary zeal for persecution, 104. His final retirement from public life, 110. Raised to the peerage as Lord Holland, 110. His character, 111. Compared with Pitt, 112
Fox, Charles James, his motion against Aldermen Oliver and Wilkes, ii. 82. His contest with Barré, 82. His contempt for the people, 82. His slow rise in debate, 83. His desire to engage in a conflict with Wilkes, 83. His dismissal, and desertion from the Tories, 149. Takes the lead in par-

FOX

liamentary license in debate, 168. His language on the American revolution, 228. His opposition to ministers, 229. Moves for a vote of censure on the Admiralty, 314. His declamation against a coalition with the ministry, 318. His duel with Mr. Adams, 340. Called to order by Lord Nugent, 387. Becomes Secretary of State, 421. His speech on Mr. Eden's motion, 427. Brings down a message from the Crown on the state of Ireland, 427. Resigns, 440, 441. His wayward conduct, 442. Rupture with Pitt, 443. Commencement of his conflict with Pitt, 443. His virulent opposition to Government, iii. 31. His India Bill, 59, 65. His speech on the Bill, 68. The Bill carried, 71. His denunciation of Jenkinson, 74. Dismissed by the King, 75. His sincerity, 82. His proceedings in the House, 88. His third India Bill, 90. His inflammatory language, 95. His difficulty in regaining his seat, 107, 108. His views on Irish reform, 125. His opposition to any further concessions to Ireland, 130. His part in the impeachment of Hastings, 146. His defence of the Prince, 159. His embarrassing position, 164. Slandered to Mrs. Fitzherbert, 166, 167. His speech on the regency question, 183. His imprudence, 185. His attempt at explanation, 187. His blunder, 188. His speech on the French Revolution, 237. His retractation, 239. His Bill to enable juries to decide libels, 249. Opposes the Canada Bill, 255. His breach with Burke, 256. His speech against Burke, 258. His complaint against Burke, 261. Inclined to retract, 281. His denunciation of the royal speech in 1792, 291. Answered by Windham, 292. Fox's irritation, 293. His speech on war with France, 301, 307. His amendment negatived, 308. His resolutions, 308. Burke's reply

FRANCE

to him, 309. His language on the French Revolution, 335. His speech as to continuing the war with France, 411. Supports the Government on the question of the establishment of the Prince of Wales, 422. His violent speech on the Act to repress public discussion, iv. 18. Proposal to prosecute him, 82. His reply to Pitt's speech on a war policy, 246. His answer to Pitt, 323.

France, preparations of England for war with, i. 13. Attack of an expedition on a French fleet, 14. Military strength of France at this period, 17. Her colonists, 17. Commencement of the war with England in 1757, 18. Minorca taken by France, 18. France concludes an offensive alliance with Austria, 19. French successes on the Continent, 26. Failure of the English expedition against Rochefort, 28. Hanover recovered from France, 31. Her losses in North America, 31, 32. Blockade of the French coast, 32. Expeditions sent from England to attack the possessions of France in the West Indies and in Canada, 33. Canada conquered by the English, 40. Negotiations of peace between England and France, 52. Difference between the two Courts, 61. Interference of France in Spanish affairs, 62. Formation of the Family Compact, 63. Results of the war with France, 70. Loss of all the possessions of France in the West Indies, 85. End of the Seven Years' War, 86. Peace of Fontainebleau, 88. Humiliating terms of the treaty, 88. Jealousy and apprehension with which France had viewed the increasing maritime power of England, 152. Contemplated invasion of England by France without a declaration of war, 228. Designs of France on Corsica, 357. Debasement of the French court at this period, 362. Condition of France since the Revolution of the last century, ii. 21. Conduct of France in relation to the

FRANCE

partition of Poland, 130. Intrigues of Franklin at Paris, 271. Rupture between England and France, 273, 274. The French disliked by the Americans, 305, 324. Alliance between France and Spain. 316, 394. Rodney's defeat of the French fleet under De Grasse, iii. 4. Negotiations between England and France for peace, 10. End of the war, 15. Negotiations. 16. Question of compensation, 17. Articles of the provisional treaty, 18, 19. The French, how treated by the Americans, 20. Concessions of England to France, 23. Signature of the preliminaries of peace, 25. Conclusion of peace, 38. Abandonment of the Methuen Treaty, 150. Conclusion of peace with France, 151. French policy in 1789, 232. Commencement of the Revolution, 235. The National Assembly, 235. Condition of France in 1792, 278. Invasion of France by Austria and Prussia determined on, 279. The Reign of Terror, 280, 329. The Jacobins, 280. The National Convention, 281. First success of the Allies, 281. Cessation of diplomatic intercourse with France, 294, 298. War declared against England, 300, 304. French breach of treaty with Holland, 306. French invasion of Flanders, 510. Alliance against France, 310. Increased energy of the French Government, 313. Proclamation of the Allies, 313. French propagandism, 315. Their losses in the East and West Indies, 323. End of the first campaign, 324. View of French democracy, 325. Murder of the Queen, 327. The Goddess of Reason, 328. Organic change necessary in France, 331. The English and French Revolutions compared, 333. The States-General, 334. Exasperation of the French against England, 338. Progress of the war, 396. Pichegru in command, 397. Savage decree of the Convention, 401. Expulsion of

FRANCIS

the Austrians and Prussians, 405. Lord Howe's defeat of the French fleet, 406. End of the Reign of Terror, 408. Resentment excited in France, 412. Expedition from England to Quiberon, iv. 1-7. Attempt of England to open negotiations with the French Government, 24. Cessation of the Reign of Terror, 24. Failure of negotiations for peace, 27. Impossible terms of the French propositions, 29. Intrigues of the French in Spain, 32. A French force in Bantry Bay, 39. And in Wales, 41. Conference at Lisle, 65. Divisions amongst the French, 65. Propositions amongst the French commissioners, 66. Rupture of the negotiations, 69. American difficulties with France, 69 note. Terms with Austria, 70. The Ionian Islands ceded to France. 70. French invectives against England, 70. Bonaparte's animosity, 71. General Humbert's invasion of Ireland, 124. The French all made prisoners, 125. Troops landed in the island of Rutland, 126. The expedition to Egypt, 187, 188. Seizure of Malta, 189. Egypt overrun, 190. Battle of the Nile, 192. Defeat at Castel Nuovo, 208. Surrender of Rome, 217. Failure of Napoleon's expedition to Egypt, 230. Intrigues of Tippoo with the French, 231. Napoleon's return to France, 240. His letter to the King, 240. Victory of Marengo, 257. Military power of France at this time, 264. Battle of Hohenlinden, 265. Desperate condition of the French in Egypt, 330. Kleber's victories, 332. Battle of Alexandria, 340. Capitulation of the French in Egypt, 342. Negotiations for peace, 343. Rumoured invasion of England, 360. Treaty of peace concluded, 367, 368

Francis, Sir P., collects materials for the indictment of Hastings, iii. 144

Franciscan Club, the, ii. 41

Franklin, Benjamin, his examination at the bar of the House, i. 207. His

FULLARTON

dialectic skill, 208. Implicated in the disclosure of the correspondence between Hutchinson and Whately, ii. 140-142. Excuses for his conduct, 145. Wedderburn's denunciations, 145. Dismissed from his office of Postmaster-General in America, 147. His misinformation to the French Government, 243

Frederick, Prince of Wales, his death, i. 4. His character, 4. His court at Leicester House, 4. His immorality, ii. 107. His death, 107

Frederick the Great, his successes and ambition, i. 20. Alliance of France, Austria, and Russia against him, 19, 20. His support of the young Pretender, 20. Commencement of the Seven Years' War, 20. Frederick's military and administrative talents, 21. Defeated at Kolin, 26. A subsidy procured for him by Pitt, 31. Defeated by the Russians at Kunersdorf, 42. His bombardment of Dresden, 43. Saves Silesia and defeats Marshal Daun in Saxony, 43, 44. Joined by the Emperor of Russia, 78, 79. Consequences of our alliance with him, 80. End of the Seven Years' War, 80, 90. His objections to Lord Chatham's proposed Northern League, 229. His impracticability, 229. His participation in the partition of Poland, 230, ii. 128

Free trade, agitation respecting, ii. 287. Class opposition, 287. Burke's views as to, 422. Pitt's advanced views on commercial freedom, iii. 128. Opposition of the trading interest, 129. Mr. Grenville's views, iv. 278

Freytag, General, defeated, iii. 318

'Friends of the People' the association so called, iii. 272

Frost, John, prosecution of, iii. 311

Fuentes, Condé de, Spanish ambassador, recalled from London, i. 75. His insolence reproved by Lord Egremont, 76

Fullarton, Colonel, his duel with Lord Shelburne, ii. 340

INDEX.

GAGE

GAGE, General, garrisons Boston, i. 299. His preparations for military defence at Boston, ii. 153, 172. Defeat of his men at Lexington, 173. Proclaims martial law, 165.
Gallantry, chivalric, in the middle ages, ii. 5
Galloway, his pacific proposal, ii. 205
Gambling, prevalence of, in the last century, ii. 14
Gardening, landscape, in the last century, ii. 18
Gates, General, sent against Burgoyne, ii. 256. His terms rejected by Burgoyne, 257. His animosity towards Washington, 292. Sent to attack Lord Cornwallis, 377. Totally defeated, 378. Superseded in his command by General Greene, 401.
Genoa, occupied by the French, and surrendered by Massena, iv. 255. Siege of, by the Austrians, 256.
George I., profligacy of the ministers of the court of, ii. 39–41
George II., his hatred of his son Frederick, i. 4. Goes to Hanover on the eve of war with France, 13. His supineness, 13. Point from which he viewed the prospect of war with France, 15. Enters into a subsidiary treaty with Hesse, and opens a negotiation for one with Russia, 15. His dislike of Pitt and Temple, 23. Who are dismissed, 23. Refuses to ratify his son's treaty of Closterseven, 29. Lord Hervey's account of his court, 105. Last moments of his queen, 106
George III., prosperity of the nation at his accession, i. 45. His early years and education, 46. Death of his father, 47. Character of his mother, 47. Waldegrave's character of him when prince, 48. As king, 49. Character of the public men at this period, 50. The King's mental capacity, 51. Attempt on the part of the Crown to recover its ancient power, 51. The 'King's Friends,' 52. The King's endeavours to break up party connection, 53. His policy,

GEORGE

54. His treatment of the Earl of Bute, 55. His speech to the Council, 58. Character of his private life, 94. His marriage, 94. His consort, 95. His treatment of the Duke of Devonshire and the Marquis of Rockingham, 100. His triumph over the Whig party, 104. His policy respecting this party, 105. His intrigues with Pitt, and his duplicity, 116. Announces to Grenville his determination to put Pitt at the head of affairs, 117. His vacillation and dissimulation, 120. His mode of gaining over the Duke of Bedford, 121. His further treacherous conduct, 122. Takes a strong personal interest in the proceedings against Wilkes, 137. His arbitrary conduct on the question of the general warrants, 137. His sudden illness, and question of a regency, 159. Misled by Halifax as to the Regency Bill, 162. Confers with Grenville and Mansfield, 163–167. His intrigues with the Opposition, 168. Sends for the Duke of Cumberland as to the regency question, 169. Puts the Duke into communication with Mr. Pitt, 170. Decision on the Bill, 171. Grenville's Insolence to the King, 171, 176. Resignation of the ministry, 176, 181. Negotiations with Mr. Pitt and with Lord Lyttelton, 170–180. The ministry recalled by the King, 181, 182. His interview with, and remonstrance of, the Duke of Bedford, 183. Formation of the Rockingham administration, 187. And of that of Lord Chatham, 219. The King's sincere support of Lord Chatham's administration, 225. His resentment against Wilkes, 265. Whom he determines to crush, 271. His design of suppressing the revolt in America, 271. His speech about the murrain, 311. His determination not to yield to the dictation of party, 323, 356. Commands Lord North to reconstruct the Government, 323. Address of the City of London to the

INDEX. 391

GEORGE

King, 336, 337. The King's answer, 339. Anger of the Court, 340. The King's answer to an address of the City of London, 357. Profligacy of ministers in the first years of the King's reign, ii. 41. Resumption of the power of the Crown by this King, 43. His part in the parliamentary proceedings against the press, 91. His consort, 103. His political maxims, 103. Death of his mother, 103. Character of the Court of Leicester House, and education of the King, 107. Death of his father, 107. His private character, 108. His brothers, 108. His opposition to royal intermarriage with subjects, 111. Increase of the Civil List, 230. Distress of the King's tradespeople, 231. Frugality of his household, 232. His inflexibility in the case of Dr. Dodd, 241. His obstinacy regarding the American war, 267, 272. His resentment at the application to Lord Chatham, 275. His intolerant spirit as to Catholic emancipation, 284. Dunning's motion for diminishing the power of the Crown, 324. The King's reluctance to accept Lord North's resignation, 416. His dislike to an oligarchy, 417. His overtures to Lord Rockingham, 420. Sends for Lord Shelburne, 421. Corrupt practices of the Crown, 434. His difficulties on the resignation of Lord Shelburne, iii. 28. Lord North's remarks on the limitation of the power of the King, 32. His supremacy at the commencement of the war with America, 42. The King's dislike of the Coalition, 66. His conduct on the passing of the Indian Bill, 71, 75. His want of openness, 76. His treacherous conduct, 77. His determination not to dismiss Pitt, 94. Termination of the struggle between the King and the Whig party, 97. His tortuous policy, 98. Obloquy thrown upon him, 99. His illness in 1788, 182. His recovery, 195, 205. His treatment during his

GERMAINE

illness, 207. His great popularity, 212. His resumption of power, 220. His interview with his sons, 221. His singular delusion, 222. Disagreements in the royal family, 223. His speech in 1792, 290. His message to Parliament as to the establishment of the Prince of Wales, 419. Outrage committed upon his majesty, iv. 16. Appeal of the Irish to him, 92. Attempt to shoot the King, 249. His strong opposition to Catholic emancipation, 286, 301. Lord Loughborough and Mr. Pitt's advice to the King on the subject, 294, 295. The King's answer, 295. Sends for Mr. Addington, 299. The King's penetration of character, 300. His mental excitement, 305. His dangerous illness, 309. His convalescence, 310

George, Prince of Wales, his marriages, ii. 113. Wears Fox's colours, iii. 108. His evil reputation at twenty-five, 153. His advantages, 153-156. His revenue, 155. Reduces his establishment, 156. His marriage with Mrs. Fitzherbert, 157, 160. His debts, 158. His falsehoods, 155, 160, 162. His debts paid, 167. His duplicity, 167. The regency question, 183 et seq. The Prince's behaviour to the Queen, 201. And to the King, 210, 222, 223. His schemes, 224. His first speech in Parliament, 275. His marriage, 414. His separation from the Princess, 417. His establishment, 418. The King's application to Parliament for his son, 419. Public indignation at his conduct, 420. Consults with Mr. Pitt as to the King's health, 307. His improper conduct, 308.

Germaine, Lord George, becomes Secretary of the Northern Department, ii. 192. His dejection and lukewarmness, 268. His remarks on General Burgoyne's conduct in America, 282. His resignation of the War Department, 282. Raised to the peerage as Lord Sackville, 411. Animadver-

GERMANTOWN

sions on, in the House of Lords, 412

Germantown, battle of, ii. 249

Gibraltar, state of, at the close of the reign of George II., i. 17. Proposal of Pitt to cede it to Spain, in consideration of her assisting England to recover Minorca, 22. Siege of, 323, 395; iii. 3. De Crillon's attempts, 12. Firmness of the garrison, 13. General Elliot's defence, 14. Floating batteries, 14. Loss of the besiegers, 15. Failure of the siege, 16. Efforts of Spain to recover Gibraltar, 23

Girondists, character of the, iii. 323

Gloucester, Duke of, his marriage with Lady Waldegrave, ii. 109. His speech on the regency question, iii. 194

Glynn, Serjeant, moves for a committee to inquire into the administration of justice in Westminster Hall, i. 379

Gordon, Lord George, his behaviour in Parliament, ii. 346. March of him and his mob to Palace Yard, 347. His behaviour in the Commons, 348. Excesses of the mob, 349 et seq. Lord G. Gordon arrested on a charge of high treason, 353. Committed to the Tower, 354. His trial and subsequent career, 359

Gorée restored to France, i. 88; iii. 23

Göttingen taken by Ferdinand from the French, i. 86

Gower, Lord, Chatham's vacillating conduct towards, i. 232. Joins the Duke of Grafton's administration as President of the Council, 253. His motion for excluding strangers from the House of Lords, 385. Resigns, ii. 335

Grafton, Duke of, appointed Secretary of State in the Rockingham administration, i. 182. His character as a statesman, 182. Resigns, 218. Placed by Pitt at the head of the Treasury, 222. His interview with the Earl of Chatham, 245. Undertakes the responsibility of prime minister, 246. Junius's abuse of, in his Letters, 280. His position

GRENVILLE

as a minister by accident, 306. Reasons for his measures, 307. His alarm, and anxiety to be relieved from the responsibility of office, 308. Treated by Chatham on his reappearance with coldness and neglect, 308. The Duke's mortification, 309. Attempts at accommodation, 309. His conduct on the Marquis of Rockingham's motion, 321. His resignation, 322. His profligacy, ii. 41. His abhorrence of measures pursued towards America, 228. Resigns, 108

Granby, Marquis of, sends in his adhesion to Granville's ministry, i. 176. Sent for by the King and tendered the reversion of the command-in-chief, 182. His resignation, 310, 320. His death, character, and career, i. 361

Granville, Earl, refuses the premiership, i. 22

Grasse, Count de, his fleet, iii. 3. Defeated by Rodney, 4.

Gratifications given by the minister to members of Parliament, i. 256 note

Grattan, Henry, his motion on the Address in 1779, ii. 331. His formal and solemn Declaration of Rights, 425, 427. His disinterestedness and patriotism, iv. 88. Overtures made to him in London, 92. Refuses to sit in the new Irish parliament, 109. His sudden reappearance in the Irish Parliament, 176. His speech, 177. Duel between him and Corry, 180

Graves, Admiral, joins Admiral Arbuthnot off New York, ii. 366

Greene, General, appointed to supersede Gates, ii. 401. Affairs in his command, 401

Grenada, island of, taken from France, i. 85

Grenville, George, dismissed from office, i. 16. Becomes leader of the House of Commons, 74. Destined for the Speaker's chair, 74. His conduct and want of tact, 74, 75. Appointed Secretary of State, 81. Resigns, 98. Becomes prime minister, 108. His

GRENVILLE

remonstrance against Bute's interference in public affairs, 102. His independence, 116. Intrigues of the King and Lord Bute to set him aside, 116. His provisional dismissal, 116. The King's duplicity, 118, 119. His dispute with the Duke of Bedford on the question of patronage, 122. His amendment on the motion of Sir W. Meredith respecting general warrants, 136. His financial schemes respecting the American colonies, 147. Innocence of his intentions, 148. Not naturally arbitrary, 149. His mitigatory measures, 149. Stability of his ministry, 157. His culpable conduct as to the Regency Bill, 163, 164. His contempt of popularity, 165. His audience with the King on the obnoxious clause in the Bill, 165. His insolence to the King, 175, 176. Resignation of his ministry tendered, 176, 181. Reconciliation between him and his elder brother, 179, 180. Conditions proposed by ministers, 180, 181. The ministry recalled by the King, 181, 182. His reply to Pitt's speech on the taxation of the colonies, 200. Attempts with Bedford to form a coalition between Bute and the Tories, 218. Reprobates the proceedings of the House of Commons as to John Wilkes, 277. His part in the debate on the Civil List, 289, 290. Reunion of the Grenville connection, 309. His Bill on controverted elections, 311. Ministerial obstructions to the Bill, 333. His death, and character, L 358

Grenville, James, in Lord Chatham's administration, i. 224. Resigns, 320.

Grenville, Thomas Lord. Operation of his Act respecting electoral corruption, i. 387. His Alien Bill, iii. 294. His reply to M. Chauvelin, 299. His answer to Napoleon's letter to the King, iv. 240. Talleyrand's reply, 242. Grenville's speech in Parliament on the subject, 244. His free-trade views, 278. His defence of the late

HARDY

ministry, 322. His attack on the Northern Convention, 365.

Grenville, Mr. Thomas, sent by Mr. Fox to Paris, ii. 436. Elected Speaker, iii. 197. Becomes Secretary of State, 223. Advanced to the peerage, 253. Becomes Secretary of State for Foreign Affairs, 253. See Grenville, Thomas Lord

Grenville, William, takes office under Pitt, iii. 85

Grey, Mr., his motion on parliamentary reform, iii. 272. His violent speech on the Address, 274, 275. Condemns the war with France, 360

Grosvenor, Mr., his motion, iii. 92

Guadaloupe taken from the French, i. 33

Guards, the Scots Fusilier, employed to quell a riot, L 267

HABEAS Corpus Act, its salutary effect, i. 129. Suspension of, in 1794, iii. 367. iv. 322 {

Hackney coachmen, their despotism, ii. 65

Hadfield's attempt to shoot the King, iv. 250. His capture and trial, 251.

Halifax, Earl of, becomes Secretary of State, i. 115. His claims for patronage, 123. Wilkes's action against him, 137. Who pleads Wilkes's outlawry in bar, 138. His conduct on the Regency Bill, 162. His impertinent advice to the King, 178. Resumes the office of Secretary of State, ii. 72

Handcock, President of Congress, ii. 217

Hanover taken by the French, L 26. Recovered by Prince Ferdinand, 31. Public dislike in England to, 77. Evacuated by the French, 88

Hardwicke, Lord, his speech on the peace of Paris, L 101. Refuses the offer of the premiership, 117. His death, 158

Hardy, trial of, for high treason, iii. 375. Acquitted, 384

HARLEY

Harley, Lord Mayor of London, his position and influence, ii. 95.

Hastings, Warren, his reception on his return to England, iii. 143. Combination formed against him, 144. Burke's charges, 144. Hastings heard at the bar of the Houses, 144. The impeachment resumed, 168. His trial, 170. Opening of the proceedings, 171. Burke's oration, 171. End of the trial, 249. Acquitted, 423. Public opinion of him, 426. His retirement, 428.

Havannah, the, taken from Spain, i. 85.

Havre bombarded by Rodney, i. 32.

Hawke, Admiral Sir Edward, attempt of the Duke of Newcastle to make a scapegoat of, i. 14. Timid measures of the ministry in their instructions to, 14. Sent to take Rochefort, 27. Returns with the fleet, 28. Blockades Brest, 35. His victory over the French at Belleisle, 41. Placed at the head of the Admiralty, 233.

Hawkesbury, Lord, Pitt's eulogy of, iv. 323.

Haymarket Theatre, opened by Foote without a license, ii. 62.

Helen's, St., meeting at, iv. 50.

Henry VII., his repression of the Barons, ii. 15.

Henry VIII., his learning, ii. 12. His attempt to revive chivalry, 15.

Henry, Patrick, at the Congress at Philadelphia, ii. 154.

Hervey, Lord, his account of the Court of George II., ii. 104.

Hesse, subsidiary treaty of George II. with, i. 15. Evacuated by the French, 88.

Highlanders, formation of the, into regiments of the line, i. 23.

Hillsborough, Lord, appointed President of the Board of Trade, i. 122. And to the Colonial Department, 254. Directs the dissolution of the Assembly of Massachusetts Bay, 293. Succeeds Lord Weymouth, ii. 337.

Hoche, General, his defeat of the Chouans, iv. 7.

Hohenlinden, battle of, iv. 263.

IMPEACHMENTS

Holdernesse, Earl of, resigns the office of Secretary of State, i. 17.

Holland, war declared by England against, ii. 382. Papers relating to, laid before Parliament, 388. Blockaded by a British squadron, iii. 11. Treaty of peace concluded on unfavourable terms, 11. French intrigues in, 232. Invaded by Prussia, 233. French breach of treaty with, 306. The Dutch population in favour of the French, 402. Conquered by the French, iv. 1. Defeat of the Dutch fleet off Camperdown, iv. 72. Expedition to, in 1799, 219. The Duke of York appointed General, 221. Difficult nature of the country, 222. The Duke's advance, 223. Failure of the expedition, 225.

Holt the printer, prosecution of, iii. 348.

Honduras, claims of England to the cutting of logwood in, i. 88.

Honour, origin of the law of, ii. 7.

Hood, Admiral, at Rodney's victory over De Grasse, iii. 4. Raised to the peerage, 4.

Horton, Mrs., married to the Duke of Cumberland, ii. 109.

Howe, General, his evacuation of Boston, ii. 204. Goes to Halifax, 205. His plans, 205. Occupies Staten Island, 212. His dilatory proceedings, 222. Challenges Inquiry into his conduct, 315.

Howe, Lord, joins his brother before New York, ii. 212. His pacific overtures, 212, 213. Sketch of his career, 216. His interview with the delegates from Congress, 217. Rejection of his terms, 219. His defeat of the French fleet, iii. 406. His popularity in the fleet, iv. 51. Redresses the wrongs of the sailors, 51.

Hudson, prosecution of, iii. 342.

Humbert, General, his landing in Ireland, iv. 124. Taken prisoner, 125.

IMPEACHMENTS, state, nature of, iii. 173.

IMPEY

Impey, Sir Elijah, motion made for his impeachment, iii. 169. Acquitted, 170

Income tax, Pitt's, iv. 236-239

Independence, Declaration of, drawn up, ii. 209. Composition of this famous paper, 210. Promulgated throughout the Union, 211

India, Lord Chatham's policy respecting, i. 234. Affairs of India in 1784, iii. 51. Ancient civilisation of, 113. Hindostan accustomed to despotic power, 114. Losses of the French Republic in India, 323. *See also* East India Company.

Indians, the American, their wars with the colonists in 1764, i. 142. French influences on them, 143

Indies, West, the French possessions in, attacked, and Guadaloupe taken, i. 33

Ionian Islands, ceded to France, iv. 70

Ireland, Lord Chatham's proposed settlement of the affairs of, i. 235. Condition of, in 1770, 351. Constitution and powers of the Irish Legislature, 351. Bill for terminating the existence of the Irish parliament passed, 353. Debate in the English House of Commons on Irish affairs, 353. Rejection of Walsingham's motion, 354. Lord Nugent's motion as to the trade and commerce of, in 1778, ii. 286. Proposed removal of prohibitory duties, 287. Difficulties in Ireland in 1779, 329. Rise of the Volunteers, 330. Meeting of the Irish Parliament, 331. Grattan's motion on the Address, 331. Disturbances in Dublin, 331. Condition of the country in 1782, 424. Repeal of Poynings' law, 424. Demands of the Irish people, 425. Grattan's motion of a formal and solemn Declaration of Rights, 425. Message from the Crown respecting the state of Ireland, 427. Objections to Irish independence, 429. Act relative to the Irish Courts of Justice, iii. 38. Condition of the country in 1784, 155. The Volunteers, 155. State of the representation at this time, 118.

IRELAND

Flood's measure, 119. Proceedings of the Irish Parliament in consequence of the illness of the King, 217. Ferocious conduct of the mob, 120. Shop-keepers and priests implicated, 120. Napper Tandy, 121. Scene at a dinner table, 121. The Catholics disinclined to reform, 124. Fox and Pitt on Irish reform, 125. Difficulty of dealing with the Irish aristocracy, 126. Reasonableness of Pitt's plan of policy, 127. Stormy debate on Pitt's Bill, 131. Defeat of the Bill, 132. Appearance of a French force in Bantry Bay, iv. 39. State of the country in 1794, 87. Corruption of the Irish Parliament, 88. Religious dissensions, 89. The United Irishmen, 90. Remedial measures, 90. Treasonable projects of French invasion, 90. The patriotic party, 91. The Duke of Portland's policy, 91. Lord Fitzwilliam becomes Viceroy, 91, 92. Overtures made to Grattan, 92. Loyal Irish addresses, 93. Changes in the Irish ministry, 94. Contrast between English and Irish Peers, 95. Bribery in Ireland, 96. Debasement of the Irish members, 97. Influence of the Beresfords, 97. The new Viceroy's acts, 98. Panic among the Irish officers, 98. Animosity against Lord Fitzwilliam, 98. Who is recalled, 100. His letters, 100. Lord Camden made Viceroy, 101. Excitement throughout the country, 101. The new Viceroy's reception in Dublin, 102. Formation of the Orange party, 103. Rival races and creeds in Ireland, iv. 104. Terrible policy of the Government, 104, 105. Violence of the Protestant yeomanry, 105. Preparations for a general insurrection, 106. Lewins's mission to France, 107. Leaders of the rebellion, 107. Sir James Stuart's proceedings, 108. Persecution of the press, 109. Dissolution of Parliament, 109. Fresh applications to France, 110. The Irish spy system, 111. Reynolds the informer, 111. Arrest

JACOBINS

of Lord Edward Fitzgerald, 112. Betrayal of the rebels, 115. Attacks on Naas and Kilcullen, 116. Sir Edward Crosbie, 117. Duff's attack on the rebels, 118. The Wexford address, 119. Defeat of the insurgents, 120. Lord Cornwallis becomes Viceroy, 121. Proclamation of an amnesty, 181. Bonaparte's distrust of the Irish, 123. Landing of General Humbert, 124. Battle of Castlebar, 125. The French taken prisoners, 125. French troops landed in the island of Rutland, 126. Suppression of the Rebellion, 127. Conflict between Catholics and Protestants, 128, 129. Union proposed, 131. Discussions on the Union, 133. Revival of agitation, 135. Opposition of the Irish bar to Union, 136. Overtures to Catholics and Orangemen, 137. Faulty Irish representation, 140. Dismissal of public officers, 141. Lord Cornwallis's disgust at his duties, 142. Lord Castlereagh becomes Chief Secretary, 143. His plan of promoting the Union, 145. Pitt's Union resolutions, 146. Character of the Union resolutions, 150. Irish opposition, 152. Lord Castlereagh's motion, 153. Prorogation of the Houses, 153. Bill of Indemnity, 154. Fitzgerald, sheriff of Tipperary, and his cruelties, 155. Use of torture in Ireland, 161. The Protestant ascendency checked, 168. Murder by the yeomanry in Wicklow, 169. And by a party of militia, 171. Disgrace of Lord Downshire, 175. Majority for Government on the Union question, 179. Duel between Grattan and Corry, 180. The Union Bill passed, 181. The articles of Union, 182. Petition of the woollen manufacturers, 183. Compensation to owners of seats, 184

JACOBINS, character of the, iii. 325. Jaffa, Napoleon's massacre at, iv. 226, 227.

KENYON

Jefferson, Mr., his appearance in the Virginian Assembly, i. 304
Jenkinson, Mr., preferred to the Board of Admiralty, i. 234. One of the go-betweens of the Court in the Commons, 404. Denounced by Fox, iii. 74
Jersey, attack of the French on, ii. 394
Jervis, Sir John, his defeat of the Spanish off Cape St. Vincent, iv. 44. Raised to the peerage, 45
Johnson, Dr. Samuel, his political pamphlets, i. 402. His parliamentary reports, ii. 72
Johnstone, Mr., appointed a 'Commissioner to negotiate with Congress, ii. 296. His indiscretion, 296. His speech on the proclamation of the Commissioners sent to America, 314
Jones, Paul, exploits of, ii. 325
Jones, Gall, conviction of, iv. 81
Judges, Act passed enabling them to hold their offices for life, i. 48. Their independence, 376. Their responsibility, 376. Attacks upon their independence in Parliament, 376-381. Their subservience at the end of the last century, iii. 349, 377
Junius, letters of, i. 279. His rancour, 279. Mysterious authorship of the letters, 280. Junius's unfounded charges, 280. His attack on Lord Mansfield and the Duke of Bedford, 282-284. His politics, 284. Becomes a classic writer, 285. Compared with Dean Swift, 285. Supposed authorship of the letters, 286. Proofs in favour of, or against, Sir Philip Francis, 287 note. Prosecution of the printers, &c., of the letter to the King, i. 374

KEENE, Sir B., British minister at Madrid, his instructions from Pitt as to Gibraltar and Minorca, i. 30. His reports from Spain, 64
Keith, his May Fair marriages, ii. 55
Kempenfelt, Admiral, his retreat from the Brest fleet, ii. 410
Kenyon, Lord, his opinion asked by the

KEPPEL

King as to Catholic emancipation, iv. 99. His ignorance, 254
Keppel, Admiral, entrusted with the Channel fleet, ii. 306. His indecisive operations, 306. His treatment of Palliser, 306. Defended in Parliament by Lord Bristol, 308. Accusations of Palliser, 308. Tried by court-martial, 309. His acquittal, 309. Resigns, 311. Review of his conduct, 311. His apology for the recall of Rodney, iii. 2
Kidgell, chaplain to the Earl of March, his disgraceful conduct, i. 132
'King's Friends,' the party so called, i. 53, 177. Burke's pamphlet on, and Lord John Russell's remarks on, 178 note
Kleber, General, his victories in Egypt, iv. 332. Assassinated, 334
Kniphausen, General, left by Clinton in command at New York, ii. 360. His fears of an attack, 361. His unsuccessful expedition, 365
Kolin, battle of, i. 26
Kunersdorf, battle of, l. 42

LAFAYETTE, Marquis de, becomes Major-General in the American army, ii. 244. His loyalty to Washington, 292. At York Town, 405
Landrecy, besieged and taken, iii. 399
Land tax, reduction of the, iv. 78
Learning in the middle ages, ii. 10. And in the sixteenth century, 11. Shakspeare and Bacon, 12
Lee, his motion in Congress that America be declared Independent, ii. 202. Captured by the English, 223. Defeated at Monmouth Court House, 301
Legge, Mr., Chancellor of the Exchequer, refuses to sign the Hessian treaty, i. 15. Dismissed from office, 16. Dismissed from the Exchequer, 57
Leicester House, court of the Prince of Wales at, i. 4. Character of the court of, ii. 107
Lennox, Colonel, his duel with the Duke of York, iii. 225

LONDON

Lennox, Lady Sarah, the King's attentions to her, i. 97
Lewins, sent over by the Irish insurgents to France, iv. 107
Lexington, battle of, ii. 173
Libel, Dowdeswell's Bill to amend the law of, ii. 100. Theory of, 131. Prevalence of libel in the last century, ii. 167. Right of juries to decide libels debated, iii. 249. Becomes a law, 251
Licensing Act, the, passed, ii. 62. Evasions of the law, 62, 63
Lincoln, American Commandant at Charlestown, ii. 360. Surrenders his garrison to General Clinton, 361
Lisle, conference as to peace at, iv. 65
Lloyd, one of Grenville's go-betweens, i. 404. Prosecution of, iii. 343
London, attempt of the Earl of Bute to bribe the City of, i. 106. Riots of the silk weavers in 1765, 175. On the election of Wilkes for Middlesex, 264. And on his imprisonment, 265. Constitution and privileges of the corporation of London, 334. The Lord Mayor's privileges, 335. The liberties of England indebted to the City of London, 335. The City 'Address and Remonstrance' to the King, 336, 337. Angry feelings of the Crown, 340. Firmness of the City members, 340. The King's answer to an Address of the City, 352. Attempts of the City to obstruct recruiting for the navy in 1770, 371. Royal edicts against the increase of, ii. 28. Causes of the increase of visitors to London, 48. Establishment of clubs, 49. Amusements, 50. Fashionable assemblies and places of assignation, 52. May Fair marriages, 55. Luxury of the London middle classes, 61. Insecurity of the streets, 62. Licentiousness and ferocity of the people, 64. Nuisances in the streets, 64. Establishment of a system of police in 1761, 65. Public outrages on decency, 66. Frequency of mobs, 66. Turbulence of the people, 67.

LOUDOUN

Public executions, 61. The pillory and public whippings, 68. Contest of the House of Commons and the City, 79. Treatment of the messenger of the House in the City, 79. The Lord Mayor summoned to attend the House, 81. His defence, 81. Proceedings of the Lord Mayor, 84, 85. Committal of the Lord Mayor to the Tower, 85. Commotion in consequence, 86. Moderation of the city magistrates, 93. The Marquis of Buckingham's visit of condolence to the Lord Mayor, 94. Discord in the City on the re-election of Lord Mayor, 97. Petition from the City on American affairs, 190. Riots in London conducted under the auspices of men of rank and fashion, 310. The 'No Popery' riots in 1780, 347. The military called out, 352. Attack on the Bank, 353. The riots suppressed, 353. Prosecution and conviction of the Lord Mayor, 355. And of the rioters, 358. Official Inquiry into the losses caused by the mob, 358. Address to the throne on the discontinuance of the war with America, 410. Popularity of Pitt in the metropolis, iii. 93. Illots and political meetings, iv. 16

Loudoun, Earl of, superseded by General Amherst, i. 31

Loughborough, Lord, his conduct on the trials of the rioters of 1780, ii. 358. Becomes Lord Chancellor, iii. 296. His breach of confidence, iv. 290. His advice to the King, 291. Remains in the Addington administration, 299. Dismissed, 315. *See also* Wedderburn.

Louis Philippe (afterwards king), accompanies Dumourier, iii. 312

Lowther, Sir James, his opposition to the continuance of the war with America, ii. 409

Lowthers, their influence in Westmoreland and Cumberland, i. 218

Loyalty, former, of the people of England, i. 397. Suspended and par-

MANSFIELD

tially revived at the accession of George III., 399

Lucia, St., island of, taken from France, i. 83. Restored to France, 88. Taken again, ii. 303. Recovered by the French, iv. 14

Luneville, negotiations for peace at, iv. 263. Treaty of, 266

Luttrell, Colonel, declared by the House of Commons duly elected for Middlesex, i. 278. His contest with Burke in the House, ii. 83. His sister married to the Duke of Cumberland, 102. *See also* Carhampton.

Lyttelton, Lord, sent for by the King to form an administration, i. 180. Excuses himself, 180. His proposals to the Marquis of Rockingham, 247

MACDONALD, General, his government of Naples, iv. 209

Macintosh, Sir James, his 'Vindiciæ Gallicæ,' iii. 263, 264

Mackenzie, Mr. Stuart, Privy Seal of Scotland, Mr. Grenville's proposal to dismiss him, i. 181. Supported by the King, 181. Dismissed, 182. Restored to his place by Pitt, 234

Malta, seized by the French under Bonaparte, iv. 189. Taken by the English, iv. 262

Malmesbury, Lord, sent to Paris to negotiate peace, iv. 27. Failure of negotiations, 28. His final propositions, 29. His dismissal, 31. Again sent to negotiate peace, 65

Manners, sketch of the development of modern, ii. 1

Mansfield, William Murray, Lord, his character and abilities, i. 8. His attorney-generalship, 12. Attacked by Pitt, 12. Raised to the peerage, 21, 22. His speech on the peace of Paris, 101. His conduct on the Regency Bill, 166. His speech on the question of levying taxes, 209. His speech on Orders in Council, 233. Junius's attack on, 282. His speeches on the Middlesex elections,

MARENGO 316, 343. Supports Mr. Grenville's Bill, 331. His conduct on the trial of Almon, the bookseller, 376. His reply to Lord Chatham, 377. Unworthy proceeding in the Lords on the matter, 378. Charges made against him, 381 note. His speech on American affairs, ii. 192. His house burnt by the 'No Popery' mob, 350. His speech on the subject, 353.

Marengo, battle of, iv. 257.

Maria-Theresa, Empress, her part in the partition of Poland, ii. 128.

Maria Antoinette, Queen, her treatment, iii. 326. Her execution, 327.

Marriage, effects of the unsettled state of the law of, in the last century, ii. 54. Cause of clandestine marriages, 55. Matrimonial contracts among the higher classes, 56. Failure of a Bill to prevent the marriage of divorced persons, 320.

Marriage Act, the Royal, ii. 111. Policy of restrictions on royal marriages, 111. German origin of the Royal Marriage Act, 114. Passes, 115.

Martin, one of the joint Secretaries of the Treasury, his duel with John Wilkes, i. 130.

Martinique, expedition against, i. 85. Surrenders to Admiral Rodney, 86. Restored to France, 88.

Massachusetts Bay, refusal of the Assembly of, to obey an enactment of Parliament, i. 242. Assembly of, its quarrels with Governor Bernard, 292. The Assembly dissolved, 293. Convention of, 297. Meeting of the General Assembly of, and its resolutions, 301. Its obstinacy in its opposition to British policy, 310. Petition of the Assembly to the Privy Council, ii. 143. The petition rejected, 146, 147. Bill for closing the port of Boston passed, 147. Alteration of the Charter of Massachusetts, 148. General Gage appointed Governor, 149. Final dismissal of the Assembly, 151. Ex-

MORDAUNT asperation of the State, 152. Formation of a Committee of Safety, 153.

Maubeuge, siege of, iii. 320.

Mauduit, Isaac, his 'Consideration of the German War,' i. 402.

May Fair marriages, ii. 55.

Maynooth question, the, in 1795, iv. 293.

M'Quirk, case of, i. 281.

Medmenham Abbey, orgies at, ii. 41.

Mentz, the Prussians at, iii. 321.

Meredith, Sir W., his motion in the House of Commons respecting general warrants, i. 136.

Methuen Treaty, abandoned, iii. 150.

Middlesex elections, riots at the, i. 264, 272, 273, 278. Petition of the county to the Crown, 278. Lord Chatham's condemnatory Bill, 342. Debate on the election, 343. Great meetings in, in 1779, ii. 334.

Military affairs in 1778, ii. 318.

Minorca at the close of the reign of George II., i. 17. Loss of, 18. Pitt's plan for recovering, 22. Restored to England, 69. Attempt of the French and Spanish at, ii. 396. Taken by the French, 411.

Mobs, frequency of, in the last century, ii. 66. Turbulence of the people, 67.

Monarchy, elective, evils of, ii. 123.

Monasteries before the Reformation, ii. 22.

Monmouth Court House, defeat of the Americans at, ii. 301.

Montcalm, Marquis de, commandant at Quebec, i. 35. His position, 35. Defeated and killed on the heights of Abraham, 39, 40.

Monckton, General, second in command under Wolfe before Quebec, i. 38. His death, 40. His operations against the French West Indies, 85. Montgomery, General, invades Canada, ii. 185. Killed at Quebec, 186.

Montreal, surrender of, i. 40.

Moorfields, the 'No Popery' riots in, ii. 349.

Morals in the middle ages, ii. 4.

Mordaunt, General, his want of promptitude before Rochefort, i. 27, 28.

INDEX.

MORRISTOWN

Morristown, meeting at, ii. 400
Morton, Mr., his motion on the Regency Bill, i. 167, 170
Motte, La, trial and execution of, iii. 372
Muir, Thomas, iii. 353. His prosecution, iii. 353. His conviction and sentence, 355
Murphy, his Government paper the 'Auditor,' i. 408
Murray, Colonel, his threat to Lord George Gordon, ii. 349
Murray, William. *See* Mansfield

NAPLES, imbecility of the Court of, iv. 203-205. Defeat of the Neapolitans in the Roman States, 207. Occupied by the French, 207. Cardinal Ruffo's march upon, 209
National debt, increase of the, from the beginning of the reign of George II. to 1763, i. 93. Increase of the, in 1797, ii. 61. Pitt's attempts to reduce the, iii. 138. The time favourable for the reduction, 139. Delusive notion of a sinking fund, 139. Price's scheme, 140. Other plans, 143
Navigation Laws, how regarded by our colonists, i. 146
Navy, state of the, in 1778, ii. 284. Sir Philip Clerke's Bill, 265. Indecisive operations of the Channel Fleet under Keppel, 306. Naval affairs in 1778, 315. Mutiny of the fleet in 1796, iv. 45. Causes of discontent, 47. Answer to the demands of the delegates, 48. End of the mutiny, 49. The mutiny at St. Helen's, 50. Mutiny at the Nore, 53. Mutinous disposition throughout the navy, 60. Ill-usage of the seamen, 60
Nelson, Commodore (afterwards Earl), at the battle of Cape St. Vincent, iv. 43, 44. Sent in pursuit of the French, 190. Gains the battle of the Nile, 192. His complaint of want of frigates, 195. His despatch, 196. Letters from Ladies Spencer and Parker, 198. Created a peer, 198.

NEW YORK

Sails for Naples, 200. His illness, 201 His reception by the Court at Naples, 201-203. His violence at Naples, 210. Goes to the Baltic, 345. His dissatisfaction with the conduct of Sir H. Parker, 347. Nelson's conduct at Copenhagen, 351. Condition of the fleet, 353. His plans overruled, 356. Appointed to the chief command, 357. His dissatisfaction, 357. His resignation, 358 Commands an attack on Boulogne, 360
Netherlands, the French in the, iii. 310
Newcastle, Duke of, his character as a statesman, i. 9. His policy, 10. Addresses himself to Mr. Fox, 11. Who is gained over by a place, 12. Attempts to throw the responsibility of his acts upon Sir Edward Hawke, 14. Fails to gain over the Earl of Chatham, 16. Dissolution of his ministry, 21, 22. Attempts to form a new administration and a union with Pitt, 24. Forms a new ministry with Pitt, 25. His exultation on the fall of Pitt, 71. His intrigues for the ruin of Pitt, 71, 72. Treated with indignity, 81. Resigns, 82. Dignity with which he retired, 82, 83. Dismissed from the lieutenancy of his county, 103. Applied to to form an administration in 1765, 186. His extension and organisation of parliamentary corruption, ii. 37. His levees in Lincoln's Inn Fields, 42
Newenham, Sir Edward, his disloyalty, iii. 121-123.
Newfoundland, claims of Spain to fish on the banks of, i. 65. Rights of the French to fish on the banks confirmed by treaty, 88. Claims of Spain relinquished, 89
Newgate destroyed by the 'No Popery' mob, ii. 350
Newspapers, Colonel Onslow's motion against the, ii. 75. Scurrility of some of the, 76. Stamp on, iii. 227
New York, refusal of the Assembly of, to obey an enactment of Parliament, 250. Suspension of, by Act of Parliament, 251. Washington

INDEX. 401

NILE

fixes his headquarters at, ii. 212.
Captured by the English, 220
Nile, battle of the, iv. 192
Nore, mutiny at the, iv. 53. Parker's behaviour, 54, 55. Parliamentary denunciation of the mutineers, 56. Suppression of the mutiny, 58. Execution of Parker, 58
Norfolk, Duke of, his disloyalty, iv. 74, 82
'North Briton,' Wilkes's, i. 124
North, Lord, in the Chatham Administration, i. 224. Declines the Chancellorship of the Exchequer, 244. But accepts it on the death of Charles Townshend, 254. Brings down a message from the Crown respecting the Civil List, 288. His construction of a new cabinet, 323. His defiance of public opinion, 323. His opinions, 324. His loyalty, 324. His contemptuous denial of grievances, 328. His addition to Mr. Dowdeswell's motion, 329. His injudicious conduct as to American affairs, 345. Signs of the longevity of his Government, 357. Burke's rudeness to him in the House, 417. Meeting at his house to consider the question of parliamentary reporting, ii. 72. His proposal, 84. Insulted on his way to the House, 86. Prompted in his course of action by the Court, 90. Dismisses Fox from office, 149. His Bill for the suspension of the Habeas Corpus Act in America, 229. Despondency of the members of his Government, 266. His desire to resign, 267, 272. His tone of dejection, 268. His Conciliation Bills, 269, 272. His overtures to the Whigs, 321. Partial change in the Administration, 335. His arguments on the inquiry into the conduct of the American war, 412. His resignation, 415. His remarks on curtailing the power of the King, iii. 32. Sent for by the King, but refuses office, 33. His opposition to Pitt's plan of parliamentary reform, 38. Joins the Coalition

OPPOSITION

Ministry, 34. Dismissed by the King, 75. His unpopularity, 101. His opposition to concessions to the Irish, 130. His motion on the regency question, 192. His death, 288. Review of his character, 288
Northampton, contest for the borough of, in 1768, i. 258
Northern League, Lord Chatham's proposed, i. 228. Defeat of the project, 230
Northesk, Earl of, his mission from the mutineers at the Nore to the King, iv. 57
Northington, Lord, Lord Chancellor in the Rockingham ministry, i. 189. Resigns the Great Seal, 219. Commanded by the King to communicate with Pitt, 219. Becomes President of the Council, 222. Retires from office, 253
Northumberland, Earl of, treatment of the, by the Duke of Bedford, i. 175. Proposed by the Duke of Cumberland as Prime Minister, 176. Raised to a dukedom, 234
Norton, Sir Fletcher, Speaker of the House of Commons, his authority set at nought, i. 328. His attack upon Lord North, ii. 341. Defeated in the contest for Speaker in the Parliament of 1780, 385. Review of his conduct in the chair, 385
Novels of the Restoration, ii. 38
Nowell, Dr., his sermon before the House of Commons, ii. 118

OCZAKOW, case of, iii. 251
Oliver, Alderman, ordered to attend in his place in the House, ii. 82. Fox's remarks on, 82. Compels Foxe to retract, 82. Committed to the Tower, 86. His position and influence, 95
Onslow, Colonel, his motion against reporters in Parliament, ii. 73. Debates on the motion, 75–77. His motion against the newspapers, 75
Opposition, mutual dissensions of the, in 1770, i. 355

VOL. IV.   D D

ORANGEMEN

Orangemen, formation of the society of, iv. 102. Their violence in 1796, 103

Oswald, Mr., sent by Lord Shelburne to Paris, ii. 436

Oswego, fort of, taken by the French, ii. 26

Outlawry pleaded in bar of civil process till 15 & 16 Vict. c. 76, i. 138

Oxford, case of the Mayor and Corporation of, i. 257

PAINE, Thomas, his 'Rights of Man,' iii. 263, 275. Prosecuted, 283, 337. Flies to Paris, 337. Appearance of his 'Age of Reason,' iv. 15

Palliser, Admiral, charges against him, ii. 307. His accusations against Admiral Keppel, 308. Court-martial on Palliser, 310. Acquitted, 310. Appointed governor to Greenwich Hospital, 387. Objections to him, 389

Palmer, Fyshe, case of, iii. 356

Pantheon, the, ii. 52, 62

Papacy, the, its opposition to freedom, ii. 24

Paris, peace of, i. 88. Conditions of the treaty, 88. Discussions in Parliament on the, 101. Majority in favour of the, 103

Parker, the mutineer, iv. 54. His execution, 58. His character, 59

Parker, Admiral, his conduct in the Baltic, iv. 346. His dilatoriness, 348. Recalled, 357

Parliament. Party jealousy, i. 4. Break-up of the Opposition in 1751, by the death of the Prince of Wales, 5. Parliamentary corruption in 1757, 26. Mode in which parliamentary government in England first developed itself, 51. Venality of Parliament in 1761, 67, 74, 97. The four political parties at this time, 74. Condition of the Court party, 96. Commencement of the struggle between prerogative and parliamentary government, 97. Prices at which votes were purchased by Mr. Fox, 98.

PARLIAMENT

Discussion on the treaty of Paris, 101. Appearance of Pitt in the House of Commons, 101. His speech, 102. Majority in favour of the peace, 103. Parliament appealed to in the matter of John Wilkes, 130. Decision of the House of Commons, 130. Conduct of the House of Lords, 131–134. Wilkes expelled the House, 135, 274. Increase of the minority in the Commons, 139. Discussions on the Regency Bill, 160, 161. Inquiry into American grievances, 207. Measures of the Rockingham administration, 214. Insubordination of state officers at this period, 216. Disorder of Parliament under Lord Chatham's administration, 243. The general election of 1768, 255. Prices of seats, 255. Gratification to Lords as well as Commons, 256. Case of the Mayor and Corporation of Oxford, 257. Proportion of electors to the population, 257. The people not represented in Parliament, 257. Popular orators always lost in Parliament, 271. Right of the House of Commons to expel a member, 276. Debate on the deficiency in the Civil List in 1769, 288. Reunion of the Grenville connection, 309. The Horned Cattle session, 311. Lord Chatham's speech on parliamentary reform, 321. The Speaker's authority set at nought, 328. Mode of getting up petitions of undue elections, 332. Main provisions of Mr. Grenville's Bill, 332. Meeting of Parliament in 1770, 371. Debate on the case of Almon the bookseller, 376. Extraordinary scene in the Lords, 383. Indignation of the Commons, 384. Results of this quarrel, 386. Powers and privileges of the Lords and Commons, 394. Former character of the Commons, 395. Parliamentary preponderance of the landed interest, 397, 401. Faulty elective system, 400, 401. A new class of members introduced into Parliament, 401. Parliamentary eloquence, 411. Com-

PARLIAMENT

parison of modern and former Parliaments, 412. And parliamentary eloquence, 414. Improvements in parliamentary departments, 415. Rudeness in debate in former times, 416. Personal attacks on the Speaker, 418. The Speaker's present authority, 418. Inordinate length of modern debates, 419. Necessity for parliamentary discussion, 420. Power of the Commons and destruction of arbitrary power, ii. 35. Parliamentary corruption introduced by Walpole, 36. Ministerial levees, 42. Resumption of power by the Crown, 43. Dissolution of the Whig Opposition in 1771, 70. Attempt to exclude parliamentary reporters, 72. Colonel Onslow's motion, 73. Debates on the motion, 73–77. Contest between the House of Commons and the City, 78. Debates on privilege, 83, 84. Arbitrary spirit of the House of Commons, ii. 84. Committal of the Lord Mayor to the Tower, 85. Popular dislike of parliamentary privilege, 87. Question of the validity of the Speaker's warrant, 88. Formation of a committee to draw up a history of the proceedings and to search for precedents, 89. Their report derided, 90. Lord Chatham's Bill for the reform of Parliament, 97, 99. Character of the constituencies in 1771, 98. Dr. Nowell's sermon before the House of Commons, 116. Petition on the subscription to the Thirtynine Articles, 119. Bill for the relief of Protestant Dissenters, 119. East Indian and American affairs in 1773–4, 157. Opposition to the Bill for determining controverted elections, 162. Debate on Horne Tooke's libel, 163. Indiscriminate conduct of the House when baffled by Horne Tooke, 168. Excessive license of parliamentary debate, 167. Discussions on the right to tax the colonies, 189. Intemperate character of the debates, 193, 198. Debates on the session of 1776-7

PARLIAMENT

on American affairs, 227. Debates on the Civil List, 232. Offensive and indecent expressions of applause or dissent in the last century, 236. Bill for the better security of dockyards, 236. Debates on the war in America, 262. Movements of the Opposition, 266. Message from the Crown announcing a rupture with France, 274. Lord Chatham's last speech in Parliament, 277. Debate on the Duke of Richmond's motion, 281. His motion defeated, 282. Agitation for parliamentary reform, Catholic relief, and free trade, 282-287. Resumption of the debates on American affairs, 313. Rupture with Spain, 316. Debate on the Spanish manifesto, 317. And on the state of Ireland, 332. Burke's economical Reform Bill, 333, 337. Presentation of the county petitions, 337. Inquiry into the pension list, 339. Violent debates and political duels, 340. Scandalous discussion between the Speaker and the Attorney-General, 341. Accumulation of petitions for reform, 341. Dunning's motion for diminishing the power of the Crown, 342. Want of parliamentary strength and union, 343. Scene in Parliament at the 'No Popery' riots, 348. Consideration of the great Protestant petition, 357. Contest for speaker in the new Parliament of 1780, 384. Vote of thanks to the late Speaker and to Lord Cornwallis, 387. Attack on Lord Sandwich, 387. Debate on the rupture with Holland, 388. And on the appointment of Sir Hugh Palliser, 388. Rejection of Burke's Bill on the Civil List, 390. Pitt's first speech in Parliament, 391. Violence of the Opposition in 1781, 392. Debates on the close of the American war, 408. Motion for an inquiry into the conduct of the war, 411. General Conway's motion carried, 412, 413. Perseverance of the Opposition, 413. Debate on vote of no confidence, 414. Condition of Ireland in 1783,

D D 2

PARLIAMENT

424. Disqualification of contractors, 430. Debate on the Civil List, 431. Intimidation of the Government and virulence of the Opposition, iii. 26. Condemnation of the treaties with France, Spain, and America, 27. Amendment to the Address, 27. Resignation of Lord Shelburne, 28. Formation of the Coalition ministry, 32. State of parties in 1783, 35. Pitt's plan of parliamentary reform, 37. India Bills and Indian affairs, 56. Excitement of the Commons on the rejection of the India Bill by the Lords, 73. Mr. Baker's resolution, and opposition to it, 73. Pitt's ministry, 84. Debate on Fox's third India Bill, 90. Virulence of the Opposition, 94. Votes of want of confidence, 94. Dissolution, 96. Agitation for reform, 117. Debate on the Prince of Wales's affairs, 158. Impeachment of Warren Hastings, 163. Prosecution of Stockdale, 174. Debates on the slave trade, 176, 226. Discussions on a regency, 183. Modes of parliamentary delay, 191. The tobacco duties, 226. Stamps on newspapers, 227. Debates on French affairs, 238. Dissolution, 245. Debate on the trial of Warren Hastings, 247. On the slave trade, 251. And on Russian policy, 252. Movements of the Opposition in 1792, 272. Mr. Grey's notice of bringing forward the question of parliamentary reform, 277. Proceedings in the House of Commons on the declaration of war with France, 308, 309. Traitorous Correspondence Bill brought in, 356. Policy of peace urged by the Opposition, 359. Sheridan's motion as to the Volunteers, 362. Defence of the Government, 363. Debate on the continuance of the war with France, 410. Proceedings of the Opposition, 412. The King's message as to the establishment of the Prince of Wales, 419. Coercive measures in 1795, iv. 16. Act to repress public dis-

PARTIES

cussion, 17. Violent debate on the measure, 18. Petitions against the Bills, 20. Loans and new taxes, 23. The Opposition against negotiations with France, 26. The new Parliament of 1796, 33. Financial affairs, 34. Parliamentary denunciation of the mutineers at the Nore, 56. Motion for a change of the Ministry, 63. Plans for invading England, 71. Factious conduct of the Opposition, 73. The budget of 1797, 75. Opposition to it, 76. Idea of presenting the chiefs of the Opposition, 82. Motion for dismissal of the Ministry, 84. Question of the Union of Ireland with England, 131. Defeat of ministers, 135. Mr. Pitt's plan of parliamentary reform, 139, 182. Debate on the Irish Union, 184. Pitt's financial measures in the session of 1799, 236. Debate on a war policy, 245. Meeting of the first Parliament of the United Kingdom, 294. Pitt's resignation, 298, 314. Mr. Addington's administration, 299, 314. Committee on Horne Tooke's case, 325. Bill to exclude clergymen from Parliament, 328. Opinion of Parliament on the peace, 364

Parliament, Irish, debates in, in 1779, ii. 331. The Short Money Bill, 332. Meeting in 1782, 428. Grattan's propositions, 428. His speech, 428. Proceedings in consequence of the King's illness, iii. 217. Prorogued, iv. 153, 173. Grattan's speech on the Union, 177. The Act of Union passed, 181. Its corruption, 88, 97. Dissolved, 109. Proceedings of the new Parliament, 132, 134. Lord Castlereagh's motion, 153

Parties, state of, in 1760-1770, i. 389-391. Disadvantages and dangers of party, 392. The constitution appealed to by party, 392. Government by party, 399. Party squabbles, 400. Employment of political partisans, 405. Impossibility of party government at the

INDEX.   405

PAUL

present day, 421. State of parties in 1783, iii. 36. Unpopularity of the Coalition Ministry, 65

Paul, Emperor, his death, iv. 355

Paymaster, emoluments of the office of, i. 112, 113; ii. 431

Pearson, Major, his repulse of the French at St. Helier's, ii. 395

Peers, privileges of, i. 394. *See* Parliament.

Pelham, Mr., his death, i. 5

Penn, Mr., draws up a petition from Congress to the King, ii. 197. His statement at the bar of the House of Commons, 197

Pension list, parliamentary inquiry into the, ii. 319

Pensions, proposal to tax, ii. 285

Pennsylvania, propositions of the home Government to the Assembly of, ii. 174

Penthièvre, betrayed by treachery, iv. 9

Periodicals, political, character of the, of the last century, i. 405

Perry, Mr., his prosecution and acquittal, iii. 350

Philadelphia, assembly of the Congress of the States at, ii. 154, 175. Captured by the British, 247. Evacuated by the British, 300

Philip Egalité, his execution, iii. 327

Philippine Islands, the, taken from Spain, i. 85

Pichegru, General, in command of the French army, iii. 397. Checked, 399. His successes, 401

Pillory, punishment of the, in the last century, ii. 68

Pitt, William (afterwards Earl of Chatham), his eloquence, i. 6. His character as a statesman, 6. His affectation, 7. His reverence for royalty, 7. In the subordinate office of Paymaster, 12. Attacks the Attorney-general, 12. Refuses the Duke of Newcastle's terms, 16. Dismissed, 16. Becomes Secretary of State in the Duke of Devonshire's administration, 22. His vigorous conduct, 22. Becomes personally distasteful to the King, 23. Dis-

PITT

missed, 23. Endeavours of Lords Bute and Chesterfield to promote an alliance between Newcastle and Pitt, 24. Which subsequently takes place, 25. All real power centred in Pitt, 26. Possessed of the confidence of the country, 26. State of the empire when consigned to his care, 26, 27. Proposes to cede Gibraltar to Spain in consideration of her assisting England to recover Minorca, 29. His vigorous prosecution of the war, 30, 32. Procures Frederick the Great a subsidy, 31. His character as a public man, 50. George III.'s treatment of him, 57. Awaits his dismissal with dignity and temper, 58. His policy as to the war with France, 58, 59. Offended by the interference of France in Spanish affairs, 63. Censured by some for having caused the Family Compact, 64. Takes prompt measures for the renewal of hostilities with Spain, 65. His vigorous policy, 65. Retires from office, 66. Review of his policy, 66. His remedy for the state of the nation, 67. His popularity, 67. His consistency, 68. Character of his subordinates and agents, 62. Intrigues of Newcastle to ruin him, 71, 72. Influence of court favour on him, 72. His wife created Baroness Chatham, 72. His consequent unpopularity, 72. His reception in the city on Lord Mayor's Day, 73. His magnanimity, 77. Mr. Thomas Walpole deputed to sound him, 96. His appearance in the House on the debate on the peace of Paris, 101. His speech, 102. Compared with Henry Fox, the first Lord Holland, 112. Attempts to form a new administration under Pitt, i. 115, 118. Who receives the royal commands, 118. Its failure, 120. Treacherous conduct of the King towards Pitt, 120-123. The Duke of Cumberland put into communication with Pitt, 170-177. Terms upon which Pitt principally insisted, 177. Failure

PITT

of the negotiation, 179. And of a new scheme, 184. Retires into Somersetshire, 185, 186. Sir W. Pynsent's bequest to him, 186. Reappears in his place in Parliament on the debate on America, 197. His speech, 198. His eloquent reply to Grenville's speech, 201. His advice, 203. His influence on the decision of the Rockingham administration as to America, 213. Overtures made by Lord Rockingham to him, without success, 218. Receives the King's commands to form a new administration, 219. His answer to Lord Northington, 219. Temple's interference, 220. Severance of their political and private friendship, 222. Composition of the new Ministry, 222. Raised to the peerage as Earl of Chatham, 222. See Chatham.

Pitt, William (son of the preceding), his first speech in Parliament, ii. 391. His speech denouncing the American War, 408. His rejection of office, 423. His motion for a committee of inquiry into the representation, 434. Becomes Chancellor of the Exchequer, 441. Commencement of his conflict with Fox, 443. Offered the Government by the King, iii. 32. His plan of parliamentary reform, 37. Becomes Prime Minister, 84. His Cabinet, 85. His India Bill, 82. His conduct on Fox's third India Bill, 90–92. His growing popularity, 93, 106. His disinterestedness, 105. His impolitic conduct as to the high bailiff of Westminster, 109. His financial measures, 109. His new India Bill, 111. His views on Irish reform, 125. His plan of policy, 125–127. His advanced views of commercial freedom, 128. Defeat of his Irish Bill, 132. His disappointment, 133. Introduces a Reform Bill, 134. Which is rejected, 136. His Bill for regulating public offices carried, 136, 137. His attempt to reduce the National Debt, 138. His conduct on Hastings's impeachment,

PITT

148. His plan for the consolidation of the Customs and Excise, 152. His denunciation of Fox's doctrine as to the Regency, 184. His resolutions, 190. Effect of his speech, 192. His resolutions on the Regency, 200. His defence of the Queen, 202. Difficulties of his position at this time, 213. His colleagues, 216. His failure to conciliate the Whigs, 286. Made Warden of the Cinque Ports, 289. His speech on war with France, 301. Disinclination of the Ministry for war, 304. Pitt's policy, 305. His conduct respecting the French Revolution, 336. His repressive measures, 338, 364. His violent speech on the continuance of the war with France, 410, 412. His proposal to relieve the Prince of Wales, 420. Undiminished confidence in him in 1796, iv. 53. His reserve as to the appropriation of the loan, 35. His supplementary loan in 1797, 62. Motion for a change in the Ministry, 63. Pitt's sincere desire for peace, 64, 68. Becomes unpopular, 77. His plan for the redemption of the Land Tax, 78. His quarrel with Tierney, 80. His opinion on Union with Ireland, 133. Defeat of ministers, 135. His plan of parliamentary reform, 139. His resolutions on the Union, 145. His support of Cornwallis, 148. His speech on the representation, 182. His defence of a war policy, 245. False confidence of ministers, 247. Pitt's vindication of his policy, 248. Success of his loan, 248, 249. Divisions in his Cabinet, 260. Discussions in the Cabinet as to Catholic emancipation, 286, 290. Mr. Pitt's measure, 289. Difficulties of the Cabinet, 292. His advice to the King on the Catholic question, 295. Offers to resign, 295. Difficulties as to the power of the Cabinet, 296. His resignation, 298, 299, 314. His conversations with the Prince of Wales as to the King's illness, 307. His support of Addington, 311. His

PITT

tergiversation as to the Catholic claims, 312. Complaints of his friends, 318. Popular dissatisfaction with him, 319
Pitt, Lady Hester, created Baroness Chatham, i. 71, 72
Pittsburg, captured by Forbes, i. 32
Plymouth, plan for the defence of, iii. 142
Poland, partition of, i. 220. Sketch of the history of the proceeding, ii. 121. Nobles and serfs, 122. Evils of elective monarchy, 123. Military condition of Poland, 125. Russian interference, 125. Death of Augustus III., 125. Character of the Polish Constitution, 126. State of Europe at the time of the partition, 126. Compulsory election of Poniatowski to the throne, 127. Execution of the Partition Treaty, 128. Apportionment of the territory, 129. Conduct of France in relation to the partition, 130. Policy of England, 130. Present opinion on the partition, 133
"Political adventurers," i. 111, 112
Poniatowski, Stanislaus, king of Poland, ii. 126
'Pop-gun Plot,' the, iv. 81
Popularity, political, i. 262
Portland, Duke of, formation of his ministry, iii. 24
Portsmouth, plan for the defence of, iii. 143
Portugal, subsidy granted by Parliament to, i. 78. Invaded by the Spaniards, who are compelled by the British to retreat, 86
Power, balance of, in Europe, i. 131. Views of the last century, 152
Poynings' law, repeal of, ii. 424
Pratt, Chief Justice, draws up the protest of the minority of the peers against the decision of Parliament in the case of Wilkes, i. 34 note. Created Earl Camden, 190
Prerogative, royal, attempt of George III. to recover the, i. 51. Commencement of the struggle between parliamentary government and, 97.

QUEBEC

Progress of the struggle, 104. Repulsive form which government by prerogative was made to assume under George III., 106. The rights and privileges of the Crown defined and arbitrary power destroyed by the Commons, ii. 35, 36. Resumption of power by the Crown, 41. Nature of royal responsibility, iii. 76
Press, indiscriminate prosecutions of the, iii. 340, 346. Their futility, 347. Persecution of the, in Ireland, iv. 109
Preston, Major, surrenders St. John's, ii. 135
Price, Dr., his system of a Sinking Fund for paying off the National Debt, 142. His part in the Revolution Society, iii. 265
Priestley, Dr., and the Unitarian Society, iii. 266. His house burnt, 268
Princeton, capture of, ii. 225
Prussia, alliance of France, Austria, and Russia against, i. 19, 20. England forced by circumstances into an alliance with, 20. Commencement of the Seven Years' War, 20. Our Prussian policy, 78. Consequence of the Prussian alliance to England, 80. End of the Seven Years' War, 86, 90. Secession of Prussia from the alliance, iii. 387. Her mercenary conduct, 404
Publishers, the, of London, at the end of the last century, iii. 347. Indiscriminate prosecution of them, 348
Puisaye, Count de, his proposal for invading Brittany, iv. 2. Failure of the plan, 27. His disappointment, 4. Defeated by Hoche, 7. De Puisaye's plans, 10
Pulteney, Mr., raised to the peerage as Earl of Bath, i. 3
Puritans, their conflict with the Royalists, ii. 18
Pynsent, Sir William, bequeaths an estate to Mr. Pitt, i. 186

QUEBEC, Wolfe sent against, i. 33, 34. Position of the city, 34.

QUEBEC

Wolfe's attack on, 35. Surrendered to the English, 40
Quebec Bill, debate on the, iii. 254
Queensberry, Duke of, i. 132 *note*
Quesnoy, surrender of, iii. 320
Quiberon, expedition to, iv. 1, 3, 5

RANELAGH Gardens, ii. 50
Rawdon, Lord, his retreat, ii. 403
Reeves, his 'Thoughts on the English Government,' iv. 21. His trial and acquittal, 22
Reform, parliamentary, Lord Chatham's Bill, ii. 97. Character of the constituencies in 1771, 98. Agitation for reform in 1778, ii. 282. Accumulation of petitions to Parliament for reform, 341. Burke's views as to, 422. His Bill, 431. Mr. Pitt's motion for a committee of inquiry, 434. Pitt's plan of reform, iii. 37. Pitt's Reform Bill, 134. Want of interest in reform, 134. Its absurd conditions, 135. Renewal of the question in 1790, 243. Mr. Grey's notice of motion, 272. Mr. Pitt's plan of reform, iv. 132. His speech, 182
Reformation, influence of the, on education, ii. 10. And on civil and religious liberty, 19. Rise of religious freedom in England, 21. Influence of the teaching of Wickliffe, 22. Religious bias of the northern counties, 23. Advantages of gradual reform, 23
Regency, question of a, on the illness of the King, i. 159. Discussions in Parliament on the Regency Bill, 160, 161. Insertion of a new clause, 162, 170. Decision on the Bill, 171. Expectations of a regency in 1788, iii. 183. Debate on the question, 183 *et seq.* Real question to be considered, 189. Proposed restrictions on the Regent, 197. Conditions of the Regency Bill, 202. The Bill abandoned, 205
Religion in the middle ages, ii. 4. Assumption of authority by the Church,

RIDGWAY

ii. 17. Church government, 17. The Royalists and Puritans, 18. Rise of religious freedom, 21. Effect of the Act of Uniformity, 27. Popular contempt for religion from the Revolution till late in the last century, 34. Effect of the Evangelical movement, 34. Evil results of irreligion, 37. The religion and morality of the middle classes in the last century, 52. Advance of the cause of religious liberty, iii. 249
Reports, parliamentary, attempt to suppress, ii. 72. Dr. Johnson's reports, 72, 73. Colonel Onslow's motion against reporters, 73. Contumacy and arrest of the printers, 74. Debates on Onslow's motion, 75-77. Contest between the City and the House of Commons on the subject, 78. Meeting at Lord North's to consider the question, 79. End of the quarrel, 90
Representative principle, the, i. 205
Restoration, state of manners at the, ii. 27. Venality of statesmen at the time, 35. Evil results of irreligion at this time, 37. Effeminacy of men of fashion, 39
Revolution, the French, considered as an appeal from traditional authority to reason and free will, ii. 20, 235
Revolution, the English, favourable circumstances under which it took place, ii. 21
Revolution Society, the, iii. 265
Reynolds, the Irish informer, iv. 111
Rhine, campaign on the, in 1794, iii. 403
Rhode Island, attempt of the French and Americans on, ii. 301. Failure of the enterprise, 301
Richmond, Duke of, becomes Secretary of State, i. 212. His motion for concluding peace with the American colonies, ii. 276-281. His inopportune motion for universal suffrage, 347, 348
Ridgway, the publisher, his prosecution, iii. 348

RIGBY

Rigby, his part in the debate on the Civil List in 1769, i. 282. Disparages Mr. Grenville's Elections Bill, 333. Acts as the Duke of Bedford's go-between, 404. Chatham's contempt of, 416. His insolence to the Speaker, 418. His impudent motion against the Speaker, ii. 234

Rights, Bill of, Society for the Support of the, formed, i. 326

Rohilla war, the, iii. 145

Robinson, Sir Thomas, accepts the seals of a secretary of state, i. 12. Removed to the office of Master of the Great Wardrobe, 16

Rochefort, expedition against, i. 27. Its failure, 28. Cause of the failure, 29

Rockingham, Marquis of, applied to by the Duke of Cumberland, i. 95. Dismissed from the lieutenancy of his county, 105. Placed at the head of an administration, 187. His political character, 187. His colleagues, 189. Timidity of the ministry as to American affairs, 195. Repeal of the Stamp Act, 211. Conciliatory measures of the administration towards the colonies, 214. Weakness of the Government, 215. Insubordination of state officers, 216. Overtures made by the ministry to Pitt, but without success, 218. Partial resignation of the ministry, 218. Resents Lord Chatham's overbearing conduct, i. 227. Resignation of the whole Rockingham party, 231, 232. His upright conduct, 242. His motion to inquire into the state of the nation, 316, 320. His sound Whig views, 355. His visit of condolence to the Lord Mayor in the Tower, ii. 24. The King's overtures to him on the resignation of Lord North, 420. Forms an administration, 421. His death, 438. His character, 439. His opposition to Lord Shelburne, iii. 24. His death, 31

Rodney, Admiral, bombards Havre, i. 32. His operations against the French West Indies, 85. His ex-

SANDWICH

ploits, ii. 379. Captures St. Eustatia, 396. His statements as to malpractices at, 398. His great victory over the French fleet under De Grasse, iii. 4. Recalled, 8. Whig dislike of him, 8. Public astonishment at his recall, 9. A peerage and pension conferred upon him, 10.

Rome evacuated by the French, iv. 217

Roses, War of the, results of, on chivalry, ii. 9

Rolls, Sir John, his motion of no confidence in the ministry, ii. 414

Royalists, their conflicts with the Puritans, ii. 18

Rosby's case, iv. 254

Ruffo, Cardinal, his march upon Naples, iv. 209

Russia, a negotiation for a subsidiary treaty with, opened by George II., i. 15. The treaty opposed by Pitt, 16. Joins Austria and France against Prussia, 20. Abandons the Austrian alliance, and attaches herself to the cause of Prussia, 72. Frederick the Great defeated by a Russian army at Kunersdorf, 42. Her interference in the affairs of Poland, ii. 125. Refusal of Russia to submit to the right of search, 331. Policy of Russia in 1789, iii. 231. Her aggrandisement, 231. Case of Oczakow, 251. A Russian embargo laid upon English vessels, iv. 270. Retaliation of England, 271. Subserviency of Russia to France, 344. Change of policy at the death of the Emperor Paul, 355. Peace with Russia, 359

SACHEVERELL, Dr., trial of, referred to, i. 322

Sackville, Lord George, supports the taxation of America, i. 243. Becomes Secretary of the Northern Department, ii. 192. *See also* Germaine.

Sandwich, Earl of, gains over the Duke of Bedford to the King, i. 121. Made Secretary of State, 122. His claims for official patronage, 123. Brings the question of Wilkes's 'Essay on Woman' before Parliament, 132. The King's mean opinion of him, i. 163. His conduct on the Regency Bill, 161-164, 172. Joins the Duke of Grafton's administration as Joint Postmaster-General, 253. His profligacy, ii. 41. Becomes First Lord of the Admiralty, 72. His defiance and contempt of the Americans, 193. Failure of an attack upon him, 316

Saratoga, Burgoyne's surrender at, ii. 257, 258. Convention of, 258, 260. Results of the Convention, 261. Evasion of the Convention, 292.

Satires, political, i. 411

Saumarez, Sir James, his exploits, iv. 361

Savannah, Count d'Estaing's exploit before, ii. 324

Savile, Sir George, refuses to join the Rockingham administration, i. 189. His language of insult and contumely in the House, 327. His attack on ministers, 329. His house attacked, ii. 350

Sawbridge, Alderman, his position and influence, ii. 95. His charge of corruption in the Civil List, 233.

Saxony recovered by Frederick the Great, i. 43, 44

Schuyler, General, his movements, ii. 255. His magnanimity to Burgoyne, 258

Scotland, the 'No Popery' riots in, ii. 345

Scotland, tyrannical proceedings in, at the end of the last century, iii. 351. Movement for parliamentary reform, 352. The 'National Convention,' 353. Thomas Muir, 353. Palmer's case, 355. Undue severity of the Scottish courts, 355

Scott, John (afterwards Lord Eldon), his absurd speech in the House, iii. 66

Seal, Great, put into commission, iii. 54

Search, right of, disputes as to, in 1780, ii. 380

Seditious publications, proclamation as to, iii. 273. Renewed proceedings against, 364

Settlement of 1688, its instability for a series of years, ii. 35

Seven Years' War, commencement of the, i. 20. Its termination, 86, 90

Shakspeare, his works and their period, ii. 12

Shears, the Irish rebels, betrayed, iv. 115

Shebbeare, Dr., his Court paper the 'Monitor,' i. 407

Shelburne, Earl of, mediates between Bute and Fox, i. 111. Resigns the presidency of the Board of Trade, 122. Dismissed from the army by order of the King, 132. Not in Lord Rockingham's administration, 190. Becomes Secretary of State in the Chatham administration, 222. Quits the Government with contempt, 271. His strong language on the conduct of the Duke of Grafton's ministry, 317. Gives the Chief Justice of England the lie, ii. 193. His defence of the Americans, 228. His duel with Colonel Fullarton, 340. Sent for by the King, 421. His conduct in the negotiations of 1782, 436. His assumption, 437. His party, 440. Accepts the premiership, 440. His declaration of his policy, 444. Opposed by the Marquis of Rockingham, iii. 25. Resigns, 28

Sheridan, R. B., his factious opposition to measures for the benefit of Ireland, iii. 130. His ribaldry, 137. His speeches on the Prince of Wales's affairs, 159, 163. And on the impeachment of Warren Hastings, 168. Cold reception of his speech on the French Revolution, 240. His motion on the enrolment of volunteers, 362. His loyal speech, iv. 84

Shoreham, electoral corruption at, i. 386. The case tried under Grenville's Act, i. 387

Sidney, Algernon, case of, referred to, i. 133

Silesia saved by Frederick the Great, i. 43

Silk weavers, depression of the trade of the, i. 174. Rejection of the Silk

INDEX. 411

SINKING

Bill by the Lords, 174. Riots in consequence, 175. Foreign silks excluded by Act of Parliament, 215
Sinking fund, delusive notion of a, iii. 139. Price's scheme, 140
Slander, prevalence of, in the last century, ii. 167
Slave trade,.debates on the, in 1788, iii. 176. Its horrors, 177. Sir W. Dolben's Bill, 179. Examination of delegates, 179. Wilberforce's speech, 225. His motion, 251. Exertions of the antislavery party, 276
Smith, Sir Sidney, blockades Alexandria, iv. 225. His defence of Acre, 227. His part in the treaty of El Arish, 332. Unjustly blamed, 333
Smollett, Tobias, his paper the 'Briton,' i. 408
Smuggling on the British coast in 1764, i. 139. Character of colonial smuggling in the West Indian and American colonies, 140
Sombrenil, De, capitulation of, iv. 9
Somers, Lord, his regard for the public welfare, ii. 35
Spain, interference of France in Spanish affairs, i. 62. Conclusion of the Family Compact, 63. Policy of England in Spanish affairs, 64. Claims of the Spanish Government on England, 64, 65. Peremptory demands of Spain on the dismissal of Pitt, 75. War declared against Spain by England, and against England by Spain, 76. Spanish professions of peaceful motives, 76. Loses the Havannah and the Philippine Islands, 85, 86. The Earl of Bute's overtures for peace, 87. Treaty of Fontainebleau, 88. Humiliating terms of the treaty to Spain, 89. Her occupation of the Falkland Islands, 357. The occupation disavowed, 359. Impending war with Spain in 1770, 383. Rupture between England and Spain, ii. 316. Prizes taken by a Spanish fleet, ii. 380. Character of the alliance between France and Spain, 394. Siege of Gibraltar, 395. End of the war, iii.

SUSSEX

16. Provisional treaty of peace, 19. Efforts of Spain to recover Gibraltar, 23. Conclusion of peace, 38. Rupture with Spain in 1790, 241. Demand made on Spain for reparation, 242. Intrigues of the French in Spain, iv. 32. Declaration of war by Spain against England, 32. Naval armament of Spain, 43. Defeat at St. Vincent, 44. British expedition to Spain, 325
Speaker. Interposition of the Speaker in the last century, ii. 78
Spithead, meeting at, iv. 45, 50
Stage, the, made instrumental to Court policy in the last century, i. 410. The comedies of the Restoration, ii. 38
Stamp Act, the, i. 143, 144. Repealed, 211. Propriety of the repeal, 212.
Stanhope, Earl, presides at the Revolution Society, iii. 265
Stanley, Mr. Hans, envoy to France for the negotiation of peace, i. 59. Recalled by Pitt, 65. Sent by Lord Chatham to St. Petersburg, 229. Abandonment of the mission, 230.
Statesmen. Venality of statesmen of the Restoration, ii. 35. Their profligacy in the first years of the reign of George III., 41. Ministerial levees in the last century, ii. 42
St. Clair, evacuates Fort Ticonderoga, ii. 254. Pursued by the British, 254. Superseded, 254
Stockdale, prosecution of, iii. 174
Stormont, Lord, his remonstrances with the French Government, ii. 273. Made Secretary of State, 337. Admitted to a seat in the Cabinet, iii. 35
Strasburg, sacrifice of, iii. 321
Stuart, Sir James, his proceedings in Ireland, iv. 108
Stuarts, mission of the, ii. 17
Suffolk, Lord, takes office in 1771, ii. 70
Sullivan, General, commands the expedition against Rhode Island, ii. 301
Sumptuary laws, futility of, iv. 280
Sussex, Duke of, his marriage, ii. 113

412 INDEX.

SUWARROW

Suwarrow, General, his victorious march in Italy, iv. 208. His treatment by the Austrians, 218
Swedes, their conduct at the battle of Copenhagen, iv. 155

TALLEYRAND, M., his reply to Lord Grenville's dispatch, iv. 242
Tandy, Napper, and the popular leaders in Dublin, iii. 121. His escape, iv. 126
Tarleton, Colonel, his service at Cooper River, ii. 361. His charge at Camden, 378. His reverse at Cowpens, 402
Taxation, theory of, i. 145. The right of the home Government to tax the colonies denied by Pitt, 192. Consideration of the question, 204. Theory of self-taxation, 205
Temple, Lord, becomes first Lord of the Admiralty, i. 22. The King's dislike of him, 23. Dismissed, 23. Supports Pitt in his rigorous policy respecting France, 65. Punished for having patronised John Wilkes, 129. His influence with Mr. Pitt, 179. His opposition to the formation of an administration under Mr. Pitt, 179. His objects, 179, 180. His perversity, 185. His interference with Pitt's arrangements, 220. His obstructive conduct, 221. Severance of his political and private friendship with Pitt, 222. Retires from public life, ii. 70.
Temple, Lord, receives the seals of office from the King, iii. 83. Resigns, 83, 84, 86. Charge against him, 87.
Test Act, proposed repeal of the, iii. 243, 277.
Thelwall, his trial for treason, iii. 391.
Thurlow, Lord, in expectation of the Great Seal, ii. 269. His support of the Bishop of Llandaff's marriage Bill, 321. His own morality, 321. His speech on the riots of 1780, 356. And on the regency question, iii. 194. His interview with the King, 220. Dismissed, 284. His conduct, 284, 285.

TOWNSHEND

Ticonderoga, fort of, unsuccessfully attacked by Abercrombie, i. 32. Seized by Arnold and Allen, ii. 184. Besieged by General Burgoyne, 283. Captured, 254.
Tierney, Mr., his opposition to Government, iv. 75. His quarrel with Pitt, 80.
Tippoo Sultan, his intrigues with the French, iv. 231. His death at Seringapatam, 235.
Tobacco duties, the, iii. 226.
Tone, Wolfe, his part in the Irish rebellion, iv. 107. His trial and suicide, 127.
Tooke, Horne, his quarrel with Wilkes, ii. 92. Debate in the Commons on the libel of, 163. Proceedings of the House against him, 164. Discharged, 166. His trial for high treason, iii. 371, 385. His effrontery, 387. Acquitted, 390. Committee on his case, iv. 325. His first speech in the House, 326.
Tories, reconciled to the Crown in the person of George III., i. 52. Called the 'King's Friends,' 53. Sketch of parties in 1760-1770, i. 389. Attempted coalition between Lord Bute and the Tories, i. 218.
Torture not allowed by the law either of England or Ireland, iv. 161.
Toulon fleet routed by Boscawen, i. 32. Besieged by the Republicans, iii. 319
Townshend, Charles, appointed Secretary-at-War, i. 57. Undertakes to carry a measure for taxing the American colonies through the House of Commons, 156. Not in Lord Rockingham's administration, 190. His explicit answer to this ministry, 216 note. Becomes Chancellor of the Exchequer, 222. Disliked by Lord Chatham, 240. His conduct as to the affairs of the East India Company, 240, 243. Reopens the wound with America, 243. His financial failures, 244. Lord Chatham's intention to procure his removal from the Exchequer, 244. His rash measures respecting the colonies, 251. His death,

INDEX. 413

TOWNSHEND

253. His talents and political character, 254.
Townshend, Alderman, his position and influence, ii. 25
Trade, free. See Free Trade
Trenton, capture of, ii. 224
Tudors, their education, ii. 12

UMBRELLAS not allowed by the hackney coachmen to be used, ii. 65
Uniformity, Act of, effect of, on civil and religious liberty, ii. 27
Unitarian Society, proceedings of the, ii. 266
United Irishmen, Society of, iv. 90. The conflicts with the Orangemen, 103. Change their tone, 104
Ushant, naval action off, ii. 305

VALENCIENNES, besieged, iii. 316. Liberation of the garrison, 317
Vaughan, General, his statement as to malpractices at St. Eustatia, ii. 398
Vauxhall Gardens, ii. 30
Vendée, La, war in, iii. 317
Vincent, St., island of, taken from France, i. 85. Recovered, iv. 14
Vincent, Cape St., battle of, iv. 43, 44
Vincent, Earl St., iv. 45. See Jervis
Virginia, protestations of, against the aggressions of the British legislature, i. 193. Meeting of the General Assembly of, 301. Appointment of Lord Bottetort governor, 303. Dissolution of the Assembly, 304
Volunteers, enrolment of, in 1794, iii. 362

WALDEGRAVE, Earl of, makes overtures to Mr. Fox, who is gained over by the Government, i. 13. Sent for by George II., 25. But fails to form a ministry, 25. Governor of George III. when prince, 47. His character of his royal pupil, 48
Waldegrave, Lady, married to the Duke of Gloucester, ii. 109
Wales, Princess Dowager of, her death, ii. 103, 104

WASHINGTON

Wales, landing of the French in, iv. 41. Lord Cawdor's preparations, 41
Walker, prosecution of, iii. 369
Walmoden, Countess de, bought by George II., ii. 125
Walpole, Sir R., his fall, i. 1. His character as a minister, 1, 2. His political morality, 3. His prudence and sagacity as to levying taxes on the American colonies, 155. His introduction of parliamentary corruption, ii. 36. His profligacy, 39
Walpole, Mr. Thomas, deputed to sound Pitt, i. 96
Warrants, general, question of the validity of, raised, i. 123. Arguments used before the Court of King's Bench, 126, 127. Decision of the court, 127. Former practice respecting those warrants, 128. Sir W. Meredith's motion in the House, i. 136. Decision of the House, 137.
Washington, George. His appearance in the Virginian Assembly, 304. Offers to raise a thousand men and lead them to Boston, ii. 150. At the Congress at Philadelphia, 154. Called to the command of the American army, 178. Difficulties of his situation, 180. His desperate position after the repulse at Quebec, 187. The first campaign, 203. Washington commissioned to exercise sovereign authority, 208. Fixes his headquarters at New York, 212. Intrenches Brooklyn, 213. Evacuates New York, and moves to Kingsbridge, 220. State of his army, 221. Loses Fort Washington, 222. Retreats into Pennsylvania, 223. Takes Trenton, 224. His reorganisation of his army, 245. Made absolute, 245. Defeated at Brandywine, 247. And at Germantown, 249. His movements, 291. Cabal formed against him, 291. Non-success of the intrigues, and magnanimity of Washington, 293. His objections to an invasion of Canada, 326. His difficulties, 327. Mutinous spirit of his troops, 363. His firmness, 363. His treatment by Congress, 364.

WATT

Inefficiency of his army, 364. His attempt on an outpost at Staten Island, 365. His probable motives for the execution of Major André. 375. Menaces New York, 400. His siege of York Town, 405. Surrender of York Town to him, 406. His apprehension of a relaxation of his countrymen's efforts, iii. 2. His difficulties, 47. His character as a general, 48. His purity, 49.

Watt, case of, iii. 371.

Wedderburn, Mr., his speech on the City address to the Crown, i. 341. Supports Serjeant Glyn's motion, 379. His moderation, 381. His account of the parliamentary decorum of his day, 412. His defection from the Whig party, ii. 71. Becomes Solicitor-General, 71. Retained by the Crown against the Assembly of Massachusetts, 145. His denunciation of the conduct of Franklin, 146. His desire for advancement, 269. Raised to the peerage and to the Chief Justiceship, ii. 358. See Loughborough.

Wellesley, Arthur, at the siege of Seringapatam, iv. 235.

West Indies. Pitt's projected expeditions against the French and Spanish, i. 84, 85. Character of the contraband trade carried on in the middle of the last century in the, 140. Successes of the French in the, in 1781, ii. 410, 411. Losses of the French Republic in the, iii. 323. Expedition to in 1794, 403.

Weymouth, Lord, joins the Duke of Grafton's administration as Secretary of State, i. 252. His imprudent letter to the Surrey magistrates, 273. Resigns, ii. 335.

Whately, one of Grenville's go-betweens, i. 404.

Whigs, their importance up to the time of the death of George II., i. 52. Causes of the reconstruction of the Whig party, 95. Commencement of the system of proscription against the Whigs, 99. Policy of George

WILKES

III. respecting the Whig party, 105. Return to office in Lord Rockingham's administration, 187. Influence of Whig jealousies and cabals in 1756, 260. The Whig opposition in 1769, 309. Their quarrel with the Bill of Rights men, 327. The Whigs as regarded by Lords Rockingham and the Earl of Chatham, 356. Sketch of parties in 1760–1770, 389. Dissolution of the Whig opposition, ii. 70. Their dissensions in 1771, 97. The party broken up, 102. Their opposition to the measures against the American Colonies, 149. Lord North's overtures to them, 321. Divisions of the Whigs upon the subject of Parliamentary reform, 435. Their dislike of Rodney, iii. 8. Their dissensions in 1783, 29. Their arrogance, 35. And factious conduct, 78, 88, 130. Termination of the struggle between the King and the Whigs, 97. Want of unanimity of the Whigs, 101. Their position after the Regency Question, 217. Divisions as to the French Revolution, 241. Breaking-up of the Whig party, 253. Failure of Pitt to conciliate them, 286. Whig accessions to office, 395. Their disloyal proceedings in 1797, iv. 71. Their violent opposition, 76, 77.

Whippings, public, in the last century, ii. 68.

Whitbread, Mr., his part in the slave-trade debate, iii. 180.

White's Club, ii. 45.

Whollaghan, his murder of Dogherty, iv. 169. His trial and acquittal, 170.

Wickliffe, John, influence of his teaching on religious liberty, ii. 22.

Wilberforce, William, returned for Yorkshire, iii. 107. His speech on slavery, 225. His motion, 251. His exertions, iii. 276. His motion in favour of peace, 409, 413.

Wilkes, John, his rise and character, i. 123, 124. His orgies at Medmenham Abbey, 124 note. His 'North

INDEX.   415

WILLIAM

Briton,' 124. His paper seized, 125. Arrested and brought before Lord Halifax, 129. Committed to the Tower, 129. Sues out writs of habeas corpus, and brought before the Court of Common Pleas, 129. Liberated from custody, 129. Vengeance of the Court in consequence, 129. Punishment of his patron Earl Temple, 129. The 'North Briton' ordered by the House of Commons to be burnt by the common hangman, 130. Wilkes's duel with Mr. Martin, 130. His 'Essay on Woman,' 132. Proceedings of both Houses of Parliament against him, 132-134. Popular sympathy for him, 134. Withdraws to Paris, 135. Expelled from the House of Commons, 135. His complaint of privilege considered by the House, 135. Decision of the House, 137. Wilkes's action against the Earl of Halifax, 137. Returns to England, 262. Elected for Middlesex, 263. Arrested and imprisoned, 265. Riots of his partisans, 265. Presents a petition to the House, which is rejected as frivolous, 272. Publishes Lord Weymouth's letter to the Surrey magistrates, 273. Brought to the bar of the House charged with libel, 274. His mode of defence, 274. His expulsion moved by Lord Barrington, 274. Which is carried, 274. His re-election, and increased popularity, 275. Gains an action against the Secretary of State, 279. Liberates the printers of the debates, ii. 75. The cause of the quarrel between Parliament and the press, 90. His declining popularity, 91. His quarrel with Horne, 92. Disliked in the city, 96. Becomes Lord Mayor, 190. His behaviour in the riots of 1780, 355. His speech on the India Bill, iii. 67. Rejected by Middlesex, 246.
William III., acceptability of, to the great majority of the nation, i. 328.
William IV., open concubinage of his early days, ii. 113.

YORK

Windham, William, his answer to Fox, iii. 292. Fox's attempts to intimidate him, 293. His speech in favour of continuing the war with France, 402.
Winterbotham, prosecution of, iii. 343.
Wolfe, Brigadier-General, appointed second in command under Lord Amherst, i. 31, 33. Appointed to form the siege of Quebec, 33, 34. His attack on Montcalm's position, 35. His repulse at Beaufort, 35. Melting away of his army, 36. His attack on the heights of Abraham, 38. His victory and death, 39.
'Woman, Essay on,' Wilkes's, i. 132.
Women, principles of chivalry in relation to, ii. 4, 5. Influence of chivalry on the female character, 6. Cavaliers and troubadours, 6. Abduction of females in former and in later times, 8. Manners and education of women in the last century, 45. Relaxation of moral and religious restraint, 53. Effects of the uncertain state of the marriage law, 54. Causes of clandestine marriages, 55. Scandalous exhibitions in the public thoroughfares of London, 66.
Woodfall, the printer, summoned to the bar of the House of Commons, ii. 164. Discharged by the House, 166. Fined and imprisoned by Lord Mansfield, 167.
Wurmser, General, in Flanders, iii. 322.

YORK, Duke of, his marriage, ii. 113. His speech on the regency question, iii. 194. His behaviour to the King, 211, 222, 223. His duel with Colonel Lennox, 225. Sent to Flanders, 313. Besieges Dunkirk, 317. Retreats, 319. Public dislike of him, 359. His rashness and losses, 399. Removed from the command, iv. 1. Entrusted with the command of an expedition to Holland, 221. Takes Bergen, 224. Failure of the expedition, 225.

YORK

York Town, siege of, ii. 405. Surrenders to Washington, 406

Yorke, Charles, Attorney-General, his argument in favour of general warrants, i. 127. The Great Seal offered

YORKSHIRE

to him, 317. His political history, 317. First declines, but subsequently accepts, the Seals, 319. His sudden death, 319

Yorkshire, great meetings in, ii. 333

www.ingramcontent.com/pod-product-compliance
Lightning Source LLC
Chambersburg PA
CBHW051741300426
44115CB00007B/649